Europe and the Politics of Capabilities

The social agenda of the European Union is shifting towards broad social initiatives that align social and economic objectives with the promotion of employment. This calls for an action framework that permits social dialogue and political deliberation to inform and complement legislative action at all levels. The debate, however, has been dominated by advocates of market-based solutions and their opponents, the supporters of traditional welfare states. This book, to break out of this sterile stalemate, demonstrates how an employment-oriented social policy in Europe can develop from a new, different set of policy principles, specifically 'a capability approach'. Taking inspiration from the work of Amartya Sen, this book focuses on the effective freedom people need to achieve their goals in life and work. The result of ongoing collaboration between researchers and social actors, it will appeal to social scientists, students, policy-makers and all those concerned with the building of Europe.

ROBERT SALAIS is Professor of Economics and Director of the Research Centre IDHE, Ecole Normale Supérieure de Cachan.

ROBERT VILLENEUVE is Director of EUREXCTER (Excellence Territoriale en Europe) and was Chairman of the Commission des Affaires Sociales, de l'Emploi et de la Formation Professionnelle of the ECPE at Brussels from 1995 to 2001.

Europe and the Politics of Capabilities

edited by

Robert Salais and Robert Villeneuve

CAMBRIDGE
UNIVERSITY PRESS

PUBLISHED BY THE PRESS SYNDICATE OF THE UNIVERSITY OF CAMBRIDGE
The Pitt Building, Trumpington Street, Cambridge, United Kingdom

CAMBRIDGE UNIVERSITY PRESS
The Edinburgh Building, Cambridge, CB2 2RU, UK
40 West 20th Street, New York, NY 10011–4211, USA
477 Williamstown Road, Port Melbourne, VIC 3207, Australia
Ruiz de Alarcón 13, 28014 Madrid, Spain
Dock House, The Waterfront, Cape Town 8001, South Africa

http://www.cambridge.org

First published 2004

Printed in the United Kingdom at the University Press, Cambridge

Typeface Plantin 10/12 pt.   *System* LaTeX 2$_\varepsilon$ [TB]

A catalogue record for this book is available from the British Library

ISBN 0 521 83604 2 hardback

The publisher has used its best endeavours to ensure that the URLs for external
websites referred to in this book are correct and active at the time of going to
press. However, the publisher has no responsibility for the websites and can
make no guarantee that a site will remain live or that the content is or will
remain appropriate.

Contents

v

18   Incorporating the capability approach into social
     and employment policies   283
     ROBERT SALAIS

Figures

Tables

Notes on contributors

PIERRE BACHMAN is expert adviser at national level of the Economic Sector of the Confédération Générale du Travail (CGT) and member of the Conseil Economique et Social Régional (CESR) of the Provence-Côte d'Azur region

JUDE BROWNE is Research Fellow at the Centre for Business Research, University of Cambridge

SIMON DEAKIN is Robert Monks Professor of Corporate Governance, Centre for Business Research and Judge Institute of Management, University of Cambridge

JEAN DE MUNCK is Professor of Sociology at the University of Louvain-la-Neuve

CLAUDE DIDRY is CNRS researcher CRS (CR1) in sociology at the Centre 'Institutions et Dynamiques Historiques de l'Economie' (IDHE), Ecole Normale Supérieure de Cachan

JACKY FAYOLLE is Director of the Institut de Recherches Economiques et Sociales (IRES), Paris and Associate Professor in Economics at the University Pierre Mendès-France of Grenoble

ISABELLE FERRERAS is Research Fellow of the Belgian National Fund for Scientific Research at the University of Louvain-la-Neuve and affiliate of the Minda de Gunzburg Center for European Studies, Harvard University

MARTIN HEIDENREICH is Professor of European Studies in the Department of Social Sciences at the University of Bamberg

EMMANUEL JULIEN is Head of Department of International and European Social Affairs in MEDEF (the Association of French Enterprises) and involved in UIECE activities

JEAN LAPEYRE was Joint General Secretary of the European Trade Union Confederation (ETUC) from 1991 to 2002

ANNE LECUYER is Researcher at the Banque de France

JANE LEWIS is Barnett Professor of Social Policy at the University of Oxford

SERAFINO NEGRELLI is Associate Professor of Industrial Relations at the Law Faculty of the University of Brescia and researcher at Fondazione Regionale Pietro Seveso, Milan

PHILIPPE POCHET is Director of the Observatoire social européen (OSE), Brussels

GILLES RAVEAUD is a PhD student on economics at the University of Paris X Nanterre

ROBERT SALAIS is Professor of Economics and Director of the Research Centre IDHE, Ecole Normale Supérieure de Cachan

ROBERT VILLENEUVE is Director of EUREXCTER (Excellence Territoriale en Europe) and was Chairman of the Commission des Affaires Sociales, de l'Emploi et de la Formation Professionnelle of the ECPE at Brussels from 1995 to 2001

NOEL WHITESIDE is Professor in Social Policy at the University of Warwick

FRANK WILKINSON is Emeritus Reader in Applied Economics and Research Associate, Centre for Business Research, University of Cambridge

PIERRE-PAUL ZALIO is Senior Lecturer at the Department of Social Sciences, Ecole Normale Supérieure de Cachan and researcher at the Centre IDHE

BÉNÉDICTE ZIMMERMANN is Senior Lecturer at the Centre de Recherches Interdisciplinaires sur l'Allemagne (CRIA), Ecole des Hautes Etudes en Sciences Sociales, Paris

Book Title: Y20

Preface

Odile Quintin
General Directorate DG Employment and Social Affairs,
European Commission

In June 2000, the Lisbon European Council set out an integrated and complementary strategy for achieving the three-fold aims of a knowledge-based economy, full employment and social inclusion. This triangular approach reflected the ongoing predominance of the European Social Model (ESM), and constituted the basis of the Social Policy Agenda adopted at Nice in December 2000, which was upheld as the right direction in the mid-term review of the Social Agenda in 2003.

A chief characteristic of this approach is the emphasis on *quality* – both quality of employment and quality of policies – supported by open and transparent processes. Quality also implies the commitment and involvement of different actors, in order to achieve the objective of a thriving knowledge-based economy, beginning at the local level. The quality of the interrelation between the local and territorial actors and their national or European-level representatives is an essential determinant of the quality and pertinence of decision-making and policy formulation at higher levels. The effective participation of territorial social partners, as with the national and European levels, in the various decision-making and implementation processes, depends on a well-functioning social dialogue. Social dialogue is an essential component of the European Social Model and, as such, is given specific recognition in the European treaties. Of the multifarious civil society players, the social partners hold a unique position, because they are best placed to address issues related to work and to negotiate binding agreements. This confers upon them a crucial role in promoting better governance, particularly in view of the enlargement of the Union in May 2004.

The European social dialogue has now achieved a new degree of maturity, evidenced by the social partners' adoption of their first autonomous multi-annual work programme for 2003–5. The work programme defines a range of themes of common interest to both sides of industry, and outlines a number of initiatives for the three-year period. These initiatives represent a vital contribution of the social partners to the implementation of the necessary measures for achieving economic and social progress.

They are now in a position to exercise influence over a wide range of areas, including the issue of social protection, and are taking an active part in the ongoing debate on the vitally important issue of the future of pension systems across the European Union.

Looking ahead, two clear trends can be identified. The first is the involvement of diverse civil society actors, and particularly the social partners, in an increasingly broad spectrum of issues, covering not only employment but social inclusion, social protection, skills and mobility, health and safety and living and working conditions. These different domains have acquired a new degree of interconnection in the framework of the Commission's Social Policy Agenda, which underlines the interrelation and mutual dependence between the three objectives of economic reform, employment and social cohesion. The relevant actors therefore have an important role in ensuring the positive correlation between the different issues in which they are involved, in order to optimise the quality and efficiency of the outcomes.

The second trend is the growing strategic importance of local actors at the territorial level, which demands a reinforcement of their capability for action. As the Commission's White Paper on Governance, published in 2001, demonstrates, today's society is characterised by increasing interdependence, requiring the commitment and active participation of all stakeholders, as the developments in the field of corporate social responsibility clearly illustrate. The work undertaken on the politics of capabilities, supported by European Community funding, has been extremely valuable, precisely because it has brought academic researchers together with the actors. This innovative approach represents the added value of the work which is encapsulated in this volume. It is therefore a welcome contribution to the policy debate, and strengthens the case for continued efforts to develop the capacity of actors to participate in the conception, implementation and follow-up of employment and social policies in the European Union.

Acknowledgements

For their help in translating chapters and for preparing this volume, we owe great thanks to Céline Ethuin, Claude Morey, Margaret Morley, Susan Taponier and Ashveen Peerbaye. This book would have not been possible without the series of meetings between researchers and social actors that have been funded and intellectually supported by the DG 'Employment and Social Affairs' of the Commission of the European Community.

1 Introduction: Europe and the politics of capabilities

Robert Salais and Robert Villeneuve

1 Introduction

Since the mid-1990s the employment and social policy agenda of the European Union has been more focused on employment promotion than on addressing Member States' systems of social protection. There has been a shift away from old concepts of welfare states towards broader social initiatives that align social and economic objectives within a coherent approach. This calls for a different framework for employment and social policy, which will permit social dialogue and political deliberation to inform and complement legislative action at all levels. The theme of this volume is to demonstrate that this framework for employment and social policy in Europe can develop from a new, different set of policy principles: a *capability approach*.

In a capability approach to work and welfare, what matters for public policies is what a person can do and be with the resources over which she has command. In other words, what matters is her achievement as a person (and, as a consequence, the effective freedom she has to achieve her goals), compared with what is judged normal (i.e. conventionally agreed) in a given society. For Amartya Sen, from whom we take inspiration, empirical evidence shows that, when faced with the same hazard, people are unequal in their capabilities of doing and being with the same basket of commodities or amount of money. The true question for social policies is thus to struggle against inequality of capabilities and to open for all an effective freedom, that is a widening of the possibilities she has the capability to achieve in her work and her life. The more fully this condition is satisfied, the more can individual and collective initiative be deployed, the more can economic efficiency and social justice be reconciled.

This volume addresses the current impact of European policy implementation while also offering a new perspective for future debate, and discussing the conditions for its development. It tries to reassess current trends critically by showing the links between social improvement and economic prosperity that result from policies designed specifically

1

to facilitate participation by all, through an enhancement of their capabilities. Hence, it breaks with approaches, mostly macroeconomic and financial, that argue for structural reforms oriented toward pure market flexibility for Europe; these reforms ultimately comprehend social welfare as counterproductive to economic prosperity. By outlining the contours of a capability approach in widely different areas of European politics, the book illustrates a 'hidden agenda' in the sense that, from the outset, this approach can inspire desirable advances in European social policies and legislation as well as in methodology – in contrast to alternative approaches that have neglected this area. Now is a good time to make this hidden agenda explicit and develop it further. At the end of 2000, the European Commission launched a new initiative, the European Social Agenda, to run until 2006 and to be renewed in 2005.

To achieve this programme, an interdisciplinary team of European social science researchers (covering economics, history, law and sociology) has worked in close collaboration with high-level representatives from agencies of the European social dialogue (ETUC, ECPE, UNICE). Following a series of collaborative seminars, research results were presented at a European conference held in Brussels in January 2001, under the presidency of the DG, 'Employment and Social Affairs'. This collaboration resulted in this book, based on original research by the participants with contributions by both researchers and actors involved in European social dialogue. Using a capability orientation, each chapter offers a critical assessment of how various European initiatives are implemented 'on the ground', thereby generating new perspectives on how future developments may be shaped. Empirical studies have been chosen to demonstrate the range of policy contexts – firms, local partnerships, social dialogue at various levels. The case studies are an opportunity to appreciate the European political process in employment and social affairs, and become aware of the varied ways in which European initiatives may be interpreted or oriented towards a politics of capabilities. In this introduction, written jointly by a researcher and a European social actor, we would like to draw the reader's attention to this 'red line' that runs through the set of contributions.[1]

The argument is developed in the following sections. Going back to the Delors project (1985–92) for social Europe, section 2 emphasises the need for EU initiatives on social issues. Section 3 develops the set of principles that constitutes a 'capability approach' and explains how it meets the requirements of a knowledge-based economy (specifically, the transformation of work). Section 4 explains why the European Employment

---

[1] Bibliographical references may be found in the individual chapters.

Strategy (EES) and its open method of co-ordination risk promoting an activation route. Europe is at the crossroads between going down an activation and a capability route. While trying to retain the best of these strategies, implementing Social Europe should follow another path, via the development of social and civil dialogue and a fresh interpretation of the principle of subsidiarity. Section 5 develops this line and advocates a 'new alliance' in favour of the development of Social Europe.

2   The need for EU initiatives on social issues

Social Europe remains the poor relation in Europe's construction. The shape and content of its future is obscure owing to a confused mixture of blockages, contradictions and potential outcomes. Strategies are unclear and their consequences risk becoming uncontrollable. The project of a Constitution for Europe has not modified this state of affairs. Under the Delors presidency (1985–92), the European Commission had a strategy, concentrating on 'the social dimension of the internal market'. This strategy has ground to a halt, at a moment when it should have been pushed forward to cope with emergent 'social objectives' on a European scale.

2.1   The Delors project: successes and failures

Whatever they may be, European norms modify national norms. But the political process and the outcomes are different depending on the options selected and the methods used. Roughly speaking, the key issue was and remains whether European policies and legislation should seek (1) to substitute, or (2) add to – or simply by focusing on new problems originating in the creation of Europe, (3) to complement – national policies and legislation. *A priori*, one would expect that the first option (substitution) would raise fundemental opposition, the second (addition) would risk being dismissed for provoking further complexity in national social and economic decision-making. The third (complement) would appear the most acceptable as it *a priori* offers relevant solutions not available at national level (even if it also creates incentives to modify national norms).

The project initiated by Jacques Delors at the end of the 1980s was something between options 2 and 3. It tried to implement a set of general principles that should and could guide the development of national legislation and policy to cope with the internal market. This set of principles was labelled a 'charter of fundamental social rights for workers'. In the spirit of subsidiarity, countries were left to translate these principles into their own model and legislation, some pressure being exercised by social actors via the mechanism of European Social Dialogue and by the negotiation of European collective agreements. For the Commission, the ambition was not (as it is in France) to make these rights effectively universal, but simply to ask the Member States to use these principles as reference points (or benchmarks) in policy development. Member States were expected first to respect selected minimal social and employment standards of their own, then to start a process of improving these standards. This assumed that social negotiation, involving intermediaries (economic, social and civil actors), could focus on new social objectives created by European economic integration (see below) and prepare the ground for European legislation.

This strategy partly succeeded and partly failed. The success was the introduction of a new title in the Treaty on the social dimension of the Union (now Title XI). This title created a new mechanism, European Social Dialogue, allowing future European legislation in this sphere to be prepared, if possible by collective agreements between European social partners, or at least following consultation with these partners. Failure was elsewhere: in a reduced scope for qualified majority voting (QMV); in more restricted possibilities for free negotiations by the social partners; in progressive blockage of the legislative process. Governments of Member States have basically resisted losing any control over programmes of social policy and national employment. At the same time, European economic integration is proceeding apace: monetary union, the single market, the creation of European champions and multinationals; the reconstruction of interest groups at a European level and the redefinition of their spheres of activity. In some respects, these trends are good reasons for governments to protect their welfare states and employment against unwelcome consequences. But doing so introduces a prisoner's dilemma in which the absence of co-operation between the Member States risks promoting *a minima* solutions at European level. It also gives incentives to put national social models in competition with each other by relocating jobs and geographically restructuring activities.

2.2   *Providing economic integration with social content*

As a consequence, a growing tension is evident between progress towards economic integration and the stagnation of social co-ordination, all the more as the enlargement of Europe is now going on. The EES, launched in 1997, is grounded on other foundations than the Delors strategy: European guidelines for national policies (placed under macroeconomic control), peer review, statistical indicators benchmarking (emphasising the macro job rate) and the open method of co-ordination (OMC).

This emphasises a switch from European strategies to national solutions, with the risk that incoherence will hamper the building of Europe. The OMC strategy, based on governance, quantitative benchmarking and co-ordination of national policies, has yet to prove its effectiveness, not to mention its coherence and efficacy. One striking aspect of the OMC strategy is that, in the long run, it seems to share the very ambitious option 1 outlined above (substituting a European framework for national frameworks) without exhibiting, nor discussing, its substantive content, or the means by which this could plausibly be achieved. In brief the OMC resembles the Delors strategy, minus what made the latter original and, presumably, relevant: the predefinition of a set of normative principles.

The conviction shared by all the contributors to this book is that, owing to its origin and specificity, Europe must endow public action with an ethical and practical orientation. Does its intervention effectively improve personal situations in terms of jobs, work and life prospects, environment and security in case of hazard? Are European policies and legislation, when combined with national ones, effectively doing more and better for people than national policies by themselves? Are they developing an atmosphere of competitiveness and justice that proves both efficient and fair in a global world? The objectives of Europe-wide participation, solidarity, inclusion and personal responsibility are essential to the success of the European project. Thus the true questions are what substantial content and direction must be given to European governance, and how this may be achieved. These questions are especially relevant for social dialogue in Europe and its role in implementing social, work and economic norms.

Facts plead in favour of such a move and for a redefinition of the stakes. On one side, the transformation of work initiated by changing markets and demands requires more responsive organisations and workers capable of initiative and responsibility, to foster the diffusion of knowledge-based technologies. Owing to their novelty and to their diverse manifestations between sectors, territories or professions, these call for collective negotiation and agreement before being introduced into European law. These objectives include, for instance: the search for positive trade-offs between flexibility and security; the promotion of secure geographical and occupational mobility; equal treatment for men and women; continual life-long learning; respect for fundamental rights; information, consultation and participation by workers and territories in economic decision-making and restructuring. On the other side, actors in Europe have accumulated experience about European matters; they are able to link these issues with their own preoccupations, interests, values and projects. By virtue of path-dependency, existing institutions have begun to frame possible choices and actions and, perhaps, to shape the 'corridor' within which social Europe can develop.

3   Towards a capability approach

Such a context of potential crisis is propitious for developing new ideas. New European data confront accumulated experience. The question is how to relate data and actors' experience to each other and exploit them to enable social Europe to progress. This book advocates a capability approach, which can serve this very purpose. In this section, we present a set of principles for public action and the main arguments in their favour.

3.1   Development as freedom: learning from Amartya Sen

The central theme of a capability approach is the construction of a *framework of active security* to cope with work transformation and economic uncertainty; this should become a fundamental objective for social Europe. This objective should be accommodated within territories, labour laws and social protection systems throughout Europe in ways specific to local practice. To achieve this, European action in each of these areas ought to establish a *focal point* towards which all should converge. The focal point to be chosen is the development of capabilities – of actors, workers, firms and territories.

The concept of capabilities in economics and law   The concept of capabilities has a long tradition in two areas of economics (the theory of production and the normative economics of well being) and in law. The concept originated from the analysis of relations between division of labour, knowledge and specialisation of the firm operating under market conditions (from Adam Smith to Alfred Marshall). Amartya Sen, 1998 winner of the Nobel prize for Economics, attached his name to the concept of capabilities in his work on social justice and collective choice. In law, the concept of capabilities refers to the endowment of persons with procedural and substantive collective rights, which permits engagement in all forms of co-operation and agreement within the security of the law. This concept is the foundation of personal responsibility that holds individuals accountable for their actions and the source of expectations as to their future conduct.

In the economics of well being, Sen argued that 'economic development can be seen as a process of expanding the real freedoms that people enjoy'.[2] This contrasts with narrower views identifying development with the growth of GNP or individual incomes. These can be very important as *means*, but means cannot be confused with the *ends* toward which attention and means must be directed. These ends, real freedoms, have as a counterpart the expansion of the *capabilities* for people to live the life they value. A politics of capabilities will aim at generating a 'virtuous process' in which '[real] freedoms are not only the primary ends of development, they are also among its principal means'.[3] More specifically, criticising John Rawls, Sen argues that, to evaluate well being, people's capabilities are more just and efficient criteria than endowments in primary goods. First, persons endowed with the same resources (notably financial) remain unequal in terms of expected outcomes. Such empirical evidence is central, for instance, to the equality of treatment between men and women, as much as for an efficient functioning of the labour market. Second, certain goods have intrinsic value, independent of individual evaluation or preference (to be suitably fed or housed, to participate in community life, to have access to a good job, to be adequately trained, etc.). Such goods are clearly fundamental rights to which public authorities should guarantee real access for everyone. These are not simply minimal rights. What counts is access to a *real freedom of choice at every stage of life*. It is about guaranteeing the security of personal development.

In the economics of production, a capability approach considers that the source of a firm's competitiveness resides not in cost minimisation, but basically in its capacity to work, organise and innovate. The organisation of industry, as George B. Richardson,[4] an influential authority, said, must be understood in terms of numerous activities (R&D, production, sales, services, etc.) which ought to be undertaken by firms offering the required *capabilities*, that is to say those 'with the appropriate knowledge, experience and skills'. It is more efficient and secure to concentrate on specific activities and to leave complementary ones to other firms. The concept of capabilities promotes a vision of the firm in terms of security and efficiency of its development. It leads to a theory of co-operation (beyond a theory of organisation aiming at controlling moral hazard, as in Williamson[5]). Long-term contracts, joint ventures (JVs), licensed agreements, etc. are efficient because they provide access to required complementary products and services. The concept thus offers the basis for a theory of endogenous territorial growth, because it

---

[2] Sen (1999: 3).   [3] Sen (1999: 10).
[4] Richardson (1990).   [5] See Williamson (1985).

emphasises specialisation in products and services acquired in which territories accumulate absolute advantages.

These origins make the concept of capabilities especially relevant for Europe. It focuses on the firm as well on the individual. The connection between the two lies in a common interest in the scope of possibilities open to an economic agent and the manner in which these possibilities are created and exploited. The vision is dynamic and contextual. A positive relationship between efficiency and equity is achievable. These studies conceive the economic agent (company or individual) as capable of co-operation, of making agreements and of keeping them. This, in one sense, stems from a recognized common interest. Each actor participates in co-ordination with others (in a firm, an industry, a territory, in her life); the satisfaction of her own objectives depends on sound development of this co-ordination. Each actor must offer adequate capabilities to both sustain her position and to ensure the high quality of the collective result.

     Situated European action and collective negotiation   In retaining the positive aspects of liberalism while removing the negative ones, a capability approach offers a credible alternative to so-called 'neo-liberalism'. The standard governance approach deals with *a priori* strictly opportunist actors. By contrast, the capability approach aims at creating a learning process of participation and of developing capabilities. It considers that the European Union is a public actor centrally concerned with common goods (more and better jobs, social inclusion, etc.) agreed upon at a European level. As such, it has an ethical and practical orientation, not solely a political and strategic one. But its premise is that common goods are achievable only by internal guidance through situated public action. By 'situated,' we mean a public action located within established negotiation and decision-making of local actors, in territories, trades, networks or firms. Such public action relies on each actor acting freely in compliance with the common good and continuing to do so, with a view to the increased capabilities and freedom of choice that she will acquire. The public authority should guide the creation of mutual expectations, which subsequently become self-sustaining. This model of collective action offers, in a sense, an end product for collective negotiation. The public actor compensates – temporarily and proportionately – for the in capacity of others. But this cannot be resolved externally, only internally redeveloped. Though this action does not comply with the model of hierarchical State authority, it remains public in the sense that it is publicly agreed upon among numerous actors (including expected beneficiaries); interested parties participate in its implementation. In principle, actors are given rights to act, in their diverse ways, subject to customary good practice. This allows the origins of European social dialogue, as recalled in section 1, to be revisited to discover new possibilities for European construction.

To conclude, a politics of capabilities would endow people and actors with adequate, fair and efficient resources: with effective rights to social deliberation and participation, with benefits and collective services focused on the development of personal and collective capabilities. In such a strategy, social Europe should fight for *equality of capabilities* between its citizens and between its firms. Doing this would gain public support for social Europe.

3.2   Some illustrations

We would like to suggest the relevance of a capability approach by offering some examples: territorial development, the employment problem and responsibility.

Collective capabilities and territorial development   The single market and the Euro do not only mean wage and price stability and pressure to cut labour costs, as the European Central Bank (ECB) and the macroeconomic view advocate. In parallel, by expanding the markets accessible to firms and making transactions easier and safer, the process of European economic integration creates an incentive to search out new opportunities for innovation, products and work competencies. These could be used as a foundation for creating employment and improving economic competition based on product and job quality. Europe-wide industries are developing their own process of territorial division of labour. This offers opportunities for new standards of work and social protection to be built on the upward trend of the EU trajectory. Studies of territorial economic specialisation indicate that many (but not all) European regions contain specialisation in specific products and services in the long run, which have accumulated absolute advantages. Their capacities in skills, innovation and production permit these regions, at least potentially, to benefit from a process of endogenous growth that could be encouraged by territorial co-ordination and adequate European structural policies. Less favoured regions merit the greatest attention from the European Structural Funds and should be involved with more favoured ones in a learning process about good economic practices. Overall, there is a need for fresh expertise on economic integration that can facilitate the development of social Europe. In particular, reforms of European competition policy that facilitate these trends should be promoted.

The employment problem   In employment questions, a capability approach would break with the standard perception that the level of employment is a process of exogenous factors, economic, financial or technological. Furthermore these factors are commonly viewed more as preventing the rise of employment rather than as facilitating it. A capability approach considers that, in a knowledge-based economy, employment becomes an endogenous input for growth and for raising productivity. In such an economy a continuous dynamic, of gradual and permanent innovation, is taking place. New products and services and new markets are generated that both create jobs and raise productivity. Reciprocally, the creation of jobs stimulates global demand and higher productivity liberates resources that can be used in new investments. Both sustain the growth of the economy. The key factor in profiting from such virtuous circles is thus to develop capabilities, at individual and collective levels, and to maintain them whatever the economic and social circumstances. Individual employability is necessary, but this is no longer enough in relation to the transformation of work: the key issue is responsibility.

Individual capabilities and responsibility   Capability-based policy principles fit well with the transformation of work that accompanies the emergence of a knowledge-based European economy. To be competitive and innovative, standards for employment require responsibility, initiative, autonomy and relational skills. The deployment of these qualities requires workers to possess initiative and the reflexive freedom of action that has no technological substitute. From the social justice point of view, widespread consensus supports claims to a fair balance between work time and private time, a fair wage, good career prospects, the freedom to choose an appropriate job and so on.

The heated debate between a neo-liberal and a capability approach focuses on whether these positive freedoms should or should not be accommodated under the law and through collective bargaining over job design and welfare provision.[6]

Neo-liberals consider that these issues are the individual's responsibility. Individuals can choose whether or not to invest in their human capital. In terms of public policy, employability has to be a strictly individual affair. This is the case, for instance, with the British 'New Deal' or for workfare policies. If necessary, the neo-liberals permit the State to create incentives and penalties to force the development of individual responsibility. Their arguments are ultimately contradictory. Labour does not move because it has no real capability to do so and remains insecure.

---

[6] The so-called 'Supiot Report' develops all these points. (See Supiot 2001.)

Other meanings of employability are more long term and collective; they are closer to capability. In this case, for employability and responsibility to be effective, explicit rules and collective infrastructure are needed to guarantee an equality of capabilities.

Far from neglecting personal responsibility, a capability approach aims to provide individuals with effective means to develop it. It acknowledges that these means should be collectively designed and provided. To some extent (to be elaborated through democratic choice), positive freedoms should be accommodated under the law – or, more flexibly, through collective bargaining over job design and welfare provision. In the wider conception of life and work and of their interaction required by a knowledge-based economy, capability is not simply human capital. Skills are only part of a wider concept of a person's potential, a broad capability to achieve her goals. This capability develops (or declines) depending on daily circumstances of life and work, at least as much as on formalised periods of education and training.

4   **Europe at the crossroads: the activation versus the capability route**

The European project is at the crossroads, in employment and social domains, between an activation or a capability route. As stated in table 1.1, two different frameworks of action (labelled, respectively, activation and capability) are currently at work. Depending on how they reach a compromise or not in European law and method, they could give rise to an activation route or to a capability route. These approaches offer contrasting content and orientation to governance and to the OMC.

Knowing that both frameworks will co-exist in the long run and that what matters is the type of compromise achieved locally, the key issue for the future is how to give priority to a capability framework over an activation framework. In institutional terms, absolute priority[7] must be given to the implementation of Title XI of the Treaty (Social Policy, Education, Vocational Training and Youth) over Title VIII (Employment), not only because Title XI historically precedes Title VIII but, above all, because respecting this hierarchy offers the only way to improve employment and active social security both qualitatively and quantitatively. In our view, this is basically what the objective of 'more and better jobs' and the call for mobilising the social and civil dialogue at all levels means in the Social

---

[7] In Rawls' terms, this requires the implementation of a 'lexical antecedence' of Title XI over Title VIII. Each decision on employment issues taken under Title VIII should respect the basic requirements deployed under Title XI and should not undermine social improvements found under this Title.

Table 1.1. *Frameworks of European action*

Juridical foundation in the Treaty establishing the European Community (EC)	Title VIII Employment	Title XI Social Policy, Education, Vocational Training and Youth
EC Objective	'promoting employment as a matter of common concern' (Article 126) 'promoting a skilled, trained and adaptable workforce and labour markets responsive to economic change' (Article 125)	'improved living and working conditions, so as to make possible their harmonisation while the improvement is maintained, proper social protection, dialogue between management and labour' (Article 136)
EC Instrument	Guidelines and political bargaining between governments	Legislative action, informed and complemented by social dialogue
Methods	OMC	Subsidiarity revisited
Benchmarks	Statistical indicators	Fundamental rights
Implementation	National policies	Collective agreements, European and national jurisprudence, Law
Approach	Employment focus	Work focus
Route	Activation route	Capability route

Agenda. We will first consider the two routes before looking at how to give priority to capability.

4.1   *An activation versus a capability framework*

The activation framework dominated the Employment Strategy at its origin in 1997 and even earlier. The objective fixed for the Union was to maximise its macro rate of employment, whatever the quality of the jobs on offer. It obeys the standard view, shared by the ECB and the macro General Directorates, that the promotion of flexible labour markets achieves maximum efficiency. In that perspective, the reform of welfare regulations must create incentives and penalties to activate insertion into jobs. A primary strategy aimed at this objective is to spend less money on social protection. A political agreement between governments is solicited, the main instruments being the co-ordination of national policies. Guidelines and benchmarking via macroeconomic indicators are used for this purpose; the hidden but strong assumption is that actors are solely rational individuals seeking to further their own interests. Thus implemented, any governance scheme would degenerate into a generalised economic and political market where public goods would be negotiated and put into competition with each other. As Europe would be identified with greater social insecurity, it would have the greatest difficulties to retain its social model and to promote the quality of products, of work – and, above all, of life.

The capability framework gives priority to the implementation of the objective 'to improve living and working conditions, to guarantee fair social protection, to encourage social dialogue.'[8] This can be achieved via negotiation between social (and civil) actors, or via European law and Directives duly prepared by negotiation. Middle-term European programmes of action are politically agreed upon for this purpose; the fundamental rights serve to benchmark national implementation. The objective is to frame a single European labour market that can be both efficient and fair. Improving social and work standards (while taking into account the diversity of national points of departure) is viewed as central to economic growth and the role of Europe in globalisation. Workers and persons have to be provided with real freedom to move, to get a job and to achieve lifetime projects anywhere in Europe. Structural policies are not designed primarily to deregulate labour markets but to improve the collective capabilities of firms, sectors and territories. The underlying but strong assumption is that actors are *capable*. They are supposed by the centre to have the capability to link their own interest with participation in and achievement of common goals. They are supposed to be capable of holding long-term stakes in a collective future. Thus, from Europe, they need rules of deliberation, of action and of access to resources that provide them with real freedom and a due exercise of their responsibility. Down such a route, its citizens could credit Europe with powers to endow them with greater capability. Europe would offer in return palpable added value for personal projects and for the achievement of common goals.

4.2   The OMC: a dead-end?

In employment and social affairs, the policy drive is currently to implement the EES through the OMC. Neither fits well with a capability approach, and even contradict it.

As stated in its series of employment guidelines, the EES is partly oriented towards a capability-friendly approach. Some emphasis is put on

---

[8] As quoted in Article 136 of the Treaty.

the quality of employment, the role of social dialogue and the implementation of this strategy at local level through the horizontal mobilisation of all relevant actors. Employability remains the major concept, but other pillars achieve importance, such as the equality of treatment between men and women and, beyond this, between categories of workers. Under the same concern for employability, the Member States implement policies utilising both frameworks of activation and capability in various ways. For instance, if the UK and Ireland understand 'employability' within a logic of activation and of flexible markets, the Continental countries by contrast interpret it within a context of social dialogue and of lifelong learning. Enhancing employability becomes in Continental countries a responsibility for the labour market that is shared between social actors and the State, hence a subject for a collective action. The capability framework has been at work in some initiatives: for instance in the Charter of Fundamental Rights of Nice, the Directive on the European Work Councils, the Directive on Information and Consultation of Workers or in the Social Dialogue agreements. The mechanism of European Social Dialogue typically obeys the principle of subsidiarity, developed in political philosophy as the primacy of collective autonomy over external State action.

But the move towards a capability approach is hindered by structural difficulties. Activation dominates. First, the call for social actors to mobilise is ambiguous in the EES, and depends on the national relationship existing between them and the State. Are they expected to act within their own terms and sphere of responsibility or simply to facilitate public policies and activation, even if these contradict their own bargaining agenda (specifically about wages and work conditions) and objectives? In other words, is their involvement designed to secure an adequate content for social Europe or to act as an appendix to the Commission or to governments? The same could be said of the mobilising of local actors. Guidelines remain dominated by macroeconomic objectives of wage moderation and of maximising the overall employment rate (both favouring labour market deregulation). A precise understanding of the links between public policy, collective negotiation and economic development is still missing, notably at territorial level. Neither public policies, nor Europe, are ends in themselves. Above all since Maastricht, OMC or not, the co-ordination mechanism has been largely intergovernmental. Democratic discussion was marginalised first (see the role devoted to the European Parliament). Growing difficulties, a lack of possibilities and low ambition have undermined European Social Dialogue. The problems do not reside in democratic or social deficits *per se*. More threatening is the no-future/no-past bargaining (both opportunistic and political) that occurs at each national Presidency and European Council. This will impede any continuity in European action and its long-term objectives. Statistical benchmarking favours policies that manipulate statistical indicators to achieve a better score. It puts countries into competition to discover, not the truly best practices but strategies which improve their statistical profile. This well-known phenomenon, a standard issue in economics, is at work for the employment ratio and the registered unemployment rate, for example. As a consequence, short-termism is promoted. Technical management and strategic bargaining cannot replace social deliberation and long-term commitment.

5 How can Europe make a capability approach a priority?

To date, in every European crisis, the setting of a new agenda has acted as a *cement* to bind together old pieces of completed institutional work and to redesign the future of this work. European construction is an endless accumulation and reinterpretation of institutions and rules. In such a process, new meanings of what has been achieved, 'new pasts', are searched for and usually discovered in close relation to future objectives. Both time arrows are mobilised, the evolutionary one descending from the past to the future and the anticipatory one coming from the future to the past. Ethical long-term orientation is essential to drive this process fairly; but as it has no ethical orientation and no memory of any such thing, as it is the subject of political bargaining, the OMC impedes this virtuous process. Something different is required.

Capability addresses a set of issues, both individual and collective, that covers a spectrum from on-the-job employability to lifelong learning, the prevention of economic and social hazards, a fair and free balance between work and private life and active social security. Capability is at the core of an agenda centred on work issues that, via collective bargaining and law, aims at developing economic competition through collective learning and quality, not between national social models via price and cost cutting. It aims to shape the labour market in such a way as not only to make it more flexible; to implement a capability approach, the advancement of such an agenda will have to escape both the EES and the OMC as they are, and find its own way. Attempting to do so will help keep the best of the EES and the OMC, and it could improve their operation. This means implementing a fresh interpretation of the subsidiarity principle: its true meaning long established in political philosophy[9] (but never developed as such in European affairs) has to be restated.

[9] See Millon-Delsol (1992), an enlightening book, unfortunately in French.

5.1   *Revisiting subsidiarity*

Subsidiarity has been distorted and interpreted as if it regulated competition between the Commission and the Member States over political
power. This was a costly mistake. Now governments, at the first opportunity, invoke this principle to repudiate any progress towards social
Europe. In political philosophy, for a public authority to act in a subsidiary way implies four characteristics. Taken together, these characteristics underline the strong similarities between subsidiary action thus
understood, situated action defined above and the politics of capabilities
that, following Sen, this volume advocates for social Europe.

Collective deliberation and action   Far from distributing administrative competencies between different levels (EU versus Member States)
in a general and definitive way, this principle organises collective deliberation and action. It adapts competencies in each case to the specific problem to be treated. As the memorandum of the Commission, commenting
on its draft for the Treaty, stated in 1991: [this principle] 'lies not so much
in choosing between social issues, distinguishing those for which Community jurisdiction is recognised, as in suggesting what, in the light of
the needs identified and the potential value added by Community action,
is the most appropriate in each case: harmonisation, co-ordination, convergence, co-operation, etc.'.[10] The philosophy of subsidiarity organises,
not policy, but *politics*. Actions are distributed among actors by giving
priority to the lowest level in order to mobilise, to the greatest extent,
the resources, initiatives and capabilities of all actors. This, in particular,
means that, *before creating a new regulation*, the centre must be sure that
other opportunities (co-ordination through mutual expectations, collective agreements at different levels) do not work. In a subsidiary State, the
centre is specifically aware of the risks of excessive regulation and looking
for flexibility and revision by learning. In our views, this is precisely one
of the major roles devoted to the European Social Dialogue.

Common norms   If regulation seems necessary, it can be established by mobilising social and civil actors for the definition of common
norms of quality, employment and social security at the relevant levels
(industry, territory, industrial group, . . .). The core would be the implementation of effective rights of information, participation and action, and
the provision of collective capabilities. As in the 'new approach' developed

---

[10] See 'Initial Contribution by the Commission to the IGC on Political Union', SEC(91)
500, 15 May 1991: 81–82.

by the Union to establish norms of quality for products, European authorities could define only basic requirements (for instance, starting from
the basic capabilities as documented in the Charter of Fundamental
Social Rights for Workers). Trade unions, employers' organisations and
associations with the help of national administrations and researchers
could have the responsibility for voluntary agreements on common norms
that satisfy basic requirements. Via the mechanism of European Social
Dialogue, its extension at sectoral and local levels and the involvement of
civil actors, European authorities can accelerate the process and make it
evolve in the long run towards tighter norms.

The subsidiarity process   As Delors stated in 1991:

La subsidiarité, ce n'est pas seulement une limite à l'intervention d'une autorité
supérieure vis-à-vis d'une personne ou d'une collectivité qui est en mesure d'agir
elle-même, c'est aussi une obligation, pour cette autorité, d'agir vis-à-vis de cette
personne ou de cette collectivité pour lui offrir les moyens de s'accomplir.[11]

The fairness of this process is guaranteed by its goal (which constitutes, simultaneously, its principle of evaluation), the effective freedom of
achievement for every person and collective and the provision of means
adequate to such ends.

5.2   An alliance between practical actors?

What makes such processes of deliberation presumably more efficient
than intergovernmental co-ordination is that they involve 'practical
actors' who have their own knowledge, expertise and jurisprudence about
work situations and stakes, about markets, about innovation possibilities
and so on. Practical actors are involved in daily co-ordination, mutual
expectations and durable relationships. In contrast to political bargaining that responds to opportunistic, general and discursive justifications,
they are subject to pragmatic tests of coherence and effectiveness in firms
and in markets; this should potentially guarantee better outcomes. Public
authorities or researchers should also participate, but primarily to help
establish the objective 'informational basis' on inequalities of capabilities
within Europe with social and civil actors, at different levels: national,
territorial, by sector, or in the face of economic and social hazards. Public social debate could then developed by building upon this basis and a

---

[11] 'Subsidiarity is not only a limit to the intervention of a higher authority in the matters
of an individual or group which can act on their own. It is also an obligation, for that
authority, to act in order to give that individual or group the means to accomplish
themselves' (Delors 1989: 9).

capability approach progressively incorporated as a European principle of reform. Nothing in the Treaties impedes the launching of such processes of deliberation and collective action, which more accurately reflect the true principles of subsidiarity. All the procedural rules needed are already available. In particular, nothing prevents the actors of the European Social Dialogue from beginning to act in this way (their Laeken joint declaration can be read in that sense).

Faced with the impasse of political opposition, the remaining opportunity is thus to develop social Europe through a 'new alliance' of pro-Europe partisans and social and civil actors. The political message of this book is that this alliance can be forged around a politics of capabilities. This alone, by addressing the expectations and needs of European citizens, can bypass the obstacles posed by national political configurations. This alone can foster a broad consensus over European labour market regulation and over welfare provision and its sustainability (hence the economic efficiency of such regulation).

REFERENCES

Delors, J., 1989. 'Le principe de subsidiarité. Contribution au débat', in Institut Européen d'Administration Publique (ed.), *La subsidiarité – principe directeur des futures responsabilités en matière de politiques communautaires*, Maastricht, 7–19
Millon-Delsol, C., 1992. *L'Etat subsidiaire*, Paris, PUF
Richardson, G. B., 1990. *Information and Investment. A Study on the Working of the Competitive Economy*, Oxford, Clarendon Press
Sen, A., 1999. *Development as Freedom*, Oxford, Oxford University Press
Supiot, A. (ed.), 2001. *Beyond Employment: Transformation of Work and the Future of Labour Law in Europe*, Oxford, Oxford University Press
Williamson, O., 1985. *The Economic Institutions of Capitalism: Firms, Market, Relational Contracting*, New York, Free Press

Part I

Products, territories and economic
activity in Europe

The purpose of part I is to illustrate through empirical examples how changing work and labour market practices are impacted by the European policy agenda. Empirical evidence is drawn from the information and consultation of workers through European Work Councils and the intervention of labour courts (Claude Didry, chapter 2); employability and labour force management in firms (Bénédicte Zimmermann, chapter 3); the creation of jobs through the stimulation of innovation and co-operation between firms (Martin Heidenreich, chapter 4); the engagement of public and private actors into pacts for employment and territorial development (Serafino Negrelli, chapter 5); encouraging local governance as a way of making State intervention more efficient and flexible (Pierre-Paul Zalio, chapter 6). These studies were chosen because they together represent the operation of core European concepts and mechanisms (information and consultation, employability, inter-firm cooperation and local governance). Part I concludes with a contribution from a participant in European social dialogue. Drawing upon European experience, Robert Villeneuve in chapter 7 advocates a more participative European governance, making employment, social dialogue and territorial development truly interact.

2 Europe tested through its products: the Renault–Vilvoorde affair and its implications for industrial and employment policies

Claude Didry

1 Introduction

Can EU law today provide a tool for the expression of an 'employment cause',[1] as a way of expressing the specific (and often not recognised) capabilities of workers in the creation of wealth? The capabilities discovered here are the outcomes of a cross-investment: the workers develop abilities and knowledge through a long-term learning that matches the investment of a firm.[2] As a result of workers' mobilisation, the expression of these capabilities is an answer to the transformation of corporate governance in the early 1990s.[3] Jobs cuts as an indicator of the search for greater labour productivity have become the corollary of a concern for increasing share value (Coutrot 1998). The 1997 Renault–Vilvoorde affair was a key illustration of this. But, at the same time, it became the symbol of what European labour law could bring to the expression of an 'employment cause'. This chapter will focus on the following issues that this highly symbolic affair revealed:

- What is the conception of employment underlying Europe's industrial and employment policies?
- What role should product policy[4] (research, innovation, development and production) play in European economic growth?
- Should product policy be the basis for centring employment policies on capabilities development?
- How can the mobilisation of EU law by social partners affect such a renewal?

[1] The notion of 'employment cause' is central to research work in France pertaining to economic situations in which mass lay-offs have been contested by works councils. These situations are analysed by Didry and Tessier (1996) and Didry (1998).
[2] On the two sides of the 'capability approach', freedom on the workers' side and economic possibilities on the firm's side, see the Introduction to this book (pp. 6–8), concerning Amartya Sen and George Richardson.
[3] It limits the monopolisation of work assessment power by the management, as shown through the concept of 'competence' by Zimmermann (chapter 3 in this volume).
[4] By 'product' we mean material product as well as immaterial product, such as services.

Section 2 recalls that the early construction of Europe was focused on the future of products such as coal, steel, planes and cars. Taking the case of the car industry, this section draws attention to the specific conception of employment which Europe was led to choose among several possible 'worlds of production', and to the difficulties in coping with new and diversified types of products and innovations such a conception has created. Emphasis in section 3 is placed on the learning process opened by the legislation on European Works Councils (EWC) in the Renault–Vilvoorde case. Section 4 examines how this mobilisation has affected the renewal of the dynamics of innovation in a sector assumed to be traditional (the car industry). The lessons that can be drawn for the European 'employment cause' are summarised in the conclusion (section 5).

2   'Product grammar' and new conceptions of employment and product evolution

The standard conception is that employment is above all the outcome of *exogenous processes*: financial and productive processes in the case of restructuring, technological processes in the case of the 'new economy'. Job elimination, like job creation, has the appearance of an 'ineluctable' phenomenon. This conception has had a long-standing history in Europe, from the restructuring of the steel and coal industries (the ECSC in the 1950s) to the restructuring of the car industry in the 1980s. Underlying this is a conception of products as mostly standardised, subject to price competition and always threatened by 'excess capacity' of production to be reduced through job cuts. To some extent, the tangible reality of the emergence of European industries as such has never been given due weight until now, save for the aerospace and aircraft industries (Airbus). What is at stake in such a Europeanisation is, first, division of labour within Europe for an industry with its range of product specialisation and capabilities anchored and disseminated in territories.[5] Within an industry, territorial developments are *de facto* co-ordinated by the way the products of this industry are evolving at the European (and often global) level. The second factor is that an ongoing dynamics of gradual and permanent innovation is taking place everywhere, giving rise to new possibilities of creating jobs that cannot be foreseen from the centre. This process of Europeanisation means that the way products can be defined and developed and the way jobs are designed and can be created are dynamically linked. All of this is visible in the transformation of the car

---

[5] On specialisation advantages and the difficulty of coping with regional development policies, see Heidenreich (chapter 4 in this volume).

industry products and in the opposite strategies that European majors follow.

In the automobile industry, the development of assembly line work was initially linked to the dynamics of product standardisation. This came to be questioned in the course of the 1980s. Strategies of product differentiation led to the development of flexibility in production processes. The objective for carmakers was to protect their market share by attempting to respond to a broad range of expectations among buyers, while maintaining the economies of scale that stemmed from standardised production. Assembly lines permitted differentiated products to be manufactured in response to the desires of a customer base segmented on the basis of socio-professional groups. Nevertheless, flexibility and the resulting product changes remain linked to a constant quest for productivity gains through rationalisation of work. Renault had a pioneering role in this respect, with the implementation of project management to guide new product development. Project management aimed at redeploying existing technical components (organs, functions, body components) into new models following customers' tastes and marketing surveys. Its limitations were rapidly perceptible, in that it considerably reduced the capacity of the automobile product to integrate innovation in the areas of organs (engines) and functions. We shall recall what could be a relevant 'product grammar' to interpret this evolution and use it to contrast the strategies of Renault on the one side and Peugeot and Mercedes on the other.

2.1   The product and its worlds

In Storper and Salais' (1997) terminology, the Renault project management corresponds to the change from an industrial world towards a market world. Other European carmakers, such as Peugeot or Mercedes, tried to incorporate elements of interpersonal and immaterial worlds in their industrial strategy; this resulted in innovation returning to the very heart of production and in the conception of a car as a new product. These of course are the stylised facts. They played their role in the Vilvoorde affair.

Economic activity is today characterised by the manufacture of a growing multitude of products and services. Work can be conceived only with a view to manufacturing products subject to varying uses and evolutions. To deal with this diversity, Storper and Salais (1997) propose to envision several *worlds of production*. They consider two dimensions in work, one being the uncertainty as to the product's capacity to find its market, and the other being productivity, understood in a broad sense as the full range of competencies called upon in manufacturing a product. The market

uncertainty dimension contrasts generic products destined for mass predictable markets to dedicated products where specific users' requirements
had to be incorporated. The productivity dimension deals with design
and organisation. It contrasts standardisation (where work is assigned
to elementary routines) and specialisation (where work is creative and
mobilises specific knowledge). The industrial world is both generic and
standard; the market world focuses on dedicated standard products; the
interpersonal world is adapted to dedicated specialised products (for
instance, special-purpose equipment) and the immaterial one aims at
developing new generic products (for instance, personal computers or
Internet). Compromise strategies are possible, and can be observed.

2.2   *Mégane: a market-survey car*

The design of the Renault Mégane, a car which was manufactured at
Vilvoorde, was driven by the corporate marketing division:

> To develop the Mégane programme, we first observed the major socio-cultural
> trends of the past 25 years in the major markets of Western Europe. The most
> noteworthy phenomenon is the transition from the group values of the 1970s
> stemming from May 1968, to the individualism and success values of the 1980s.
> This re-centring of the individual to focus on self, networks of family and friends
> and their values, manifested itself with the emergence of a need for differentiation
> in the automobile industry. (Deconinck 1998: 68)

The orientation towards a market world, combining satisfaction of consumers' tastes and product standardisation, is clearly revealed. In this
context, *habitability* is a key factor; innovations are found primarily in the
body, the sheet metal.

Fundamentally, this strategy is very basic and presents nothing new.
It was given its most complete expression by General Motors as early as
the 1930s (Chandler 1977, Fligstein 1990). Process innovation is turned
towards finding flexibility in assembly lines, without significant questioning of work practices. Yet this product policy hinders more systematic
innovation in the cars' components, and especially in the engines.

2.3   *The return of innovation (the cases of Peugeot and Mercedes)*

In the 1990s, manufacturers officially began exploring other pathways to
restore basic innovation – particularly in engines and vehicle functions – to
a position which project management had undermined. The inadequacies
of the market world orientation were perceptible, and led manufacturers
of mid-range and luxury cars to direct their attention towards research

and innovation and towards the dimension of product *specialisation*. Within the Peugeot group, the 'avant-projet' (the phase preceding project elaboration) was given fresh attention (Ciavaldini 1998: 25). Prior to the gathering of existing data within the firm, the 'avant-projet' engages competing innovative ideas for a new model in a co-operative deliberation. It specifies the choices that need to be made – in particular, between marketing, style and technical studies.

Capitalising on experience is another key factor; it organises the feedback of information from the process of production. The several professions which make the product are put in a position to learn and improve on their practice (Moisdon and Weill 1998). This was impossible under the standard *'contractual'* structure between the design department and the production division that prevailed in the past. In such a structure, the design department is considered as a set of consultants in an external position (Charue-Duboc and Midler 1998), which impedes 'integrating downstream needs' in product design and taking advantage of the 'learning effect' that comes from the analysis of problems encountered during production (Foray and Mowery 1990). Here, Mercedes' strategy appears exemplary. Mercedes extended its product range downwards with the Smart and Class A models, but this was not achieved by abandoning high up-market requirements. As they were in the best position to meet the problems, engineers of the four-wheel drive department were asked to solve the difficulties encountered by models in which the centre of gravity is higher than in a conventional sedan. Mercedes' capacity to make the Smart and Class A models benefit from the experience acquired with other models (four-wheel drive) is a proof of the firm's more general capacity to build on experience. Mercedes took the time required to improve these new products both technically and in terms of the targeted market. The Hambach plant can now count on a development of the Smart model that was previously uncertain.

Within the Renault group, the workers' struggle that grew up around the closing of the Vilvoorde plant revealed the limitations of a 'product policy' whose imprisonment in the market world was basically imposed by submission to financial markets. In effect, this strategy seemed financially secure as it combined standardisation with an eye to market needs. What is striking is that, in reality, the struggle highlights the incapacity of Renault, and maybe of part of the European automobile industry as a whole (excepting Mercedes), to innovate and to confront the challenges raised, particularly by the protection of the environment and the traffic congestion of urban roadways, in Europe and world-wide. The core problem is to be able to view the car as a new product, as a source for new activities and employment. These questions will be raised further in section 4. Let us first look at the Vilvoorde affair and the lessons that can be drawn from that case.

3   Mobilising the European Works Council in the Vilvoorde affair

The conflict sparked off in 1997 by the decision to close the Renault plant in Vilvoorde marks a shift from a local to a European scale, in terms of both the stakes and the legal means deployed. For the first time, EU law constituted a resource for the building of an employment cause on the scale of a group of international and European dimensions: Renault. This cause was expressed via two sets of legal action, one in Belgium representing the employees of the plant located there, and the other representing the Europe-wide group's EWC, located in France, the country of the group's corporate headquarters.

Specifically, the EWC enabled the 'ineluctable' nature of job cuts to be questioned for the first time, and in this respect it constituted a tool for the initial expression of a European employment cause, hence its exemplary nature. After a phase of discovery and experiment 3.1, the law served as a resource for the mobilisation of workers 3.2.

3.1   Discovery and experiment of the prerogatives of the EWC

The Renault EWC was established by an agreement concluded on 5 April 1993 between the Renault executive management and the representative labour unions holding majority positions in the group's plants. Beyond their own organisations, the union representatives signed 'for the European Metalworkers' Federation'. The preamble to the agreement recalls that the EWC takes its meaning with regard to the Single Market instituted on 1 January 1993. The general framework of this contractual act refers in the preamble to the fundamental norms of the Union, the EU Charter of Fundamental Social Rights and the Treaty of the European Union (TEU). The EWC is defined as a 'structure for information and dialogue on the subjects of the group's strategic orientation at the European level concerning economic, financial and social issues, as well as the significant trends in EEC subsidiaries insofar as they have an impact at the European level' (Article 1). The agreement specifies the nature of the information to be communicated by management, and sets an annual timetable for meetings and composition of the EWC. A new agreement was negotiated in 1995 to take into consideration the implementation of the Directive adopted in 1994.[6]

---

[6] CEC (1994).

The dialogue and information structure enabled the social partners to become mutually acquainted, and over four years (1993–6) they took the measure of the stakes at the European level. In 1996 a CGT[7] administrator sitting on the company's board informed the Vilvoorde labour union members that their site was threatened. The FGTB[8] representative on the Renault EWC was able to question the CEO about the future of the Vilvoorde plant, and in 1996 received assurances, before an audience comprising his European colleagues, that the site would be preserved.

The planned closing of the Renault Vilvoorde plant was presented by the group's management at a press conference held at the Brussels Hilton Hotel on 27 February 1997. On Saturday 1 March the members of the European group works council met with the Belgian workers in Vilvoorde. An exceptional meeting held on 11 March 1997 mandated the secretary of the EWC to take legal action against the management on behalf of the council. The European Commission began to move, with a meeting of the Commission headed by Jacques Santer on 5 March 1997. On 6 March 1997 the Commissioner for Social Affairs and Employment, Padraig Flynn, called for a stronger social Europe, highlighting the flagrant infraction of EU law by Renault. Moreover, the Belgian authorities (informed by Renault's management of the closing of Vilvoorde on 21 February 1997) reportedly agreed with the European Competition Commissioner, Karel Van Miert (a member of the Belgian Socialist Party) to look for a way to take Renault's management to court.[9]

On 19 March, using an emergency law procedure, the Renault EWC asked the judge to halt the closure proceedings, since the council had not been consulted before the proceedings were launched. The hearing was held on 26 March. The decision handed down on 4 April by the judge at the Court of Nanterre (near Paris) was founded on European legislation and looked favourably upon the EWC's request. Priority was given to consultation of the European group works council, ahead of other bodies of employee representation, and notably ahead of the Renault Vilvoorde works council. Furthermore, as stipulated in the Directive and in the contractual form under Article 13, the EWC emerged as a body capable of undertaking legal action in an autonomous fashion.

---

[7] The 'Confédération Générale du Travail' (CGT, General Labour Confederation) is the main French union. It was formerly close to the Communist Party. It remains the most important union in Renault, after having been hegemonic from 1945 to the 1980s. CGT entered ETUC in 1999.

[8] The 'Fédération Générale des Travailleurs Belges' (FGTB, General Federation of Belgian Workers) is one of the two main unions in Belgium, the other being the 'Confédération Syndicale Chrétienne' (Christian Union Confederation). It belongs to the ETUC, and is close to the Belgian Socialist Party.

[9] See *EIROnline* (March 1997: 2).

The management appealed against this decision, which was upheld by the Court of Versailles on 5 May 1997. This allowed a new actor to enter the dispute. The European Metalworkers' Federation was heard by the Court of Versailles as a labour union having an interest in the regular operation of the Renault EWC. The ruling highlights the 'useful effect' to be expected from consulting and informing workers. It is grounded in the 1989 European Charter of Workers' Fundamental Social Rights (Moreau 1997), but it is also grounded in the 1994 Directive, and this was decisive for the appeals case. The free-market interpretation offered by the group's management was disallowed, rejecting the argument that, as the Renault EWC was created prior to the 1994 Directive and governed by the Directive's Article 13, it was thus not bound by the obligations created under the Directive. The 1993 and 1995 agreements constituting the European Council were considered as contracts binding on the parties. These agreements became the mandatory reference framing the disputes between the parties, this reference being itself subject to the law, both national and European.

3.2   From the rule of law to the workers' mobilisation[10]

The EWC played a major role in setting a medium-term agenda, the annulment of the closure, for the mobilisation of the Vilvoorde workers. This was first due to a personal initiative of EWC members, who arrived in Vilvoorde on the day immediately following the announcement of the closure. It was also due to the EWC's active commitment to legal action. Thirdly, it relied on the mobilisation of the rules that define the EWC.

And yet, in early 1997, the mobilisation of the Vilvoorde workers was far from being ensured. The workers felt they had been betrayed by the unions after the concessions granted with respect to flexibility in 1993. They remained shocked by the precedent of the closure of the Delacre plant, also in Vilvoorde, in 1996. The workers had resisted the closure of this reknowned Belgian cookies factory with the result that, faced with a refusal to negotiate, the management had closed the plant without any compensation. At Renault, throughout the conflict from March to July 1997, many workers leaned towards a rapid negotiation of compensatory indemnities and early retirement, via 'pre-pension' plans rather than pursuing a long strike and occupation of the plant. But as the legal actions punctuated the movement, they regularly rallied it; these legal actions also helped block any negotiation of possible financial compensation for job losses.

---

[10] This section analyses the mobilisation of European law in the Renault–Vilvoorde case.

The strike had begun without difficulty, with the occupation of the lot where the Clio and Mégane vehicles were parked. After five weeks of conflict, marked by actions in Belgium and in France at different Renault sites, as well as 'Euro-strikes' and 'Euro-walks', the labour leaders, and the Belgian labour leaders in particular, began to realise that they were involved in a long-term conflict. The workers voted to return to work five weeks after the closure was announced, maintaining the occupation of the lot and limiting output to one-third of normal volume. In early April, several successive court rulings in France and in Belgium asked for, and at the same time postponed, the implementation of a new information and consultation procedure at Vilvoorde. Noting the fact that the factory closure had been announced to the press by the CEO before the meeting of the EWC at the Vilvoorde plant, the Belgian judge ordered that the consultation procedure be started over again from scratch. This decision made it impossible for the Vilvoorde workers and their representatives to negotiate a social plan to accompany the eventual loss of jobs, insofar as the management's project was blocked by the courts, at least temporarily. The legislative campaign period that followed the dissolution of the French National Assembly in April gave hope to the Belgian workers, to the extent that the representative of the winning party in the elections, Lionel Jospin, had pledged to reopen the case if the Left won the elections. The annulments of the closure and lay-off procedures in Belgium and in France, and the victory of the Left in the elections in France, strengthened the partisans of a 'struggle for jobs' to oppose the planned closure.

This struggle for jobs took two complementary forms. The first was to reject the site closure and to struggle to save the jobs, as laid out in the contractual commitment made by Renault in 1993. The second consisted in looking for an alternative to the elimination of jobs within the group, by reducing the hours worked. In this respect, the Volkswagen accords stand as a benchmark. An expert (from Bernard Brunhes Consultants[11]) was appointed in July by the French government. Her report was delivered at a time when it had become impossible for the workers to continue their mobilisation against the factory closure. The report reiterated the management's economic arguments without discussion: the aim of closing the Vilvoorde site was to pursue the concentration of production of each model around a limited number of plants. On the basis of this argument the proposal to cut hours worked across the group, initially backed by

[11] Bernard Brunhes has created a consulting group on organisational issues, working especially in the public firms. He was part of the Gyllenhamar group after the Renault Vilvoorde crisis.

the Confédération Française Democratique du Travail (CFDT), was set aside. The report, however, is a sort of 'memorandum' of arbitration, in that it integrated the FGTB's call to maintain 400 jobs at the site and keep the employment contracts for all employees for two years, so as to prepare substantial training schemes.[12] The final agreement negotiated by the Belgian unions integrated these two proposals which, for them, were a substantial victory over a pure and simple site closure. In addition to the conservation of employment contracts over two years Renault agreed to pay for the training that the workers desired.

4   The European automobile industry between over-capacity and innovation

The Renault–Vilvoorde affair brought to light the importance of defining a European line of thought and policy with regard to the automobile industry. This line unexpectedly echoed the criticism voiced by the European Parliament of the Commission's focus on competitiveness 4.1. What is at stake here is to find a way out of the price war between European carmakers and to move towards a policy for new European automobile products. This 'new automobile' has to incorporate the desire to satisfy emergent living standards in Europe, notably with respect to the pollution problems caused by cars 4.2. The Renault–Vilvoorde affair also shed lights on the *territorial* dimension of European employment policies and the need to focus on capabilities development 4.3.

4.1   The race for the market

The strategy of the Renault group's executive management closely espoused the hypothesis of permanent over-capacity in a 'mature' market. This strategy led Renault to undertake an 'aggressive restructuring programme' in the 1990s (Hancké 2000). Its objective was to steadily lower the profitability threshold (expressed in terms of the minimum number of cars to be produced) by reducing the labour force via externalisation and by raising productivity through work flexibility. Economies of scale

---

[12] Maintaining jobs at the site was a strategy that had been tried some ten years earlier by Belgian metalworkers in the region, in the fight against the closing of the Philips factory in Louvain; thanks to this strategy, activity resumed at the site ten years later. The retention of employment contracts for two years was inspired by the Billancourt factory closure in 2003: 'We had in mind the Renault Billancourt closing, where the closing was spread over five years' (Interview with Karel Gacoms, secretary of the FGTB metalworkers' federation in the Brabant region).

were sought by producing one model per factory. Less explicitly than at GM Europe, the production sites were subject to benchmarking on the basis of unit wage costs, which pitted them against each other. In 1996, as Renault's market share fell in Europe, the aim shifted to lowering the price of the units produced, implying continued and accelerated reduction of costs. The fluctuation of Renault's share price on the financial markets in late 1996 and early 1997, linked to the carmaker's loss of market share, was stabilised by the announcement of the Vilvoorde plant closure that led to the elimination of over 3,000 jobs, and by the announcement of a massive lay-off affecting 2,764 jobs, announced to the central works council in April 1997. Beyond the strong signal sent by elimination of over 5,764 jobs, the expertise acquired by Renault in this domain over fifteen years further reassured the markets.

This decision was in line with the Commission's industrial policy which maintained the spectre of 'one carmaker too many' and fostered the fight between manufacturers. In the division between the new and the old economies, the automobile industry was generally ranked among the declining industries. The future of the European automobile industry was generally understood through an hypothesis of market saturation. This assumption was given force by a report drawn up in 1997 by 'Analyse Auto' an expert working with the European Commission's DG Enterprise, entitled *'Excess Capacity in the European Car Industry. Report Prepared for the European Commission'*. It was commonly accepted that there was one carmaker too many in Europe; the assertion that Renault and PSA were seen as not attaining a 'critical mass' compared to other manufacturers, in particular Volkswagen, made it even more probable that this 'extra carmaker' would be French.

4.2   The foundations of an innovation policy in the automobile industry

The mobilisation around the Vilvoorde closure appeared in a context in which economic actors were largely convinced that they had little room to manoeuvre. The Vilvoorde affair contributed to a criticism of the way in which economic information was disseminated, via the resolution adopted by the European Parliament on 13 March 1997, following the report by the MEP Alan John Donnelly (see Donnelly 1997). Both the resolution and the report were critical of the Commission's inaction regarding innovation. The Parliament declared that it was

worried by the narrow scope of the missions assigned to the Commission Task Force on 'Cars for Tomorrow', in light of the range of challenges facing the automobile industry regarding investment and research–development, and the key role that this task force must play in preserving the competitiveness of the industry in question and in serving as a rallying point for collaboration and solidarity in this sector. (Resolution adopted 13 March 1997[13])

The role of a task force in thinking about the 'car of tomorrow' would be, among other things, to engage carmakers in co-operation to work on materials and engines that help cut pollutant emissions.

Donnelly's report and the Parliament's resolution highlight the prior assumptions of the analyses focusing exclusively on competitiveness: the product is taken for granted, so that competitiveness can be enhanced only by downward pressure on production costs, and within these costs on the element that constitutes a guarantee of good management in the eyes of financial markets – labour costs. Countering these assumptions, Donnelly's report puts forward the need for an innovation-based strategy in the automobile industry.[14] It cites as an example the Partnership for a New Generation of Vehicles (PNGV) created by the Clinton Administration in 1992 and largely funded by the US government, and calls upon the 'industry/research task forces' existing in Europe to commit themselves to the design of the car of the future. Such an initiative is all the more necessary in Europe as carmakers are caught up in a process that some experts have called the 'Great Car Wars'.

The tardiness of Europe with respect to innovation in the automobile industry is thus highlighted. The work of the research task force for fundamental research led to the targeting of specific objectives, with the Technologies for Carbon Fibre Reinforced, Modular, Automotive Structures (TECABS) programme, 'which associated Volkswagen (project leader), Renault and Volvo', with 'the aim of developing by 2004 an industrial prototype vehicle that could be produced at a pace of 50 units a day (as opposed to 2,000 for a conventional series)'.[15] Toyota, however, has marketed the first hybrid vehicle powered by electricity and gasoline, already available in Japan and in Europe.

4.3   Territorial governance risks serving the ends of social dumping

In a market perceived to be hypercompetitive, the persistence of the Vilvoorde plant up to 1997 proves the Belgian workers' capacity to achieve

---

[13] European Parliament, Plenary Session, Minutes of 13/03/1997 – Final Edition, 'Industrial competitiveness (A4-0052/1997), Resolution on the communication from the Commission to the Council, the European Parliament, the Economic and Social Committee and the Committee of the Regions 'European Automobile Industry 1996' (EP 1997).

[14] See also *EIROnline* (April 1997: 1).

[15] 'Automobiles, New Materials and Computers, Digital Simulation Prepare the way for Composites', *La Tribune* (27 March 2001).

production meeting international standards. In this respect the Renault factory is not an exception: car manufacturing is a major speciality of the Belgian economy.[16] Indeed, of all European countries, Belgium has the highest density of workers linked to the automobile industry. Within the Renault group, the strength of the plant was high productivity tied to product quality, which counterbalanced the high level of wage costs in Belgium owing to high remuneration and costs for social protection.[17] In 1993, talks between management and unions led to an agreement on flexible hours. In exchange for flexibility the management pledged to invest 8 million Belgian francs[18] to build an assembly line for the new line of Mégane models. In the context of sharply competitive benchmarking between production sites, the Belgian unions succeeded in laying the groundwork for an orientation of human resources management over the longer term. The level of investment made it reasonable to anticipate a perspective of several years before the existence of the site would be called into question.

Yet the high competencies and specialisation of Belgian workers in carmaking were undermined by the incoherence of the European Structural Funds policies and their absence of co-ordination with other European policies. There was much perplexity at Vilvoorde and elsewhere when, on 6 March 1997, the day after the closure was announced, the European Competition Commissioner Karel Van Miert announced that Renault would receive a subsidy of 7 million ECU from the Fonds Européen de Developpement Regional (FEDER),[19] in order to enlarge its plant in Valladolid in Spain. The Spanish site was also supported by the Spanish government and the regional government, to a total of 11 million ECU in subsidies to finance its extension. Emerging in the aftermath of the closure of the Vilvoorde site, the subsidy-hunting practices of European industrial groups favoured by these policies were brought to light. Outside of the industrial groups, this put in question the coherence of EU territorial policy. European regional policies see the territories as autonomous units, without conceptualising their integration into the European Union as a whole.

The notion of 'governance of territories' proved to be inadequate for founding a European policy to strengthen the Union. The problem lies in

---

[16] 'Assembly, a Belgian Speciality', *EIROnline* (30 March 1997: 3) and 'Le secteur va mieux grâce à VW Forest, l'automobile emploie 8.400 personnes à Bruxelles' in the Belgian newspaper *Le Soir* (6 February 2003).

[17] 'The Belgian social, fiscal and salary systems make the effective cost of an hour of work 30 per cent higher than in French factories', Louis Schweitzer, minutes of the extraordinary session of the European group works council (11 March 1997).

[18] 1.4 million French francs.

[19] In English, the European Regional Development Fund (EFDR).

the fact that, as stated in the Introduction, the construction of Europe does not consist in adding up countries with the idea that this will suffice to equalise their levels of development,[20] nor in encouraging competition between territories with a reduction of public action to promoting the market mentality.[21] The construction of Europe has now entered the Single Market phase, marked by an ongoing and deepening division of labour across the EU itself. This creates a complex and interlocking web of co-operation and competition between firms, between order givers and suppliers and between territories, etc. A set of interdependencies in innovative activities must be grasped to promote industrialisation and employment. In the aftermath of the Vilvoorde crisis, the Gyllenhamar report emphasised that for public action in Europe today: 'The point of departure is constituted by the setting up of the single market, replacing 15 different national sets of regulations pertaining to goods and services with a unique set of EU provisions guided by accompanying policies' (Gyllenhamar 1998: 4). Following Gyllenhamar's proposal, the creation in 2001 of the 'European Monitoring Centre on Change'[22] was an important step towards data collection and the observation of an emerging 'EU Economy' to which nations and regions can contribute via their specialisation. But contemplation is not action. In the case of the automobile industry an EU initiative remains necessary to push the industry towards a product policy for 'new European cars'. This should be done in a variety of forms with help from all existing European instruments, and will require active co-ordination between the multiple fields of European action.

5   **Conclusion: employment and the need for European product politics**

The social struggle provoked by the closure of the Renault plant in Vilvoorde remains on the agenda, as 400 jobs still exist onsite. This mobilisation of the Vilvoorde workers is not simply a defence of the status quo in the automobile industry. The support for the EWC reveals, by the debates it elicited, the need for European product policies focusing on innovation, quality competition, co-ordinated regional development and workers' and firms' capabilities. Macro policies of stabilisation cannot cope with this need, nor can pure market competition policies. The danger is that of halting the construction of the European economic space half-way

---

[20] See chapter 9 by Jacky Fayolle and Anne Lécuyer in this volume.
[21] See Pierre-Paul Zalio's presentation of the Marseilles' case in chapter 6 in this volume.
[22] Within the European Foundation for the Improvement of Living and Working Conditions.

if innovation policy is restricted to sectors thought to be advanced (such as information technology, communication or biotechnology), while leaving sectors considered to be traditional to slowly die out without giving them a chance to respond to the requirements of the future. In all 'old' and 'new' industries and services, and especially in the car industry, new products should be developed on a European scale that permit new ways of combining work and personal development, achieving common goods such as a clean environment and quality of life, improving the quality of products, etc.

This implies a broad action on the European level, action which is today far from having found its field of operations. Indeed one can say that, in some respects, Europe has joined the 'employment cause' in its own fashion since the Luxembourg employment summit in 1997. But to help build up a durable industrial advantage for European countries, employment policy should not be restricted to only restructuring and an 'ineluctable' adaptation to exogenous economic factors. Employment policy has to focus on the development of work capabilities everywhere and at all levels, and to consider appropriate job creation as an endogenous input for growth and productivity. Among other things, this means that it is not enough to decentralise employment policy at a local level. Co-ordination between territories must be sought, as well as between European, regional and innovation policies. This domain constitutes a key case for developing a mainstreaming approach truly focused on a European 'employment cause'. The last, but not least, lesson from Vilvoorde is that *social dialogue* at all levels must be actively involved in this approach. Social dialogue has to overcome the danger of a specialisation in the social treatment of restructuring, and has to open itself to economic development in a broad sense, at a European level. It also has to face globalisation. By confining the social partners to a limited, 'social', domain, and keeping them out of projects for a European constitution, one runs the risk of seeing European discussions being once again monopolised by experts, in this case experts in constitutional law.

The contribution to the organization of globalisation through the defence and enhancement of the European social model is a perspective for Social Dialogue[23] that goes back to the roots of the Val Duchesse process launched by Jacque Delors in 1985. At that time, social partners were deeply associated by the new President of the Commission with choices such as the achievement of the Single Market or the Single European Act (SEA). They had to take up positions on the foundations of the European construction and were active in all the reforms of the Delors

---

[23] See chapter 11 by Jean Lapeyre in this volume.

era (SEA, Maastricht Treaty). It was by being part of the global process of building Europe that social partners were able to promote the adoption of important social directives later on (e.g. EWCs, workers' participation in the organs of European limited companies, information and consultation of workers). Europe then began to take on some reality in the workers' daily lives.

REFERENCES

Analyse Auto, 1997. *Excess Capacity in the European Car Industry, Report prepared for the European Commission*, Antwerp, Analyse Auto
Chandler, A. D., 1977. *The Visible Hand: The Managerial Revolution in American Business*, Cambridge, MA, Belknap Press
Charue-Duboc, F. and C. Midler, 1998. 'Au-delà du management de projet, une évolution des métiers de conception, l'exemple des métiers de conception', in N. Bertrand, J.-M. Pointet and J.-C. Thenard (eds.), *La Politique du produit*, Noisy, GIP Mutations industrielles, 231–244.
Ciavaldini, B., 1998. 'L'avant-projet: dans quelle organisation naît une voiture? Les évolutions au sein du groupe PSA Peugeot-Citroën', in N. Bertrand, J.-M. Pointet, and J.-C. Thenard (eds.), *La Politique du produit*, Noisy, GIP Mutations industrielles, 35–56
Coutrot, T., 1998. *L'entreprise néo-libérale, nouvelle utopie du capitalisme*, Paris, La Découverte
Deconinck, R., 1998. 'Innovation, différenciation et performance économique dans le développement des nouveaux projets', in N. Bertrand, J.-M. Pointet and J.-C. Thenard (eds.), *La Politique du produit*, Noisy, GIP Mutations industrielles, 61–72
Didry, C., 1998. 'Les comités d'entreprise face aux licenciements collectifs, trois registres d'argumentation', *Revue Française de Sociologie*, 39(3), 495–534
Didry, C. and L. Tessier, 1996. 'La cause de l'emploi, les usages du droit dans la contestation de plan sociaux', *Travail et emploi*, 69, 23–36
Donnelly, A. J. (rapporteur), 1997. *Report on the Communication from the Commission to the Council, the European Parliament, the Economic and Social Committee and the Committee of the Regions 'European Automobile Industry 1996' (COM(96)0327-C4-0493/96)*, Report A4-0052/97 of the European Parliament, Committee on Economic and Monetary Affairs and Industrial Policy
European Industrial Relations Observatory (EIRO), 1997/2000. *EIROnline*, www.eiro.eurofound.ie.
European Commission, 1998. 'Proposal for a Directive Establishing a General Framework for Informing and Consulting Employees in the European Community', 11 November
Fligstein, N., 1990. *The Transformation of Corporate Control*, Cambridge MA, Harvard University Press
Foray, D. and D. C. Mowery, 1990. 'L'intégration de la R&D industrielle: nouvelles perspectives d'analyse', *Revue Economique*, 41(3), 501–531

Gyllenhamar, P., 1998. *Gérer le changement, rapport final du groupe d'experts de haut niveau sur les implications économiques et sociales des mutations industrielles*, Brussels, European Commission

Hancké, B., 2000. 'European Works Council and Industrial Restructuring in the European Motor Industry', *European Journal of Industrial Relations*, 6(1), 35–59

Moisdon, J.-C. and B. Weill, 1998. 'La capitalisation technique pour l'innovation: expériences dans la conception automobile', in N. Bertrand, J.-M. Pointet and J.-C. Thenard (eds.), *La Politique du produit*, Noisy, GIP Mutations industrielles, 209–230

Moreau, M.-A., 1997. 'A propos de l'"affaire Renault"', TGI Nanterre 4 avril 1997 et cour d'appel de Versailles 7 mai 1997', *Droit social*, 5 May, 493–503

Pointet, J.-M., 1998. 'La politique du produit Mercedes: addition de projets et dysfonctionnement du processus d'innovation des Smart et Classe A', in N. Bertrand, J.-M. Pointet and J.-C. Thenard (eds.), *La Politique du produit*, Noisy, GIP Mutations industrielles, 73–90

Storper, M. and R. Salais, 1997. *Worlds of Production: The Action Frameworks of the Economy*, Cambridge, MA, Harvard University Press

3   Competences-oriented logics and the politics of employability

Bénédicte Zimmermann

1   Introduction   MSO M12

Since the early 1990s, the concept of 'competences' has experienced new developments within the world of labour. This has produced – in France particularly, but also in other European countries such as Germany – a set of new management practices, which are now the object of attempts to systematise them into a 'competence-oriented logic'.[1] The scope of these attempts is all the more important as the concept of competence often goes along with that of 'employability'. In particular, the logics of evaluation and classification of persons which result from them are placed at the core of a 'politics of employability'. The notion of employability has been promoted by European employment policy as one of the 'four pillars' for reforming the labour market (EC 2000c).[2] It is therefore interesting to look into the modes of implementation of one of its possible practical expressions. One of the aims of this chapter is to explore the implications, but also the limits, of a politics of employability too exclusively centred on the logic of competence. Indeed, the concept of competence tends on the one hand to locate employability on the side of the individual – the individual is responsible for updating and developing her competences – and to construct employability primarily upon an internal competence market within the company on the other. A politics of employability developed thus is first oriented towards the needs of companies and only in second place towards the needs of employees as regards career development.

A politics of employability directed towards both the needs of the company and of the employee cannot rest only on a competence-oriented logic mainly determined by a strategy of individualisation of the management of human resources. Such a politics requires *collective framing* – bringing into play the quality of employment and collective guarantees as regards fair treatment or transferability of acquired competences from one

---

[1] 'Logique de compétences' in French.
[2] On the European Employment Strategy, see Gilles Raveaud's chapter 8 in this volume.

company to another, for example. However, such collective guarantees, in the midst of a capabilities approach as sketched out in this volume,[3] are absent from the competence-oriented logic, as empirical results seem to show.

The competence-oriented logic as implemented by firms is indeed characterised by its increasing integration into work practices. This entails a tension for the employees between company-based demands for individual adaptability, and public – especially European – exhortations to lifelong training and career development. Contrary to what one might think at first glance, our observations show that the competence-oriented logic implemented at firm level is unable to reconcile both demands. The tension produced by this twofold injunction upon the employee calls for collective solutions reaching beyond the firm's boundaries. Furthermore, the study quite clearly shows that in order to implement a politics of employability whose scope is not limited to a logic of competence development at managerial level but also constitutes a politics of capabilities, a *collective and institutional framework* needs to be set up which can be backed by procedures of social dialogue.

Section 2 is devoted to identifying the different elements of the debate on competence in France. Section 3 seeks to analyse the practices used in formalising, identifying and deriving value from competences in the workplace. This section draws on surveys conducted in twelve selected French companies in four different sectors – metalworking, agribusiness, insurance and pharmaceuticals,[4] and seeks to study the production of competences 'in situ', i.e. related to actual workplace contexts. Section 4 attempts to re-examine, in the light of these case studies, the issue of competences as a focus of employability politics and collective framing.

2   Competences: the individual versus the collective?

The ways in which the concept of competence is used in the work sphere are ambiguous. They simultaneously confer value on the person and individualise her treatment. This is because competences are attached to the employee, to her abilities and career path, and therefore entail a type of personnel management driven by a logic that is no longer focused on posts but on persons (Zarifian 1999). The relationship between the individual and the collective in the workplace therefore needs to be reconsidered (Garsten and Jacobsson 2003). However, such a focus on persons does

---

[3] See especially Robert Salais' chapter 18 in this volume.
[4] The survey was based on an examination of documents and on semi-structured interviews conducted between April and June 1999 with trade union representatives and human resources managers.

not mean that collective contractual constraints are obsolete, contrary
to the assertions of those who reduce, a little too hastily, the individ-
ual/collective relationship, which is intrinsic to a competence-oriented
logic, to an opposition between the sovereign power of the employer and
collective regulatory control. Practices of individualisation that take into
account the competences of employees are not incompatible with collective frameworks – on condition, that is, that such practices are not
called upon merely to assist the employer in the managing of economic
contingencies. This is precisely where all the ambiguity of the uses of
'competence' as a concept in the work sphere is to be found. Such uses
are productive of a tension between the individual and the collective which
implies in the long run either a slackening of the forms of collective regulation, or their reinvention.

The MEDEF (*Mouvement des entreprises de France*), which placed competences at the very heart of its *Journées internationales de la formation*
(International training days) in October 1998, highlights the need for
employee accountability and insists on a definition of competences given by
companies themselves. Does this mean that competence is to be considered as a managerial concept whose ineluctable logic of individualisation
would allow employers to escape collective regulatory control while developing new forms of subordination?[5] If competence really corresponds to
'the taking of responsibility in a workplace situation' (Lichtenberger 1997:
14), everything depends on the conditions under which that responsibility is assumed. If the context is one in which the individualisation of
personnel management aims at freeing the employer from collective constraints, responsibility goes along with lack of job security for staff and
exclusion from the company of those unable of keeping their competences up to date. However, if it genuinely involves taking into account
the person, responsibility calls for the construction by both employer and
employee of 'work organisations relevant to the company and protective
of employees' (Fairise and Gérard 1998). But the need remains to create
the conditions for such a joint construction, since competence-oriented
approaches – with a few exceptions – tend more towards individualisation
as a technique for personnel management than towards concerted action
by employers and the workforce.

In order to consider the conditions under which a competence-oriented
logic both efficient for the company and providing security for employees might emerge, two issues need to be raised: the role of the collective
dimension in the building of competences, and the guarantees of fair

[5] On the 'managerial revolution' based on a competence-oriented logic promoted by
employers see 'Compétence', 2001 (Special Issue of *Sociologie du travail*).

treatment that the former can introduce into individualising practices. Who are the actors and what are the means for the acquisition, assessment and recognition of competences? These are core issues. They call for a response from the collective rather than a unilateral definition by the employer, which some may wish to institute. But what does 'the collective' mean here? What are its constituents? At what level is it located? The MEDEF seeks to define – or, indeed, to confine – competences to their deployment at corporate level: 'It is the company's task to identify, evaluate, validate and valorise them' (MEDEF 1998). However, to say that the company is the locus for competence validation has strong implications both for traditional certification procedures and for the regulatory activity of a series of collective authorities, such as those representing industrial sectors and the public authorities (Maggi-Germain 1999: 693).

The essential ambivalence of the concept of competence – which allows diverse interpretations for employees – does in fact make the issue all the more problematic as it affects the whole spectrum of the firm's activities, ranging from wages to work organisation and including internal structures of management and job categorisation (Eyraud *et al.* 1989), training and domains hitherto outside the company such as the certification of knowledge. Competence-oriented logics are in many ways synonymous with a *redistribution of power and responsibility*, not only between employers, employees and their representatives, but also between the latter and the State, and therefore embody high stakes.

This ambivalence is exacerbated by the difficulty of defining with any precision the boundary between the concept of competence and the related notions of 'qualification' and 'ability' (Dubar 1996). Depending on the authors, or actors, one notion encompasses the other or vice versa. Thus, while some refer to qualification as validated expertise, and therefore a component of competence, in the same way as experience for example (*Le Monde* 1999), others define a person's qualification as 'the whole range of his or her applied competences, along with all the individual's acquired theoretical and practical knowledge, expertise and experience, not all of which are inevitably used in his or her work' (CFDT 1995: 6). For its part, the MEDEF makes a distinction between professional qualification, which 'guarantees the potential abilities placed at the employer's service by the employee . . . and from which value is derived by a profession in standard situations', and professional competence, defined as 'a combination of knowledge, know-how, experience and behaviours applied in a given context' (MEDEF 1998).

One can get a glimpse of the political stakes behind such semantic games. The concept of 'qualification', whose meaning was for a long time controversial, has now reached a consensus based on the idea of certification validated by public authorities outside the firm. This entails that to withdraw the notion of competence from the scope of qualification is to withdraw the former from the historical forms of collective control associated with the social codification of qualification. On the other hand, to include competence under the heading of qualification is to reassert the necessity of socially recognised and guaranteed procedures for the evaluation of individual abilities. How to identify and evaluate such abilities is the core issue. Whatever the chosen option, 'ability' is generally understood as a set of intellectual, practical and relational resources which can be developed by a person. In short, it corresponds to a *potential*. But whereas the qualification-based approach focuses on abstract norms – i.e. detached from daily working practice – and aims at identifying and evaluating this potential with a concern for objectivity, general applicability and transferability, the competence-oriented logic inscribes such recognition in specific work practices inside the firm.[6] Although the idea of inscribing the assessment of individual abilities in actual workplace situations might be seducing in many ways, socially recognised methods for its validation must still be found (Feutrie and Verdier 1993). The designation of the company, or rather the workshop or the office, as the locus of such recognition makes large-scale solutions defined for qualification hard to transfer to this level. It is therefore wrong to see qualification as opposed to competence. The relationship between them is better expressed as one of *complementarity*, for both companies and employees.

The notion of competence refers in its very etymology (Latin: *competentia*) to the concept of *relationship*. In France in the sixteenth century, 'competence' took on the legal meaning of 'the legally acknowledged capacity of a public authority to carry out a given action under defined conditions', becoming in the seventeenth century 'in-depth, recognised knowledge conferring the right to judge or to take decisions in certain areas' (*Le Petit Robert* 1988: 349). Two constant themes can be noted from this historical development: first, a reference to the conditions under which competence is used, and secondly a need for recognition. This leads us in this chapter to consider competence from a finalised point of view, as the validated use by a person in the workplace of abilities that are of pragmatic, intellectual and relational nature. This definition, which highlights the contextual dimension of competence use and evaluation, assumes that the issue is dealt with from the point of view of the actual practices of economic agents, rather than on the basis of abstract and speculative definitions. It implies that competences should be identified

---

[6] For a discussion of the relationship between the concepts of qualification and competence, see notably Schwartz (1992), Tanguy (1998).

where they are used, according to the principles of dynamic evolution and periodical readjustments.

Competence is not, however, solely to be sought in individuals carrying out activities: it is the result of a joint process of construction by employees and the company: the former supply their abilities and the latter the conditions allowing them to be expressed and kept up to date. As many writers on this subject have emphasised, competences require the simultaneous presence of three components: knowledge, will and the power to act, the latter being to some extent outside the control of the employee and dependent on workplace organisation (Lichtenberger 1997: 14, Le Boterf 1998: 150). Furthermore, another fundamental yet too often neglected element needs to be added to this list, which is the fact that competence cannot be considered in isolation from the judgement of the person who testifies to its existence (Eymard-Duvernay and Marchal 1997; Richebé 2002). Indeed competence does not exist by itself, but is always the result of a process of *evaluation and recognition* performed by others. This essential link between competence and judgement by others leads us to raise the issue of competence production and identification even before we question its validation.

3   Competence implementation in firms

One can observe at least three different steps in the implementation of a competence-centred logic in companies. The first is an *inventory of duties or jobs* within the firm in order to classify them. This step is one in which the qualification and know-how required by the firm are identified notwithstanding the persons who may exercise them. It is broken down into a series of operations: job inventory, job description, job analysis (with standardised profiles and a defined set of reference criteria) and lastly the definition of a scale for measuring each job. At this first stage, corporate practices closely conform to national agreements on classification.

The second step consists in *positioning each employee* individually within the classification structure thus obtained. The third step deals with the *evolution of job classifications and employee grading* over time. In contrast to the first stage, which is structured by national classification criteria agreements, the following two are shaped more by corporate policies, since the employer enjoys control over individual human resources management. However it is primarily onto the mechanisms produced in these last two phases that a competence logic can to be grafted.[7]

---

[7] For this reason, our remarks will concentrate here on these two last phases. For a more detailed analysis of the phase of classification of jobs and functions, see Zimmermann (2000).

From this perspective, it is significant that no implementation agreement for classification criteria or competence-centred logics has ever been signed in any of the companies studied, even in those cases where management and trade union representatives have worked together to define tools for implementation. In the most favourable circumstances, such collaboration has developed on joint employer/employee implementing committees, whose proposals have been validated later by management. When it exists in companies, social dialogue on competences occurs in an atmosphere more akin to deliberation than to negotiation. Whereas negotiation involves bargaining on the basis of the respective interests of the parties within a predetermined cognitive framework, deliberation is here more a matter of collective construction of the necessary cognitive framework and the search for common interests with a view to co-ordinating action.

3.1   *Employee evaluation: a core issue*

The second step above – i.e. the grading of workers – is particularly problematic. It is, in the four sectors studied – metalworking, agribusiness, insurance and pharmaceuticals – governed by national classification agreements based on grading criteria.[8] Grading criteria were first developed in the metalworking sector in the 1970s, in order to break the rigidity of the 'Parodi' classification tables introduced at branch level after 1945 (Parodi was the French Minister of Labour when the classifications were negotiated). The introduction of grading criteria in national agreements on classification went along with a shift in the evaluation and grading of employees from sector level to firm level, and by doing so led to a greater individualisation of their treatment.

To put it briefly, this new type of classification is based on grading levels which correspond to predetermined criteria, such as levels of knowledge, responsibility, autonomy, versatility, technical nature, etc. It is the definition of these criteria – and no longer the specification of jobs as was the case in the Parodi tables – which is the subject of national agreements at branch level. Job description and specification is a task which is now taken up by firms, and is based on national criteria as well as the firms' own specific productive constraints. Moreover, posts are no longer the sole referent of the classification and the employee's personal contribution can be more easily taken into account. All these arrangements aim at turning grading criteria-based classification into an evolutional system, appropriate for both the company and the employee, in order to permit

---

[8] 'Accords à critères classants' in French.

a more global and flexible recognition of changing qualifications, in relation to the ever-changing needs of the firm. But employee evaluation – that is to say the assessment of individuals' actual competences and work practices in relation to the work required – raises numerous problems in companies. The union representatives' uneasiness about this issue reveals how hard it is for any trade union, as a collective organisation, to enter this territory.

Many company case studies emphasise a lack of transparency in the evaluation process. Trade union representatives do not intervene at this stage unless an employee lodges an appeal. This allocation of roles does in fact seem to be backed by a consensus between management and unions, who are not particularly keen on judging employees. As a general rule, supervisors at $n + 1$ level are crucial players here. This key role of supervisors is nevertheless not beyond question; staff at this level are frequently poorly prepared and resourced to take on the new role of assessor. Classification criteria make supervisors at level $n + 1$ key agents of corporate human resources policy, especially in a competence-oriented logic. This decision to devolve power to supervisors is based on the proximity of the assessor to the assessed; It aims at providing the right conditions for better informed and more transparent judgements, but it has encountered some resistance within the ranks of the supervisors themselves. With the exception of Sollac in the steel industry and one agribusiness firm, none of the staff members in our sample had received specific training in this area.

Various cases need to be distinguished to reflect the degrees to which the evaluation procedure is formalised. Where the procedure is most advanced, the management has defined an evaluation criteria table to be filled in by supervisors during a mandatory individual interview with each of their subordinates. While such a framework for the evaluation procedure would seem necessary and logical, it is in fact a situation which is encountered in only a few companies. All the ingredients are rarely found together: either the supervisor is able to do without an assessment interview, or no evaluation tool is provided. Some companies combine both failings. This is true of one pharmaceutical company, where the lack of formalisation tools, plus the absence of any training for the supervisors, is said by a union representative to have resulted in 'real deterioration in the evaluation and grading programme'. This example provides an illustration of the fact that 'competences do not exist independently of the evaluation practices that seek to determine them' (Le Boterf 1998: 144), and argues for the definition of tools to frame these practices, and ensure a degree of codification, not of the assessments, but of the approach and criteria leading to them (Thévenot 1997).

Once the evaluation is made by an assessor close to the employee, it must then be validated by the personnel manager and, depending on the case, by the supervisor at intermediate level $n + 2$. The aim of this added level of validation is to protect employees against the risk of a dishonest or hostile supervisor. The fact that assessors are themselves monitored by their own supervisor is meant to provide a further barrier against abuse. However, if despite all this an employee still feels that she has been unfairly treated, an appeal can be lodged, which will be processed either by the human resources management or by a joint employer/employee committee in the company. Agribusiness companies are the only firms who register a large number of individual appeals. Elsewhere, the number is negligible.[9]

The evaluation process entailed by the grading of employees crystallises in an exemplary way a whole range of issues that inevitably arise in a competence-oriented approach. Specifically, it raises the issue of the codification of employee evaluation and grading and of the definition of collective rules or tools that may be applied to a plurality of individual cases, in relation to principles of justice and equity.

3.2   *The gap between competence-oriented logic and employability politics*

The stages described above aim at producing a classification, i.e. a snapshot of the division of labour in a company at a given moment. They can thus, record or stabilise the results of a competence-centred logic, but cannot be the locus of its implementation. The assessment of a corporate logic focused on competence and employability, which takes into account the possibilities for ongoing development of employees within the classification system, must be undertaken at another level.

However, except when there is a national agreement specifically focused on competences, as in the steel industry and the pharmaceutical sector, no genuine competence and employability dynamic is to be found. Even in the pharmaceutical sector, where conditions might appear conducive to the flourishing of such a dynamic, given the existence of agreements on prospective management of jobs and competences (*Gestion prévisionnelle de l'emploi et des compétences*, GPEC) and training, the companies studied do not succeed in getting any competence dynamic off the ground: the two latter agreements are simply not applied in practice. Why is this so? Most of the union representatives say that they have been held

---

[9] This does not mean that all employees have expressed satisfaction at their grading. The internal conditions under which appeals can be made in each company merit closer examination.

back by timetable constraints arising particularly from the introduction of the thirty-five-hour week. Should we then conclude that the issue has merely been postponed, and abandon any surmise that they might be reluctant to venture down this road?

As in the preceding stage, supervisors are required to play a key role in the deployment of a competence and employability dynamic once the classification criteria have been established. The A.CAP 2000 agreement, signed in January 1991 in the steel industry, underlines this point, stating that the competence-oriented logic necessarily entails 'a suitable conception of the role of the supervisor' (Title II). A study of its implementation at Sollac reveals the importance of the tools proposed to supervisory staff to assist them in the carrying out their new task. Supervisors first receive regularly updated training in how to conduct personnel interviews. The scheme is based on an interview for each employee at least once every two years. This interview is meant as an assessment but is also a way of defining objectives (for training, career, activities, etc.). A reference set of job profiles, an interview form and an individual employee log recording the acquisition of expertise are used to standardise the procedure and render it more transparent. The expertise acquisition log, which follows each employee throughout her career, recording the career path as it unfolds, is a major component of the competence scheme. Employees enjoy a right of appeal with respect to the vocational interview, either to supervisor at level $n + 2$, or, in the event of non-compliance with the procedure, to a joint employer/employee committee set up specifically for this purpose.

To seek out the presence of an evolutive competence dynamic in the practical reality of classification of employees is to touch the raw nerve in most corporate practices. It is a raw nerve because it raises the issue of access to qualification and recognition of competences that make an employee more valuable (Osty 2002). It is also a blind spot because, with the exception of Sollac, it is usually ignored by companies. However, insofar as competence-centred logic is associated by employers with the requirement to render their employees accountable where their career and training are concerned, it is important that these latter have the tools allowing them to shoulder this responsibility. It is precisely here that the shoe pinches. Formalisation of the career paths for the various jobs identified in the company, plus notification of the competences required and the ways they can be obtained, is an example of such a tool. Without this type of scheme, and without genuine guarantees of the possibility of vocational development and mobility, the competence-centred logic is totally worthless for employees, and is nothing more than double-speak justifying managerial practices which isolate individuals and institute competition between them. This seems to be the dominant scenario today: competences are first and foremost a tool for management.

4   Competence-oriented logic and collective framing

The competence-oriented logic inevitably entails individualised treatment of employees. By encouraging a shift in the evaluation of employees' abilities toward companies and away from collective bodies such as those representing industrial sectors, or the public authorities, it also contributes to a strengthening of the prerogatives of the employer in the field of human resources management (HRM). The surveys conducted show how far the trade union movement, accustomed to defending collective causes, finds this domain uncongenial. Various types of problems seem to converge there, some of which are related to the specific nature of the competence logic. Some union representatives do in fact fear that individual treatment might lead unions to merely pander to individuals and groups. Others feel that it is not their job to work in a field perceived as belonging to the employer. The second type of problem derives from employers' dominance in HRM. When sector-wide agreements make no stipulations guaranteeing conditions for involvement of employees and their representatives, the actual participation of the latter depends on management's goodwill. This is why the firm is not necessarily the best place to provide collective responses to the challenge posed by the idea of competence – that is, in a context in which corporate practices are not governed by a broader collective framework.

Out of the four sectors studied, only two have collective agreements seeking to codify competence-oriented logic more closely: the agreements on the prospective management of jobs and competences in the pharmaceutical sector (GPEC, 28 June 1994) and the agreement on development of vocational activities in the steel industry (A.CAP 2000). These two agreements are the only ones to propose definitions of competence. According to a classification glossary for the pharmaceutical industries, competence is 'a broader concept than qualification since it is based on a combination of different types of expertise as validated by experience (knowledge, know-how, personal approach, etc.)'. The pharmaceutical sector agreement makes competences a core classification principle. It opens up a domain for the identification of employee competence – i.e. skills as related to the individual – through the distinction it makes between 'required work' and 'effective work'. The agreement is nevertheless far from informative on the arrangements whereby 'effective work' can be taken into account, leaving to companies the task of defining them.

In the steel industry, A.CAP 2000 goes even further, setting as its objective a 'competence-based logic' which it defines as follows:

Competence-centred logic leads:
- to [Taking] into account the knowledge and experience of employees in the various trades in the sector, and not the qualification required for each of the duties actually performed;
- to the creation of the conditions needed to ensure that employees can apply their competences in practice;
- to a drawing of all the consequences entailed for employees in terms of classification, remuneration and career. (A.CAP 2000 agreement, Title II: 10)

This agreement provides for the definition of a career path for – and in collaboration with – each employee (cf. Titles IV and V), starting out from the status quo and anticipating the objectives to be attained. The value of training is stressed as 'one of the means whereby the individual and collective competences of the workforce can be developed; it is the foundation upon which careers can unfold' (Title VI).

However, even in these two cases, where a national agreement on competence does exist, the reasoning is done in terms of an internal corporate market, with the company being seen, at least as far as this point is concerned, as an organisation that is fairly closed to the outside world.[10] In such circumstances, what is to be made of the ideas of employability politics and lifelong competence development and training (EC 1995a), if workforces are highly mobile, moving between companies or even between sectors? None of the agreements and practices studied here considers this issue of *know-how transferability* and *acquired competences*.

When they do not remain silent on the topic of competences, national agreements are in fact framework agreements guaranteeing much room for discreet implementation by the firm. They define no new collective rights, but at best open the way to 'a right of individual access to a defined procedure' (Besucco and Tallard 1999: 123). Even then, employees and their representatives must be in a position to take advantage of this right and to make use of it in companies and this, with the exception of Sollac in the steel industry, is far from being self-evident in the companies of the survey, including the pharmaceutical industries.

4.1   *From individualisation to secure career paths*

The deployment of a competence-oriented logic may, depending on the employer, be directed at a number of different objectives. In some cases,

---

[10] For a critique of the restrictive conception of the company as an organisation, see Salais and Storper (1997).

and this is particularly true of the metalworking trades, this type of logic makes it possible to promote the figure of the *polyvalent employee* required by new forms of workplace organisation. In other cases, it is a tool for wage policy, or a public relations instrument for management. In most cases, adding value to employees' expertise is far from being the main objective.

This brief outline of possible motivations is suggestive of the differences in the meaning given to the competence concept by different companies, or even by different divisions in the same company. Depending on its use as an instrument by management, this may yield very diverse effects, which will however be overshadowed by one common characteristic: individual treatment of employees. Since in each case it is adjusted to specific circumstances, competence-oriented logic nonetheless is for the employer, in the name of this principle of individual treatment, a way of managing contingencies, and constitutes an important lever for injecting flexibility into work practices. In this perspective, the overall picture hardly seems beneficial to the employee (Dugué 1994). However, competence-oriented logic could be used as an instrument for contingency management by employees as well, if it was combined with schemes for training, for validation of acquired expertise and dispositions permitting their transferability from one company to another. On these conditions only can a logic of competences offer the core elements of an employability politics which will not be reduced to a principle of activation of employees' individual accountability (Chassard and Bosco 1998).

If it is to be effective for employees, and not merely a process of individualisation exploited unilaterally by the employer, the competence-centred logic must be combined with a genuine training and career management policy. In such circumstances it can be an adequate instrument for ensuring secure career paths for employees.[11] However, this means the elaboration of a collective framework for competence-oriented logics. Such a collective framework could seek to create the conditions for adjustment of professional competences not only as a means for the management of economic contingencies, but also to secure individual career paths. This would entail neither joint corporate management nor require withdrawal on the part of the unions (an alternative rejected by some union representatives), but rather necessitate the provision of collective guarantees for channelling practices of individual treatment of employees. In other words, the aim would be to create the conditions for ensuring the

---

[11] On this notion of secure career paths, see Supiot (2001); also Noel Whiteside's chapter 16 in this volume.

equivalence of such practices, thereby preventing them from becoming discriminatory. However, companies alone cannot create the whole set of conditions needed to provide such security and guarantees.[12] It is also important that agreed certification standards which are able to ensure competence-transferability from one company to another, be produced at a more general level, on top of the companies' internal competence validation procedures.

4.2   From a logic of competences to a politics of capabilities

The development of more general framing agreements can be seen here to be of great importance, first to create the conditions in which the workforce's representatives can provide input to companies, and secondly, to lay down the procedural components to be applied uniformly to all employees.[13]

The issue of the collective framework also arises on completion of the competence development process, but in other terms. It raises the question of *collective guarantees* which may ensure the taking into account of expertise acquired by employees in considering classifications, wages and careers. If competences are to be recognised outside the company, it appears necessary also to define ways in which acquired expertise can be transferred, authorities to which employees can appeal and so on.

To conclude, we would stress three important points which derive from our French survey, but which can be transposed to a wider context:
• First, the effectiveness of collective frameworks channelling the management of competences inside companies, as a rule, depends on the quality of the collective guarantees created outside the company. The weaker the latter, the less competences are subject to identification and validation procedures upon which employees can rely in managing their careers or possibly to lodge appeals.
• Secondly, where such a collective framework does exist, it takes the form in companies of deliberation rather than negotiation, making competences and the development of formalisation tools the subject of a shared learning process.

---

[12] As shown by Claude Didry's chapter 2 in this volume on the Renault–Vilvoorde affair.
[13] For example, during our inquiries we observed the following competence formalisation tools: sets of reference criteria for jobs and competences; vocational development paths (indicating possible bridges between jobs and the expertise or training required); periodical vocational assessment interviews (overview, evaluation and definition of objectives) mutually binding on the signatories (the employee and a supervisor committing the management); vocational interview record sheets; expertise acquisition logs accompanying the employee throughout her career; monitoring and appeals committees.

- Thirdly, if competence-centred logic is also meant to provide a means for secure career paths, it is important that such logic be associated with schemes for training, validation, certification and transferability of acquired expertise.

A positive competence-oriented dynamic is thus characterised by two requirements: the need for a flexible instrument for the management of classification systems, which can take into account individuals' expertise and their ongoing development, and the need for means such as training or validation capable of ensuring such development. The deployment of a competence-oriented logic protective for both company and workforce is therefore part of a complex interplay between different levels of action and control, between different views of social dialogue and public action. These levels are professional – companies, sectors – as well as territorial – districts, regions, nation-states, European Union. They are not exclusive, but provide complementary means of shaping a politics of capabilities, in an interplay between social dialogue and public action, employer's and employees' interests.

In other words, a competence-oriented logic aiming at security and positive outputs for the employee must be reconsidered in terms of a politics of capabilities bringing together different professional and territorial levels and their specific rationales. Support for the capabilities concept requires a collective dimension of social construction of competences, which is in general lacking in competence-oriented logics as they are implemented by companies. It is in this politics of capabilities, and not a strict competence logic, that the foundations for the development of a social responsibility of companies (EC 2001e) should to be sought. But empirical studies show that, beyond declarations of principle, much still remains to be done in this area.

REFERENCES

Besucco, N. and M. Tallard, 1999. 'L'encadrement collectif de la gestion des compétences: un nouvel enjeu pour la négociation de branche', *Sociologie du travail*, 41, 123–142
Chassard, Y. and A. Bosco, 1998. 'L'émergence du concept d'employabilité', *Droit social*, 11, 903–911
'Compétence', 2001. *Sociologie du travail*, Special Issue, 1, 3–66
Confédération Française Démocratique du Travail (CFDT), 1995. *Guide sur la qualification*, Paris, June
Dubar, C., 1996. 'La sociologie du travail face à la qualification et à la compétence', *Sociologie du travail*, 2, 179–193
Dugué, E., 1994. 'La gestion des compétences: les savoirs dévalués, le pouvoir occulté', *Sociologie du travail*, 3, 273–292

Eymard-Duvernay, F. and E. Marchal, 1997. *Façons de recruter. Le jugement des compétences sur le marché du travail*, Paris, Métailié

Eyraud, F., A. Jobert, P. Rosenblatt and M. Tallard, 1989. *Les classifications dans l'entreprise: production des hiérarchies professionnelles et salariales*, Paris, La documentation française

Fairise, A. and L. Gérard, 1998. 'Compétences. Un débat qui pourrait être fructueux demain', *Entreprises et Carrières*, 450, 4, 6–12

Feutrie, M. and E. Verdier, 1993. 'Entreprises et formations qualifiantes: une construction sociale inachevée', *Sociologie du travail*, 4, 469–492

Garsten, C. and K. Jacobsson, 2003. *Learning to be Employable: New Agendas on Work, Responsibility and Learning in a Globalizing Labour Market*, London, Palgrave

Le Boterf, G., 1998. 'Evaluer les compétences. Quels jugements? Quels critères? Quelles instances?', *Education permanente*, 135, 143–151

Le Monde, 1999. 'Du diplôme à la formation tout au long de la vie', 6 January, 'Initiatives', series, II

Le Petit Robert, 1988. Paris, 'Le Robert' Dictionaries.

Lichtenberger, Y., 1997. 'La compétence comme prise de responsabilité', Paper given at the ETMT seminar, Dijon, 2–3 October

Maggi-Germain, N., 1999. 'A propos de l'individualisation de la formation professionnelle continue', *Droit social*, 7/8, 692–699

Mouvement des entreprises de France (MEDEF), 1998. *Objectif compétences*, Deauville, International training days

Osty, F., 2002. *Le désir de métier. Engagement, identité et reconnaissance au travail*, Rennes, Presses universitaires de Rennes

Richebé, N., 2002. 'Les réactions des salariés à la "logique compétence": vers un renouveau de l'échange salarial?', *Revue française de sociologie*, 1, 99–126

Salais, R. and M. Storper, 1997. *Worlds of Production: The Action Frameworks of the Economy*, Cambridge, MA, Harvard University Press (first published in French, *Les mondes de production. Enquête sur l'identité économique de la France*, Paris, Editions de l'EHESS, 1993)

Schwartz, Y., 1992. 'De la qualification à la compétence', *Flash Formation Continue*, 339, 10–16

Supiot, A. (ed.), 2001. *Beyond Employment: Changes in Work and the Future of Labour Law in Europe*, Report for the European Commission, Oxford, Oxford University Press

Tanguy, L., 1998. 'Définitions et usages de la notion de compétence', in A. Supiot (ed.), *Le travail en perspectives*, Paris, LGDJ, 545–562

Thévenot, L., 1997. 'Le savoir au travail. Attribution et distribution des compétences selon les régimes pragmatiques', in B. Reynaud (ed.), *Les limites de la rationalité*, 2, *Les figures du collectif*, Paris, La Découverte, 298–321

Zarifian, P., 1999. *Objectif compétence. Pour une nouvelle logique*, Paris, Editions Liaisons

Zimmermann, B., 2000. 'Logiques de compétences et dialogue social', *Travail et Emploi*, 84, 5–18

4 Regional capabilities and the European Employment Strategy

Martin Heidenreich

J68 R23 J08

1 The regional dimension of the European Employment Strategy

The European Employment Strategy (EES), among other things, was designed to improve the integration of groups which are currently under-represented into the labour market. Women, older workers, the long-term unemployed, young people, early school leavers, low-skilled workers, people with disabilities, immigrants and ethnic minorities are explicitly mentioned in the 2003 Employment Guidelines. The creation of a more inclusive national employment order is being pursued above all through a new, more open method of co-ordination, based on the definition of common targets, and a common evaluation of the outcomes and mutual learning processes (see Philippe Pochet's chapter 12 in this volume; De La Porte, Pochet and Room 2001; Hodson and Maher 2001; Ferrera, Matsaganis and Sacchi 2002; Scharpf 2002).

Initially, the EES was focused mainly on the national level. In 2000, the foundations for local and regional employment policies were laid. Since 2000, the importance of the regional level has not only been emphasised in the Employment Guidelines, the European Commission also calls for a 'local dimension for the European Employment Strategy'.[1] This was legitimated with a high share of government expenditures at the local and regional level, the employment potential of smaller businesses and the large impact of the third sector, the non-profit organisations.

Until now, the effects of this decentralisation have been extremely limited, according to the Commission in an evaluation of the EES in 2002.[2]

---

[1] EC (2000a).

[2] 'Since European policies tend to reach the local level not so much at the policy track but in the context of funding operations, respective incentive measures and, particularly the ESF [European Social Fund], have played a major role . . . The EES, which is itself partnership based, tries to stimulate *a partnership approach* also at local level, visible for instance in the promotion of Local Action Plans for Employment (LAP), which proved that such an approach is feasible. Local authorities are expected to play a major role in this context, but there is still a significant lack of information not only with regard to

This may be the result of defining a given region too narrowly – a definition that focuses on the social and ignores the productive dimension of the region. Regional employment and unemployment disparities are at the centre of the regional dimension of the EES.[3] Regions are considered as areas of social services and social exclusion, but not as areas of entrepreneurial activities and innovation strategies. The Commission seeks and promotes the involvement of regional and local authorities, public employment services, social partners and civil society, but it does not mention the involvement of entities such as regional companies and business associations. Regional innovation policies are also not mentioned.[4] The productive and economic prerequisites for the creation of regional jobs have not yet been incorporated into the EES; it thus risks limiting its territorial dimension to a mere symbolic practice, or to a policy which mainly exists to redistribute funds (via the structural funds).

Our thesis is that a more comprehensive approach to regional employment and unemployment policies requires that *the region has to be regarded as a productive system.* Such a system has to be characterized by a set of horizontally and vertically interrelated companies and a regional order (public authorities, educational facilities, research and development institutes, industrial relations and business associations . . .) facilitating the creation of new, and the recombination and path-dependent development of existing, productive capabilities. By these means, the productive bases of regional disparities can be directly addressed without having to rely merely on redistribution policies. *Regional capabilities* are the crucial basis for regional employment. Regional employment strategies should therefore not only concentrate on redistribution and on patterns of social exclusion, but should also address the origins of unsatisfactory

techniques and instruments, but also with regard to their role as such . . . The role of the social partners in local strategies is less pronounced, and that of businesses and other groups in society even less.' (Impact evaluation of the European employment strategy supporting EC 2002b.), emphasis by the author.

[3] In the 2003 Commission proposal for the 'Guidelines for Employment Policies of the Member States' it is stated: 'Member States should implement a broad approach towards reducing regional employment and unemployment disparities. The potential for job creation at the local level, including in the social economy, should be supported and partnerships between all relevant actors should be encouraged. Member States will:
– promote favourable conditions for private sector activity and investment in regions lagging behind;
– ensure that public support in regions lagging behind is focused on investment in human and knowledge capital, as well as adequate infrastructure.
The potential of the Cohesion and Structural Funds and the European Investment Bank should be fully exploited' http://europa.eu.int/comm/employment_social/ employment_strategy/ prop_2003-gl_en.pdf; accessed on 17 July 2003.

[4] See chapter 7 by Robert Villeneuve in this volume.

regional employment performance by enhancing regional productive competences.

There is also a second way in which the EES could profit from an increased involvement at the regional level. In section 4, we will show that more inclusive labour market regimes are empirically linked to higher educational levels and more knowledge-based forms of production (for example, advanced services). Supporting regional production networks may therefore, also be an indirect way of increasing the inclusiveness of labour markets.

This chapter is based on the analysis of regional innovation systems (Braczyk, Cooke and Heidenreich 2004). It will thus focus on the *collectively* created, institutionally and organizationally reproduced productive capabilities of a region or territory. How can these capabilities be linked to labour market structures?

In section 2, the institutional and organisational bases of regional capabilities and their path-dependent evolution will briefly be summarised. We will then (section 3) analyse the two-dimensional structure of regional capabilities and discuss their possible connection to regional patterns of labour market exclusion. In section 4, we will address the possibilities of political support for regional innovation systems. Section 5 briefly concludes.

2   The evolution of regional capabilities

The regional concentration of industrial competencies is a well-known phenomenon – at least since the classic work of the British economist Alfred Marshall (1982 [1890]). Observing the early industrial districts of England, he wrote:

The mysteries of the trade become no mystery; but are as it were in the air . . . Good work is rightly appreciated, inventions and improvements in machinery, in processes and the general organisation of the business have their merits promptly discussed: if one man starts a new idea, it is taken up by others and combined with suggestions of their own; and thus it becomes the source of further ideas. (Marshall 1982: 225)

These regional capabilities are not a characteristic of early industrialisation; industrial competencies are still regionally concentrated today. This is true for traditional industries as well as for the information technology (IT) and multimedia industry, finance services, advertising and biotechnology. In Germany, for instance, the multimedia industry is concentrated in Cologne, Munich and more recently in Berlin; the microchip industry is based in Munich and Dresden and their immediately surrounding areas. In Hamburg, the advertising industry plays a considerable role in the city-state's economy, and nearly all German kitchens are manufactured in eastern Westphalia. The automobile and mechanical engineering industries are of major importance in the Stuttgart region, and the German biotechnology industry is concentrated in Munich and around Heidelberg. Financial services are concentrated in Frankfurt, textile mechanical engineering in the Krefeld region and medical technology and instruments are produced in the Tuttlingen region.

This regional concentration and accumulation of industrial capabilities is addressed in the discussion on industrial districts, on regional and national clusters (Cooke 2002), on learning regions and on regional innovation systems (Storper and Salais 1997, Braczyk, Cooke and Heidenreich 2004; see the overview in Storper 1997 and Amin 1999). While the discussion on clusters is focused on the industrial structure of a region and the existence of territorially concentrated, socio-culturally embedded and institutionally stabilized interorganizational networks that facilitate the accumulation, recombination and utilization of technical knowledge in specific technological fields, the discussion on regional innovation systems addresses the *institutional order* of a region and the provision of regional 'collective competition goods' (Le Galès and Voelzkow 2001).

These regional innovation systems (RIS) can be defined as

places where close inter-firm communication, socio-cultural structures and institutional environment may stimulate socially and territorially embedded collective learning and continuous innovation . . . Basically, [a] regional innovation system consists of two main types of actors and the interaction between them . . . The first actors are the firms in the main industrial cluster in a region including their support industries. Secondly, an institutional infrastructure must be present, i.e., research and higher education institutes, technology transfer agencies, vocational training organisations, business associations, finance institutions, etc., which hold important competence to support regional innovation. (Asheim and Isaksen 2002: 83–84)

The basis of regional capabilities is the experience and implicit knowledge that regional businesses and employees have accumulated through their close involvement in the production of a specific product or the use of a specific technology. Such implicit, context-specific, non-tradable competencies can best be passed on through direct interactions and regional co-operation networks facilitated by close geographic proximity. Regional capabilities are therefore anchored in the institutions and networks that facilitate such patterns of *inter-organisational learning*.

Regional capabilities are not only the result of current organizational or political strategies. Many regional case studies have demonstrated that regional capabilities are developed in a sometimes century-long history of co-operation and competition, and that accidental factors often have a much stronger impact than planned political interventions. Regional trajectories, regional variation, selection and stabilisation processes (see Nelson 1995; Cooke 2004a), sub-optimal, cumulative and path-dependent learning processes (Edquist 1997) and regional inertia and lock-in-effects have to be taken into account so as not to overestimate the contribution of a regional innovation policy in improving the performance of regional employment. An evolutionary framework is useful because it points to the limits of political interventions: simply put, not every major university can establish a biotechnology district, and not every country can establish a Silicon Valley or a global financial services centre.

An evolutionary perspective on regional innovation systems has to show what the basic units of the regional innovation system are, and what the 'mechanisms' of regional variation, selection and stabilisation processes are. First, similar to organisational rules and routines that determine the capabilities of organisations (see Chandler 1992; Teece, Pisano and Shuen 1997; Teece 1998), the capabilities of a region are anchored in institutionally stabilised patterns of co-operation and competition (*basic units*). These patterns are the 'memory' of a region and are often the result of long-lasting interorganisational experiences of co-operation and conflict. The accumulation of implicit knowledge in a region results from these recursive processes of interaction; they are crucial for shaping the learning and innovation opportunities that regional firms have.

Second, the *variation* of regional capabilities requires the development of new intercompany patterns of relationship and co-operation. This can be accomplished through the creation of start-ups or new regional institutions, for example.

Third, new patterns of relationships can be more easily established when they have the benefit of being able to rely upon previous regional capabilities, relationships and institutions (*selection*). This refers to the path-dependent nature of regional capabilities. Previously developed productive capabilities constrain certain trajectories and facilitate the development of others. For instance, a region such as Stuttgart, which is dominated by the automobile, electronics and mechanical engineering industries, film, entertainment and multimedia firms would have very few opportunities to co-operate with established industrial companies, and this would considerably reduce their chances of survival. On the other hand, the chances for production-related services would be excellent (Strambach 2002).

Fourth, patterns of co-operation and learning between firms can be stabilized by regional institutions or governance structures (*stabilisation*).

Ethnic or professional communities are possible means for attaining such a stabilization. Such a phenomenon has been demonstrated in the central Italian industrial districts, the former Parisian and New York clothing districts and the current Frankfurt banking milieu. An alternative to such a *socio-cultural* basis of trust is the idea of regional and national institutions such as employers' professional and business associations, trade unions, schools and universities, public research and development institutions or public technology transfer institutions, which work to stabilise regional patterns of communication, co-operation and mutual learning by the provision of collective competition goods.

In conclusion, regional capabilities are a possible focus for strategies which could be implemented to improve the regional employment and unemployment situation. Regional capabilities are one example of a collective investment in people's capabilities, which are at the centre of a capability approach. The goal of this approach is not only to increase the number of regional jobs, but also to increase the technical content, the innovativeness and the sustainability of these jobs. While an employment-centred approach tries to reduce individual and regional disparities in income and employment opportunities, a capability approach tries to increase the *quality* of these jobs by, among other methods, the creation of a collective investment in regional productive competencies (in the sense of the 'highroad' strategies analysed by Sabel *et al.*, 1989). Such investments have to take the evolutionary, path-dependent nature of regional capabilities into account.

In section 3, we will argue that a shift from an employability-centred to a capability-centred approach may also be useful for another crucial objective of the EES, the creation of more inclusive labour markets.

3 Regional capabilities in Europe: is there a link between innovativeness and inclusion?

The EES aims to improve the employment possibilities, especially for females and younger and older people, thus making the European labour market regimes more inclusive. This reflects a project of societal modernisation, which is characterized by a shift from particularistic to universalistic orientations, from ascription to achievement and from diffuse to specific obligations. The intended modernisation of European labour markets can be criticised from two, partially complementary; points of view. First, this project ignores the existence of path-dependent patterns of evolution: the central objective of European employment strategies is a higher inclusion of females and older and younger people, and this means a radical change–especially for Mediterranean and some Continental European labour market regimes. Second, if such a shift from exclusive to inclusive labour markets is nevertheless possible, it may undermine the specific competencies linked to exclusive, segmented labour markets (for example internal, professional or vocational labour markets). The strategies of social closure, which are the principal target of employability-centred strategies, are also the basis for specific industrial relations and strategies which have been analysed as flexible production (Piore and Sabel 1984), 'diversified quality production' (Streeck 1991) or 'co-ordinated market economies' (Hall and Soskice 2001). More inclusive labour markets also require a different institutional and organizational environment: a different production model. An employability-centred strategy, such as that implemented by EES, cannot be implemented without the development of different forms of regional capabilities.

This thesis will now be discussed based on the available regional data for the so-called 'NUTS-2' regions of the European Union.[5] On this basis, the diversity of regional capabilities and the corresponding patterns of exclusion and inclusion can be analysed, even if longer time series are not available and even if the available indicators for regional capabilities are extremely limited.

On the basis of the five variables described in table 4.1, a factor analysis was performed for 203 of the 211 European NUTS-2 regions. This analysis explains 82 per cent of the initial variance. Two factors with an eigenvalue of more than 1 emerged, each of which strongly correlated with three of the variables (see table 4.1). These correlations suggest that the first factor can be used as an indicator for the basis of the region in terms of qualification. A high level of employees with an upper secondary or tertiary qualification, a high share of research and development expenditure (GERD) and a high share of employment in knowledge-intensive services indicate the importance of formally certified, abstract qualifications and systematic innovation activities. The second factor points to the relative impact of industrial- in comparison to service-based forms of production and organization. As will be shown later, this factor refers also to the relative importance of tacit, especially production-related competencies.

The values for the two factors can be calculated for each region. These regional factor scores cluster within a nation: the total regional variation can be reduced by 82 and 29 per cent if the 'nationality' of the respective region is known. For illustrative purposes the values for the 203 regions can be aggregated on the national level (table 4.2).

[5] The nomenclature of territorial units for statistics (NUTS) established by Eurostat is a hierarchical classification that sub-divides the EU-15 Member States into seventy-eight regions at NUTS-1 level and 211 regions at NUTS-2 level. The UK, for example, is subdivided in twelve government office regions and thirty-seven counties or groups of unitary authorities.

Table 4.1. *The two-dimensional structure of regional capabilities in 203 European regions: the results of a factor analysis*

	Descriptive statistics		Factor analysis		
	Mean (weighted)	Standard deviation (weighted)	Factor loadings of the first factor (formal knowledge)	Factor loadings of the second factor (service orientation)	Communality
Share of persons ages 25–59 with a high or medium educational attainment (% of the total age group; 2000)	66.44	17.61	**0.87**	0.05	0.75
GERD (1997)	1.61	1.02	**0.84**	0.04	0.70
Share of employment in knowledge-intensive services (ISIC Rev.3: I61, I62, I64–I67, K70–K74, M80, N85, O92; % of total employment; 1999)	32.00	8.08	**0.72**	**0.60**	0.89
Industrial employment (% of total employment; 2000)	28.89	7.15	0.15	**-0.93**	0.89
Service employment (% of total; 2000)	66.73	8.66	0.40	**0.86**	0.89

Notes:
No. of European NUTS-2 regions: 203.
GERD: Gross domestic expenditure on research and development in % of GDP.
ISIC: International Standard Industrial Classification.
Method of extraction: Principal components analysis.
Method of rotation: Varimax.
Sources: Own calculations on the basis of data provided by European Communities/Eurostat, various years: *Regions. Statistical Yearbook.* Luxembourg: Office for Official Publications.

Table 4.2. *Regional capabilities in EU countries: nationally aggregated regional factor scores*

Country	Formal knowledge (factor 1)	Service orientation (factor 2)
Austria	0.09	−0.51
Belgium	0.05	0.87
Denmark	0.88	0.57
Finland	0.69	0.14
France	−0.02	0.12
Germany	0.75	−0.79
Greece	−1.66	−0.03
Ireland	−0.39	−0.35
Italy	−0.83	−0.10
Netherlands	0.35	0.94
Portugal	−1.92	−0.39
Spain	−1.20	−0.29
Sweden	1.72	0.47
UK	0.61	0.44

Sources: Own calculations on the basis of the factor analysis described in table 4.1 and in the text.

This data shows that the Scandinavian, Dutch, Belgian and British regions are characterized by a relatively strong service sector and a qualified labour force, whereas the Mediterranean regions are characterized by a higher proportion of low-skilled inhabitants and a higher share of industrial employment. Germany, Austria and France are in an intermediary position. Their service sector is much smaller while the formal qualification of their population is as high as in the service-oriented economies of northern Europe.

In the next step, we will analyse the patterns of inclusion and exclusion within this two-dimensional space of regional capabilities, taking as an indicator selected age- and gender-specific employment and unemployment rates. In the case of older people, the difference between the employment rates of the 55–64-year-old population and the core age group (35–44 years) is taken as an indicator. For younger people, the unemployment rates are a more adequate indicator for exclusion processes, because the low employment rates of younger people can also be the result of prolonged participation in the educational system. Women can either be constrained to non-paid jobs (childcare, etc.) or they can be unemployed. These two forms of exclusion are indicated by gender-specific differences of the employment and unemployment rates.

In table 4.3, the results of five linear regression models are shown. The dependent variables are the total employment rate and the four exclusion variables just mentioned. The independent variables are the two factors described in table 4.1. GDP *per capita* is used as a control variable. These regressions show that the inclusion of women in the labour market is strongly correlated with the first factor, indicating the effects of a higher education. This confirms that women are the principal winners of the educational expansion. The same is true for younger people; their inclusion in the labour market is facilitated by formal qualifications. This explains why the total employment rate strongly depends on the share of persons with a high or medium educational attainment. This variable, however, does not significantly influence the relative share of older employees. Other aspects of labour market institutions, for example public pre-pension schemes, may be more important.

However, the labour market involvement of women and young people also depends on whether the respective region is service- or industry-oriented. In service-oriented regions, the relative *employment* rates of women and older people as well as the *unemployment* rates of younger people are higher. For a thorough interpretation of these facts, much more detail on the regions and their labour markets would be necessary. A reasonable first interpretation of these results could be that employment in industry-oriented sectors is accompanied by specific forms of labour market segmentation, which accounts for the exclusion of female and older employees and the inclusion of younger ones. These forms of labour market segmentation are the result of strategies of social closure, which limit the access to privileged occupational positions to skilled male industrial workers. Younger workers are also relatively privileged by these patterns of segmentation because the transition from school to work is facilitated in German-speaking and Scandinavian countries by a system of vocational training. On the one hand, these forms of labour market segmentation are the basis for the exclusion of women and other groups, on the other, they are the basis for the accumulation and intergenerational transmission of work-related, experience-based skills. This is a major advantage of closed labour markets, examples of which are the professional and internal labour markets. Even if segmented labour markets are not specific to industrialized regions, industrial forms of production are apparently more dependent on the accumulation of experiences and practical skills than services.

In conclusion, the available data show that two dimensions of regional capabilities can be distinguished for more than 200 European regions. The first dimension is *formalised knowledge*, which is the product of systematic education and of systematic research and development activities.

Table 4.3. *Regional capabilities and labour market exclusion of women and younger and older people (203 European NUTS-2 regions)*

	Employment rate (% of population aged 15–64; 2000)	Difference between the employment rates of men and women (% of total; 2000)	Difference between the unemployment rates of men and women (% of total; 2000)	Difference between the average and the youth unemployment rates (% of total; 2000)	Difference between the employment rates of the 35–44 and the 55–64-year-old population; (2000)
Constant	61.18***	16.57***	4.83***	13.73***	35.34***
GDP/head (PPS): 2000; EUR15 = 100	0.04	0.02	−0.02	−0.05*	0.09*
Formal knowledge (factor 1)	3.91***	−6.59***	−3.21***	−2.82***	−1.02
Service orientation (factor 2)	−0.39	−1.23**	−0.002	1.71***	−1.97*
R^2 (corr.)	0.283***	0.574***	0.468***	0.24***	0.035*

Notes:
Linear regression models. Level of significance: *: 5%; **: 1%; ***: 0.1%.
Sources: See table 4.1.

The second is *industrialised forms of production*, where tacit, experience-based forms of knowledge apparently play a somewhat larger role than in service-based forms of production. The first factor is strongly negatively correlated with the exclusion of female and young people; indicating the inclusive nature of regional capabilities based mainly on formalised, explicit knowledge. The second factor is linked to the exclusion of female and older people and the inclusion of younger employees, thus illustrating the specific patterns of labour market segmentation mainly in the highly industrialised, German-speaking European countries.

For the EES, this means that a higher level of inclusion of females and younger and older people in the labour market may threaten the production-related, experience-based skills that have been previously generated and transmitted in segmented, exclusive labour markets. The development of an alternative, less exclusive labour market regime, especially in Mediterranean and Continental European countries, therefore requires not only a reorganisation of the labour market, but also different educational and production concepts. Forms of production more strongly based on explicit, transferable qualifications will be required to facilitate a shift to a more inclusive labour market, which is the primary target of the EES. This could be achieved if the organisations and regions involved increase their innovativeness. Therefore, the 'employability' approach of the EES should be complemented by a 'capability' approach, which attempts to strengthen the innovative capacities of regional production systems. Whether or not, and how, this may be possible will be discussed in section 4.

4 The political support of regional capabilities: limits and possibilities of cluster policies

Besides the provision of an adequate regional 'knowledge infrastructure' (research and development, technology transfer infrastructures, education, training), regional patterns of co-operation and competition are a crucial feature of regional innovation systems. These patterns can be politically facilitated on three different levels. First, the state can create institutions on the national level that promote the development of *co-operation and relationship networks* across the boundaries of an industrial branch. Secondly, the same idea can be applied on the regional level. Thirdly, attempts can be made directly to create *interorganisational co-operation networks*. Cluster policies can therefore be concentrated on the national level, on the regional level and on the micro level of actual co-operation networks. Their main objective is the selection and sometimes the creation of new, promising networks. We will illustrate the corresponding political conceptions with the aid of some case studies reported in Braczyk, Cooke and Heidenreich (2004) and OECD (1999).

4.1   National cluster policies

A national cluster policy could be particularly interesting for countries with close interindustrial production and value chains. In this case, it would be important to overcome traditional industrial boundaries through an economic, research and technology policy that fosters patterns of co-operation across the traditional boundaries of branches and areas of technology. An example of this is Denmark, a country with a relatively high share of smaller businesses. In Denmark (nearly) the entire economy has been divided into six 'resource areas'. These areas are separated into groups based on their commonly known characteristics: food, consumer goods and leisure, construction and housing, communication, transport and supply industries, medico/health and general supplier businesses. In each of these resource areas, a co-ordination group has been founded with the participation of businesses, employee representatives and public authorities. These co-ordination groups develop policy recommendations taken from the respective legislator or from specific committees.

In Finland, national economic policy is also designed to support knowledge-based economic clusters. The public authorities promote the telecommunication cluster, for example, through targeted research and education politics and through the active support of the development of international standards for the industry. The state also acts as a demanding customer for domestic industry; this does not mean primarily favouring domestic firms, but promoting products and standards that will also be attractive to foreign customers. A cluster policy on the national level therefore aims to orient the 'knowledge base' of a country, its firms, research, training and education facilities, towards new demands and co-operation opportunities.

4.2   Regional cluster policies

On the regional level, public policies can be used to stimulate interorganisational patterns of co-operation and regional innovation networks through research and technology centres and technology transfer facilities. An example of this is Wales (Cooke 2004b). After the decline of the mining industry, foreign companies opened new engineering, electronics and automotive plants. Through innovation and technology transfer centres, science and technology parks, supplier networking initiatives, and joint research initiatives and education facilities, the Welsh Development

Agency (WDA) and other public authorities tried to promote new linkages and networks between the newly settled production plants and local firms and institutions which were already in place. In this way, the foreign plants were used as focal points for the creation of new industrial clusters. At the end of the 1990s, job losses in the larger manufacturing firms exposed the limitations of these attempts.

Another example of a regional cluster policy is the ERVET system in the central Italian region of Emilia-Romagna. The industrial districts of this region are based to a considerable extent on small enterprises. Over 40 per cent of the regional industrial personnel work in enterprises with fewer than twenty employees. Such firms do not have the production-related services necessary for the development and subsequent global commercial exploitation of new products. However, many firms in the same branch are concentrated around one single town. The food industry is concentrated in the province of Parma, clothing in Carpi and Modena, shoes in Fusignano, furniture in Forli and ceramics in Sassuolo. The region therefore decided to support these industries through nine regional competence centres, concentrated in the ERVET organisation. Part of ERVET is a quality control centre, a centre for the shoe and leather industry, a centre for agriculture machines and a centre for the textile and clothing industry. These centres are jointly administered by the region, the relevant business associations and by nearly 1,000 firms. Costs were divided almost equally between private firms (34 per cent), the region (36 per cent) and national and European sources (30 per cent). The main function of such centres is to provide information and services that small regional firms cannot feasibly manage or adequately finance alone. Such competence centres strengthen the economic profile of a region, they are the expression of a common local pattern of development, thus facilitating the co-ordination, orientation, motivation and legitimisation of local entrepreneurial efforts. However, this example also demonstrates the limits of an exclusively regional orientation: regional competence centres cannot overcome deficiencies in national infrastructures, particularly in the fields of education, professional training and research.

4.3   Local cluster policies

At the local level, public authorities can attempt to directly create and stabilise interorganisational patterns of co-operation. A prominent example for this is the promotion of networks between small enterprises by the Danish Technology Institute. In the years 1989–92, a programme was created and initiated to support intercompany networks. The participating firms and forty network moderators (comprising local consultants, agencies and associations) created over 300 such networks. The aim of this programme was to improve the flow of information and co-operation between smaller businesses, and thus overcome some of their more notorious weaknesses: small purchase volumes, inadequate marketing capacities and limited research and development potential. These networks made it easier for the smaller businesses to observe market and technological development, and to initiate joint research projects and share expensive equipment. This also permitted these firms to specialise in complementary tasks. The network moderator programme was broadened to other areas (tourism, environmental technology, export support) after 1992. However, a further evaluation of the network programmes exposed their disadvantages; the costs per network were very high, and numerous networks could not be stabilised after the end of the initial public financial support. This points to the important role of common institutions such as the Joint Venture Silicon Valley Network, the Italian ERVET system or the German chambers of commerce in effectively stabilising such intercompany networks.

The experiments with cluster policies conducted in Germany, mostly since the mid-1990s, are mainly oriented towards the direct creation of co-operation networks. For illustration purposes, we will mention three of them: structural policies in North Rhine-Westphalia and the national Bioregio and Innoregio programmes. North Rhine-Westphalia, our first example, has the longest experience of regional economic and structural policies. Regional innovation and technology projects have been developed since 1987 as a reaction to the crisis of the coal and steel industry in the Ruhr area. An evaluation of these projects questioned the strong similarity between different regional development projects, because they did not reflect regional specificity. It also stressed the overwhelming importance of more basic and conventional improvement measures such as upgrading the traffic infrastructure, providing sites for new firms and setting up technology transfer facilities (Heinze and Voelzkow 1997). In 1994, a second generation of thirty-five regional projects was started. This time, the major objective was to create and strengthen networks between firms, associations, research and development centres, public authorities, schools and universities (Rehfeld, Baumer and Wompel 2000). In 1996 the Federal Research Ministry started the successful Bioregio project designed to support the most efficient biotechnology regions in Germany. It has been claimed that this programme has produced considerable regional synergies and has brought these regions closer to the level of the more advanced European and American biotechnology regions. In 1999 the Federal Research Ministry once again initiated a similar programme, the Innoregio project. The target areas are twenty-five selected regions in eastern Germany, and various branches are addressed. These regions will be supported until 2005 to the tune of 250 million Euro. The Federal Ministry anticipates that this programme will foster the creation of interorganisational networks and co-operation. In all three cases, the aim is to create new regional capabilities by linking regional actors in different ways. The Bioregio programme was especially successful because it was able to create new patterns of co-operation between existing universities, clinics, research institutes, pharmaceutical and chemical companies.

In conclusion, cluster policies can successfully support strategies which are implemented to react to new challenges within the continuity of previous regional capabilities and development trajectories. In many cases, however, completely new technologies and organisations are needed in order to successfully cope with new situations. For example, the current strength of the manufacturing industry in Baden-Württemberg seems to be the result of the successful merging of old and new technologies – of mechanical engineering, car production, IT, new materials, micro-system technology and opto-electronic systems. There are therefore no simple recipes for a successful cluster policy. Just as spatial proximity is no guarantee for close co-operation between firms and their clients, suppliers and competitors, stable co-operation networks are no guarantee for reciprocal learning. Intercompany networks may also prevent learning and even support unsuccessful technological trajectories.

The theoretical basis for cluster policies should be an evolutionary understanding of regional strengths, weaknesses and trajectories. On one hand, it would be absurd to assume that political intervention could create a successful economic cluster in the middle of nowhere. Experience in eastern Germany has shown that even with an enormous amount of money it is difficult to create a competitive industrial base. On the other hand, there is no room for political fatalism. Political intervention can have a considerable, if sometimes unintended, impact on the development of new clusters.

5   Conclusion

The crucial objective of the EES is to create more inclusive labour markets. More specifically, the employment rates for women and younger and older people should be increased. Currently, the local and regional levels of the EES play a minor role in comparison with the national level. This is a major disadvantage, for three reasons. First, the regional level is essential in the creation of jobs in the social services area. The second disadvantage is that the regional level is the best-suited target for innovation-centred policies. Finally, increased regional innovativeness has the potential to increase the inclusiveness of the labour markets.

The possible link between *innovation and inclusion* has been discussed in three steps. In the first step, it was pointed out that productive and innovative capabilities are very often regionally concentrated. This was reported not only for the jewellery, steel, coal, ceramics, wood, paper, leather, shoes, clothing and textiles industry, but also for the vehicle and mechanical engineering industry, for financial services, IT, multimedia, biotechnology, advertisement and other cultural products. The reason for this occurrence can be divided into four groups, which were originally proposed by Alfred Marshall: the availability of local resources, transaction cost advantages, specialisation advantages and learning and innovation advantages. These regional capabilities evolve in a path-dependent manner.

In the second step, it was demonstrated that the regional level may play also a major role for labour market inclusion. We have tried to show that regional capabilities in more than 200 European NUTS-2 regions can be analysed in two dimensions. These dimensions are the 'knowledge dimension', in which Mediterranean were distinguished from other European countries and which points to the importance of formal, explicit knowledge – in higher education, in research and development or in knowledge-based services, for example; and the second dimension which distinguishes between regions with a higher share of service employment and regions with a high share of industrial production (especially in southern and Continental European countries), thus highlighting the role of implicit knowledge usually created and reproduced in relatively closed labour markets. These forms of implicit knowledge seem to continue to carry more weight in industrial production than in service-based forms of production. A higher level of inclusion of females and younger people is positively correlated with a higher educational level in the regional population, higher research and development expenditures and a higher share of service production. More inclusive labour markets may therefore require an all-embracing reorientation of industrial and educational strategies – for example, a shift towards more knowledge-based forms of production and services.

Finally we illustrated the possibilities and limitations of successful political initiatives that can work to promote regional innovation systems. The success of economic regions depends to a considerable extent on previously accumulated competencies and on previously established patterns of co-operation. Political interventions can influence innovative capabilities only where previous regional trajectories have already laid the appropriate foundation. Nevertheless, a cluster policy can influence the development of regional competencies and patterns of co-operation both directly (through the political support of co-operation networks) and indirectly (through the creation of national and regional institutions). A regional cluster policy can therefore play an important role in creating jobs within a European strategy for employment that aims to facilitate the required, complementary reorientation to knowledge-based production forms. The political support of regional learning and innovation processes could work to facilitate a higher inclusion of relatively disadvantaged groups. The creation of more inclusive labour market regimes and the intended shift towards a more knowledge-based forms of production therefore could be mutually reinforcing – especially at the regional level.

REFERENCES

Amin, A., 1999. 'An Institutional Perspective on Regional Economic Development', *International Journal of Urban and Regional Research*, 23, 365–378

Asheim, B. T. and A. Isaksen, 2002. 'Regional Innovation Systems: The Integration of Local "Sticky" and Global "Ubiquitous" Knowledge', *Journal of Technology Transfer*, 27, 77–86

Braczyk, H.-J., P. Cooke and M. Heidenreich (eds.), 2004. *Regional Innovation Systems*, London, UCL Press

Chandler, A. D., 1992. 'Organisational Capabilities and the Economic History of the Industrial Enterprise', *Journal of Economic Perspectives*, 6, 79–100

Cooke, P., 2002. *Knowledge Economies: Clusters, Learning and Cooperative Advantage*, London and New York: Routledge

2004a. 'Introduction: Origins of the Concept', in H.-J. Braczyk, P. Cooke and M. Heidenreich (eds.), *Regional Innovation Systems*, London, Routledge, 1–18

2004b. 'Global Clustering and Regional Innovation: Systemic Integration in Wales', in H.-J. Braczyk, P. Cooke and M. Heidenreich (eds.), *Regional Innovation Systems*, London, Routledge, 214–233

De La Porte, C., P. Pochet and G. Room, 2001. "Social Benchmarking, Policy Making and New Governance in the EU", *Journal of European Social Policy*, 11(4), 291–307

Edquist, C. (ed.), 1997. *Systems of Innovation: Technologies, Institutions and Organizations*, London, Pinter

Ferrera, M., M. Matsaganis and S. Sacchi, 2002. 'Open Co-ordination against Poverty: The New EU "Social Inclusion Process"', *Journal of European Social Policy*, 12(3), 227–239

Hall, P. A. and D. Soskice (eds.), 2001. *Varieties of Capitalism: The Institutional Foundations of Comparative Advantage*, Oxford, Oxford University Press

Heinze, R. G. and H. Voelzkow (eds.), 1997. *Regionalisierung der Strukturpolitik in Nordrhein-Westfalen*, Opladen, Westdeutscher Verlag

Hodson, D. and I. Maher, 2001. 'The Open Method as a New Mode of Governance', *Journal of Common Market Studies*, 39(4), 719–746

Le Galès, P. and H. Voelzkow, 2001. 'Introduction: The Governance of Local Economies', in C. Crouch, P. Le Galès, C. Trigilia and H. Voelzkow, *Local Production Systems in Europe: Rise or Demise?*, Oxford, Oxford University Press, 1–24

Marshall, A., 1982 [1890]. *Principles of Economics*; reprint of the 8th edn., Philadelphia, Porcupine Press, 1920

Nelson, R. R., 1995. 'Recent Evolutionary Theorizing about Economic Change', *Journal of Economic Literature*, 33, 48–90

OECD (ed.), 1999. *Boosting Innovation: The Cluster Approach*, Paris, OECD

Piore, M. J. and C. F. Sabel, 1984. *The Second Industrial Divide: Possibilities for Prosperity*, New York, Basic, Books

Rehfeld, D., D. Baumer and M. Wompel, 2000. 'Regionalisierte Strukturpolitik als Lernprozess', *Graue Reihe des Instituts Arbeit and Technik*, 11/2000, http://iat-info.iatge.de

Sabel, C. F., G. B. Herrigel, R. Deeg and R. Kazis, 1989. 'Regional Prosperities Compared: Massachusetts and Baden-Württemberg in the 1980s', *Economy and Society*, 18(4), 374–404

Scharpf, F. W., 2002. 'The European Social Model: Coping with the Challenges of Diversity', *Journal of Common Market Studies*, 40(4), 645–670

Sen, A., 1993. 'Capability and Well-being', in M. Nussbaum and A. Sen (eds.), *The Quality of Life*, Oxford, Clarendon Press, 30–53

Storper, M., 1997. *The Regional World: Territorial Development in a Global Economy*, New York and London, Guilford Press

Storper, M. and R. Salais, 1997. *Worlds of Production*, Cambridge, MA, Harvard University Press

Strambach, S., 2002. 'Change in the Innovation Process: New Knowledge Production and Competitive Cities – The Case of Stuttgart', *European Planning Studies*, 10(2), 215–231

Streeck, W., 1991. 'On the Social and Political Conditions of Diversified Quality Production', in E. Matzner and W. Streeck (eds.), *Beyond Keynesianism: The Socio-Economics of Production and Full Employment*, Aldershot and Brookfield, VT, Edward Elgar, 21–61

Teece, D. J., 1998. 'Capturing Value from Knowledge Assets: The New Economy, Markets for Know-How, and Intangible Assets', Special Issue on Knowledge and the Firm, *California Management Review*, 40, 55–79

Teece, D. J., G. Pisano and A. Shuen, 1997. 'Dynamic Capabilities and Strategic Management', *Strategic Management Journal*, 18, 509–533

5 The territorial pacts in Italy: the competitive corporatism assumption in question

Serafino Negrelli

1 Introduction

From the 1990s onwards, several collective agreements labelled as 'social pacts' have been concluded in Europe between social partners at different levels and on various topics (mainly: wage moderation, work conditions, employment and flexibility). Beyond their heterogeneity, what unites them is they are explicitly linked to the construction of Europe: at the beginning, to the process of convergence towards the Euro that started at Maastricht in 1991 and to the monetary stability advocated and supervised by the European Central Bank (ECB). They are all calling for a fresh interpretation of what could become the industrial relations in the near future of European countries. This chapter would like to pose the terms of this question in its full scope. A well-established theory is a candidate for such an interpretation – the so-called 'neo-corporatism', which was very much in favour in the 1970s. Is a simple adaptation of this assumption needed – for instance, toward more decentralisation and micro-bargaining – or have we to search for a more radical move?

Section 2 recalls the main features of neo-corporatism in industrial relations and suggests that the social pacts and other similar agreements in the 1990s do not fit very well with this approach. In order to confront to empirical evidence, section 3 describes the process of decentralising the social concertation in Italy, its numerous types of agreements and the diversity of their relevant features. The search in Italy for a 'new programme' – that is, a method for achieving a better effectiveness of public objectives via multi-level agreements – is presented in section 4. This draws attention, for a given amount of public resources (whatever they are), to the efficacy by which local actors of a pact transform these resources into desirable and effective outcomes. Following the main line of argument of the volume, we shall call this the (very unequal, as we will see) power to convert public resources into outcomes, the *collective capabilities* that local actors deploy when implementing their agreement (see Salais and Villeneuve's chapter 1 in this volume). Decentralized social

73

concertation and territorial pacts are still at work in Italy with the present Berlusconi government of the Centre-right, even if the 'new programme' policies and the 'co-ordinated bargaining programmes' were launched by the Centre-left government in the second half of the 1990s. Section 5 focuses on territorial pacts (funded or not by the European Union) in Italy, and tries to find out the main factors behind the inequality of these collective capabilities. The theoretical debate evoked in section 2, can thus be reformulated in the conclusion (section 6). Roughly speaking, there are two options. The first is to refine global corporatism into *multiple competitive territorial* corporatisms. The second is to conceive the development of local pacts as part of a wider process of *exchange and benchmarking of good practices* at the European level. The stakes in such a process would not be downward economic competition between territories but the improvement of collective capabilities to make an efficient use of public (European, national or local) resources.

2   Social pacts: the relevance of the neo-corporatism assumption

The common elements characterising the social pacts in Italy and Europe during the 1990s made them substantially different from traditional, social neo-corporatist agreements based on the 'political exchange' (Pizzorno 1977). But at the same time they are radically opposed to the neo-liberal solutions of the 1980s (Negrelli 2000a). Their *structures* are based more on equilibrium between centralisation and decentralisation, that is to say 'controlled decentralisation' with micro-social concertation playing an essential role (Visser 1998), whereas the fundamental elements of the neo-corporatist structures were a high degree of centralisation and a system of representing interests in 'hierarchically organised' units (Schmitter 1974; Schmitter and Streeck 1985). A main difference lies in their objectives. The previous neo-corporatist systems had favoured the expansion of the welfare state, support for collective bargaining, full employment and regulation of the labour market (Boyer 1996). This happened in a general context of strong national regulation of the economy, consistently stable market growth and accommodating monetary policies, within the 'Fordist model' of economic convergence. The social pacts, instead, encompassed strategies predominantly oriented towards the joint definition among collective actors from a minimum 'threshold' of social protection to the search for a 'fair' combination between economic flexibility and social solidarity, between fairness and efficiency. They shifted from a 'demand-side' towards a 'supply-side' approach. Social dialogue now developed through situations of market globalisation with slower, more unstable growth, an ageing population and rigid monetary constraints (EMU), it will have to become increasingly engaged in industrial relations focused on wage moderation. Social dialogue is more and more involved with reorganising the welfare state and promoting growth, all of this being regulated by labour market flexibility in order to encourage both corporate strategies and public policies against unemployment (Fajertag and Pochet 2000; Regini 2000; Traxler 2000).

After 1998, social pacts entered a second, equally important and no less critical phase of social dialogue, whereby new objectives were linked to economic growth – namely, innovation and development of companies, employment, as well as social and economic infrastructures. This new phase is also the logical evolution and result of national social pacts. Social dialogue has to extend to a more decentralised level in order to stimulate change and local economic development. This implicitly draws attention to 'collective territorial capabilities', while encouraging a 'situated public action', with more negotiation and decision-making by local actors, territories, industrial districts, networked firms or clusters (see chapter 4 by Heidenreich and 6 by Zalio in this volume). These capabilities presuppose *decentralised systems of social infrastructures for innovation, for regulation and for governance of local economies*. As we will see in sections 4 and 5, institutionalising such systems is one thing, making them effective is another, and by no means the least one.

In Italy, besides the specific 'Pacts for Employment and Competitiveness' (PECs), laid down by the European Union, many other collective agreement initiatives have developed at the decentralised and territorial level. They involve a wider and more active participation of partners that represents the interests of entrepreneurs, trade unions, governments and local communities. They cover a wide range from 'territorial pacts' to 'area agreements', to 'programme contracts', to 'pacts for major cities' (for example, Milan) and, finally, to agreements related to a more traditional kind of company and territorial collective bargaining. The role of social and institutional partners *vis-à-vis* local development has emerged in many successful instances, whether at the macro or the micro level.

The spreading of territorial pacts throughout Italy and the rest of the European Union may be viewed as the major indicator of the evolution in social pacts at the macro level. Different 'models' and 'histories' of territorial capabilities may be found at the local level, and several 'diversities' may be identified within the same 'structure' and 'strategy', possibly explaining the different level of performance and success of decentralised social agreements.

3   Decentralised social concertation in Italy: local models and histories, diversified structures and strategies

As it has emerged in most macro-national social pacts, decentralised social dialogue is usually analysed by suggesting the existence of specific models and histories combined with competitiveness, employment and partnership. However, the case of Italy underlines the necessity also to refer, beyond models and histories, to the existence of different structures and strategies.

If reference is made to three main indicators of *structure* – i.e. level of decentralisation, economic resources and 'social ownership' (or quality and number of participating collective partners) – nine types of formalised social agreements can be identified at the decentralised level in Italy:

(1) *Regional pacts*, for example in the Marches or Piedmont regions, and thus with an intermediate level of decentralisation.

(2) *'National' territorial pacts*, mainly involving private investment, with the participation of many collective partners (from a minimum of fifteen, as was the case with the pact of Palermo, to a maximum of 179, in the pact regarding the Canavese area (Cersosimo 2000).

(3) *Pacts for Employment and Competitiveness (PECs)*, predominantly based on EU resources and with more formalised rules of social dialogue.

(4) *Area agreements*, mainly based on public financial resources (up to 70 per cent), as defined in the 'Pact for Employment' of 1996 and the Budget Act of 1997, with an important role played by institutional partners (i.e. Treasury Ministry, Labour Ministry, etc.).

(5) *Programme contracts*, which are focused on major Italian companies and far-reaching projects with the aim of integrating economically depressed areas (Italian Law 64, 1986).

(6) *Pacts for major cities*, such as Milan, Turin, Rome, Ferrara, etc.

(7) *Collective company agreements*, regarding the second level of the bargaining structure, as established by the Ciampi Protocol of 23 July 1993.

(8) *Collective territorial agreements*, regarding the second level of the bargaining structure, alternative to the company level, always within the framework of the Ciampi Protocol of 23 July 1993.

(9) *Local collective agreements*, within a given industrial district (i.e. around the cities of Prato, Carpi, etc.) or concerning areas of 'networked' firms or clusters, closely related to a major production site (such as automotive suppliers based in Melfi or Turin).

The diversity of these agreements is even more pronounced with regard to the major goals and objectives of their *strategies*.

Only *'national'* *territorial pacts* and those promoting employment initiated by the European Union have the explicit and formalised aim of 'building relations based on trust and collaboration between public and private local partners' in common. *Area agreements* are limited to incentives for business initiatives developed in so-called 'economic crisis areas', although they do involve more formalised agreements between employers' associations and the trade unions, with public administrations intervening only to check their effects. *Programme contracts*, on the other hand, are experiencing a difficult transition period. Having initially had the status of 'extraordinary intervention' instruments, they are becoming a new element for reforming 'co-ordinated economic programmes', basically also to attract investments from other countries.

Pacts for major cities follow ad hoc strategies. Take, for example, the Pact of Milan. This agreement entails temporary wage reductions to facilitate the introduction into the job market of immigrants, long-term unemployed (aged 40 years or more) and disabled persons. The Pact of Ferrara, by contrast, involves 'first-time job contracts', stages and fixed-term work contracts (maximum one year) for young people with a diploma or University degree, allowing them to work in companies and earn a minimum salary with funds from the European Union.

The aims of decentralised agreements arising from more traditional applications of collective bargaining are also quite varied. For those cases referring to the second level in the bargaining structure, either *company-related* or *territorial*, the aim is to regulate every four years the distribution of gains in production, quality and profitability at the company or local area level. In the case of *'district' agreements* or agreements *'closely related' to a major production site*, the aim is mainly to harmonise work protection standards between the companies of a given territory (within a 'community' of districts – for example, Prato – or owing to the leadership of a major manufacturing firm in the sub-contracting area, such as Fiat at Melfi). In addition, this harmonisation of standards avoids unfair competition or the opportunistic behaviour of companies with regard to social protection and trade union rights.

One has to reconstruct *models* of social relations that refer to several specific groups of decentralised pacts on the basis of related events and behaviours of the collective actors.

With regard to *territorial pacts* (for example 'national' or PECs), a great deal of literature and empirical research has pointed out the existence of some polarisation between models with a *strong leadership* and those with a *weak leadership*, regardless of who is capable of ensuring this leadership (Cersosimo 2000). Instead, in the case of *pacts for major cities*, different models seem to emerge depending on whether *separate* or *mainstream* trade union agreements were signed (for example, the Pact of Milan was not signed initially by the Confederazione Generale Italiana del Lavoro, CGIL, the main Italian trade union; the Pact of Ferrara and many other agreements were signed by all trade unions).

In the case of second-level *collective company agreements*, what still remains is a more traditional form of dualism. This dualism places, on one side, the prevailing *participatory* model of industrial relations based on extensive consultation activities and mixed committees formed by representatives from labour and management (for example, the cases of Electrolux–Zanussi and the Fiat plant in Melfi mentioned earlier) (Fortunato 2000) and, on the other, a widespread '*distributive* model' based on trade union antagonism and direct relations between management and labour (Walton and McKersie 1965; Negrelli 1998). In the case of second-level *collective territorial agreements*, what remains is another type of dualism partly inherited from the politico-ideological traditions of employers and trade union associationism in the regions – for example, between the politically moderate 'white Veneto' model and the politically left-wing 'red Emilia Romagna' model (Trigilia 1986; Giaccone 2000).

Finally, in the case of *district agreements* or those *closely related to a major production site*, the *employer-led* model of governance harmonising work standards (for example, the model introduced by Fiat in the area of Melfi, Pulignano 2002) is contrasted with a *union-led* model of governance of this harmonisation process (recall, for example, 'production site delegates' or the agreements on company functions externalised at Iveco in Brescia or Turin, Marchetti 2000, Piotto 2001, Negrelli 2004).

4   Bargaining for territorial economic programmes: the Italian 'new programme'

Owing to extreme differentiation of models, strategies and structures in local agreements, it is worth highlighting that in Italy the growth of public policy instruments, namely the 'new programme' policies, has fostered better orientation towards order and rationalisation, at least as far as territorial pacts, area agreements and programme contracts are concerned.

A report published by the Italian Treasury Ministry (Ministero del Tesoro 2001) on actions carried out in the so-called 'depressed areas' of Italy[1] summarises the relevance of this policy in addition to the important results achieved. In particular, the report points out how 'for the

---

[1] The eight regions of the *Mezzogiorno* (Campania, Apulia, Basilicata, Calabria, Sicily, Sardinia, Abruzzo and Molise), are recipients of community funds for areas with a regional *per capita* GDP 75 per cent lower than the European average (Objective 1); plus areas of the Centre-North, recipients of community funds owing to reasons of economic difficulty (Objective 2).

first time, after reinforcing decentralised levels of governance and introducing a new role for technical assistance and control at the centre, State intervention in favour of development is finally moving at the same pace as society and the market'. The 'new programme' policies were launched in 1998; their main purpose is to modify the objectives of public action in favour of development. They intend to progressively move from State action purely 'compensating' for territorial disadvantages within an economic and social context – in the past characterised by infrastructures policies and employer or employment incentives – to a more complex, integrated State action aimed at 'removing' these same territorial disadvantages. This seems to be closer to policies aiming at providing territorial actors with effective capabilities to overcome these disadvantages by their own action. Such removing of territorial disadvantages, in effect, requires qualified public investments, a reinforcement of decentralised governance, new technical assistance and centralised control, fast implementation of territorial pacts and the renewal of programme contracts.

Although instruments to offset local disadvantages in depressed areas still exist, priority has been given to 'co-ordinated bargaining programme' instruments, especially territorial pacts and programme contracts. These programmes are considered as decisive for the second objective aimed at reducing structural imbalances (quoted above). 'Co-ordinated bargaining programmes' are viewed as the most valid and innovative solution for eliminating the disadvantages of a given economic location, for implementing joint projects locally between public and private partners and between local institutional authorities and social partners representing the different interest groups. It could be also viewed as a real 'capability framework' more than an activation one (see chapter 13 by Brown *et al.*, 14 by de Munck and Ferreras and 18 by Salais in this volume, as well as Salais and Villeneuve's chapter 1).

Yet the implementation of these new public action objectives in depressed areas has been relatively slow. This is mainly due to bureaucratic and procedural problems which have not yet been resolved. The procedural course of co-ordinated bargaining programmes is rather complicated, four phases have been created that, in turn, are more complex and a source of further constraints and delays, not always understood by the private partners involved. In fact, the first phase – whereby funds are allocated by the CIPE (Inter-Ministry Committee on Economic Programme) to the various instruments – is followed by a second phase to select action via an evaluation process mainly carried out by public administrations, particularly the Treasury. The third phase allocates funds, and the fourth phase entails the spending of funds on the part of private

Table 5.1. *Potential resources and resources effectively allocated for programmes financed in October 2000 (excluding Community-related pacts) (billion lire)*

Instruments	Overall 'active' commitments	Potential resources (pr)	Allocated resources (ar)	Ratio ar/pr (%)
Territorial pacts	3,038	1,300	549	42.2
Area agreements	3,104	1,368	803	58.6
Programme contracts	1,770	1,516	678	44.7
Total	7,912	4,184	2,030	48.5

Source: Ministero del Tesoro (2001).

or mixed private/public local partners. During the transitions between these phases, some initiatives are lost and many appropriations are not finalised. According to the estimates of the Italian Treasury Ministry (January 1998–October 2000), of overall 'active' commitments for co-ordinated bargaining programmes totalling roughly 7,900 billion lire (excluding Community-related pacts), resources 'suitable for allocation' amounted to roughly 4,200 billion lire (about 2,160 million Euro) and out of these only a mere 2,000 billion lire (48.5 per cent) were 'effectively allocated' (see table 5.1).

According to several analyses conducted by the Department for Development and Cohesion Policies (DPS) of the Treasury Ministry and other research institutes, at least four reasons explain this partial failure:

(1) Bureaucratic and procedural factors associated with the limited capabilities of *central public administrations* to supply the potential resources in time.

(2) Inability of *local authorities* to promote adequate spending services; these problems are in the process of being solved.

(3) *Unequal cohesion* among territories between private interests and local administrative functions; the same could be said for local integration. The difficulty in promoting effective interaction between the various interest groups involved in the projects seems to characterise the Italian experience of territorial pacts, placing it still in an experimental phase (Cersosimo 2000).

(4) Different levels of *business capabilities* in providing investments and availability of resources to be allocated to the various projects. These problems may also stem from the very limitations of public action, as defined in items 1 and 2 (Ministero del Tesoro 2001).

Nevertheless, 'co-ordinated bargaining programmes' are gradually strengthening their role in regulating the local economy in Italy, owing to the number of initiatives introduced, the surface area and related population covered, not to mention the number of municipalities and social and institutional partners involved.

As far as the new '*territorial pacts*' are concerned, activities at the end of 2000 involved twenty pacts in the Centre North and forty-one in the Mezzogiorno, where the municipalities concerned account for 18.4 per cent of the total (just under one-third of the total number for Southern Italy, but with peaks reaching almost 50 per cent in Apulia as well as Tuscany and Umbria). The total surface area covered is 25.7 per cent (more than one-third of the total amount for the South and almost one-fifth that of the Centre-North, but with peaks of 61 per cent in Apulia and close to 50 per cent in Sicily, Tuscany and Umbria). The population involved accounts for 21.7 per cent of the nation's total (with 41.7 per cent in the South and 10.3 per cent in the Centre-North, and peaks of 71 per cent in Apulia and 49 per cent in Sicily (table 5.2).

The 'typical' Italian territorial pact (based on average characteristics) therefore involves twenty-four municipalities, a surface area of $1,270$ km^2 and a little over 200,000 inhabitants. The average number of municipalities involved is higher in the Centre-North, with thirty-four versus twenty in the South. Likewise, the average surface area covered is higher in the Centre-North, with $1,639$ km^2 versus $1,090$ km^2 in the South. The average population involved is relatively similar for territorial pacts in the Centre-North (188,527) and in the South (212,659). Worthy of notice is the fact that territorial pacts in several regions are characterised by a high number of municipalities involved (67 in Piedmont, 54 in Molise, 53 in Abruzzo and 44 in Sardinia). In other regions, territorial pacts are characterised by an 'extensive' average surface area covered (with Umbria $1,924$ km^2, Abruzzo $1,860$ km^2 and Sardinia $1,850$ km^2); in others again they are distinguished by the 'density' of the population (i.e. Apulia 290,275; Sicily 250,255; Lazio 221,336).

The importance of 'co-ordinated bargaining programmes' in local Italian development is also shown by the growing use of two more instruments – '*Programme contracts*' and '*Area agreements*'. The 'programme contracts' were first introduced within the framework of 'extraordinary intervention' measures promoted by Italian Law 64, 1986, that favoured the implementation of large-scale integrated projects in economically depressed areas. Together with industrial investments, their aim was to develop infrastructures, research, training and other necessary activities. Their management was handed over to the Treasury Ministry in 1993, when extraordinary intervention policies were abolished. Italian Law

Table 5.2. *Territorial pacts in progress: number, surface area covered and population involved, October 2000*

Regions	No. of pacts	% involved with pact over regional total			Average regional characteristics		
		No. of municipalities involved	Surface area (km²)	Population	No. of municipalities involved	Surface area (km²)	Population
Piedmont	4	22.1	19.0	11.2	67	1,204	120,506
Veneto	3	13.3	17.1	11.5	26	1,046	171,882
Liguria	1	12.8	14.0	9.2	30	757	149,541
Emilia R.	2	9.4	15.0	7.5	16	1,656	148,081
Tuscany	7	44.6	50.9	34.0	18	1,672	171,280
Umbria	2	41.3	45.5	30.7	19	1,924	127,981
Marche	2	20.7	23.7	14.3	26	1,148	104,116
Lazio	3	15.6	17.0	12.6	20	972	221,336
Centre-North	*20[a]*	*12.3*	*18.4*	*10.3*	*34*	*1,639*	*188,527*
Abruzzo	2	34.8	34.5	33.1	53	1,860	211,257
Molise	1	39.7	35.5	40.6	54	1,575	133,708
Campania	8	21.6	25.8	26.0	15	438	188,048
Apulia	10	45.7	61.3	71.0	12	1,186	290,275
Basilicata	2	22.9	31.5	29.6	15	1,571	89,883
Calabria	6	37.2	37.3	39.9	25	936	137,265
Sicily	10	36.4	45.0	49.1	14	1,158	250,255
Sardinia	2	23.3	15.4	15.1	44	1,850	124,878
Mezzogiorno	*41*	*31.6*	*36.3*	*41.7*	*20*	*1,090*	*212,659*
Italy	*61*	*18.4*	*25.7*	*21.7*	*24*	*1,270*	*204,747*

Note: [a] The total number is less than the sum, because in the Centre-North some territorial pacts are interregional.
Source: Ministero del Tesoro (2001).

662, 1996, not only assigned this instrument specifically to co-ordinated bargaining programmes, but also envisaged the financing of related initiatives with funds intended for depressed areas.

Programme contracts within the realm of co-ordinated bargaining programmes are focused mainly in the fields of agriculture, agro-industry and tourism; their real launch was only in 2000, after a delay of two years due to the unavailability of resources to be allocated to these new projects, and only after approval by the Commission of the European Union (July 2000). Programme contracts have been approved by the CIPE for Pirelli, Snam, Bosch, 7C Italia, Tct, Madia Diana and Ati/e-Sud.

'Area agreements', created under the 'Pact for Employment' of 1996, were created and officially launched in the Budget Act of 1997 (Article 2, sub-section 203, Italian Law 662/96) promoting new businesses in crisis areas. In particular, it is explicitly stated that the creation of new business initiatives should take place via the creation of a more favourable institutional framework, better co-operation in industrial relations, ad hoc 'soft' loans and tax breaks. Allocation of incentives was conditional on the observation of such institutional commitments. The investment must also be accompanied by firm agreement between management and trade unions at the local level (together with agreements between public administrations in order to accelerate these procedures, this is an integral part of area agreements), especially when it comes to jointly regulating actions relative to the cost of labour and labour market flexibility.

5   Territorial pacts in progress and collective capabilities

The 'new programme' was designed for achieving better effectiveness of public objectives through multi-level agreements. What evaluation can be made of the collective capabilities that local actors showed for innovating and regulating local development? We will focus on the sixty-one territorial pacts that were implemented at the end of 2000. There is enough information and material to make an initial evaluation of their scope and effectiveness, although such pacts started off quite differently and at different times:

(1) Twelve 'first-generation' territorial pacts in the Mezzogiorno, approved between 1996 and 1997, became active only in 1999, involved 347 active initiatives concerning businesses and infrastructures and 715 billion lire in planned incentives involving 5,479 additional persons employed out of a total employment of 8,284 persons.

(2) Thirty-nine 'second-generation' territorial pacts, active since 1999, involved 2,090 initiatives, roughly 6,100 billion lire in overall investments 2,472 billion lire in facilities, and 21,681 additional persons employed out of a total of 143,433 persons.

(3) Ten territorial Pacts for Employment and Competitiveness (PECs), approved at the end of 1998 according to EU procedures, became active in 1999 with roughly 900 billion lire granted by the CIPE for a total of 6,404 employees.

The overall conclusion to draw is that this model of governance for local development is still in its infancy, not only because of its recent start-up, but also because of the role and ambitious aims that the 'co-ordinated bargaining programmes' assigned to it.

In one of its documents, the Italian Treasury Ministry (Ministero del Tesoro 2001: 102) clearly specified the 'final' and 'intermediate' objectives of these territorial pacts. The former are characterised by 'the building of relations between public and private partners based on trust, with the dual purpose of designing and implementing projects for the development of infrastructures and for the improvement of services, giving life to integrated business initiatives'. Financing is therefore provided for the management activities of the 'actor in charge of' the consortium handling the pact and related infrastructures, as well as investment facilities for participating companies. The degree of efficacy of these pacts 'must therefore be measured in terms of this final goal, hence in terms of the ability to offer better services to companies, infrastructures, quality improvement actions for local life, environmental clean-up, as well as the implementation of agreements for improving contractual conditions with banks or the local labour market'.

In order to meet these intermediate and final goals, the first requirement is to offer facilities without delay to companies that participate in the selected and approved pacts. However, this condition was not complied with in the past, especially at the very beginning, though important improvements have been reported more recently, namely to streamline the procedures and develop a learning process within central public administrations as well as the local authorities (Ministero del Tesoro 2001, figure III.11). Overall, there are still some strong limitations in and divergences among the territorial pacts. In particular, if we take the fifty-one national territorial pacts (excluding EUPECs), the level of effectively allocated resources compared to those that may be allocated is still lower than average (42 per cent versus 48.5 per cent). However, this mean value of 42 per cent is matched by strong divergences: ten pacts exceeded 60 per cent while nine pacts actually remained below 10 per cent. We may add that such percentages refer to average levels, which means that they may be the result of a combination of winning and losing effects concerning the different initiatives within a single territorial pact.

According to the Italian Treasury Ministry, this divergence could be, first, an indicator of some local difficulty, particularly due to administrative weaknesses and limited capability of managing such pacts, despite the soundness of the projects initially selected; secondly inadequate project quality level for some specific initiatives that had been carefully evaluated and selected, but perhaps too hastily; and lastly, inefficiency of the companies involved (Ministero del Tesoro 2001: 105).

In addition to the limitations of the public administration mentioned above, it is therefore possible to affirm that the Italian experience with territorial pacts has increasingly raised the existence of divergent local collective capabilities, whether at the interterritorial or infraterritorial level. Nevertheless several elements seem promising. A survey on forty-six territorial pacts conducted during the first months of 2000 by 'Sviluppo Italia' on behalf of the Department for Development and Cohesion Policies of the Italian Treasury Ministry (Ministero del Tesoro 2001: 109–110) highlighted the consistently positive attitude of a majority of local social partners who took part. In particular, 84 per cent of 'internal' businessmen (those who actively participated in territorial pacts) expressed a positive evaluation that pacts have the ability to increase the advantages of a given location from the viewpoint of production activities, although this is not always visible (only 15 per cent spoke negatively). Likewise, 41 per cent of 'external' businessmen gave a positive evaluation (while 40 per cent did not express an opinion). 'External' businessmen seem ready to join the pact at a later date, whether it be to obtain incentives (roughly two-thirds) or to implement or join specific initiatives through agreements or protocols. For many, however, joining the pact is subordinate to a streamlining of the procedures, to the dissemination of more information, and to less 'political hype' surrounding the pacts.

This generally favourable attitude of businessmen towards territorial pacts points to a strong consensus with regard to decentralised social concertation. On the one hand, this represents the logical evolution of macro-national pacts and, on the other, the end to former public policies of 'extraordinary intervention'.

But territorial pacts still largely remain a 'gamble':
• Are public incentives capable of igniting a virtuous cycle?
• Can they help establish new 'rules of the game' for employers and local development and favour social behaviour geared to improving co-operation so as to promote widespread use of this public aid?
Several research studies conducted on the creation of new businesses and the relative institutional approach adopted in Italy have reported that these two questions are at the heart of the growth of capitalism in Italy (Pagani 1964) as well as the recent promotion of women in business (Negrelli 1999). Indeed, the success of territorial pacts is closely linked

to the granting of State aid and to the social partners actively taking them into consideration in their business calculations.

Among the few studies geared to measuring this impact, the research in the field conducted by the DPS of the Italian Treasury Ministry in 1998 on eighteen territorial pacts and three area agreements (Cersosimo 2000). However, besides the many positive effects derived from the introduction of new co-operative rules, numerous cases have been reported of 'false dialogue' or 'collusive coalitions' launched in an instrumental way only to obtain public funds, as well as cases of highly bureaucratic 'inclusive coalitions' with agreements signed by a multitude of actors hardly inclined to any form of integration, or steps taken towards partnerships without any real project or strong leadership.

The widespread participation of social actors representing local interests groups is central for building a 'social infrastructure' supporting the collective capability of innovation and regulation of local economies. An excessively high number of institutional, social, public and private 'owners' of pacts runs the risk, however, of causing 'social disorder'. This can hinder the formation of a legitimate leadership, and thus nip in the bud the very development process of decentralised social dialogue. The high number of actors signing the agreements, which could also be seen as a relevant indicator of participation and local democracy, in reality has a tendency to reduce the 'quality' of projects when faced with 'undifferentiated and non-specific populations of institutional subjects gelled together by the expectation of receiving public funds (for example, 100 billion from the CIPE) for each member territory' (Cersosimo 2000: 233).

These elements of social disorder and pact-oriented bureaucracy may be accentuated in the transition from the preparatory phase, where there are predominantly social partners and representatives of interest groups, to the phase of the *pact management*, when businessmen and personnel approving funds allocation play a prominent role. As illustrated by Cersosimo (2000: 240–241), the social 'sponsors' who first designed and promoted these initiatives will give way to stronger, more decisive 'men with bowler hats' owing to the financial implications.

There are considerable limitations also in the economic effects. The DPS research mentioned earlier, for example, reports that

rarely in private investment projects does one see the local development project itself. Actually, quite often the plan is a mere juxtaposition of projects without any real functional or business-related connection. The infrastructures that invested into these pacts often do not appear to be 'closely functional' or related to the investments provided in the pact, nor do they comply with, even very slowly, growth objectives and physical and economic agglomeration. (Cersosimo 2000: 222–223)

Moreover, it has been reported that out of 830 business initiatives, 797 were related to investment projects for expanding, modernising and restructuring already existing enterprises, whereas only thirty-three (4 per cent) referred to new businesses (essentially area agreements). The effects in the labour market have also been quite modest – roughly fifteen employees involved for every initiative set up as a territorial pact, with an average investment of 5.4 billion lire, so very minimal financial commitments for businesses. Even more tenuous is the contribution of public resources for every new job created (a mere 73 million lire), which reaches 100 million lire if one includes all of the national and PEC pacts. This is decidedly lower (virtually half the number) compared to the estimated amount in public financing provided for young people starting their own businesses based on Italian Law 44, 1986. These contradictory elements should not make us lose sight of many pacts in which a selective coalition of a few players (essentially among those selected by the province, municipalities, employers' associations and trade unions) have achieved a considerable use of resources congruous with the objectives of territorial projects. In this case, the existence of effective costs and well-targeted projects have contributed significantly to limiting opportunistic behaviour.

6   Conclusion: competitive territorial corporatisms or a learning process by benchmarking?

Many problems of the central public administrations and local authorities and their capabilities in Italy were or could be solved by a learning process. But what sort of learning process? Through which procedures or co-ordination could it be implemented? In the light of evidence shown in this chapter, we can return to pursue the discussion begun in section 2. Is a simple refinement of the neo-corporatist assumption needed, or should we look for a more subtle definition of what could be a learning process in Europe on this matter?

In the past, the standard hypothesis was that the learning process could be based on competition among macro-national social pacts. Visser and Hemerijck (1997), for instance, underlined the importance of the political and social learning process in the 'Dutch miracle'. Regarding political developments as an intelligent puzzle about what to do during an uncertain situation and as a political struggle among interests in competition, they strongly argued that the 'internal' dynamics of the institutional change were the decisive factor in the Dutch case. There was a crucial change of mentality and of political economy by the social actors who adjusted, strengthened and reorganised the old system of social dialogue.

Yet a closer look suggests that even these examples have little to share with 'regime competition' between European economic and (more or less corporatist) social systems. This idea carries a negative connotation of competition at the lowest level of social protection (without a socially accepted threshold). But, generally, the European countries, as indicated by Streeck (1992: 6), 'are institutionally rich societies where markets are deeply embedded in an array of co-operative, redistributive and regulatory institutions', which marks the path towards 'diversified quality production' and a 'highway' of economic development.

The idea of a *competitive* or *supply-side corporatism* (Traxler 1997) or of competitive territorial corporatisms, which means that some risks in social protection exist but can be absorbed or reduced by new opportunities influencing or reacting to the challenges of economic globalisation and flexibility could be more useful. This perspective takes reactions, adjustments or new strategies from traditional neo-corporatism, but also from the neo-liberal systems of the 1980s that entail a more considered balance between centralisation and decentralisation, between flexibility and solidarity and between public policies and free-market policies. Many political agendas of the European governments from the 1990s (Prodi's 'Ulivo Programme' in Italy; Blair's 'Third way' in the UK; the 'Soziale Marktwirtschaft' in Germany; the Social Pacts in Spain, etc.) are searching for such strategies. All of them rely upon the idea that with the advent of the Euro and of national income policies and co-ordinated collective bargaining on wages, only at the decentralised levels of territories and enterprises will it be possible to distribute the output of productivity and to negotiate on wages and social protection. All things being equal, especially with regard to the unequal capabilities of territories to profit from public resources and to transform them in positive outcomes in economic development and employment, there is a growing risk that more competition among decentralised levels of social dialogue will imply more wage stagnation and stricter work conditions. As several past examples have shown, large companies will have more opportunities to compete with non-European territories for their future investments and locations.

This raises the question of how to implement a process of learning from territorial experience that would not lead to negative effects and risks but would maximise the positive effects and new opportunities that can be expected from territorial development and economic specialisation. Such 'maximisation' refers to collective capabilities – that is, the power to *convert public resources into favourable outcomes*. This question is two-sided. It is addressed first to the actors, above all, with regard to how they build agreements at territorial level and commit themselves to achieve agreed expected outcomes. But one must not forget that public resources and tools are not necessarily designed or oriented to maximise the expected outcomes. Our chapter tried in the case of Italy to shed light on the main factors that, on both sides will influence the course of events. This highlights a political question for Europe, connected to governance and to the implementation of the open method of co-ordination (OMC) on territorial and social dialogue issues (see chapter 12 and 8 by Pochet and Raveaud respectively, in this volume). How can we develop at European and national level instruments of evaluation and of benchmarking that can focus on territorial capabilities, their inequalities within Europe, and their improvement? Lessons from these instruments should be drawn not only for collective actors, but for the adjustment of public policies as well.

REFERENCES

Boyer, R., 1996. 'The Convergence Hypothesis Revisited: Globalization but Still the Century of Nations?', in S. Berger and R. Dore (eds.), *National Diversity and Global Capitalism*, Ithaca, NY, Cornell University Press, 29–59
Cersosimo D., 2000. 'I patti territoriali', in D. Cersosimo and C. Donzelli (eds.), *Mezzo Giorno. Realtà, rappresentazioni e tendenze del cambiamento meridionale*, Rome, Donzelli, 209–251
Fajertag, G. and P. Pochet, 2000. *Social Pacts in Europe – New Dynamics*, Brussels, ETUI
Fortunato, V., 2000. 'Il caso Fiat-Sata di Melfi', in S. Negrelli, S. (ed.), *Prato verde, prato vosso. Produzione snella e partecipazione dei lavoro nella Fiat del duemila*, Soveria Mannelli, Rubbettino, 55–140
Giaccone, M., 2000. 'Contrattazione territoriale come infrastruttura dello sviluppo locale', *Quaderni Rassegna Sindacale*, 3, 13–46
Marchetti, A., 2000. 'Il caso Fiat Iveco di Brescia', in S. Negrelli (ed.), *Prato verde, prato rosso. Produzione snella e partecipazione dei lavoro nella Fiat del duemila*, Soveria Mannelli, Rubbettino, 141–210
Ministero del Tesoro, 2001. *Terzo rapporto sullo sviluppo territoriale 1999–2000. Relazione di sintesi sugli interventi realizzati nelle aree depresse e sui rispettivi risultati*, Allegato alla Relazione previsionale e programmatica per il 2001, www.tesoro.it
Negrelli, S., 1998. 'Le relazioni industriali e la gestione delle risorse umane nelle imprese', in G. Cella and T. Treu (eds.), *Le nuove relazioni industriali. L'esperienza italiana nella prospettiva europea*, Bologna, Il Mulino, 257–96
(ed.), 1999. *Istituzione e imprenditorialità*, Milan, Guerini
2000a. 'Social Pacts in Italy and Europe: Similar Strategies and Structures; Different Models and National Stories', in G. Fajertag and P. Pochet (eds.), *Social Pacts in Europe – New Dynamics*, Brussels, ETUI, 85–112
(ed.), 2000b. *Prato verde, prato rosso. Produzione snella e partecipazione dei lavoratori nella Fiat del duemila*, Soveria Mannelli, Rubbettino
2004. 'The Outsourcing "Prince": Models of Supply Chain Governance in the Italian Automobile Districts', *Industry and Innovation*, 11, 1–2, 109–126

Pagani, A., 1964. *La formazione dell'imprendi torialità*, Milan, Comunità

Piotto, I., 2001. 'Dal just in time alla produzione modulare. Rapporti tra imprese e problemi di relazioni industriali', *DSS Papers*, Soc. 4–01, Brescia, Dipartimento di Studi Sociali, Università di Brescia

Pizzorno, A., 1977. 'Scambio politico e identità collettiva nel conflitto di classe', in C. Crouch and A. Pizzorno (eds.), *Conflitti in Europa. Lotta di classe, sindacati e stato dopo il '68*, Milan, Etas, 407–434

Pulignano, V., 2002. 'Relazioni industriali e gestione delle risorse umane nel settore della fornitura dell'auto in Basilicata', in R. Botticelli and D. Paparella (eds.), *Sistemi territoriali della produzione automobilistica: il Piemonte e la Basilicata*, Milan, Angeli, 133–166

Regini, M., 2000. *Modelli di capitalismo. Le risposte europee alla sfida della globalizzazione*, Bari, Laterza

Schmitter, P., 1974. 'Still the Century of Corporatism?', *Review of Politics*, 36, 85–131

Schmitter, P. and W. Streeck, 1985. 'Comunità, mercato, stato e associazioni? Il possibile contributo dei governi privati all'ordine sociale', *Stato e mercato*, 13, 47–86

Streeck, W., 1992. *Social Institutions and Economic Performance. Study of Industrial Relations*, London, Sage

Traxler, F., 1997. 'The Logic of Social Pacts', in G. Fajertag and P. Pochet (eds.), *Social Pacts in Europe*, Brussels, ETUI

2000. 'National Pacts and Wage Regulation in Europe: A Comparative Analysis', in G. Fajertag and P. Pochet (eds.), *Social Pacts in Europe – New Dynamics*, Brussels, ETUI, 401–418

Trigilia, C., 1986. *Grandi partiti, piccole imprese*, Bologna, Il Mulino

Visser, J., 1998. 'Two Cheers for Corporatism, One for the Market. Industrial Relations, Unions and Labour Markets in the Netherlands', *British Journal of Industrial Relations*, 36(2), 269–292

Visser, J. and A. Hemerijck, 1997. *A Dutch Miracle*, Amsterdam, Amsterdam University Press

Walton, R. E. and R. B. McKersie, 1965. *A Behavioral Theory of Labor Negotiations*, New York, McGraw-Hill

6 Mobilising local capabilities for a European economic project: the case of Marseilles

Pierre-Paul Zalio

1 Introduction

Since the 1960s, building Europe has constituted one of the horizons framing the economic choices of the Member States, and has contributed to redefining regional productive specialisation. In the case of France, two periods can be clearly distinguished. A first period started with the constitution of the six-country European Common Market in the 1960s, during which centralised economic policies were framed by a new technocratic body, DATAR.[1] These policies aimed at reshaping the economic geography of France according to two principles: eliminating 'production overlaps' (and, more broadly, restructuring regional economic fabrics deemed archaic or not competitive enough) and creating 'national champions' able to face European and international competition. In the early twenty-first century, the issue is framed in rather different terms. Instead of being State-driven, the economic destiny of a region now simultaneously plays out at the local level of 'territorial' authorities and at the more global level of corporate strategies. As a result, the State's ability to define the public interest – i.e. its capacity to assign objectives whose achievement, after due deliberation, seems profitable to all actors and to the collective as such – is now questioned at the local level.

In such a context, the notion of 'territory' has gained theoretical importance. However, it lacks a clear definition, being at best considered as the supposedly relevant level at which an efficient economic policy should be elaborated and conducted. Searching for the specific relevance of such a notion is all the more important as territorial dialogue procedures have been endowed with every conceivable virtue – for instance, that of providing better 'governance'.

This chapter focuses on the metropolitan area of Marseilles in France, an area which provides a vantage point for observing these trends and for understanding the issues at stake in a territorial approach to politics. On two distinct occasions, thirty years apart, large-scale economic

[1] DATAR: Délégation à l'aménagement du territoire et à l'action régionale.

91

projects supported by the French State have been deployed there: the harbour and steel industry project in Fos-sur-Mer in the 1960s, and the 'Euroméditerranée' development project in the 1990s. The latter was supported by various sources of French public funding as well as the European Community (EC), and aimed at creating a tertiary activity pole in Marseilles. The main issue at stake here is one of redefining the State's role as part of a public action involving several public and private actors. It is therefore important to know who are the actors involved in deliberation when the economic destiny of a local territory is taken into account, by scrutinising the procedures of collective choice at a local level, in the way they operate and the outcomes they have.

Section 2 is a brief reminder of how the Euroméditerranée project was set up to overcome a deep crisis in the urban economy of Marseilles, and the two phases the project underwent. In the first period (1995–8) the operation simply put fresh wine in an old bottle. Following a scheme elaborated by DATAR, State intervention in the territory sought to confer upon Marseilles the attributes of a southern European capital within the Latin Arc. In the second period (1998–2003) private sector actors, both local and national, were involved. Conception and implementation of the economic strategy of the project were 'sub-contracted' to them by the State (Section 3), permitting them to allocate public money toward ends they deemed both workable and profitable. This illustrates how a public scheme can become, for the sole actors that have been entitled to participate, a locus of expression of tensions and of search for compromises that open the way to a range of possible economic solutions (Section 4). In conclusion (Section 5), lessons will be drawn for public action.

2   'The Commando State' or a dialogue under command

The Fos-sur-Mer operation in the 1960s was at the heart of the economic strategies of the Gaullist State. With the installation of a waterfront steel complex, the State intended to bring Marseilles' economy (which it deemed to be archaic and in crisis, as the streams of colonial income had dried up) into the concert of Fordist modernisation, and to prepare it for entry into the European Common Market. Up to the 1960s, the economic system of Marseilles was grounded in Port trade and industry (processing of raw materials from the colonies: oils and fats, food processing, chemicals).[2] Its failure resulted in a dynamic but fragmented regional economy, mainly constituted of petrochemicals around the Berre

[2] Zalio (1999).

Marsh and a pole of microelectronics not far from Aix-en-Provence. This redeployment of productive specialities went along with a separation between Marseilles and the new industrial area that was meant to become a hinterland of the city.[3] The de-industrialisation of the city was not compensated by an equivalent increase in employment in services, and the city became increasingly impoverished, even though it was located at the very heart of a prosperous metropolitan area. The municipality's tax resources, which had always been insufficient in relation to the size of a vast working-class city, left the local government with little room for initiative. This situation led to the conviction that only 'shock therapy' could revitalise the economy of Marseilles, and that only massive State support could bring this about. Hence the Euroméditerranée project. Through a public planning and infrastructure development corporation, EPAEM,[4] in charge of overseeing an 'operation in the national interest', the project aimed to revitalise the economy of Marseilles by attracting tertiary sector companies to a degraded district bordering the Port and the city centre. It also aimed to upgrade a vast urban zone made up of struggling neighbourhoods.

Let us first look at the specificity of the project (2.1) and then examine its pseudo-deliberative nature (2.2).

2.1   A local project entrusted to the State

It all began with a private initiative. In 1989, when the economic situation of Marseilles was at its lowest, a major French real estate group (SARI) decided to acquire the 'Docks de Marseille', a vast nineteenth-century building set alongside the Port basins. With the prospect of the TGV (high-speed train) line coming in 2001, the idea of making the zone between the station and the Port a pole of tertiary development gradually took shape. At that time on the local level, no one had a clear idea of the economic strategy to be devised for the site.

The project was local only in appearance, being hardly a matter of relying on the local economic forces, which were perceived as non-existent. The prevailing notion was that the city space had to be reorganized (through rehabilitation of transport lines and the built environment) in order to attract investors acting on a European scale. The project, formally initiated by the city government, led to the creation of a public corporation, the EPAEM, thanks to which the city was ensured that the State would take part in project funding and in future negotiations with private partners and local authorities. From the State's point of view, this

---

[3] Morel (1999).   [4] Etablissement public d'aménagement d'Euroméditerranée.

solution was a way to get the partners (city, department, regional government, Chamber of Commerce, Port Autonome authorities) to work together, despite their very different expectations and their traditional inability to agree upon anything. The various partners were committed to support a scheme involving the site between the Port and the train station (both were State-owned utilities). Therefore, local actors, through the voice of municipal councillors, for instance, were not the ones to elaborate the development project before looking for the partners needed to carry it out. The mission of thinking out the future of the site was entrusted to a ministerial task force led by an engineer from the Ponts et Chaussées school. This task force established an initial cost estimate for the operation, decided on its philosophy and devised a schedule for dividing up funding between the State and other levels of government.

With the creation of the EPAEM public corporation, the scheme was endowed with a substantial budget: from 1.7 billion francs in 1995 (including 800 MF from the State), the allocation rose to 2.4 billion francs for 1995–2006. The European Union contributed 130 MF to this total under ESF Objective 2 (1997–9) and under the European Regional Development Fund (ERDF). While the State provided half of the scheme's funding, the city was responsible for 25 per cent, the regional and departmental governments contributed 10 per cent each and the 'Marseilles-Provence-Métropole' community of towns 5 per cent. This sharing followed a partnership model, neither the State nor the city wanting to take on sole financial and political responsibility for the scheme. Urban planning rules and permits were modified in favour of the State, thereby releasing the municipality from some of its authority. It was the Prefect (named by the government), and no longer the mayor (elected), who issued the various permits. On the Board of Directors, the State (via high-level civil servants, many of whom came from the Infrastructure administration) and local authorities were equally represented, but the essential power was wielded by the director-general, an engineer trained at the Polytechnique and Ponts et Chaussées schools, and appointed by the State.[5] In many respects the scheme was really and truly State-driven.[6]

The pre-configuration mission (1994) called for formulation of a 'detailed timetable' for the operation. EPAEM asked workgroups to define this framework, notably its economic content. These groups would

---

[5] The Board of Directors has twenty members: nine represent the State, four represent the City of Marseilles, two represent the regional government, two the departmental government and one represents the 'Marseilles-Provence-Métropole' community of towns. The last two members are a representative of the *Port Autonome* and a qualified individual appointed by the Prime Minister (a Marseilles banker).

[6] Dubois and Olive (2001).

be 'made up of experts or competent individuals, taking part in this work in a personal capacity, independently of all institutional representation, and having to define the content of the operation'.[7] The procedure was thus *formally* a partnership, based on the public corporation's efforts to foster co-operation between a multitude of actors who came from the institutions taking part in the operation, the regional offices of central administrations and actors of the local economy and society. The make-up and architecture of these workgroups shows that EPAEM had in reality chosen to maintain a discreet control over the deliberative process. With eight workgroups of ten–twelve members each, focusing on very broad objectives, headed by a steering group in which the representatives of the various authorities associated with the operation appeared once again, and centralised by a co-ordination unit entirely controlled by EPAEM, the arrangements gave the public corporation plenty of room for set-ting up compromises and keeping the lead with respect to the scheme's content.

2.2   A caricature of deliberation

The mandates assigned to these groups reflect an abstract conception of the division of deliberative work in a project of this sort: three work-ing groups covered the 'supply' side (content, operations, quality) and included for the most part representatives of the administrative bodies who would have to work with urban planners. Three groups covered 'demand': a 'long-term' group brought together economic forecasters, sociologists and experts from the sectors of maritime transport, logis-tics and telecommunications. A 'medium-term' group included promot-ers, real estate specialists and bank representatives. A 'short-term' group, meant to express the immediate demand, included local businessmen, notably in the branches of the 'trade/logistics/service target'. Lastly, to these six groups EPAEM added two others to take into account the cul-tural and social dimensions of the project, while making sure these groups were cut off from deliberation on the infrastructure construction and the economic vocation of the project. A 'daily life' group, described as made up of 'residents, shopkeepers, social workers, teachers', was entrusted with the task of 'evaluating how residents might experience the operation', and an 'imagination' group, made up of 'artists, writers, communica-tion professionals, citizens' was asked to 'dream about Euroméditerranée without any constraints'.

---

[7] All the quotations that follow are taken from the summary notes written in June 1996 by the working groups.

In 1996 the workgroups produced only a vague and abstract formulation of the economic orientations for the scheme. The question of the synergy between the Port and the scheme had however been raised: 'In terms of economic strategy, the workgroup raised the question of the extent to which the fate of Euroméditerranée and the Port would have to be reconciled by mixing activities, letting territories interpenetrate, encouraging permeability. "Tear down the gates to the Port" can be seen as symbolically summarising this intention.' This contained the premises of a conflict between the Port and EPAEM, affecting the very definition of the economic identity of the scheme. The lack of clarity in the economic choices was therefore largely due to the operational mode of the public corporation. The devising of an economic strategy was devoted to a small team of high-level civil servants, some of whom had experience in economic conversions. Some had shouldered their first responsibilities in Lorraine with the Prefect delegated to head the economic conversion effort, Jacques Chérèque. From this they retained, in the terms used in our interviews, a culture of the 'Commando State' and the 'State thug', employing their personal contacts, informal structures and discretionary powers supported by the appropriate budgetary measures. Applied to the situation in Marseilles, these methods rapidly proved counterproductive, in particular by provoking the hostility of the Chamber of Commerce and Industry. Disconnected from actors of the local economy, they focused their efforts on decentralising public bodies, and above all on hunting down the big companies, French or foreign, that could set up headquarters serving as a beacon for southern Europe. This European-scale hunt led the EPAEM team to rally its national networks (particularly those tied to friendships within the corps of Ponts et Chaussées engineers). But this fruitless quest only worsened the image of a project bereft of any local meaning, and managed in an overly technocratic fashion.

3   The return of the territory in the scheme: sub-contracting the public interest to the private sector

As the scheme was not making progress, it was subject to much criticism. Its lack of content was the foremost reproach; locally, the prevailing feeling was one of a tremendous waste. An audit by the Cour des Comptes was conducted in January 1998, which highlighted points of malfunction, following which the director-general was asked to leave, he being the person who, rightly or wrongly, locally personified the heavy hand of the highest level of State servants.[8] His successor did indeed have

---

[8] Blanc and Cavallier (1997).

quite a different profile. A graduate of the Institut d'études politiques de Paris, he was also a naval architect and a city planner. He knew Marseilles well, having worked in the 1970s as a city planner in another major public corporation in the region related to the Fos-sur-Mer scheme. This change in management marked a new focus on urban development issues in the scheme. It also manifested a renewed control of the State, faced with a noxious local political climate. Henceforth a small group directed the scheme under the authority of the Prefect (a group including the director-general, the chairman, the mayor of Marseilles – or, rather, the first deputy mayor – a representative of the departmental government and a representative of the regional government). But the decision taken was to build upon broader co-operation with actors in the private sector of the economy.

The 'new equilibrium between plan and market' is presented first (section 3.1) and then how it organised some sub-contracting of the State objectives (section 3.2). Finally we will discuss to what extent this offered a way to express tensions between competing interests at the local level (section 3.3).

3.1   A 'new equilibrium' between planned programme action and market forces

As early as 1996 the summary report of the scheme indicated that it was necessary to find an 'equilibrium between planned programme action and market forces'. Henceforth the economic project was renewed on the basis of intense co-operation with private sector actors. The deliberative procedures increasingly called on business leaders to reformulate the scheme's economic strategy. Contacts initiated during the preceding period were reactivated and a *Club d'initiative pour le rayonnement d'Euroméditerranée* (CIPRE) created for the purpose of bringing local business leaders and EPAEM executives face to face.

In just a few months the private sector actors drew up a fairly detailed economic strategy. In February 1998 the Prefect (who had regained some authority over the scheme) set up four workgroups. Three of these were made up of business leaders and private sector actors who turned in their report in September; a final synthesis was written in October. The first group, chaired by the chairman of the Chamber of Commerce, Claude Cardella, formulated proposals dealing with trade (international, Port activity); the second group chaired by the banker Bernard Maurel drew up proposals on the development of the top-level tertiary sector; the third group, called the 'group of Parisians', included the heads of major French companies (more or less professionally or personally connected to Marseilles), who were to give their point of view.

For the entrepreneurs, this forceful entry into the scheme was seen as a return to a fairer state of affairs:[9]

There is significant risk in favouring only exogenous development (companies coming from outside) while neglecting the development of SME–SMIs [small- and middle-sized enterprises and industries] that are already implanted; businesses must be supported when they are setting up, but also as they develop . . . The major local businesses feel they have not received enough attention and support from the political and administrative spheres. They must be included in order to reap the local profits, which are already substantial, of the trickle-down effects of the policies they have initiated[10]

The mobilisation of local economic resources was thus preferred to secrecy and to waiting for decentralisation moves by public sector bodies or private industrial corporations.

These workgroups comprised leading businessmen, who were chairmen or regional directors of their respective corporations. The groups were marked by the place held by new information and communication technology companies (France Télécom, Cégétel, Matra-datavision, etc.), banking and finance (Bernard Maurel played a central part along with a representative of the Lazard Frères bank). These local actors received advice and support from top French executives who were familiar with Marseilles, and were members of the 'Parisian group' – including Frédéric d'Allest (Aérospatiale), Pierre Bellon (Sodexho), Serge Tchuruk (Alcatel) and Jean Peyrelevade (Crédit Lyonnais). The 'regional' group met once a month, whereas the 'Parisians' met for lunch three times a year 'to have a regular update on the advancement of Euroméditerranée and Marseilles'. These meetings aimed at deliberating the Euroméditerranée strategy, as well as co-ordinating steps to make contacts, attract investment and lobby certain administrations, the European Commission or the French government. The 'Parisian group' undertook to obtain DATAR's tertiary development allowance ('prime d'aménagement tertiaire' or PAT). The minutes regularly recorded how group members helped out EPAEM by using their networks: 'M.S. pledges to give EPAEM a list of useful contacts in some large companies.' The formal structuring of a lobby in Brussels was even considered. Executives closest to the high governmental and administrative levels volunteered to intercede with the latter for a stronger support of the State to the scheme. In the words of Frédéric d'Allest: 'It must be constantly repeated that Euroméditerranée

---

[9] The following quotations are taken from working group notes written between February and October 1998.
[10] 'Le développement du tertiaire supérieur sur Euroméditerranée', summary report of the working group instituted by the PACA Regional Prefect (October 1998: 4).

is a national scheme, driven by national authorities; the lobbying effort must be intensified in order to get one or two operations that will prime the pump of Euroméditerranée; some of us could speak out firmly in this direction at the highest level.'

3.2 The public corporation sub-contracts the definition of some of its objectives to the private sector

At the local level, the workgroups tried to unite the resources of actors in the local economy. This effort was all the more critical as the local business leaders lacked a locus of centralised co-ordination, an aspect indicated by the fragmentation of the structures devoted to promotion of the local economy.[11] Gradually a network took shape – the 'network of ambassadors' – integrating the pre-existing networks: the CIPRE and the Chamber of Commerce network.

These groups not only exchanged information and services; they also provided a locus for dialogue. The deliberations of the meetings show how the economic vocation of the scheme came to be progressively built, taking the shape of picking a 'winning combination'. In 1996, the project provided for eight sectors that could be of interest to the scheme: telecommunications and information technology; audio, video and multimedia industries; water and environmental services; corporate support services; finance; training; tourism and urban leisure activities. This broad spectrum concealed a lack of decision and of clear identification of economic resources in the territory. As was pointed out by the top Parisian executives in the minutes of their meetings: 'Marseilles no longer has a clearly proclaimed vocation. Major choices must be made in order to give the city an "economic soul."' The first aspect of this redefinition – and not the least conflicting one – was the calling into question of the harbour's role in the scheme.

Whereas before the First World War 70 per cent of the goods that arrived on the docks of Marseilles was processed by local industry, the de-industrialisation of Marseilles led to a crisis of Port industry in the 1960s. The Port statistics concealed this fact for a time owing to the tonnage of hydrocarbons refined around Fos. In the 1980s the question of the economic viability of the docks of Marseilles was raised, and with this question came that of the transfer of all the activities of the Port Autonome de Marseille to Fos.[12] Despite successive crises (decline in

[11] Zalio (2001).

[12] The Port Autonome, established in 1966, is a public corporation that, like Euroméditerranée, is under the authority of the Infrastructure Ministry.

ship repair, falling market share for containers, labour conflicts delaying reform of the status of Port cargo handlers, etc.), it was stated that the docks of Marseilles were viable. The problems of co-ordination between the Port and Euroméditerranée were mainly territorial in nature: maintaining the Port zone under Customs authority (the maritime domain) was in part incompatible with one of the aspects of the scheme, which was to 'give the sea back to the people of Marseilles', i.e. extend public access to the piers. The Euroméditerranée scheme itself was not very clear about the issue. In 1992 the Port, whose territory was not bound within the scheme's perimeter, was nonetheless included in the first protocol of agreement. Two years later, in the first pre-configuration report, it was said that 'Euroméditerranée is 80 per cent devoted to Port activity. It will be a centre of decision and sophisticated logistics adapted to a major distribution platform for receiving, processing, packaging and redistributing merchandise.' On the other hand, one of the developers' prime focuses was to reconcile the Port and the city. This aspect constitutes a leitmotif of urban development schemes in many Port cities; in the case of Marseilles, however, it raised an important issue, as the city (to the south) and the Port (to the north) had tended to develop in two opposite geographical directions. While it seemed natural to give public access to docks that seemed to draw fewer and fewer boats, the project was to give rise to a profound crisis between the Port and the city.[13]

In order to redefine the productive activities of the Port city in relation to the development scheme, a forum was needed to debate the pattern that had governed the economy of Marseilles for 150 years – an economic model which was based on the Port. EPAEM came to constitute this forum for the expression of tensions that ran through the local social body. Institutions' inability to work together, as well as rivalry between promotion agencies 'blurred' the image of Marseilles in a way that was not likely to attract investors. The local business community was fragmented, owing to the crisis in modes of social integration and to the downturn in Marseilles' economy. In such a context, it was impossible to reach a consensus as long as EPAEM sought to monopolise the debate by expressing the views of a few civil works engineers from Ponts et Chaussées. Reaching a consensus on the procedures of dialogue themselves (and hence the procedures of conflict) was the first step allowing the actors to overcome their differences and their conflicts of interest. By relying on the input of private sector actors, the scheme was to progressively foster better

---

[13] Although a protocol of agreement was signed between the Port and EPAEM in 1997, the interaction remains tricky between Port activity in the course of redeployment and the use of urban infrastructures on the same shores.

co-ordination between the partners, i.e. between the municipal, departmental and regional governments, the Chamber of Commerce, the Union Patronale and the Port.

3.3   The scheme as a forum for expressing tension between interests and redefining productive activities in the territory

What were, roughly speaking, the main features of the conflict that divided actors with regard to the economic future? This conflict concerned both the role of public actors and the forms of investment by private partners (local entrepreneurs, representatives of the business community and investors from outside Marseilles). In addition to the opposition between the Port and EPAEM, a conflict emerged between the proponents of a strategy aimed at attracting headquarters or subsidiaries of major international groups for their southern European activities and the proponents of a strategy of support for existing economic dynamics, notably SMEs. This overlapped with an opposition between actors with different horizons of action: high-level civil servants and local executives of major groups on the one hand, and the heads of local SMEs on the other (some of whom had an interest in renewed Port activity, others not). It is noticeable that a whole range of economic activities present on-site were ignored during these deliberations, i.e. all the activities of small foreign-born entrepreneurs who conducted commercial trade activities (textiles, automobile parts) with other Mediterranean cities but who were on the fringe of the underground economy, and thus incompatible with the scheme's profile. A whole segment of local economy actors – the most modest but also the most active, and in some ways the most global[14] – were absent from the theatre of deliberations.

The definition of possible productive choices depended on considerations on the regional economic identity and on the opportunities that could be seized as the information and communication industries, notably related to the Internet, began to rapidly expand in 1998. In giving up the idea of waiting for a few prestigious 'front offices', the economic actors began to consider the advantages of the territory in terms of cost-effectiveness (particularly land prices and wages), in order to attract mid-level 'back office' activities (tertiary administrative services, sales follow-up). At the same time, while a fabric of advanced industries, notably in microelectronics, was growing in the nearby Aix district, the notion that the city should bank on the information industry began to dawn upon actors in Marseilles.

[14] Peraldi (2001).

The need to focus the economic promotional appeal on a few major sectors of activity, calling for specific products, is confirmed . . . In this framework telecommunications, information technology and multimedia can be grouped under a common heading, that of 'information industries'. Call centres and educational multimedia publishing are activities to be specifically developed within this branch.[15]

Little by little a 'winning combination ticket' was drawn up, the three winners being: information industries (telecommunications, tele-services, IT and multimedia); southern France or southern Europe base offices (back office, decentralised administrative centres, regional or divisional corporation offices, call centres and telephone platforms); and international trade (Port, maritime shipping, logistics).

This choice of content-oriented information industries corresponded to several levels of expectations and objectives. The national operators could expect the installation of infrastructure (notably in terms of broadband telephone and Internet networks), partly backed by public funds, and enabling the development of activity in these fields. The talks referred to this in passing: 'As underlined by the chairman of Vivendi, without this content the telecommunications pipelines will sound hollow.'[16] This strategic orientation in fact encompassed two types of activities with different capital structures (and different localisations). The docks were to host the call centre activities (sales prospecting, customer service on behalf of other companies) and communications hubs (platform associating infrastructure operators and telecommunications service providers). An on-site industrial wasteland (Friche de la Belle de Mai) was set aside for the creation and support of start-ups specialised in multimedia activities which, objectively, externalised some of the production risk for some of these major corporations.

4   Public action caught between major corporations and local dynamics

The company directors to whom was given *de facto* the task of defining the economic strategy for this public scheme considered that EPAEM should 'behave like a firm.'[17] Echoing this conviction, the group of Parisian executives recalled that 'entrepreneurs are the ones who create wealth', and not technocrats. They called for the State actors to adopt a market-oriented approach: 'The priority must be to concentrate on targets that

---

[15] 'Tertiaire supérieur Euroméditerranée' Group, meeting minutes, 22 June 1998: 2.
[16] 'Tertiaire supérieur Euroméditerranée' Group, meeting minutes, 22 June 1998: 9.
[17] 'Le développement du tertiaire supérieur sur Euroméditerranée', Executive summary, October 1998.

stem from a market approach, without nonetheless underestimating the impact of the creation or transfer of public institutions and services if they constitute an attractive element for private-sector activity.'[18] There ensued an appeal to a more flexible management, which would be less restrictive in terms of regulations and limitations, and more favourable to private sector profitability, whilst being nonetheless supported by public measures. For instance, it was deemed important 'not to regulate the sales of land and buildings under too rigid an urban development scheme; the "knock-on" effect from a few strategic locations must be maximised, without missing out on unanticipated opportunities.'[19] Going against the initial orientations of the public planners, the executives insisted on the need to focus the strategy not on public development but rather on taking advantage of real estate opportunities in a pragmatic fashion: 'We have to have real estate opportunities, and thus a very firm public/private partnership upstream of the development process.'[20] At the same time public support was constantly sought for this market-oriented strategy, whether it be direct subsidy – 'It will be essential that DATAR confirm its willingness to support the call centre implantation applications, by means of the tertiary development allowance' – or development assistance measures – 'Development support policies, especially those undertaken in the framework of the State–region planning contract, should be extended to the Euroméditerranée priority sectors, and notably to the content provider industry.'

This wavering between market-oriented development and rhetoric, and a systematic search for public subsidies, could also be found in the conception that these actors had of the economic resources of local territorial entities. Even if some wording seems to refer to the construction of a new economic identity – 'Regionals must create their own wealth, derived from their own veritable assets (to be clearly identified and chosen: health, leisure, tourism, living conditions, etc.)' – in most of the discussions the resources of the territory were thought of in terms of their comparative advantages (quality of infrastructure, real estate and salary levels less costly than in the Paris region): 'There is no strategic reason for the administrative functions of large corporations to stay in the Paris region which is costly for them . . . These functions are therefore a potential target for Euroméditerranée which can present them with a less expensive metropolitan environment.'[21] Likewise, Parisian business leaders highlighted the fact that 'while the front office cannot be

---

[18] *Ibid.*: 5

[19] 'Tertiaire supérieur Euroméditerranée' Group, meeting minutes, 18 May and 27 May 1998: 2.

[20] *Ibid.*: 4.   [21] Meeting minutes 20 July: 2.

transferred out of the capital, the back office can be implanted anywhere, under certain conditions: fiscal issues (identical to free zones, local tax on businesses and corporate income tax); annual rent for "smart building" office space at less than FF1000/m²'. During a meeting a major banking executive presented as a service rendered to EPAEM the possibility of installing a telephone platform on the cost conditions given above, given the existence of ad hoc telecommunications infrastructure at the site. It was up to the public developer to set up a rapid and cost-competitive network. In the minutes of later meetings it became clear that the bank in question had already planned two platforms of this kind for the coming two years. From this point of view, the private actors appropriated the objectives of public action, in more ways than one.

From all these talks there emerged a consensus in favour of giving priority to information and telecommunications industries, to the implantation of southern European bases for the tertiary sector and lastly to Port services.[22] These choices, contrary to the Port interests, clarified the stakes by reopening certain old conflicts (between EPAEM and the Chamber of Commerce, between the Port, the city and EPAEM), and forced each of the actors to take a position. These conflicts also had the merit of revealing the limitations and ineffectiveness of the old special-interest networks. Local actors were forced to accept a mode of regulation guided by functional collaboration rather than by allegiance to notabilities. Several theatres of deliberation were operating at different levels:

• First, major corporations via the network of 'Parisian' executives defined strategies at a global level, aiming to have at their disposal lower-cost locations in southern Europe for essentially secondary activities (back office, customer service via call centres, etc.).

• Secondly, on their own small scale, actors in the local economy sought to redefine the specialisation of Marseilles as a place for business.

The economic success of Euroméditerranée would depend upon the articulation of these two levels and scales of action in the context of a crisis in the configuration of local society and the opportunities of new economic sectors.

This success is attested today by the corporate presence at the site and by the dynamic economics of the scheme. The real estate offerings have been taken up, and while unemployment remains very high in the area, the pace of job creation in the zone of the scheme is twice that of the city as a whole. This presence corresponds, in part, to the arrival of major

---

[22] The installation of the headquarters of the large French shipowner CGM–CMA, headed by a Marseilles resident of Lebanese extraction, was to be undoubtedly the only emblem, highly symbolic, of Port interests in the whole operation.

telecommunications companies that moved into the docks. For the most part, however, they are newly created companies. One-third of the businesses at the site are less than three years old and employ an average of 2.5 people; only 10 per cent of the activity generated by the scheme is due to the transfer of businesses within Marseilles. There has thus been a profound renewal, turned towards 'new economy' activities (information and communication technology, telecommunications operators, multimedia).

The site remains characterised by a fairly low-skilled population suited to jobs in construction and public works. As the companies had to hire to carry out the major infrastructure works, they were required to work with the State employment agency and with the local jobs insertion bureau. Emphasis was placed on very small enterprises (VSEs, fewer than ten employees). Actors who had previously remained aloof social workers, non-profit organisations in charge of insertion, Euroméditerranée executives and local authorities, local business leaders and banks – had to set up a vast structure for talking and working together.[23] Finally, a whole series of measures to facilitate creating business were offered, with the intervention of all the partners (local initiative platform, PACA-Entreprendre, etc.). Attention to the dynamics within the territory replaced the policy of local authorities that had focused on subsidising 'poles of excellence' in high-tech activities (Sophia-Antipolis and the microelectronics around Aix). Through local initiative platforms and public/private risk-capital arrangements, the representatives of banks, local businesses, traditional business leaders and local authorities evaluated the business plan of each project.

5   Conclusion: local capabilities and the State

According to classical analyses, 'territorialised' public action is now characterised by a process of concerted thinking between public and private actors, instead of a clearly identified leadership entity.[24] As far as the French State is concerned, 'territorialisation' of public action is viewed as a way to reduce the scope of its action and as constituting the territorial segment of a broader policy of flexibility. In the case of Marseilles, the State, as embodied by EPAEM, continued to play a central role: in the wake of the failure of an authoritarian territorial government strategy, a new mode of action has emerged, relying to a greater extent on a

---

[23] Marseilles has been involved in the European Equal Credit (Regions and Cities for Europe-Recite-II-ERDF) and Emploi-Integra (ESF) programmes.
[24] Duran (1999).

range of partners such as the external branches of administration, local authorities, business community institutions and informal investor networks. EPAEM attempted to set up instances for negotiation between partners, and in so doing became a locus for the expression of tensions. The crisis in the fabric of local society had come to a point that made it possible to elicit new arrangements between the actors. These conflicts, far from being a constraint, allowed actors to take an objective view of local resources and opened the way to new productive solutions. The prevailing model in Marseilles' economy for more than a century and a half was broken, but local capabilities were developed.

By 'local capabilities' one should understand, in our view, not only financial resources but relational and deliberative resources as well, that constitute for local actors (notably heads of businesses) a way of determining and effectively implementing economic action. These capabilities are 'territorial' in the sense that the territory constitutes both a space and a social configuration, i.e. a set of locally interdependent actors. Actors are caught up in concrete situations of deliberation and action.[25] In this context, public funding provided from outside of the territory will not have full effect unless it mobilises these capabilities. Having at one's disposal places where local capabilities are created and their use deliberated helps foster a common awareness of the opportunities available and allows a redefinition of the local economic identity.

To such an extent we could speak of governance, meaning the set of procedures for agreement between partners, notably private sector players, which gradually replaced the elaboration of an economic policy.[26] In that respect, some problems appeared, mainly induced by the substitution of spheres dominated by private sector actors for the representative elected officials.

First, lack of democracy cannot be simply resolved by the recourse to partnership with non-profit groups and associations. Relying on the initiatives of the private sector within local territorial entities assumes that a local social fabric truly exists. This is problematic in territories where the economy is in the throes of major realignment and where, limiting ourselves to the employers and without mentioning workers' interests, several heterogeneous business worlds are juxtaposed that do not necessarily form a community. Building a public space involving a wide and problem-relevant participation of all actors concerned should be the political purpose of at least local authorities, public corporations, Chambers of Commerce, employers' unions and federations and the not-for-profit

---

[25] Elias (1991).   [26] Pinson (1999: 130–139.)

sector. But its effectiveness relies upon forms of local regulation and upon some awareness of belonging to a territory, whose existence has to be assessed. As in the case of Marseilles, crises are key moments to observe these processes. More generally speaking, in contexts of diverging interests, it might be up to the local representative of the central State (the Prefect) to co-ordinate, if not to lead, the making of a local public interest and to guarantee the equity of modes of agreement.

Secondly, the construction of Europe and the subsequent need to redefine Marseilles' place in the European economic geography led its economic actors to counter the marginalisation that threatened their territory at the southern border of Europe. The preference given to territorial and regional dynamics (over central State governments), as well as to principles of governance, must not obscure the risk that territories at the margins of Europe may not find a place in the new geography. Already stricken by conversion of their industrial sites, and/or gravely handicapped by unemployment, they risk greater difficulties from the trend towards competition between territories and market-oriented public policies aiming at creating territorial 'supply'. Faced with the globalisation of trade, this focus on territories' policies can constitute an opportunity if it opens the way to a redefinition of regional productive specialisation. This nevertheless constitutes a challenge and a gamble, since reaffirming territorial specialisation could go hand in hand with a greater indifference manifested by large companies as to their territorial localisation and with the crumbling of specific territorial assets. This highlights the need for a regional development policy at European level that overcomes any risk of downward competition. Some signs in our chapter suggest that these dangers deserve some attention on the part of policy-makers and social actors.

REFERENCES

Blanc, A. and G. Cavallier, 1997. *Rapport d'audit sur l'opération d'intérêt national Euroméditerranée à Marseille*, Paris, November
Dubois, J. and M. Olive, 2001. 'Euroméditerranée: un grand projet d'aménagement à l'épreuve du débat public', in A. Donzel (ed.), *Métropolisation, gouvernance et citoyenneté dans la région marseillaise*, Paris, Maisonneuve & Larose, 421–444
Duran, P., 1999. *Penser l'action publique*, Paris, LGDJ
Elias, N., 1991 [1970]. *Qu'est-ce que la sociologie?*, Paris, Éditions de l'Aube
Morel, B., 1999. *Marseille, naissance d'une métropole*, Paris, L'Harmattan
Péraldi, M. (ed.), 2001. *Cabas et containers. Activités marchandes informelles et réseaux migrants transfrontaliers*, Paris, Maisonneuve & Larose

Pinson, G., 1999. 'Projets urbains et construction des agglomérations. Echelles fonctionnelles et politiques', *Annales de la Recherche Urbaine*, 82, 130–139

Zalio, P.-P., 1999. *Grandes familles de Marseille: enquête sur l'identité économique d'un territoire portuaire*, Paris, Belin

2001. 'Les "mondes" patronaux de l'aire métropolitaine marseillaise. Une perspective de sociologie économique', in A. Donzel (ed.), *Métropolisation, gouvernance et citoyenneté dans la région marseillaise*, Paris, Maisonneuve & Larose, 19–35

7 Employment and social dialogue at the European level: a different approach to governance of territories (EU)

Robert Villeneuve

1 Introduction

The topic of employment and social dialogue has been a familiar one for sector-based and interprofessional social partners in Europe since Val Duchesse, the Luxembourg process and the social chapter of the Treaty of Amsterdam.

Today, this topic is inseparable from the debate opened by the Commission in its White Paper on European Governance.[1] Following the European Convention's submission of a draft Treaty establishing a Constitution for Europe, and prior to the 2004 intergovernmental conference (IGC), this document calls for a thorough transformation of the functioning of European, national and regional institutions. This transformation aims at increasing the participation of stakeholders in order to bring Europe closer to its citizens, improve the conception and implementation of EU policies, contribute to global governance and refocus policies and institutions on their essential role.

This chapter will attempt to show that the link between the actors in employment and social dialogue and those involved in research corresponds to another, less visible, EU policy option. This option is nonetheless a strategic orientation for the mutual strengthening of the former's capacity to act and of the relevance of the research produced by the latter, without this relationship jeopardising the autonomy or accountability of the parties involved.

The reasoning presented here and illustrated in action undertaken in recent years is based on promoting ties that are as direct as possible between European social dialogue and social and civil dialogue at the territorial level, so as to stimulate employment in a sustainable development framework.[2] This hypothesis also posits the principle of parallels

---

[1] EC (2001f).

[2] This is the goal of the EUREXCTER project – Territorial Excellence in Europe – which was active in five Member States between January 1997 and December 2000, with a total budget of €6 million (EU and partners); see www.eurexcter.com.

between the forms of governance conceived at different levels, and in this chapter particularly between the European and the territorial level. This approach does not seek to discount the specific attributes and responsibilities of States, but rather seeks to introduce a break in the traditional linear relationship (Europe, State, territory), and envisions a 'triangulation' that identifies these three relationships by pairs. The discussion also looks at the instruments required to ensure the coherence of these relationships while respecting the attributions of each level (which vary widely from one State to another within the Union).

Reflecting the views of an actor in the social dialogue, this is also a pragmatic approach that aims to 'take a second look at subsidiarity' and contribute to an 'alliance between actors in the field' according to experimental forms of deliberation that seek a middle road between the open co-ordination method (OMC) and the approach based on 'capacities' that is envisioned in the introduction to the White Paper.

2   Governance, employment and social dialogue

Employment, even though it continues to be a prerogative of Member States, is covered by a European co-ordination procedure set out in the Luxembourg process and refined in treaties and summits over the years. This procedure, referred to by the Lisbon summit as an illustration of the OMC,[3] fixes the national and European timetable for employment policy and largely determines its content, through annual guidelines, multilateral monitoring and peer evaluation, the joint report on employment and the Commission's recommendations to Member States.

While the focus of the present research encompasses the unwanted side-effects and the limitations of this strategy, the procedural dimension has proven to be a strong form of co-ordination that ensures the best possible convergence of national employment policies, while respecting the diversity of national situations and without overriding government responsibilities.

The Commission and the European Committee for Social Dialogue made up of interprofessional partners (Union des Industries de la Communauté Europeénne (UNICE), European Trade Union Conference (ETUC) and European Centre of Enterprises with Public Participation and of Enterprises of General Economic Interest (CEEP)) have taken

---

[3] 'The open method of co-ordination is used on a case by case basis. It is a way of encouraging co-operation and exchange of best practices and agreeing common targets and guidelines for Member States, sometimes backed up by national action plans as in the case of employment and social exclusion. It relies on regular monitoring of progress to meet those targets, allowing Member States to compare their efforts and learn from the experience of others' (EC 2001f: 21).

pains to associate national and European social partners, starting with the first generation of guidelines issued in late 1997 and the preparation of the resulting National Action Plans for employment in 1998. This exercise was the first to articulate a tripartite social dialogue at the national and European level.

2.1 Employment Guidelines, 2001: an important step towards territorialisation of employment policy

Since 1998 the formulation of employment guidelines has given rise to in-depth debate at the European and national level. The organisation based on four fundamental pillars— employability, entrepreneurship, adaptability, equal opportunity— has been and continues to be a strong structuring outline that induces policies made of several heterogenous elements, with 'organ-pipe' effects and segmentation that undermine an integrated approach and encourage partners to focus only on the topics that interest them to the detriment of other subjects.

It quickly became clear that some guidelines were general and transversal in nature, and could not bear fruit unless they were systematically mentioned in the policies segmented within each pillar. The transversal nature – or 'mainstreaming' in Brussels parlance – of the fourth pillar regarding equal opportunity was the first to be recognised, but the Commission did not want to go any further, for fear of blurring its message.

CEEP argued for the importance of a territorial employment policy from the outset in 1998, in which integration of the four pillars would be the rule and the autonomy of local partners accepted for this typically subsidiary exercise. A proposal was made to introduce a fifth pillar, consisting of a single guideline and a single sentence, specifying that:

In the light of the strong development of local public/private partnerships, the Member States will encourage initiatives that implement the four pillars of the guidelines under territorial agreements focusing on employment and sustainable development.

The recurring annual debate over this position, the lessons drawn from the EUREXCTER project and no doubt a maturation of this issue in Europe have led to the emergence of territorial governance as the prime domain for action to support employment in a framework of sustainable development. The Commission communication entitled 'Acting Locally for Employment: Giving a Local Dimension to European Employment Strategy' constitutes an unambiguous expression of a new-found awareness:[4]

---

[4] EC (2000a).

There is an increasingly keen awareness of the possibilities of local employment . . . To date European employment strategy has relied essentially on activities carried out at the national level, and to a lesser extent regionally.

The present communication aims to

- recapitulate the changes that have led Member States and the European Union to increasingly turn to the local level to develop employment;
- examine ways in which different local actors . . . can contribute to job creation or the preservation of employment at the local level.[5]

Without significantly modifying the overall structure of the guidelines, the Commission thus introduced a debate, according to the principles of open co-ordination, that continued throughout 2000 and was summed up in a conference held in Strasbourg on 30 November – 1 December, during the French Presidency.

2.2   *A constructive critical approach to territorialisation of employment policies*

While stressing the importance and relevance of the initiative, in its opinion on the Commission's communication, CEEP highlights five weaknesses in the text, with reference to a bolder approach to territorial governance and to the role of research:

(1) 'An institutional viewpoint' on 'public EU policy' that is not directly transposable to the local level.

(2) A questionable distinction between development of employment and sustainable development of the territory.

(3) Poor knowledge of the role of services in the general economic interest.

(4) Exogenous development, as a useful phase, not an endpoint.

(5) The role of research and its contribution to action.[6]

Let us look at each of these points, to reveal the difference in conception and implicit model of governance developed by the Commission in its communication, and to outline an alternate vision. As a social partner, I would like to submit this alternative to the research community, urging researchers to draw up an alternate theoretical framework that will enhance its analytical capabilities.

The limitations of method transposition   The communication mentions in several places the idea of applying the Luxembourg method locally. Drawing analogies between EU policies at the national and local levels is undeniably useful, as long as the effects of the change of scale and

---

[5] EC (2000a, Summary: 4).   [6] CEEP. 2000/SOC. 109: 22/08/2000: 8.

of the nature of the problems are analysed. Despite greater implication of social partners, EU policies are above all public policies with indirect and complex effects; furthermore businesses, like local trade union actors and local territorial authorities, are largely unaware of and ill-informed about these effects.

At the local level employment is primarily due to business activity linked to the economic situation and to local or sector-based management of human resources. Asking territorial public authorities to draw up *local employment plans* for which they would assume responsibility would lead to a temptation to establish local public policies, with the risk of restricting employment to public and para-public sectors, the social economy and services, while businesses would continue to control within their own sphere the jobs that are directly productive in the competitive and market sectors. There would be no chance of resolving the powerful equations encountered in fighting unemployment – competitiveness and employment, flexibility and security, employment and lifelong training, active security and professional agendas.

Furthermore, local transposition of the European method underpins the method of associated indicators. Without actually saying so, employability, for instance, is transferred from the European to the local level, precluding deliberation on this topic among the actors at this level. The risk is that local governance could turn out to be a pale version of European governance.

Boosting employment and sustainable territorial development   The communication focuses on employment, and not on sustainable development. The introduction draws attention to this distinction, referring to the Commission's numerous proposals pertaining to development (initiatives for local development and employment) and rejecting the idea of a new local development programme.

The risk involved here is to make job creation an end in itself, and to place a priority on public action, seeking to persuade actors in civil society that the virtues of such an approach are in their own interest. While this reasoning is more understandable at the EU and national level, at the territorial level it becomes schematic and questionable.

In our view, while EU and national employment policies can and must stand alone, locally they must be articulated directly and inseparably with respect to a policy for sustainable territorial development. This message, far from undermining the goals of territorial co-ordination of employment policy, will on the contrary ensure their credibility, by proclaiming social cohesion as their ultimate objective, and their necessary reliance on a sustainable development policy.

The alliance between actors regarding territories is meaningful for each partner within a global project: employment is a compartmentalised approach at the territorial level; deliberation assumes that the actors share the same objectives; employment is not a shared objective (an adjustment variable for firms, not an end in itself), whereas sustainable development is.

The role of services in the general economic interest ignored   This 'omission' leaves out an actor (perhaps the only actor) that in all contexts must take on business objectives (competitiveness, development) and assume the responsibilities of a public agent (employment and social cohesion). This actor must both comply with the rules of the marketplace and honour the obligations of public service. General interest services thus find themselves in a framework that imposes constraints which the notion of 'corporate social responsibility' discussed in a 2001 Green Paper is very careful not to impose on firms.[7]

In addition the social cohesion and competitiveness of territories are highly dependent on the nature and quality of the services in the general interest that the territories can offer to businesses.

Fortunately this issue has moved higher on the EU agenda, and in Article III-3 of the draft Treaty the Convention proposes that services of general economic interest should operate under principles 'defined by European law'. In this regard, in its ruling concerning *Altmark Trans GmbH*[8] the Court of Justice refused to consider subsidies granted to a firm providing public city transport as 'State aid', stating that 'such subsidies are to be considered as compensation in exchange for services provided by the recipient companies in execution of public service obligations'.

'Nesting territories' and the limitations of an endogenous vision of territorial development   For quite some time now, in Europe as in the USA, public and private local actors have taken initiatives targeting employment and local economic development. At first the emphasis was on exogenous development. Endogenous development, highlighting the intrinsic potential of territories, followed with more success when the local circumstances were favourable. But this also entailed an increase in interregional disparity that was strongly underlined in the second Commission report

---

[7] EC (2001e).

[8] Ruling dated 24 July 2003: 'Règlement (CEE) n°. 1191/69 – Exploitation de services réguliers de transports urbains, suburbains et régionaux – Subventions publiques – Notion d'aide d'État – Compensation représentant la contrepartie d'obligations de service public.'

on social cohesion,[9] and that will not be reduced by enlargement, quite the contrary.[10] Better results were obtained when all actors were able to rally around a common project. But it is easier to promote the idea of a 'project territory' than bring it into existence.

The communication rightly grants SME–SMIs a key role in job creation; it highlights 'local production systems' (industrial districts in Italy, clusters in the USA) as characteristic of the emergence of the local sphere, but it makes no mention of the role played by large multinational and global corporations and the precarious wealth they bring to territories. The Green Paper (EC 2001e) on corporate social responsibility does indeed refer to industrial restructuring 'in a socially responsible perspective', a polite way of saying that pain must be inflicted with as light a touch as possible.[11] In fact, when a firm is a global company with a world-wide strategy, neither the State nor the territory is a partner of equivalent rank. In the unequal contest of negotiation between territory and global business, the outcome is predictable, barring special circumstances. It is clear, however, that employment and its stability in the territory are derived from both the endogenous and exogenous components of development.

The vision of the employment policy system proffered by the communication is based on a construction of nesting levels of regulation: Europe, Member States, regions and territories. While transnational co-operation is mentioned, it hardly goes beyond the exchange of best practices between territories or cross-border exchange between neighbouring territories. Why not imagine forms of co-operation on employment between States that would be comparable to the 'reinforced co-operation' under discussion in the context of the construction of Europe, and why not give interregional co-operation a shared economic dimension, and not just objectives limited to comparing practices?[12]

Research and the actors for development and employment   The results of research and experiments in research–action are outlined in an interesting appendix to the Commission's communication devoted to the factors for the success of a local employment development policy. Even though these results are useful, they have been adopted with difficulty by

---

[9] EC (2001a: 11), 'The decisions made in 1988 and 1992 for reinforcement of EU support for regions experiencing structural difficulties were based on the observation that wider economic integration would not necessarily reduce regional disparities and could, initially at least, aggravate them'.

[10] See Jacky Fayolle and Anne Lécuyer, chapter 9 in this volume: 'Given the low level of labour mobility in Europe, territorial imbalance is therefore likely to continue into the future, especially when membership is widened to include the CEECs':   .

[11] EC (2001c), § 36: 11.

[12] See Martin Heidenreich's chapter 4 in this volume.

development actors, and this has perpetuated a dangerous gap between research and action that is inadequately informed of research results.

Actors in development and employment should maintain direct relationships with researchers, fostering a joint conception of research topics and themes and jointly appropriating implementation of these results, without altering the role and responsibilities of each party. My current involvement as a social partner (with the participation of UNICE and ETUC, and support from the Commission) in the research that has led to the present chapter, spurs me on, in the spirit of the 'knowledge society' called for in Lisbon, particularly in areas such as employment development in territories.[13]

2.3   National Action Plans for employment: the case of France

Each member State draws up a National Action Plan (NAP) document under a national consultation process that takes into account specific forms of social dialogue and relationships between public authorities and social partners. While the social partners were only symbolically associated with this process at the start, they had reached a good level of involvement in the 2001. The latter constitute a point of equilibrium in the implementation of the Luxembourg process, as reported in the evaluation in early 2002.

The case of France, with which the author is more familiar for having been directly involved, shows how social dialogue intervened and modified the conception of employment policy at the national level, in relation to the general European framework.

At the end of 1998 the Ministry for Employment and Solidarity set up a Social Dialogue Committee (CDSEI), to address European and international issues, composed of members representing trade union confederations, public and private sector employers, artisans, farmers, professions and farmers' mutual insurance companies and health insurance organisations.

Initially the preparation of the NAP under the Luxembourg process was conceived as an exercise involving the public authorities, in which consultation of social partners, albeit undertaken methodically, was nonetheless secondary for an outcome that was in the end arbitrated by the public authorities alone, and evaluated by their peers and the Commission itself. This stance was the result not only of the attitude adopted by the administration in charge of the process, but was and continues to be

---

[13] 'Social Dialogue, Employment and Territories', July 2000, an international research project involving the three European social partners.

shared by certain employers and trade unions that are unwilling to engage their independence as social partners in situations that escape their final control.

Several significant trends emerged during the 2001 NAP exercise. Following a committee meeting, a letter signed by the Minister and addressed to the committee members marked a strong methodological break, by accepting that the NAP was no longer produced under the responsibility of the public authorities alone, since it now included specific contributions that were the sole responsibility of the social partners, and thematic contributions that were the outcome of debate between public authorities and social partners within the committee. The results of the national collective bargaining process pertaining to employment policy supported by the social partners could thus be integrated into the NAP. The plan was no longer an administrative 'object' but a document representing the different and complementary points of view and the results of tripartite discussion on subjects chosen out of a common accord.

Prior to the final arbitration, the NAP was discussed in talks between members of CDSEI and the Commission in Brussels. During this initial evaluation the viewpoints of the public authorities and the social partners were debated with the Commission, quite transparently, establishing an example of 'triangulation' that is analogous to the European – national – territorial relationship evoked in the introduction to this chapter.

Lastly, the committee members all wanted the entire 2001 NAP elaboration process to be subject to real-time observation by a researcher invited to attend all the national and international technical and policy meetings.[14] The research findings nurtured the implementation of the 2002 NAP process.

3   In summary . . .

The Luxembourg process and its developments have considerably modified, at all levels (European, national and territorial) the approach to the three dimensions covered in section 2:
- governance
- employment
- social dialogue.

In section 3 we shall briefly illustrate some ways to move forward on these issues that have been tested in EU-funded projects investigating the 'triangulation' of the three levels of intervention in the area of employment and sustainable development: Europe, Member States and territories.

[14] See chapter 8 in this volume.

3.1   *Governance, sustainable development and cross-border co-operation*

The White Paper on governance (EC 2001f), which advances the significance of the relationship with networks and proposes target-based tripartite agreements between regions, States and the Commission, has opened up interesting directions for a 'triangulation' approach. EUREXCTER, a not-for-profit operator with experience in transnational and inter-regional co-operation between Member States, bolstered by its close relationship with European and national social partners, is a force acting to make proposals, alone or with other institutions, to the Commission, Member States and territorial partners.

Two projects co-funded by the Commission aim at responding to the issues studied here, and at bringing to bear expertise and applied research in social sciences, in keeping with the goals framed in the White Paper pertaining to scientific analysis.

3.2   *EUROCAP: social dialogue, employment and territories,* en route *for a European policy of capabilities*

The EUROCAP project has been proposed to the Commission under the technological research and development programme and refers to the key action 'Development of basic socio-economic knowledge'. The project is sponsored by IDHE (Institutions et Dynamiques Historiques de l'Economie), a unit of the Ecole Normale Supérieure in Cachan which is a principal member of CEEP, grouping ten scientific institutions from five Member States and a European social partner. The project grew out of a series of seminars co-conducted by researchers and social partners which also led to the writing of this chapter.

The ultimate goal of the project is to promote a European policy of 'capabilities' (following the theory of Amartya Sen) in keeping with EU legislation and in the framework of a knowledge-based society. This approach is designed to stimulate social dialogue at all levels, particularly in territories, in a labour market turned towards 'active security'. The social partners are associated with the structuring of the research programme, as they help define relevant issues and choose sites for empirical research. This relationship driven by CEEP respects the roles of each party.

The project seeks to respond to three concerns of European citizens:
- Can employment, economic reform and social stability in a knowledge-based society be achieved in the framework of EU policies, notably at the territorial level?

Table 7.1. *The COPARSOC project: related actions*

Society and on-going change
Law and Contact
Education and Enterprise: what kind of employability?
Economic Sector and Enterprise: what kind of Collective Agreement?
Economic Sector and Local Area: what kind of Employment Policy?
Social cohesion and Mobility
Working life, Family life and Private life: what kind of Conciliation and
  with whom?

What is a good practice and which method for the project
Exchanges on Practices: no benchmarking neither Useless Chat
Autonomous and international debate on Employment friendly Practices
Compulsory Compliment for the balance between Law and Contract
Mobilisation to support the Project Execution

- How can a movement combining economic efficiency and social equity
  be set up in the sectors of economic activity in Europe?
- How can citizens be integrated in a Europe that embraces knowledge
  and provides them with employment in an environment of active security throughout their lives?

3.3 The contribution made by national social partners to the Luxembourg process: COPARSOC

Following the experiment with consultation concerning the 2001
National Action Plan for Employment (NAPE) the social partners that
take part in the CDSEI in France decided to propose an experiment with
a European impetus to the Commission and to the French Ministry for
Employment and Solidarity. The results are published in five languages
on the association's website http://www.eurexcter.com.

This project is based on two related actions:

(1) Dissemination of the Compendium of best practices for employment
    drawn up by the partners in the European interprofessional social
    dialogue.
(2) An evaluation of the employment process and of national employ-
    ment action plans under the auspices of an experimental network of
    associated European social partners.

This project, which brought together the social partners of all the Member States enabled them to arrive at a common assessment of dynamic
balances that are factors in transformation – *Society and On-Going Change*;

and to validate a method for deliberation – *What is a Good Practice and Which Method for the Project,* (See table 7.1).

4   The overall process

Section 2 of this chapter aimed to demonstrate the progress accomplished at the EU level on issues of governance, employment and social dialogue, drawing attention to the fact that sustainable development and cross-border and inter-territorial co-operation had not been sufficiently taken into account.

Section 3 illustrated the ways in which European and national social partners were engaged in projects designed to:

- Bring researchers and social partners together in order to work towards establishing a theory of the economy at intermediate levels (territories) that will contribute to European employment policies.
- Create a shared culture and knowledge of the system of national employment policies as part of the Luxembourg process.
- Develop synergistic interterritorial actions among partners with a strong European policy impetus, to test the contribution of territorial networks to employment policy and the renewal of governance.

This process is built upon the twin pillars of European social dialogue and action in the field. It aims to be a demonstration of expertise that the Commission can draw upon, as set out in the White Paper on governance. Several chapters in this volume illustrate this synergy. One of these is the 'capacity-based approach as a principle of European reform' that Robert Salais elaborates in chapter 18, emphasising work as a value, and the operational character of the capacities-based approach and its integration into the European process in order to endow the OMC with the ethics of objectivity, notably in the relationship between indicators and policy.

Salais concludes by proposing that a deliberation procedure

on the basis of proposals emerging from research work, a contradictory and far-reaching debate, be organised among social, political and civil actors. The scope of the debate would be the cognitive frameworks for such a basis, and the procedures to achieve it.

Let us hope that this proposal is adopted.

Part II

Assessing EU procedures and
European initiatives

The purpose of part II is to critically assess the development and outcomes of key European procedures and initiatives in employment and social affairs: the European Employment Strategy (EES), the European structural funds, European Social Dialogue and the Open Method of Co-ordination (OMC). The benchmark is their capacity to reform themselves, first by overcoming the emerging difficulties they often contributed to create, second by dealing with new objectives in relation with the future of Social Europe. From a 'cooperative growth strategy', as advocated in the 1994 Delors White Paper, EES has degenerated into employability and activation policies at the expense of a capability approach (Gilles Raveaud, chapter 8). The European structural funds, although promoting a catching up between countries, have failed to correct imbalances at regional level. This calls for more ambitious mechanisms for redistribution, redesigned to deal with inequality of regional capabilities (Jacky Fayolle and Anne Lécuyer, chapter 9). Emmanuel Julien and Jean Lapeyre – social actors, respectively, on the employer (UIECE) and on the union side (ETUC) – argue in chapters 10 and 11 for a greater degree of autonomy and innovation in the agenda and processes of European social dialogue which, they say, should be less constrained by the Commission's strategy. Seen in the light of the principle of subsidiarity, the OMC, however, develops other political lines. Its impact on European governance, especially on European social dialogue, remains unclear, depending on the scenarios that actors come to adopt in the future (Philippe Pochet, chapter 12).

8 The European Employment Strategy: from ends to means? (EU)

Gilles Raveaud

JO8 J68

> Increasing employment cannot be but at the very top of the list of things to do. It is amazing that so much unemployment is so easily tolerated in contemporary Europe. (Sen 1997: 168)

> The purpose of economic activity is to increase the well-being of individuals . . . This proposition might seem anodyne . . . Yet, the policies that are pursued often turn out to be antithetical to it. (Stiglitz 2002: 9)

1 Introduction

The greatest achievement of the European Union so far is the creation of the Euro. But Europe is often pictured as a one-eyed man, preoccupied only by economic issues – and forgetful of the social aspects of life. The purpose of the European Employment Strategy (EES) was to counter this criticism by showing that the European Union could actively fight unemployment. Yet, far from counterbalancing the restrictions imposed on growth by stage three of the European Monetary Union (EMU), the EES limits its action to this predefined framework. How is this possible? History can tell us a lot. In fact, the conditions that prevailed when the EES was first elaborated explain why this policy is still largely dominated by the fight against a now disappeared ghost (inflation), when its true enemies (poverty and unemployment) are still alive and kicking. We will successively look at the origins of the EES (section 2), at how it works and how to evaluate it (section 3) and finally, at the future for Europe it could open (section 4).

2 The origins of the EES

2.1 The limited promises of the 1993 White Paper

Shaping the market in a liberal view? Part A of the 1993 White Paper, called *The Challenges and Ways Forward into the 21st Century*

A first version of this chapter was presented during a seminar at the IRES (Paris). The discussion with the participants, in particular Florence Lefresne, helped me correct many mistakes. Robert Salais has read and criticised the successive versions. Thanks to them all.

(EC 1993a), acknowledged the 'responsibility of governments and of the Community to create as favourable an environment as possible for company competitiveness'. The White Paper proposed three main strands of action:
- Completing and simplifying the Community's legal rules
- Making it easier to set up and run small- and medium-sized businesses
- The 'accelerated establishment of Trans-European infrastructure networks'.

But the main aim of the White Paper was to make the labour market work better. The first line of argument followed the conservative criticisms of the welfare state of the 1980s, which attributed the high level of unemployment in Europe to 'Eurosclerosis'. It recalled that 'the social welfare system [was] being re-examined in many Member States to improve efficiency and reduce costs through greater responsibility and selectiveness' which meant, in particular, the reduction of unemployment benefits.[1] The White Paper thus pleaded for a less 'passive' and more 'active' welfare state, that is one that does not hinder the flexibility of the labour market, but on the contrary promotes it. Legal rules were to be adapted, as 'the inflexibility of the labour market [was] responsible for large parts of Europe's structural unemployment.' This was supposed to be to the benefit of the worse off, as undeclared workers would turn to declared work (Northern countries), and precarious workers would get more stable positions, if 'the conditions under which workers on unlimited contracts may be laid off' were 'made more flexible' (Southern countries). Lastly, the 'heavy burden of statutory charges' (40 per cent of GDP in the Union in 1991, compared to 34 per cent in the USA[2]) was to be reduced, as its rise was seen as 'a cause of the economic slowdown and especially of the increase in unemployment'.

Solidarity within the workforce   In its chapter 8, *Turning Growth into Jobs, the* White Paper openly criticised past wage arrangements:

Existing collective bargaining . . . and labour cost arrangements have the effect of causing gains from economic growth to be absorbed mainly by those already in

---

[1] As if in an afterthought, the authors noted that 'unemployment benefits are still essential . . .' and that 'they can only be reduced so far before the poverty line is reached'.

[2] Even if the relevance of the comparison of gross figures is highly questionable, as Adema (2001) shows. This has been recently acknowledged by the Commission, for whom 'the European social model . . . is not distinguished from social systems in other countries by its levels of expenditure, but by its methods of funding. The main difference . . . between Europe and the US is that funding is public in Europe, and much more private in the US'. As a result, 'the benefits appear to be much more evenly spread in Europe than they are in the US' (EC 2001a: 5).

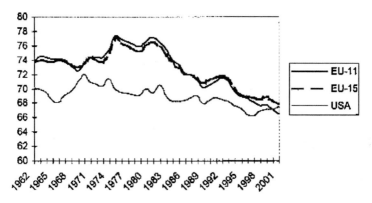

Figure 8.1. Evolution of the wage share in GDP, 1962–2001

employment, rather than creating more jobs. To change this would mean seeking political and Social Partners' agreement on keeping hourly wage increases below the growth of productivity.

But this change is no easy task. A 'large consensus on the necessary course of action to be followed [needs] to be achieved' because it is not simply a matter of wages, but of solidarity:

The new model of European society calls for less passive and more active solidarity. Solidarity first of all between those who have jobs and those who do not. This key concept has not figured at all in the collective discussions and negotiations of the last ten years. That is why we are proposing a sort of European social pact, the principle of which is quite simple . . . ; new gains in productivity would essentially be applied to forward-looking investments and to the creation of jobs.

Why this insistence in the White Paper on wage moderation? Factual elements alone cannot give an answer. Both the discourses and practices of the European social actors were in line with this approach for many years. In November 1986, they had written, in their *Joint Opinion on the Co-operative Growth Strategy for More Employment*, that in all countries, 'moderate growth of real per capita wage costs below productivity gains should be maintained for some time' (UNICE, CEEP, ETUC 1986) – i.e. the part of wages in GDP should diminish. But not only did they call for wage moderation, they did it. In fact, as figure 8.1 shows, in 1993, the *total* cost of labour in the Union represented only 71.3 per cent of GDP, far below its 1975 peak (77 per cent of GDP), but also below its general level in the pre-inflation 1960s (around 74 per cent).

Finally, the White Paper proposed deploying effective means to fight unemployment. This implied, first, an important increase in spending by public employment services, at 0.5 per cent of GNP. Financial targets were thus proposed from the very beginning, in a procedure similar to that which prevailed for monetary union, but this led to little progress.[3] Second, the White Paper also proposed to 'establish a Community-wide guarantee that no young person can be unemployed under the age of 18'. Last but not least, the White Paper suggested that unemployed people 'should be involved' in talks re-defining their rights and duties.

The White Paper also indicated that 'Pressure to increase labour market flexibility without countervailing action has . . . often reduced [rather] than increased the incentives for firms and individuals to invest in much needed training and retraining . . .' Here, the conservative criticism of the welfare state can be seen as going against 'long-run competitiveness'. In fact, long-term efficiency requires 'investing in people', not diminishing social spending, as the European Social Agenda recognises (EC 2000b).

2.2   Towards the Luxembourg process

The White Paper was a balanced approach, which offered a convincing 'New Deal' to Europeans. But it was balanced only insofar as the liberal reforms of the labour market were balanced by a guarantee of a rise of public and private investment. But, following the 1993 European recession, the promised investment did not take place. The monetarist framework of the construction of EMU also imposed a continuous restriction on wages growth, a priority that was to be followed, along with a continuous stress on the reform of the labour market.

The Essen summit (9–10 December 1994)   The Essen summit identified five priorities:
• To improve workers' employment opportunities by promoting investment in vocational training
• To make growth more employment-intensive
• To reduce non-wage labour costs
• To develop a more effective labour market policy
• To strengthen measures in favour of groups particularly affected by unemployment.

---

[3] The total spending on unemployment and active labour market policy remained roughly the same between 1989 and 2000 in the EU 15, at around 2.5 per cent of GDP, despite a *higher* unemployment rate (8.2 per cent in 2000, 7.7 per cent in 1990). The share of active spending has not progressed: at 40 per cent of total spending, it is no more than 1 per cent of GDP (OECD 2001).

The only element of the 1993 White Paper to survive in its original form was the reduction of labour costs. The project of European networks was abandoned. The social dialogue policy remained on the agenda, as the general responsibility of the social partners was renewed, but with a view to perpetuating moderate wage growth. As far as the vocabulary is concerned, two changes are worth noticing. First, the question was no longer one of raising the number of jobs, but of promoting 'employment opportunities'. Second, the *employment* policy was dubbed an *active labour market* policy. The question was no longer one of creating jobs more or less directly, but of raising individual opportunities through a well-functioning labour market. By preventing bottlenecks, skills mismatches, the removal of disincentives to work and labour contracts rigidities, etc. structural reforms of the labour market were to make GDP growth more employment-intensive, but GDP growth was no longer a target in itself.

The Essen process also laid down the procedure which was to be followed later, namely the annual writing by Member States of 'action plans on employment' and their review by the Commission.

The Dublin Declaration on Employment (13–14 December 1996)
As Tina Weber (1997) recalls, the idea of a Confidence Pact on Employment was first raised by President Santer on 31 January 1996 in a speech to the European Parliament. He pleaded for a Trans-European network and strengthened co-ordination between Member States, in order to achieve a 'multiplier effect in employment'. In October 1996, the economic and finance ministers of the EU refused supplementary funding for the networks.

The European social partners, in their *Action for Employment in Europe. A Confidence Pact* (ETUC, UNICE, CEEP 1996), still persisted in supporting the 'necessary reforms in the area of flexibility and the functioning of the labour market'. They were aware that the current policies of high exchange rates and high real interest rates, following German reunification, were not favourable to employment. They stressed 'the importance of avoiding EMU becoming associated in the public mind with unemployment'. In a context of monetary turbulence and lack of co-ordination between national monetary and budgetary policies, they thought that 'the achievement of the EMU, by definition, [would] eradicate the obstacle to growth stemming from intra-EU currency turbulence . . . Thus, the realisation of EMU [would] in fact help to achieve the employment objectives of the White Paper' – that is, halve unemployment rates between 1993 and 2000. A few weeks later, the *Dublin Declaration on Employment*, annexed to the Dublin European Council conclusions, repeated the confidence of the national leaders in the structural reforms of *all* markets to combat unemployment:

To secure the maximum benefit in employment terms from the economic growth . . . the European Council endorses . . . the necessity to pursue . . . policies of structural reforms aimed at redressing deficiencies in Europe's labour markets and those in the Single market for goods and services.

This was congruent with the simultaneous adoption of the principle and main elements of the Stability and Growth Pact (SGP), which wished to 'avoid excessive deficits', and which would be made official a few months later.

The Stability and Growth Pact (Amsterdam Summit, 16–17 June 1997)   Many, notably the recently elected socialist French Prime Minister Lionel Jospin, feared that the SGP would not promote enough growth. So, in Amsterdam, in order to 'keep employment firmly at the top of the political agenda of the Union', a separate *Resolution on Growth and Employment* was adopted on top of the *Resolution on the Stability and Growth Pact*. They support each other: 'sound macro-economic and budget policies go hand in hand with strong and sustainable growth in output and employment.'

In practice, if they go hand in hand, one hand leads the way, as the *Resolution on Growth and Employment* makes clear: 'The Council is . . . called upon to take the multi-annual employment programmes . . . into account when formulating the broad guidelines, in order to strengthen their employment focus.' For instance, as 'taxes and social protection systems should be made more employment friendly', they will be incorporated in the Broad Economic Policy Guidelines, adopted by the ECOFIN Council, which will thus be allowed to make recommendations on wages, social security contributions, unemployment benefits, etc. That is, employment and social policies do not conflict with, nor even balance, the SGP. They widen its scope, by extending the 'market making' logic of the European Union (Streeck 1995) to another 'market': the labour market. As the *Resolution on Growth and Employment* indicates:

more attention will be given to improving European competitiveness as a prerequisite for growth and employment, so as to, among other objectives, bring more jobs within the reach of the citizens of Europe. In this context, *special attention should be given to labour and product market efficiency* . . . Full attention should also be given to training and education systems including life-long learning, work incentives in the tax and benefit systems and reducing non-wage labour costs, *in order to increase employability*. (Emphasis added)

Far from being 'decommodified' (Esping-Andersen 1990), labour is to be apprehended as a commodity, exchanged on a market (Deakin 1996). This is why *structural* changes are necessary: they are 'structural' in the precise sense that they aim at the creation of a new *structure* of individual interaction – an ideal labour marketplace. For instance, 'employability' makes its first appearance in an official document.

However, Member States refused to set any binding target (Trubek and Mosher 2003). In other words, they accepted the need to be accountable for their levels of public deficit, debt and inflation (as planned by the SGP), but not for their level of unemployment, nor even for the means devoted to active labour market policies – i.e. means effectively enhancing the employability of individuals.[4] If Ireland was publicly blamed for its excessive inflation in February 2001, the Council had no means to blame, say, France and Germany, for their excessive levels of unemployment.[5] Shamelessly, the conclusive sentence of the *Resolution* designated some responsible actors: 'The European Council asks social partners to fully face their responsibilities within their respective sphere of activity.'

3   The EES at work: a soft policy in a straight jacket

3.1   *The progressive building of a collective cognitive framework*

The Amsterdam Treaty (2 October 1997)   The Amsterdam Treaty defined the content and procedure of the EES (or 'Luxembourg process', as it was adopted at the extraordinary Luxembourg summit of November 1997). It introduced the new Title VIII Employment, which made the promotion of employment 'a matter of common concern' between Member States (Article 126). The purpose of the EES was not to harmonise national employment policies, nor to make them converge. The range of action available to the Community was limited to '*encouraging co-operation* between Member States by supporting and, if necessary, complementing their action. In doing so, the competencies of the Member States shall be respected' (Article 127, emphasis added).

---

[4] In a similar vein, Bosco (1998) mentions "the 1993 Belgian Presidency proposition [of] a monitoring mechanism which appeared far too binding as explicit reference was made to the 'European social snake'". It was not adopted.

[5] In June 2000, the Council recommended that Ireland raise its budgetary *surplus* for 2001 (4.7 per cent of GDP in 2000), in order to diminish inflation (which finally reached 5.6 per cent in 2000). It was ignored by the Irish government. In the meantime, the rate of unemployment in Ireland was 4.2 per cent, compared to 9.5 per cent in France and 7.9 per cent in Germany (EC 2001c). In these two countries, the rate of inflation was, respectively, 1.7 per cent and 2.4 per cent.

Finally, in its Article 128, the Title presented the procedure that was to be followed yearly:
– drawing up of guidelines by the Council, acting by a qualified majority
– annual National Action Plans (NAPs) by the Member States on the measures taken in the light of the guidelines for employment
– potential recommendations (adopted since 2000 by the Council by a qualified majority, on a proposal of the Commission) from the Council to Member States following the examination of the NAPs.
These recommendations are not binding. All Members States have to do, each year, is to produce a NAP indicating what they will do in order to follow the guidelines and answer the recommendations made to them.

The definition of the 'open method of co-ordination' (Lisbon, 23–24 March 2000)   This method was later labelled the 'open method of co-ordination' (OMC) at the Lisbon summit. It consists in a periodic monitoring of the results achieved by each country, notably through the use of quantitative targets (rates of employment, etc.) and the exchange of qualitative 'best practice' (schemes for the inclusion of youth, systems of job rotation; etc.). Following the Lisbon conclusions, this method is now used in a variety of fields, such as pensions, education and social inclusion. Maria João Rodrigues, a social scientist, explains the philosophy of the method she invented:

The open method of co-ordination is a concrete way of developing modern governance using the principle of subsidiarity. This method can foster convergence in [the] common interest and in some agreed common priorities while respecting national and regional diversities. It is an inclusive method for deepening European construction. (Rodrigues 2001)
    The purpose of the open method of co-ordination is not to define a general ranking of Member States in each policy, but rather to organise a *learning process* at the European level in order to stimulate exchanges and the emulation of best practices as well as to help Member States improve their own national policies. (Rodrigues 2003: 23)

This is the sunny side of the story. But there is also a darker one, that Maria Rodrigues does not hide. If the OMC was invented, it is mainly because the European Union could not do otherwise:

This method was created to overcome a strong political difficulty identified in the preparation of the special European Council of Luxembourg on employment in 1997, because it was impossible to adopt a common target for unemployment reduction, as a counterpart of the common targets for inflation, deficit and debt reduction. But, under the political pressure of the summit, it became possible to adopt common qualitative guidelines instead.(Rodrigues 2001)

Since then, the OMC has led to a proliferation of analysis and comments. For Janine Goetschy, it is 'probably the most subtle answer for a new balance between convergence and respect for national diversity' (Goetschy 2003: 93). She enumerates its potential qualities:

• Enlargement of the EU agenda to employment matters
• Comprehensive approach to employment and unemployment problems
• 'Flexible integration' of the Member States in the process
• Adoption of a medium-term perspective
• Development of an evaluation culture that may 'serve as a catalyst for the efficiency of national employment policies' (p. 92).

Still, Goetschy recognises that the use of non-compulsory EU guidelines may not only prove ineffective, but even dangerous, as it may undermine the classical Community method which rests on 'hard' law and not 'soft' co-ordination. Indeed, it is important not to fall into the 'governance myth', in which learning effects between Member States will by themselves lead to co-ordinated changes in national employment policies (De La Porte and Pochet 2003: 32). For instance, empirical studies show that the EES is unknown to actors involved in employment policy at a local level (Jacobsson and Schmid 2003).

But one clear result seems to be a new 'conventional wisdom' (De La Porte and Pochet 2003: 14) on the benefits of active labour market policy.

3.2   The convergence towards activation

Employability: an initial patchwork of national approaches   From the start until the reform of 2003, employment guidelines were organised under the four following 'pillars':

• Improving employability
• Developing entrepreneurship
• Encouraging adaptability of businesses and their employees
• Strengthening equal opportunities policies for women and men.

The relative importance of these pillars in the NAPs varies greatly. Here, we will concentrate on the employability pillar, quantitatively the most important (Lefresne 1999), and the best entry into the *logic* of the EES. In 2002, the employability guidelines were as follows:

• Activation of the unemployed (offering a 'New start' for every young and long-term unemployed person and reaching a global rate of activation of 20 per cent)
• Reform of benefit and tax systems, in order to reduce 'poverty traps' and give incentives to older workers to remain in work
• Reform of educational and training systems, through social dialogue
• Fight against discrimination and social exclusion.

These guidelines are varied, as they reflect the national approaches to employability used by the different states in 1997. In order to make sense of them, it is possible to use the typology proposed by Esping-Andersen (1990). For him, three ideal-typical configurations of welfare state systems can be identified:

- The *'liberal regime'* is in a position of subordination to the market, whose development is not to be hindered by excessive rules and social welfare
- The *'conservative-corporatist'* regime embeds the market in legal and collectively agreed rules that protect workers and unemployed people
- The *'social-democratic'* regime constrains the market as much as possible, and even substitutes itself for it when it is failing – for instance, through massive public employment in the case of persistent unemployment.

The employability pillar combines these approaches in varying proportions. The liberal approach dominates, with the stress on the removal of disincentives, in order to stimulate the supply of labour by the old, the unemployed, etc. But social dialogue, central to a corporatist way of thinking, is also put forward, in the cases of lifelong learning and matching on the labour market. Finally, if the social democratic 'commitment to a full-employment guarantee' (Esping-Andersen 1990: 28) is not observed, the fight against discrimination and social exclusion implies a form of collective responsibility for the fate of the weakest. Indeed, one should not forget that it is countries like Sweden, Denmark, Finland and the Netherlands which have invented active labour market policies – i.e. which first recognised the necessity to spend more and better on the unemployed (EC 2002a). The EES, promoted on the political side by Jean-Claude Juncker, who was Prime Minister, Finance Minister and Labour Minister of Luxembourg, was for an important part a Swedish initiative, led by Allan Larsson, former Swedish Minister of the Economy and future Head of DG Employment.

A frequent question is, then: is it possible to identify a common trajectory in the policies led by these countries? Working on the first three years of the EES (1998–2000), we found a plurality of employability policies in the NAPs (Raveaud 2001). For instance, we could define an *individual employability*, best illustrated by the UK, where conditionality and incentives are combined to make people seek and accept work. This is opposed to what can be called a *socially shared employability*, as the responsibilities of the Swedish municipalities in the fight against unemployment[6] or the French programme 'New Start' (*Nouveau Départ*) seem to illustrate.

---

[6] 'If the young person has not obtained meaningful employment within 90 days, responsibility then passes to the municipalities, which will offer suitable measures' (1998 Sweden NAP: 11).

But the UK does not have the monopoly of this logic of individual responsibilities. It is followed, for instance, by the Netherlands, where 'adequate financial stimulation for individual jobseekers to accept work or a training programme' has been put in place (1998 Netherlands NAP: 10). And this is seemingly the direction towards which the policies of countries such as Denmark, Sweden, Finland and Germany are evolving,[7] even if they are still mainly characterised by what we have called 'collectively shared responsibilities' in the promotion of employability. The liberal turn, even if it takes very different forms between countries, thus seems well documented, the latest example being the 'Agenda 2010' in Germany.

The EES as an intellectual agenda   In its evaluation of the first five years of the EES, the Commission notes a 'clear *convergence* towards the active labour market principles' (EC 2002b, emphasis in the original). This is illustrated by the recommendations addressed to the Member States. They gradually evolved from the requirement of creating these policies towards a need to improve their quality and effectiveness.[8] This trajectory is typical of Belgium, Germany and France. According to the Commission's evaluation, they have 'adopted completely new approaches in labour market policies as a direct effect of the implementation of the guidelines'. In Greece, Spain and Italy, the progress is less significant, but the Commission still considers that they have 'reoriented their labour market policies by shifting towards more preventive, individualised and diversified approaches'.

In 2003, the UK was the only country which did not comply with the target of proposing an active measure to at least 20 per cent of the unemployed. This is quite surprising, as in 1998 the UK had launched

---

[7] In Denmark, 'a refusal to accept a reasonable training offer will mean that the young person forfeits the right to receive unemployment benefits' (1998 Denmark NAP: 35). In Finland, 'The employment office offers designated employment to unemployed jobseekers within their own commuting area [the size of which was expanded and standardised], and unjustified refusal of such an offer leads to sanctions' (2000 Finland NAP: 12). In Sweden, 'Unemployment insurance is being reformed with the aim of reinforcing its role as an adjustment insurance. The requirement that individuals make efforts to seek work will be clarified while there is an increase in requirements in terms of occupational and geographical mobility' (2000 Sweden NAP: 14). In Germany, the idea was also to 'strengthen the incentives to work, the help given to people to help themselves', in a context where 'tax-financed social benefits payments should be concentrated on those people really in need' (1999 Germany NAP: 28).

[8] This is confirmed by the fact that, in 2001, all countries but one (the UK) complied with the 'activation target' of at least 20 per cent of the unemployed benefiting from an active measure. Even if the figures need to be handled with care, as the definition of activation policies is not harmonised, one can note that the scores vary between 14 per cent (UK) and 60 per cent (Sweden) (EC 2003a).

its 'New Deal', whose purpose was precisely to offer a 'new start' to the young and the long-term unemployed. Actually, the UK claims that no less than 100 per cent of the long-term unemployed, whether young or adults, benefit from active measures.[9] But for the Commission, 'The UK only achieved a rate slightly over 12 per cent, when excluding intensive counselling from the measures'.

There is thus a debate on the definition and scope of 'activation' policies, which are indeed varied (Raveaud 2001). But there seems to be a general agreement between the Commission and the Member States on the need to 'activate' the unemployed, although several researches challenge this view (Abrahamson 2000). It is indeed possible to identify an 'ideological convergence' in these policies, consisting in:

the portrayal of unemployment as something for which the individual is responsible. The individual is seen as being responsible for managing risk (for example, job loss), and this risk is considered to be an inevitable fact of life. (Serrano Pascual 2003: 153)

This is the line of the *Third Way Manifesto*, which intends to 'promote a new entrepreneurial spirit at all levels of society'. Indeed, for its authors, the purpose is no longer to protect people from risks, but to 'transform the safety net of entitlements into a springboard to personal responsibility' (Blair and Schröder 1999).

But even if this is the case, what is the responsibility of the Union in these developments? Serrano Pascual recognises that 'the European institutions do not seem to have been playing an important role' (2003: 162) in the implementation of such policies. Still, for her, 'the role of the union should not be underestimated, as the EES is promoting and popularising a certain diagnosis of the problem (interpretation and causes), legitimisation principles, targets of intervention and definition of the role to be played by the state' (2003: 151).

This perspective is reinforced by the now complete integration of the EES into the broad economic policy of the Union.

3.3   The integration of the EES into the Broad Economic Policy Guidelines

The necessity of a structural reform of the labour market   The adoption of the Euro, at the beginning of 1999, brought to the forefront the need for increased co-ordination in policy, at both national and European

---

[9] This example, not so exceptional, points to the possible manipulation of indicators in the EES framework, as the Commission does not check the origin and construction of national data (Salais 2004).

level. This is why in Cologne in June 1999, the European Council decided to launch a 'macro-economic dialogue based on mutual trust', between the Council, the Commission, the European Central Bank (ECB) and the European social partners. But it remained an 'exchange of views', in which the requirements of the ECB on price stability, wage moderation and the flexibility of labour markets were communicated to the other participants, without much information going in the opposite direction (Dufresne 2001). This poses a major problem, 'as . . . it is, to say the least, problematic to delegate decision-making to an independent central bank which is unrepresentative of the various groups affected by macro-policy, which is dominated by financial interests, and which pays little if any attention to employment' (Stiglitz 2002: 19).

The *European Employment Pact*, adopted simultaneously, validated this approach. Its purpose was to combine the newly created macro-economic dialogue with two existing processes: the 'Cardiff process' (1998), whose purpose is to 'improve competitiveness and the functioning of the markets in goods, services and capital', and the EES. But this co-ordination led to what could be called a *cognitive merger*, implying the generalisation of the market-making logic. This is illustrated by the fact that *all* aspects of economic life are now considered as 'markets', whose 'structural reform' is the priority. As the text of the *Conclusions* indicates, the aim of the *Pact* was a 'comprehensive structural reform and modernisation to improve the innovative capacity and efficiency of the labour market and the markets in goods, services and capital'. This departs from the Keynesian tradition, for which labour is never exchanged on a market (Fitoussi 1995). But it is 'One of the great 'tricks' . . . of neoclassical economics to treat labour like any other factor of production' (Stiglitz 2002: 10).

As Dufresne (2001) explains, co-ordination is in fact in a hierarchy, starting from the requirements of the ECB and those of the SGP, to which the EES is subordinated. The specific nature of work relationships is thus neglected, the only question being to deregulate labour markets, like other markets. Indeed, for Blair and Schröder, 'flexible markets' are 'a modern social democrat aim' (Blair and Schröder 1999). This was echoed by José Maria Aznar during the Spanish Presidency:

In my opinion, the greatest adversary for a jobless person is the rigidity of the job market. The greater the rigidity, the higher the unemployment rate. There is no greater adversary for someone looking for a job than the rigid rules that prevent him from taking advantage of opportunities or prevent him from accessing that necessary flexibility in the labour market. (Aznar 2002)

This is the general context in which the more progressive elements in the EES, introduced in 2000, are to be evaluated.

Raising the quality and quantity of jobs?   The euphoria of the late 1990s, with the myth of a 'new economy' (Gadrey 2002) did not only hit stock markets. It made victims among European leaders as well, who wanted to 'prepare the transition to a new knowledge-based economy and society' at the Lisbon summit, the first of the newly created Spring summits for 'employment, economic reform and social cohesion', held in March 2000. Lisbon was also the stage of the come-back of a nearly forgotten notion: 'full employment', which was to be reached through the 'realistic prospect' of a yearly growth of GDP of 3 per cent. All these objectives were packed in a grand sentence: the EU was 'to become the most competitive and dynamic knowledge-based economy in the world, capable of sustainable economic growth with more and better jobs and greater social cohesion'. More precisely, this summit saw the introduction of *targets for employment rates* for the first time. The aim was to raise the employment rate from an average of 61 per cent in 2000 to 'as close as possible' to 70 per cent by 2010, with a target for women at 60 per cent (51 per cent in 2000). The subsequent Stockholm summit (March 2001), introduced intermediary targets of 67 per cent and 57 per cent, respectively, in 2005.[10] But this is not all: not only was full employment to be achieved, but it should be reached through 'better jobs'. The catch-phrase 'quality of employment' thus appeared at the end of many of the 2001 guidelines.

But the fact of putting together conflicting objectives in a single sentence does not erase their incompatibility. For instance, the conclusions of the Barcelona Spring Summit (2002), stated that:

The revised Employment Strategy should focus on raising the employment rate by promoting employability and by removing obstacles and disincentives to take up or remain in a job, while preserving high protection standards of the European social model.

That is, Member States should at the same time reduce welfare payments (the other name for 'disincentives'), while still offering 'high protection standards' to their citizens. Beyond rhetoric, it is not hard to know which of these two objectives will be given priority in real life, especially as the first objective coincides with the priorities of most current European governments.

The fate of the theme of the 'quality of work' does not predispose to optimism. While the original Communication from the Commission was ambitious (EC 2001c), the four indicators finally selected do not

---

[10] In 2001, the latest data available at the time of writing, the figures were 63.9 per cent and 54.9 per cent, respectively, according to the 2002 *Employment in Europe* report.

include any serious element, starting with the level of wages and the type of contracts offered, or trade union representation.[11]

Conclusion: the future of the EES – has anyone found the European Social Model?

Looking for explanations for the European successes in employment at the end of the 1990s, the Commission estimated that 'wage moderation is considered as one key factor' (EC 2002b). This is in line with the permanent recommendations made in the Broad Economic Policy Guidelines (BEPG). It is therefore logical to assume that, for the future of the EES, the Commission recognises the BEPG as 'an overarching economic policy co-ordination instrument' (EC 2003a).

Since 2003, the EES has three top priorities:
• Full employment
• Quality and productivity at work
• Cohesion and an inclusive labour market.[12]

Here as so often, these objectives partially contradict one another. For instance, under the heading 'Promoting adaptability in the labour market', one can read that:

Flexibility should continue to be encouraged, in particular in terms of the availability of different contractual or working time arrangements. At the same time, steps should be taken to prevent a segmentation of the labour market between different types of workers and to facilitate transitions between different forms of work.

The problem is that some qualified observers have different views on what 'flexibility' means:

In short, the mantra of increased labour market flexibility [is] only a thinly disguised attempt to roll back – under the guise of 'economic efficiency' – gains that workers had achieved over years and years of bargaining and political activity. (Stiglitz 2002: 13)

The role of the EES could thus have been to tell us what precisely are the expected costs and benefits of flexibility. In fact, most of the communication is devoted to procedural aspects (simplification and stability of

---

[11] They are only indicators of transition between various states (employment, unemployment, non-employment), and are only a 'context indicator'. On the other hand, the number of accidents at work is a 'key indicator'.

[12] Three changes in the content of the guidelines itself are noticeable in their 2003 version: the stress on 'active ageing'; and the fights against 'undeclared work' and 'regional employment disparities'.

the guidelines, etc.). This is no doubt valuable, but it does little to help to start defining what the 'European Social Model' may well be.

In its 2003 Recommendations, the Council of the European Union, dealing with the case of Sweden, wrote:

The Swedish labour market is characterised by very high employment rates, including among older workers and women, and all the EU-wide targets have already been exceeded . . . Despite the ongoing tax reform, the tax burden on labour is still the highest in the EU. Benefit schemes are relatively generous in an international perspective and include tight eligibility criteria. However, further efforts appear necessary to improve incentives to work.

Is it possible to do better (or worse) than this nonsensical statement to show that, all along the long road from 1993, the European Union has mistaken the *ends* for the (wrong) *means*?

REFERENCES

Abrahamson, P., 2000. *The Active Turn in Scandinavian Social Policy: The Case of Denmark*, Paper presented at the DREES Conference, 'Comparing Social Protection Systems in Europe', Paris

Adema, W., 2001. *Net Social Expenditure*, Labour Market and Social Policy Occasional Papers, 52, Paris, OECD

Aznar, J. M., 2002. 'Economic Reform and Progress with the Lisbon Process', *El Escorial*, Madrid, 6 February

Blair, T. and G. Schröder, 1999. 'Europe: The Third Way', London. Labour Party, 8 June, http://www.socialdemocrats.org/blairandschroeder-6-8-99.html

Bosco, A., 1998. 'Putting Europe into the Systems: A Review of Social Protection Issues', in E. Gabaglio and R. Hoffmann (eds.), *European Trade Union Yearbook 1997*, Brussels, ETUI, 305–334

Deakin, S., 1996. 'Social Rights and the Market', in U. Mückenberger *et al.*, *A Manifesto for Social Europe*, Brussels, ETUI, 17–40

De La Porte C. and P. Pochet, 2003. 'A Twofold Assessment of Employment Policy Co-ordination in Light of Economic Policy Co-ordination', in D. Foden and L. Magnusson (eds.), *Five Years' Experience of the Luxembourg Employment Strategy*, Brussels, ETUI Editions, 13–68

Dufresne, A., 2001. 'Oskar Lafontaine's Dream: An Opportunity for Economic Policy Co-Ordination?', in C. Degryse, and P. Pochet (eds.), *Social Developments in the EU 2001*, Brussels, ETUI, 85–113

Esping-Andersen G., 1990. *The Three Worlds of Welfare Capitalism*, Princeton, Princeton University Press

ETUC, UNICE, CEEP, 1996. *Action for Employment in Europe. A Confidence Pact*, 29 November, Joint Contribution to the Dublin European Council; available at http://europa.eu.int/comm/employment_social/soc-dial/social/euro_agr/data/en/961129.doc

Fitoussi, J.-P., 1995. *Le débat interdit – Monnaie, Europe, pauvreté*, Paris, Arléa

Foden, D. and L. Magnusson (eds.), 2003. *Five Years' Experience of the Luxembourg Employment Strategy*, Brussels, ETUI Editions

Gadrey J., 2002. *New Economy, New Myth,* London, Routledge

Goetschy, J., 2003. 'The Employment Strategy and European Integration', in D. Foden and L. Magnusson (eds.), *Five Years' Experience of the Luxembourg Employment Strategy*, Brussels, ETUI Editions, 69–110

Jacobsson, K. and H. Schmid, 2003. 'The European Employment Strategy at the Crossroads: Contribution to the Evaluation', in D. Foden and L. Magnusson (eds.), *Five Years' Experience of the Luxembourg Employment Strategy*, Brussels, ETUI Editions, 111–140

Lefresne, F., 1999. 'Employability at the Heart of the European Employment Strategy', *Transfer*, 4/99, 460–480

OECD, 2001. *Employment Outlook*, Paris, June

Raveaud, G., 2001. 'Dynamics of the Welfare State Regimes and Employability', in D. Pieters (ed.), *Confidence and Changes: Managing Social Protection in the New Millennium*, The Hague: Kluwer Law International, 5–26

Rodrigues, M. J., 2001. 'The Open Method of Co-ordination as a New Governance Tool', in M. Telò (ed.), 'L'evoluzione della governance europea', Special issue of *Europa/Europe*, 2–3, 96–107

2003. 'Introduction: For a European Strategy at the Turn of the Century', in M. J. Rodrigues (ed.), *The New Knowledge Economy in Europe*, Cheltenham, Edward Elgar, 1–27

Salais, R., 2004. '*La politique des indicateurs. Du taux de chômage au taux d'emploi dans la Stratégie européenne pour l'emploi*', in B. Zimmermann, 2004. *Les sciences sociales à l'épreuve de l'action: le savant, le politique ét l'Europe*, Paris, Editions de la Maison des Sciences de l'Homme, 287–331

Sen, A., 1997. 'Inequality, Unemployment and Contemporary Europe', *International Labour Review*, 136 (2), 155–171

Serrano Pascual, A., 2003. 'Towards Convergence of European Activation Policies?', in D. Foden and L. Magnusson (eds.), *Five Years' Experience of the Luxembourg Employment Strategy*, Brussels, ETUI Editions, 141–166

Stiglitz, J., 2002. 'Employment, Social Justice and Societal Well-Being', *International Labour Review*, 141, (1–2), 9–29

Streeck, W., 1995. 'From Market Making to State Building? Reflections on the Political Economy of European Social Policy', in S. Leibfried and P. Pierson (eds.), *European Social Policy: Between Fragmentation and Integration*, Washington, DC, Brookings Institution, 389–431

Trubek, D. M. and J. M. Mosher, 2003. 'New Governance, Employment Policy and the European Social Model', in J. Zeitlin and D. M. Trubek (eds.), *Governing Work and Welfare in a New Economy*, Oxford, Oxford University Press, 33–57

UNICE, CEEP, ETUC, 1986. *Joint Opinion on the Co-operative Growth for More Employment*, 6 November

Weber, T. 1997. 'European Social Partners Issue Joint Declaration on Confidence Pact for Employment', EIROnline; 28 February, www.eiro.eurofound.eu.int

9 Regional growth, national context and the European Structural Funds: an empirical appraisal

Jacky Fayolle and Anne Lecuyer

R11

L52   R32

1   Introduction

Studies[1] on the location of industrial activity within the European Union usually point to an undeniable tendency toward industrial specialisation, but also to a more doubtful trend toward greater geographical concentration of activity, both measured at a *national level*. The rise in importance of intrasector trade, increasing returns to scale and commercial or technological externalities are all viewed as favourable factors conducive to increased revenue owing to a combination of comparative advantages and strong industrial links.

As this chapter will argue, this is a rather hasty conclusion. Such studies fail to look, first, at a regional interpretation of industrial specialisation or, secondly, at the consequences of the observed geographical heterogeneity on revenue disparities within Europe. The interdependence of economic agents in Europe, the customer/supplier links between companies, as defined by the theoreticians of the new economical geography point, for example, to a regional, rather than purely national, specialisation in activities. This means that geographical heterogeneity in Europe needs to be interpreted from the local and transnational points of view.

In addition, the lesser concentration of activities in Europe compared with the USA is accompanied by greater inequality of regional development, as assessed by the yardstick of *per capita* income (Puga 1999). However, these two characteristics of European economic geography cannot be accounted for in terms of comparative advantage using traditional theories of trade. According to the latter, perfect competition in markets will help ensure fair distribution of activities over the whole of the territory – in other words, territorial imbalances will not exist. The approaches used by the new economic geography seem to be the most pertinent in accounting for the complex relationship between the concentration of economic activities and levels of income. If such concentration goes hand in hand

---

[1] For instance, Midefart-Knarvik *et al.* (2000). See also Bradley (2000).

140

with high labour mobility, it will be conducive to the spread of high wages, thus tending to equalise income levels. Conversely, geographic compartmentalisation may act as a brake on such concentration, as well as helping income disparities to persist. Concentration is not automatically a source of territorial inequality, but it will be if the mechanisms for the primary dissemination of productivity gains and increased wages within the geographical space are not operative. Given the low level of labour mobility in Europe, territorial imbalance is therefore likely to continue into the future, especially when membership is widened to include the Central and Eastern European (CEE) countries.

This chapter sets out to arrive at a comparative assessment of growth performance in different European regions over the 1986–96 period. It looks at the dependence of such performance on the Member State to which the regions concerned belong and their access to European Structural Funds. The specific character of the chosen period needs to be underlined: on the one hand, the conjunction of the process of European integration and of restrictive policies make this a period of complex transition, impeding the ability of countries and regions to catch up steadily with the European leaders; on the other, this is a period in which the role of the Structural Funds was expanded, in the expectation that they would help mitigate the handicaps affecting regions at risk or lagging behind. Multi-year budget planning at EU level began in 1988 and the Structural Funds committed in the first two programming periods (1989–93 and 1994–99) are examined here. The specific character of the period considered certainly makes it an interesting one for an objective appraisal of the effectiveness of the Structural Funds, but it would be far from prudent to draw overgeneral conclusions from it. For example, the macroeconomic policies adopted during the period probably interfered with the effectiveness of the Structural Funds *per se*. Lastly, the starting point for our study is 1986–7, two years immediately preceding the first budget period, but the final year, 1996, the last for which we had regional macroeconomic data, does not coincide with the end of the second budget programming period.[2] The Structural Funds committed throughout this second period were obviously not completely spent in 1996. Nevertheless, comparison of the development of the different European regions reveals phenomena continuing after 1996. Section 2 presents the principal features of

---

[2] GDP figures for 1996 come from Eurostat regional data (News Release, 11/99. 9 February 1999) and those for 1986–7 from the statistical annexes of the 4th periodical report of the European Commission (Regional Policy DG) on regions. Structural Fund data come from the publications of the European Commission: in the case of 1989–93, from the DG for Co-ordination of Structural Policies (*Community Structural Assistance, Statistical Bulletin*, 3 and 4, July and December 1992), and for 1994–9, from the statistical annexes of the *9th Annual Report on the Structural Funds*.

catching-up in Europe. Section 3 develops the role of Structural Funds. Section 4 presents a short econometric evaluation of their effectiveness. Some explanation for their apparently disappointing effectiveness will be provided in section 5. The challenges that the structural policies face with regards to the new European geography are summarised in a brief conclusion (section 6).

2   Specific national effects on regional catching-up

The logical starting point is to look in detail, for the 1986–96 period, at European and national patterns in catching-up by less developed regions. Figures 9.1–9.5 plot initial *per capita* GDP in 1986–7 for countries or regions – expressed in terms of purchasing power parity (PPP) and relatively to the EU mean – against growth in those same countries or regions between 1986–7 and 1996, once again compared with the EU mean for growth. These graphs illustrate the concept of absolute β-convergence developed in the economics literature.[3] GDP *per capita* (y) for a set of N countries or regions (index i) verify just such a property of β-convergence if their growth, over a period between first year 0 and final year T, is governed by the following equation, the β coefficient being positive:

$$\log(y_{iT}) - \log(y_{i0}) = \alpha - \beta \log(y_{i0}) \quad i = 1 \dots N \tag{1.1}$$

If we think in terms of relative *per capita* GDP, that is to say expressed as a ratio to the mean *per capita* GDP $\bar{y}$ for the group under consideration $y_{it}^r = y_{it}/\bar{y}_t$, β-convergence can be expressed even more simply if we assume that all the elements making up the geographic set are governed by the same equation:

$$\log \left(y_{iT}^r \right) - \log \left(y_{i0}^r \right) = -\beta \log \left(y_{i0}^r \right) \quad i = 1 \dots N \tag{1.2}$$

If this absolute β-convergence prevails, the more the countries or regions are disadvantaged at the outset, the faster they will grow. The value for the β-coefficient indicates the rate at which the region or country is catching-up. The development gap will narrow to zero over the period considered if the value is 1 and the annual catch-up rate is expressed by the ratio β/T.

The series of figures 9.1 to 9.5 illustrates the relevance of equation (1.2), since the X and Y axes correspond precisely to the logarithms for initial relative *per capita* GDP and relative growth, which appear, respectively, to right and left of the equation.[4] If the equation were verified for a

---

[3] For a general survey of this, see Fuss (1999).
[4] The scales for these two axes therefore represent, respectively, subject to logarithmic approximation, the percentage gap between initial *per capita* GDP for each country or

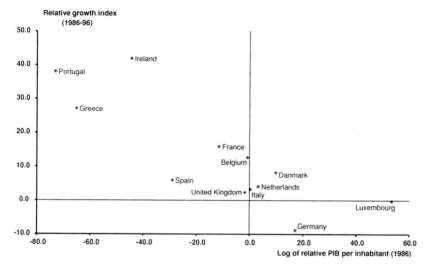

Figure 9.1. The catching-up of European countries, 1986–1996

given set of countries or regions, they would be spread along a negative-slope, straight-line plot passing through the point of origin of the axes. The absolute value of the slope will correspond to the rate β with which the regions or countries are catching-up. The shape of the plot provides an immediate indication of the reality of β-convergence over the period analysed.

Figure 9.1 presents this equation for the twelve Member States of the European Community over the entire period. It suggests not only that it is not possible to rule out a relationship of inter-state β-convergence within Europe, but also that the reality of such convergence is highly dependent on the relative performance shown by three modestly sized states (Greece, Ireland and Portugal), as well as on the appearance of a degree of comparative decline in Germany. If we replace the Member States by the 131 regions[5] making them up, the general shape of the plot (cf. figure 9.2) remains suggestive, although the slope of the resulting plot seems to be less marked for initially prosperous regions, which hardly decline at all in relative terms. However, this suggestive aspect disappears completely

---

region and the EU mean, on the one hand and, on the other, between their cumulative growth over the period 1986–96 and mean growth in the Union.

[5] The regions studied here are the NUTS-2 regions as defined by the European nomenclature, with the exception of Germany and the UK, for which we keep to NUTS-1, for reasons related to the availability of data. Denmark, Ireland and Luxembourg have not been broken down: these countries are considered to consist of a single region. Lastly, the EU mean relates to the former Europe of 12, excluding the Eastern Germany Länder and the newest Member States (Austria, Finland and Sweden).

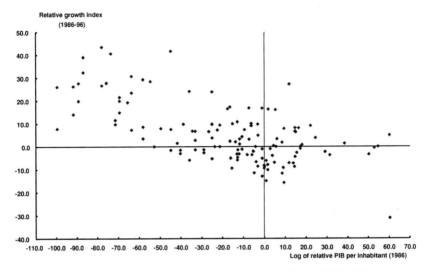

Figure 9.2. The catching-up of European regions, 1986–1996

if we remove from the sample the regions making up Greece, Ireland and Portugal, along with the French overseas departments (Guadeloupe, Martinique, French Guyana, Réunion), the Spanish enclave Ceuta and Melilla in Morocco and, lastly, the Dutch region of Groningen, a rich region whose development falls back sharply. The plot is no longer clearly structured around a β-convergence relationship (figure 9.3). The plot is roughly centred around the point of origin (average prosperous regions show average growth) but there is no clear relationship between the initial level of wealth, on the one hand, and relative growth on the other. This goes to show just how far the reality of catching-up is conditional upon the performance registered by the regions belonging to three countries in particular and by outlying regions.

This over-dependence of the appearance of catching-up on the chosen sample encourages a closer look at the reality country by country, once again in relation to the EU mean. A correct reading of such close-ups on individual states requires attention to the shape of the national relationship and to the location of the national regions within the overall plot. It then becomes obvious that regional convergence is closely dependent on the State to which a given region belongs. The patterns governing how regions develop and catch up with others are not identical from one country to another. A series of brief comments on some contrasting individual States will serve to detail these differences.

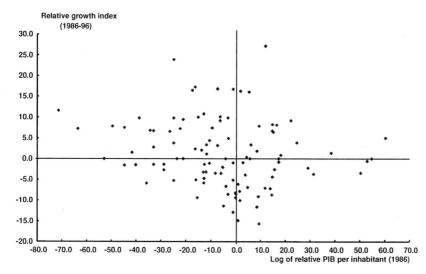

Figure 9.3. The catching-up of European regions, 1986–1996, except French overseas districts, Greece, Ireland, Portugal, Ceuta y Melilla and Groningen

- **Greece and Portugal** Greece (figure 9.4) and Portugal[6] provide the two clearest examples of effective, although imperfect, catching-up by regions. In Greece, relative growth is noticeably stronger in the most backward regions. However, this relative growth seems to peter out all too quickly, diminishing virtually to zero for the most developed regions (Peloponnese, Sterea Ellada), despite the fact that they are very far below the EU mean. In Portugal, all regions catch up significantly with the EU mean, but the catch-up rate correlates poorly with the scale of the initial gap. In particular, the two island regions (Azores, Madeira) have great difficulty in catching-up at a rate commensurate with their initial gap.
- **Spain** Spain (figure 9.5) and Italy are the two major examples that run counter to the idea that regions are actually catching-up. In Spain, once the two outlying regions of Ceuta y Melilla and the Balearic Islands have been eliminated, there is no definite relationship between the size of the initial backwardness and the rate of catching-up. This rate remains within a fairly narrow band irrespective of the initial position and the two relatively developed regions, Madrid and Catalonia, show good relative growth figures. As for Italy, the pattern is clear: the Mezzogiorno,

---

[6] Data and graphs for countries are available from the authors.

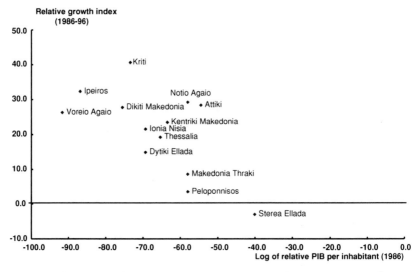

Figure 9.4. The catching-up of European regions, 1986–1996: Greece

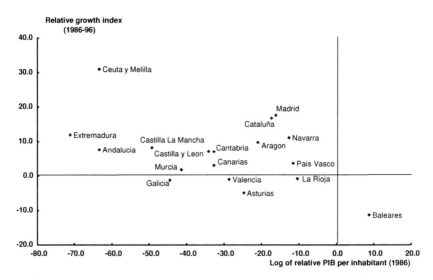

Figure 9.5. The catching-up of European regions, 1986–1996: Spain

Basilicata excepted, is catching-up neither with the EU mean, nor with the developed regions of Italy, which are themselves above the EU mean. Among the latter, the dynamic growth is concentrated in the Northeast regions with high-performance small firms.[7]

This major influence of the national context on regional convergence[8] is thus important in two ways: first, each region benefits, all other things being equal, from the economic performance of the State to which it belongs; secondly, and less trivially, the degree of inequality in regional development varies widely from one country to another. For example, regional catching-up is much more visible in Portugal and Greece than in Spain or Italy. The dynamics of regional inequality is highly specific to the country of which the region is part.

If studies show that there is a degree of interregional convergence within Europe, it is largely because inter-State convergence prevails, overriding purely cyclical factors, and because the regions of a country in the process of catching-up with the others will benefit by that fact. The most backward regions benefit all the more if the national level can act as an effective conduit for the interregional catching-up process, but this is not generally true of all European countries. Lastly, interregional convergence follows the same trends as interstate convergence – i.e. fairly marked from 1950 to 1970, but diminishing in the decades that follow, despite the expanding role of the Structural Funds.[9]

3   The nationally conditioned effectiveness of the Structural Funds

Problems of method are raised by the determination of the specific effectiveness of the Structural Funds where regional development is concerned. If, for example, the distribution of Structural Funds were perfectly proportional to the initial development gap of each region, as assessed by *per capita* GDP, and assuming the β-convergence equation described above reveals, for the chosen period and sample of regions, an effective catching-up by those regions, how could we distinguish which factors among those underlying such catching-up are due to the Structural Funds and which can be put down to other, more general factors? The catching-up will be seen to correlate with the distribution of Structural Funds, but there would be no guarantee that these were a real

---

[7] These Italian characteristics are confirmed for the period examined here by the detailed study of Quarella and Tullio (1998).

[8] See studies conducted at different regional aggregation levels (see Capron in Beine and Docquier 2000).

[9] See Armstrong and Vickerman (1995), Fagerberg and Verspagen (1996).

explanatory factor for it, and, conversely, we could not rule out the conclusion that this assistance was no more than a windfall in regions which would have caught up in any event.

Differences in the performance of regions with similar starting points allow us to hope that some clues may be gleaned as to the interaction between Structural Funds and catching-up. This is because the distribution of the Structural Funds is governed by a set of announced criteria and actual practices which cannot be reduced to a calculation based solely on *per capita* GDP. Some underdeveloped regions have received, *per capita*, a level of structural assistance that is little different from that received by more advanced regions. The financial redistribution effected by Structural Funds is far from perfect. Three sets of factors help explain why this should be so:

- First, *financial redistribution* is only part of the purpose of the Structural Funds. In the first two budget programming periods, their resources were divided between several objectives. Only Objective 1, which relates to regions whose *per capita* GDP was initially under 75 per cent of the *per capita* GDP for the Union as a whole, relates strictly to the objective of narrowing development gaps. Objective 2, which comes in second place, relates to aid for conversion and diversification in regions affected by industrial restructuring, these often being initially prosperous. It is clear that the distribution of funds assigned to objective 2 has no clear link with any initial level of *per capita* GDP.

- *Structural Fund distribution*, which relates solely in this instance to less developed regions (Objective 1), correlates only very imperfectly with the size of the initial gap. Figure 9.6 testifies to this fact. It compares relative *per capita* GDP for 1986 in the regions and the cumulative total of Objective 1 Structural Funds committed to each region over the two budget programming periods, as expressed in 1997 ECU *per capita* and compared with the EU mean (100 will therefore correspond to a region that has received, *per capita*, an amount of Objective 1 Structural Funds identical to the EU mean, that is to say the ratio between the total for all such structural assistance divided by the total population of the Europe of 12). Criteria other than *per capita* GDP alone obviously come into play in targeting fund distribution, and institutional bargaining between the Union, national and regional levels, has a substantial influence on the ultimate allocation of Structural Funds. Member States still retain considerable powers to shape the detailed geographical distribution of Structural Funds.

- Lastly, the *additionality* rule means that European Structural Funds intended for defined projects must be duly supplemented by national and regional co-funding. This rule helps ensure that projects are

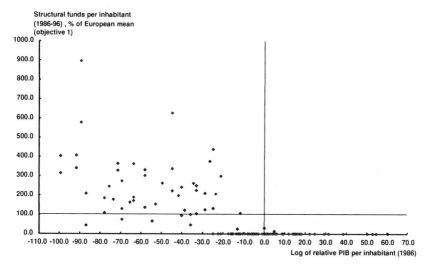

Figure 9.6. The initial backwardness of European regions and their access to Structural Funds (Objective 1)

managed by genuine partnerships. But if we calculate the level of such co-funding – that is to say the ratio between all funds committed, European and local, and European funds alone – the level of co-funding is very roughly indexed to the initial wealth of the region (figure 9.7). It is rare that co-funding manages to double the EU financial input for poor regions, whereas it may treble or quadruple that input for average or very wealthy regions, even leaving aside a small number of exceptionally well-endowed regions. Money attracts money! There is nothing surprising in this observation: wealthy regions are in the best position to provide back-up for structural assistance. However, we might well wonder how hard national States try to correct this anti-redistributive bias, especially as control of the application of the additionality principle remains problematic.[10]

When all these factors are taken into account, it can be readily understood that the distribution of Structural Funds is linked only vaguely to catching-up in the regions. Figures 9.8 and 9.9 illustrate this link. They compare, for all the regions, the cumulative total for Objective 1 Structural Funds committed, *per capita*, expressed as a percentage of the

---

[10] These remarks should, however, be treated with a degree of caution. Apparent levels of co-funding may be biased by presentational phenomena linked to institutional practices, and the difficulty of deciding clearly between priorities. Announced co-funding may be actually implemented to a variable degree and a comparison in terms of the funds really spent might lead to significantly different conclusions.

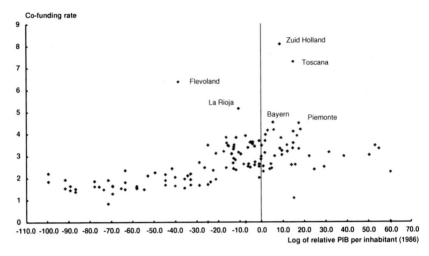

Figure 9.7. The initial backwardness of European regions and the co-funding rate of Structural Funds

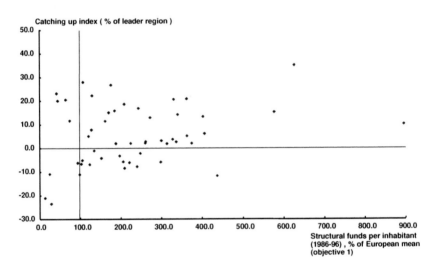

Figure 9.8. The catching-up of European regions and their access to Structural Funds (Objective 1)

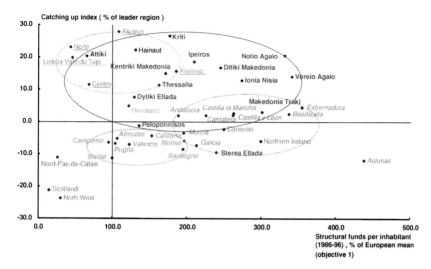

Figure 9.9. The catching-up of European regions (except 'insular' regions) and their access to Structural Funds (Objective 1)

EU mean, and an indicator for the rate of catching-up with the NUTS-2 leading region (which is, in 1996 as in 1986, Hamburg, whose lead over the EU mean is in fact increasing). This index is calculated according to the following formula (in which y^r_{it} expresses the ratio $y_{it}/y_{Hamburgt}$ between the *per capita* GDP of region i and that of the Hamburg region at date t):

Catching-up indicator between 0 and T

$$= -100 \times \frac{\log\left(y^r_{iT}\right) - \log\left(y^r_{i0}\right)}{\log\left(y^r_{i0}\right)} \tag{1.3}$$

The indicator will be positive if region i is catching-up with the lead region, and otherwise negative. The value of the indicator will be commensurate with the rate at which the region is catching-up or lagging behind, in terms of a percentage of the initial gap between itself and the lead region. If the β-convergence equation was totally verified, the indicator would simply be identical to the coefficient β itself (expressed as a percentage) and it would be the same for all regions. Figure 9.8, concerning only regions eligible to Objective 1, shows that this is far from being the case. The dominant trend is significantly in the direction of the catching-up, but some regions are lagging behind and the link with the level of funds received is hardly self-evident.

If outlying regions are left out of account, the overall diagram for all regions, plotted both for the level of Structural Funds received in relation to Objective 1 and their catch-up index, does not show any particular shape (figure 9.9). The information it provides does, however, become clearer when the national context of each region is included. Although it is not automatically the case, regions in the same country are often close together in the plane formed by the two criteria. National ellipses can be drawn freehand to cover the majority of regions in a given country. If we move across the plane in a clockwise direction, starting at 12 o'clock, we encounter a series of four countries whose situations are markedly different. The first is Portugal, whose regions, receiving overall an average level of Objective 1 funds, have performed noticeably well in catching-up with other areas. Next comes Greece, whose regions, although fairly dispersed, received high levels of Structural Funds and have often performed respectably. The regions of Spain also receive high levels of funding, but their performance in catching-up is very limited, or even negative. Asturias is a region that falls outside the ellipse, providing a more than adequate example of such disappointing results (it should, however, be remembered that not all regions in a country such as Spain are eligible for Objective 1 funding and only those regions that are eligible are plotted). Lastly, the southern Italian regions, which tend to receive more than average structural funding, are in no position to catch up – they are falling behind compared with the leading European region.

This national ranking does not permit any conclusion as to the effectiveness of the Structural Funds *per se*, but it is quite clear that effectiveness is linked to the economic and institutional context specific to the individual Member State, which determines the distribution, application and use of the funds.

4   Broad econometric assessment of the regional effectiveness of Structural Funds

The *Sixth Report on Social and Economic Evolution and Development of Regions* (EC 1999a) contains a review of the various evaluations of the contribution to growth made by the Structural Funds based on four different macroeconomic models. It concludes that the contribution made was significant in the first two budget programming periods, 1989–93 and 1994–9. In the four so-called 'cohesion' countries (Spain, Greece, Ireland and Portugal), the estimated impact of the Structural Funds on growth, although variable according to the model applied, is definitely positive, possibly amounting to one yearly growth point in Greece and Portugal. Nevertheless, as the Commission's report points out: 'given the data which exist, the models can only really be applied effectively to analyse developments in individual Member States rather than in different regions within countries.' This is obviously a major constraint on analysis, since the effectiveness of the Structural Funds in either microeconomic or macroeconomic terms cannot guarantee that they are contributing to regional development. A well-designed and well-executed project in a disadvantaged region may end up being more beneficial for developed regions in the same country. The producers in the latter areas may satisfy demand financed by the Structural Funds and provide more intense competition for local producers if improvements in infrastructures facilitate penetration of their products; the productivity gains associated with the project may fund increased income levels outside the designated beneficiary region. The Commission report shows that the catching-up is more significant in terms of productivity than *per capita* GDP, and that many regions eligible under Objective 1 are not succeeding in converting their productive modernisation into new jobs. While it seems likely that the Structural Funds have contributed a great deal to remedying the development gap in less advanced countries, their impact on regional development – a broader concept than that of modernisation of production alone – is more doubtful.

The aim here is simply to apply some preliminary tests suggestive of the factors at work in regional catching-up in Europe. The intention is only to indicate ways forward to a more detailed evaluation of the regional effectiveness of the Structural Funds.

Following on from the notion of β-convergence employed in the present chapter, it is possible to look at the introduction of explanatory factors for differences in regional catching-up. Without prejudging the 'ultimate stationary state' of each region, which is difficult to imagine on the basis of such a limited period, we can attempt to estimate the influence of various factors on the observable rate of β-convergence over the period 1986–96. The comments above have shown that this rate, as assessed by the catch-up indicator (1.3) seems to be highly variable from region to region, with no clearly established link with the level of funds received, although the role played by national context appears to be important for the effectiveness of such funding.

The equation tested here thus aims at providing a direct explanation of the catch-up indicator (which continues to be measured in relation to the leading Hamburg region):

Catching-up indicator between 0 and T

$$= -100 \times \frac{\log\left(y_{iT}^r\right) - \log\left(y_{i0}^r\right)}{\log\left(y_{i0}^r\right)}$$

$$= \beta_0 + \sum_j \beta_j X_{ij} \quad i = 1 \ldots N \tag{1.4}$$

where X_{ij} is the value taken in region i by factor j governing regional convergence.

The j factors introduced with some degree of success into the equation are as follows:

- The *level of Structural Funds* committed over the two budget programming periods, expressed in 1997 ECU *per capita* and compared with the EU mean for this ratio (variable FS). If the value of variable FS were equal to 1, this would mean that the region concerned received structural funding equal to the mean for the EU.

- Using the same measurement method, the *relative provision of Structural Funds* under Objective 1 (FS1) and Objective 2 (FS2).

- The level of *co-funding*, added to the total for committed Structural Funds. This variable, CF, will be nil in the theoretical case of an absence of co-funding (and also, naturally, in the absence of structural funding) and its value will be equal to 1 if the co-funding provided increases the Structural Funds by 100 per cent, i.e. if it doubles EU input.

- *National context*: there are as many j factors as there are countries. Variable X_{ij} for national context will be equal to 1 if region i belongs to state j, and 0 if not. Each such variable is simply designated using the name of the relevant country.

Table 9.1 sets out the results for a small number of regressions of interest, obtained by the ordinary least square (OLS) method applied to the complete sample of 131 regions (the results for a limited sample, after elimination of outlying regions and mono-regional states, are not significantly different, other than in the special cases described later). In these four regression (columns (1)–(4), table 9.1), irrespective of the other variables introduced, the relevant level of structural funding has a significant and positive influence on catch-up performance. The coefficient of variable FS appears fairly stable, between 4 and 6.5: if this variable rises from 1 to 2 – that is to say if funding rises from the average for the EU to twice that value – the catch-up indicator will rise by roughly 5 points (which is, expressed in yearly terms, a rise of 0.5 per cent per annum in the convergence rate). Column (2) suggests that this result can be attributed solely to objective 1 Structural Funds. Column (4) indicates that the

Table 9.1. *Testing the explanatory factors for the rate of regional catch-up (column (4))*

Equation variables	(1)	(2)	(3)	(4)
Constant	−10.1 (4.6)[a]	−7.0 (2.6)		
FS	6.5 (3.9)		4.0 (2.2)	4.8 (2.5)
FS1		4.2 (3.4)		
FS2		−1.6 (1.2)		
CF				2.3 (1.4)
Germany[b]			0.2 (0.0)	−4.1 (0.6)
Belgium			−1.5 (0.3)	−5.5 (0.9)
Denmark			4.5 (0.3)	−0.5 (0.0)
France			−18.5 (5.0)	−23.8 (4.4)
Greece			6.4 (1.2)	4.0 (0.7)
Ireland			16.2 (0.8)	9.8 (0.5)
Italy			−10.9 (2.6)	−15.9 (2.9)
Luxembourg			−76.1 (4.3)	−82.3 (4.5)
Netherlands			−10.6 (2.1)	−17.4 (2.4)
Portugal			10.1 (1.3)	7.3 (0.9)
Spain			−4.9 (1.0)	−9.5 (1.6)
UK			−20.5 (3.8)	−27.4 (4.1)
R^2	0.10	0.13	0.37	0.38

Notes:

[a] The numbers in brackets correspond to the Student-t values.

[b] When the national origin variables are present, we can no longer include a constant in the equation if we wish to avoid collinearity: the constant is a linear combination of these twelve variables. In fact, their inclusion boils down to a differentiation of the constant by country.

specific effect of the Structural Funds is probably amplified by the level of co-funding, although the returns of such funding may be decreasing in relation to the Structural Funds it supplements. The modest impact of co-funding does nevertheless indicate that presentational practices may probably be exaggerating the amount of funding actually spent.

The variables for regional origin are not all equally significant, but some national contexts seem to be a significant handicap for regional catching-up. Such a national handicap is clearly apparent for French, Italian and UK regions, but less so for the Spanish regions. If the region of Groningen is removed from the sample, the Netherlands join Germany and Belgium as archetypal examples of the neutral character of national context for regional development. Luxembourg, a mono-regional state, is a case apart: this wealthy region was initially close to the leader, Hamburg, but has since stagnated in relative terms, while Hamburg has continued to progress. If we leave Luxembourg out of the sample, the coefficients for the other national context variables hardly change at all. Lastly, the poor performance of France remains unaffected by elimination of the Departments d'Outre-Mer (DOMs) and Corsica from the sample.

This is obviously a long way from accounting for all the factors in regional convergence, which would require the dynamic impact of the advantages and handicaps specific to each region, expressed in suitable variables, to be made explicit. But outcomes suggest that the specific effectiveness of the Structural Funds for regional growth is bound up with the *national context* of the beneficiary regions. National idiosyncrasies exert an influence on regional catching-up and in this respect are something of a handicap in some major states (Spain, France, Italy, UK), despite the fact that the reasons are not the same in every case: industrial decline in the UK affects all that country's regions; in Italy, the relative decline of the old industrialised regions in the north is associated with an absence of catching-up in the south, the upshot being that Italy's dynamic energy is concentrated in its north-eastern regions. In France, the polarisation favouring the Ile-de-France area remains a handicap for all too many regions. In Spain, the virtues of European integration were felt initially in already relatively prosperous regions. When the national context is neutral or positive (this is the case for Portugal and Greece, whose coefficients for national context are positive, although not truly significant), the Structural Funds can act to full and unimpeded effect.

A more detailed econometric study of the years 1989–97, covering other factors in regional development, comes to similar conclusions.[11] It incorporates additional factors: innovative activities in the regions concerned, as assessed by the yardstick of the percentage of the national workforce engaged in research and development; their potential for the dissemination of technology as measured by the initial level of GDP; supplementary factors influencing the capacity for this dissemination, such as long-term unemployment, the relative contributions of agriculture and industry to total employment, population density and data on infrastructure (km of road per km^2). It then can be seen that the Structural Funds have a positive effect on regional growth, but not a significant one. If national context is left out of account, the effect on growth of the Structural Funds does, however, begin to look more significant (twice as high as when the impact of the national level is taken into account). The nation-state does therefore seem to be impeding the effectiveness of EU structural policy.

[11] See Cappelen, Verspagen and Fagerberg (2000).

5   Factors explaining the limited effectiveness of the Structural Funds

The European Structural Funds are thus of limited effectiveness in correcting regional divergences, despite the fact that this is their stated aim. They do not simply redistribute financial resources but set out to act positively on the factors in regional development. Such an assessment casts doubt neither on the microeconomic effectiveness of the projects financed from the Structural Funds, nor on their macroeconomic effectiveness – quite the contrary, since several recent studies confirm the positive impact of the Structural Funds on the growth and the ability of the less developed states in the European Union to catch up with the others.[12] It simply demonstrates that possible microeconomic or macroeconomic success is not automatically synonymous with benefits for the development of disadvantaged regions. For example, when a project financed from the Structural Funds improves local productivity, it is not certain that the allocation of the relevant productivity gains will in the end benefit the geographical area directly involved in the project.

In explaining the partial and disappointing effectiveness of the Structural Funds where regional development is concerned, the nature of the economic and institutional relations between the different levels of the Union, the individual state and its regions is relevant:

• The distribution of the Structural Funds may not be taking sufficient account of the *European geographic dynamics* which needs to be interpreted at transnational and territorial level.[13] The integration of a region within the changing geography of European networks does in fact highlight the advantages and disadvantages specific to that individual region. The unequal development of the regions which may result is part of the overall dynamics of European growth. A region's development relates to the roles played by national context and that region's specific advantages compared with the other areas of the European Union. Specifically territorial factors (geographical location, proximity to Europe's centres of activity, externalities between neighbouring regions) contribute to those advantages.[14] If it is the case that the interaction of European and national dynamics does not guarantee equality of opportunity between the regions, EU structural policies need to take account of that fact.
• Considerations of *efficiency* may encourage limitation of the primary redistribution associated with the Structural Funds. Certain regions

[12] See Cour and Nayman (1999), De la Fuente and Domenech (1999).
[13] An argument developed in chapter 7 in this volume by Robert Villeneuve.
[14] See Quah (1995).

with wealth close to the EU mean receive fairly high levels of structural funding because it is expected that support for their development will drive national growth and growth in less developed regions. A more redistribution-directed allocation of structural funding would attenuate regional inequalities spontaneously, but it might also hold back collective growth.[15] Indeed, the stated aim of certain components of the Structural Funds (notably Objective 2, which relates to restructuring of regions suffering from industrial decline) is to counter the decline of regions which may have hitherto been relatively prosperous. Although its effectiveness is far from guaranteed, such action is legitimate. An exaggerated egalitarianism in intra-EU redistribution would ratify the decline of old industrial or rural regions that were once wealthy. Conversely, the practice of co-funding, based on the additionality rule, appears to attenuate the redistributive character of European funds to some degree. The level of such national co-funding, expressed as a ratio to EU fund input, is usually seen to rise along with the wealth of the region.

- *Ex post*, the funding allocated to *poor regions or regions in decline* may benefit even more those regions in the same country that are rich or dynamic, because it is the market supply from those regions that will meet demand financed by European funds, or because the development of infrastructures in poor regions benefits producers in more favoured regions, who can then market their products more easily.

- The setting up of projects financed by Structural Funds and the allocation of funds between projects sometimes involve *tortuous interaction* between regional, EU and national institutions. Programme definition, implementation and monitoring are often highly centralised activities in Member States. The management of the Structural Funds is insufficiently decentralised to take account of the reality of regional dynamics. In France, for example, DATAR and the regional préfets, whose activities are part of a programme of de-concentration rather than decentralisation, play key roles.[16] In countries with more decentralised traditions, institutional practices could be hardly any more effective. In Germany, combining national and European funding is virtually a monopoly of the ministries of the economy in the *Länder*, which operate at the interface between regional, national and EU policies. In addition, the tight bureaucratic linkage between the *Land* and federal levels generates a strong tendency to compartmentalise fund allocation, to the detriment of a 'bottom-up' approach and intersectoral co-ordination of regional policies taking due account of regional capacities.

---

[15] See for Spain, De la Fuente and Vives (1995).
[16] See, for an example, chapter 6 in this volume by Pierre-Paul Zalio.

Despite the fact that they co-finance the programmes, regional governmental administrations take a back seat where their definition and management are concerned. The official line talks in terms of co-operative partnership and additionality of funding, seeing regions very much as subjects of the Union. Despite this, actual practice remains dominated by national organisations which have difficulty in perceiving the lines of force in the geographical dynamic, precisely because that dynamic is strongly determined by factors at a European, or even wider, level. The quality of the co-ordination between EU, national and regional bodies determines the effectiveness of the Structural Funds.

6   Conclusion

The fact that the nation-state is now a very imperfect organisation for the correction of internal imbalances should be used as an argument for redistributive and regional policies of a more integrated kind at EU level. The simultaneously unified and heterogeneous character of European space is a durable feature and that same heterogeneity will increase with the accession of new members from Eastern Europe. It would seem to be difficult to guide the dynamic of European heterogeneity in the absence of appropriate procedures at EU level, given that it is to some extent at that level that the dynamic originates. An *inequality of opportunity* prevails between the regions of Europe, which no doubt stems from their intrinsic advantages and handicaps, but it is also the result of the way in which they are integrated into the European geography and it is possible to modify this. In other words, equality of regional capabilities has to be searched for in regional policies at the European level.

Consequently, it seems reasonable to envisage the maturation of more ambitious mechanisms for redistribution between European regional areas, or even between individual European citizens – i.e. progress in the direction of redistributive European budget. It is also reasonable to move toward a more integrated territorial policy at EU level, along the lines of the INTERREG cross-border programmes, which take more explicit account of geographical imbalances when allocating Structural Funds. Today, the whole range of programmes supported by the Structural Funds resembles too closely a series of *negotiated sectoral interventions*. Better transnational co-ordination of regional policies could strengthen the effectiveness of EU polices in the area of regional convergence. For this reason, what needs to be promoted at EU level is a logic based on interterritoriality.

In accordance with a logic of decentralisation and as the Committee of the Regions (CoR) has emphasised, it becomes necessary to closely associate the territorial governments, the involved actors of the private sector and the non-governmental sphere, in the implementation and monitoring of programmes financed from the Structural Funds, in order to develop regional capabilities.[17] The aim would be to promote collective projects conducive to the empowerment of individuals active in private enterprise or not-for-profit associations, even if not elected. Local and regional governments could, for example, be signatories of the Single Programming Document. The management committees (including non-elected actors) for programmes could be empowered to take decisions relating to programme management, including modifications made necessary by social and economic conditions in the regions.

More generally speaking, thinking structural policies through in the light of the new European economic geography is a challenge to *institutions*: the task must be to think out a mode of regional governance that will make it possible to avoid the negative integration that stems from competition between the most dynamic regions, to go beyond the issue of efficiency and to create positive integration based on the improved interfacing of the various institutional levels. In the most dynamic regions, the setting up of partnerships is the best way of defining appropriate strategies for growth and creating networks that can exert a positive influence on European growth. In the case of the most disadvantaged regions, what is essential is to improve co-ordination between the EU and regional levels and to build horizontal partnerships between territorial areas. The balance of power within the European Union would in this way evolve towards a multi-leveled governance.

Such institutional aspects determine the consequences of a major part of the spatial and thematic concentration of Structural Funds, as confirmed by the Berlin summit in the Spring of 1999, for the programming period 2000–6. The number of objectives has been reduced from five to three:

- catching-up by regions whose development is lagging (regions whose *per capita* GDP is less than 75 per cent of the EU mean)
- Support for conversion programmes in regions undergoing radical change
- Development of human resources.

The population covered by regional objectives, equivalent to half the total population of the EU, would then be closer to one-third, despite the transitional smoothing measures introduced by the Berlin summit. If this increased concentration goes hand in hand with improved efficiency, the

---

[17] See chapter 5 by Serafino Negrelli and chapter 4 by Martin Heidenreich in this volume for examples of such involvements.

beneficiaries will not only be those who receive the funds, but the entire Union. The combination of more decentralised management of the funds and of the definition of an integrated regional policy could contribute to that outcome by encouraging a better balance between concerns for solidarity and efficiency. Reinforcement of the concentration of the Structural Funds, by hardening the eligibility criteria, risks only triggering a zoning policy – i.e. an accurate split in eligible areas (down to urban districts!) – which could undermine the concerns of global efficiency, without being an especially democratic procedure. While subsidiarity has a role to play in regional and structural policies, we may wonder whether the European Union is able today to do without a more effectively integrated regional policy, so that the partnership and additionality rules lead genuinely to a more balanced consideration of European geography. Marrying integration to decentralisation is a requirement which tackles deep-rooted habits of the nation-states.

REFERENCES

Armstrong, H. and R. W. Vickerman, 1995. 'Convergence and Divergence among European Regions', *European Research in Regional Science*, 5

Beine, M. and F. Docquier, 2000. *Croissance et convergence économiques des régions, théorie, faits et déterminants*, Brussels, De Boeck

Boldrin, M. and F. Canova, 2001. 'Inequality and Convergence in Europe's Regions: Reconsidering European Policies', *Economic Policy*, 32, 207–253

Bradley, J., 2000. 'Policy Design and Evaluation: EU Structural Funds and Cohesion in the European Periphery', in F. den Butter and M. Morgan (eds.), *Empirical Models and Policy-Making: Interaction and Institutions*, London, Routledge

Cappelen, A., B. Verspagen and J. Fagerberg, 2000. 'Regional Convergence, Clustering and European Policies', Paper for the Regional Science Association World Congress 2000, Maastricht Economic Research Institute on Innovation and Technology

Cour, P. and L. Nayman, 1999. 'Fonds structurels et disparités régionales', *Lettre du CEPII*, 177, 1–4

De La Fuente, A. and R. Domenech, 1999. 'The Redistributive Effects of the EU Budget: An Analysis and Some Reflections on the Agenda 2000 Negotiations', CEPR Discussion Paper, 2113

De La Fuente, A. and X. Vives, 1995. 'Infrastructure and Education as Instruments of Regional Policy: Evidence from Spain', *Economic Policy*, April, 11–54

Fagerberg, J. and B. Verspagen, 1996. 'Heading for Divergence? Regional Growth in Europe Reconsidered', *Journal of Common Market Studies*, 3, 431–448

Fuss, C., 1999. 'Mesures et tests de la convergence: une revue de la littérature', *Revue de l'OFCE*, 69, 221–250

Midefart-Knarvik, K. H., H. G. Overman, S. J. Redding and A. J. Venables, 2000. 'The Location of European Industry', *Economic Papers* 142, European Commission

Puga, D., 1999. 'The Rise and Fall of Regional Inequalities', *European Economic Review*, 49(2), 303–334

Quah, D., 1995. 'Regional Convergence Clusters across Europe', CEPR *Discussion paper*, 274

Quarella, S. and G. Tullio, 1998. 'Economic Convergence of Italian Regions: The Role of Organised Crime and of Public Expenditures, 1960–1993', University of Brescia, June, mimeo

10   Sketching European social dialogue freehand

Emmanuel Julien

(EU)

I 30

In memoriam Stellan Artin.

1   Introduction

On 28 November 2002, UNICE, UEAPME, CEEP and ETUC adopted a *Work Programme 2003–2005* comprising nineteen actions as a 'useful contribution to the European Lisbon Strategy and to preparation for enlargement'. But European social dialogue has long been involved in governance without knowing it. Since the adoption of the White Paper on governance,[1] the most serious introspective exercise ever undertaken by the Commission, observers who have habitually tended to be sceptical have understood the path-breaking role that European social dialogue has played since the 1980s.

The European Council in Laeken on 14–15 December 2001[2] granted the European social partners three seats as observers to the 'Convention composed of the main parties involved in the debate on the future of the Union'. This sounds very much like the supplementary, and logical, recognition by States of the altogether particular role played by UNICE, CEEP and ETUC. This co-operation led, in a satisfactory way, to a reinforcement of the authority invested in these actors in the 'Draft treaty establishing a Constitution for Europe'.[3] These actors appear to have passed all the stages of acquiring full legal legitimacy, which confers a major responsibility upon them.

Has social dialogue achieved autonomy? Will European social dialogue be successful in avoiding the pitfalls of constructivism? What is the governance needed for social dialogue in the EU process? What body of law is available to the actors? This chapter will attempt to answer all of these questions.

[1] EC (2001f).   [2] SN 300/01 ADD 1, 14 and 15 December 2001.
[3] CONV 850/03, 18 July 2003, Articles 47, 104.4, 105 and 106.

2   Has the European social dialogue acquired autonomy?

There is no need to review the history of European social dialogue.[4] Suffice it to recall that from the first joint opinion on employment on 6 November 1986, to the joint contribution for the European Year of People with Disabilities, the European social partners have adopted forty-eight texts, including three agreements transformed into Directives. And yet, for some observers (fewer and fewer), European social dialogue is not at its full capacity because it is struggling with insufficient autonomy. At this point, some distinctions must be made.

In negotiation phases the autonomy of the EU social dialogue is nearly optimal. It is subject to no major constraints, whether financial, administrative or legal. Recognition of the stakes introduces a degree of uncertainty, notably if no agreement is reached. But as Stellan Artin, former director of the defunct Swedish employers' confederation SAF, remarked at the conference on the European Social Model organised by the Dublin Foundation (10–11 September 2001): 'in order to negotiate, there must be a mutual uncertainty as to what will happen if the parties fail to agree.'

Furthermore, after having achieved an agreement, the autonomy of Social partners to choose the way they will implement it has no formal equivalent anywhere in the world. Article 139.2 of the Treaty establishing the European Community (TEU) reads as follows:

Agreements concluded at the Community level shall be implemented either in accordance with the procedures and practices specific to management and labour and the Member States or, in matters covered by Article 137 [social competencies], at the joint request of the signatory parties, by a Council decision on a proposal from the Commission.

Not only do the social partners choose the form of implementation they deem most relevant, if they request validation from the Council the latter is not authorised to modify the terms of the agreement.

By contrast, it is true that the social partners are driven by an 'urge' for autonomy when it comes to setting priorities. Contesting the right of initiative conferred upon the Commission by the treaties is out of the question. But the capacity of the social partners to together gauge the significance of the stakes must be developed, independently of the political project outlined by the Commission or the Council. The Commission's decision to adopt the Social Policy Agenda,[5] then the eponymous decision by the European Council of Nice six months later with a slightly different content, can be interpreted as a sign of the intent to take back the lead from the social partners, and direct their work.

[4] See chapter 11 by Jean Lapeyre in this volume.   [5] EC (2000b).

The national or regional context has often been invoked to hasten or slow down social dialogue, or both at once. No one can deny that the context is important. But how can more light be cast on this debate?

'I demand that before all else man learn to live, and use history only in [the] service of life thus learned', wrote Nietzsche in the second of his *Untimely Meditations*, an indictment of the excesses of the historical prism in Germany in the 1870s. 'The sense of history, when it can reign unbridled and draw all the consequences of its domination, uproots the future, because it destroys illusions and deprives existing things of the atmosphere that surrounds them and which they need to survive.' 'When the sense of history no longer preserves life, but mummifies it, then the tree dies, and it dies in a way that is not natural, starting with the branches and moving down to the root, so that the root itself also ultimately perishes.'

The obsession with national cultures and practices might have been the downfall of European social dialogue if the latter had not acquired its autonomy with respect to the past. In taking on the task of prolonging the existing situation, in opting to be the advocate of conservatism, social dialogue might have missed the boat. In the wake of the adoption of its first autonomous work programme, the task at hand continues to be to focus its thinking on the social aims, tools and solutions for tomorrow. In acquiring functional autonomy European social dialogue is little by little acquiring the intellectual autonomy that alone will allow it to steer its course. It will be a long haul.

Social partners experience their autonomy in relation to other actors every day. This autonomy is exercised with respect to EU institutions and with respect to civil society. This more operational form of autonomy is nearly complete; the social partners possess it under the terms of the Treaty, and strengthen it each time they exercise their responsibility. Social dialogue is also autonomous with respect to itself, because it proceeds at several levels that are not systematically articulated.

Some observers, unfamiliar with employers' structures, do not understand that UNICE refrains from giving instructions to its members . . . or to its non-members like branch organisations! It seems too early to conclude in this regard, because any scheme suggested would unfailingly copy the traditional scheme praised by observers: articulated multi-level negotiations (company/sectoral/national). But will the European Union of tomorrow, covering several million km^2 and a population of several hundred million people with significant differences in purchasing power, political and social organisation, really need an articulated collective bargaining system to manage advances acquired at the EU level?

Even if Europe were to find this scheme necessary, its form would remain to be determined. It is doubtful that the solution would be all that similar to those adopted in countries with strong cultural cohesion. For this reason, it is obvious that social dialogue should be able to emerge on different topics, within variable perimeters, with unequal coverage and even differences in benefits reflecting degrees of performance. It is up to elected public authorities to find democratic trade-offs, establish the bounds of public order, build the foundations and outline the shape of solidarity. In a political space as vast as the European Union the rest will have to be grounded in local action, to avoid another political crisis and increasing disorder in the wake of blurred responsibilities.

In our performance-oriented societies, it is the capacity for concrete achievement, its role in constructing a project larger than itself, that gives legitimacy to a segment of civil society, as much its representativeness. Social partners have a good degree of concurrent representativeness in the Union; they must now merit the confidence that the States have shown in granting them legislative powers. In a fairly short span of time European social dialogue has already set up a decision-making process, and has tested it in a number of ways. It would be risky to underestimate this progress.

3   Finding a contractual space avoiding constructivism for Europe

The European Commission thinks, a bit too loudly, that idleness is the mother of all vice. Fighting inch by inch against the States' appetite for revenge, especially since the Maastricht period (1992), echoing public opinion in Europe that is imaginary but, luckily, avid for new rights, administering a superstructure that has not yet recovered from the departure 'by invitation' of Jacques Santer, the Commission belches forth proposed directives as others run kilometres after kilometres without any apparent effort. It assures the social partners of its 'balanced support',[6] but practises textual harassment, pursuing, above all, its own satisfaction. As for the other party, it is summoned to respond to the unvarying instruction: *negotiate or wait for the directive.*

We were told that this blackmail was due to the ongoing practice of feet-dragging, a UNICE speciality. The accelerated pace of social dialogue since 2000 amply contradicts this statement, all the more as the increasing engagement of UNICE in social dialogue has not given businesses any advantage, since it was intended only to avoid the worst solutions. Signing agreements with trade unions hinges on the presence of an

---

[6] Article 138.1 of the Treaty stemming from the European Council of Amsterdam.

implementation clause, called a 'non-regression' clause in the jargon, which by definition prohibits any reform.[7]

The Supiot report (Supiot 2001) solicited by the Commission and first published in 1999, aimed 'to conduct a prospective and constructive survey on the future of work and labour law within a Community-wide, intercultural and inter-disciplinary framework'.[8] This report, although it is the only high-quality European study on these issues, goes quite far in the direction of constructivism. While the regulatory community should turn its attention to any new social object, ostensibly to protect workers, it is also necessary to elaborate 'a framework for observation and evaluation which is suited to economies which are becoming structured by a requirement of flexibility in a context of uncertainty'. 'Certainly it is a challenge of European social dialogue to find an agreement on this framework'. The thinking that follows this suggestion is not without relevance, nor without menace: there is no change in society that does not require a 'framework', no social dialogue to which third-party intellectuals may not submit their programme and even the criteria of observation of reality must be agreed upon between social partners!

The Commission is aware that the accumulation of proposals is damaging for its credibility, and even for its neutrality. The habit has therefore developed in recent years of submitting questions to groups of experts where people keen on regulating (trade unionists, academics, politicians, etc.) are structurally in the majority, even if the group is diversified. These groups release excellently crafted reports, but more often than not they lead to proposals for regulation.

The Veil report on free circulation of individuals, the Davignon report on *European Systems of Workers' Involvement*, the Gyllenhammar report on the economic and social implications of industrial transformation[9] are all illustrations of the Commission's attempt to bolster the legitimacy and the expertise of its proposals by calling upon outside 'high-level' personalities to formulate them. By arranging for the rapporteurs of these groups to be persons close to the Commission, the latter also managed to keep control of their content.

European social dialogue is at all times funnelled into this channel: required to construct to prevent (inevitably unbridled) liberalism from allowing isolated businesses to cut loose their social obligations. Constructivism has three features:

---

[7] See for instance clause 6 in the agreement on part-time work (EC 1997b).
[8] Supiot (2001).   [9] Issued in March 1997, May 1997 and May 1998, respectively.

- a *universal standard*, because no one should be deprived of its benefits
- the answer to an *immediate problem*, even a temporary or isolated one
- a *restriction of competition* because the latter is pernicious.

Because the standard must be universal, the only option is social dialogue leading to formal agreements. Because politicians believe that they are subject to the scrutiny of public opinion for the least of their acts – which no doubt relativises in their eyes the shortcomings of their primary missions – the standard must latch onto the convulsions of current events and extend their application to all the actors in the economy. From this point of view, European constructivism is a close rival to similar national practices, even if the sense of urgency is sometimes justified.[10]

The desire to restrict the field left open to competition via social legislation is an ongoing problem in the European Union. The social empowerment approach could be a much more interesting alternative, but it requires a total change of paradigm on the part of the Commission, from a law-based standard to a tool-based standard (see section 4 below). There is some evidence, however. In December 1996 a directive on the freedom to propose services was adopted, listing the areas in which outside workers must benefit from the same conditions of employment as local workers.[11] This intelligent scheme does not harmonise levels of protection; it establishes equal treatment for a limited number of working conditions. Competition is thus given free play, on the understanding that a company cannot pay a foreigner less than the minimum wage simply because the worker is a foreigner. The same holds for paid annual holidays, maximum working time and so forth. Going any further would have impeded competition, which is allowed to play freely on aspects that are not fundamental to the employment relationship.

Neither directives or social dialogue should serve as a backup force in a grand attempt to restrict and, ultimately to impede any competition in the market. If all employees' rights were defined at the European level there would be nothing recognisable left, as in Balzac's short story *Le Chef d'œuvre inconnu*, where only a hand emerges in the painting which the hero madly strove to perfect.

4   Advancing from social dialogue to contractual governance in Europe

The alternatives can be summarised in a binary fashion to identify the main forces which, like tectonic plates, cause shifts in the European social

---

[10] For example in health matters, foreign policy, or the common security and defence policy (ESDP).
[11] 96/71/CE, 16 December 1996.

dialogue. For businesses, the aim of the European social dialogue is to create a European labour market. The Commission quite rightly adopted a communication entitled *New European Labour Markets, Open to All, with Access for All* which is too little known.[12] For labour unions, the aim is clearly the elaboration of a European statute for employees. The talks on temporary employment that failed in the early Spring of 2001 clearly showed how much importance ETUC placed on the notion of 'comparable worker' and on the need for a single intangible definition of the so-called 'user company' and the 'temping agency'.

European social dialogue remains fragile, despite its importance; it brings into play antagonistic strategies which are still too dependent on the initiatives of the Commission. The Commission's method of pressuring partners to negotiate is logical for an institution that has to prove its usefulness and renew its project in the view of other Community institutions. But this practice cannot establish confidence.

Fortunately, the Commission is a complex world that leaves no room for caricature. It was the instigator of an enlargement of the scope of open co-ordination. According to the Commission, in its Agenda, 'open policy co-ordination involves *establishing policy guidelines, setting benchmarks, concrete targets and a monitoring system* to evaluate progress via a peer group review'. This is not politically insignificant, because open co-ordination has been incriminated as being a threat to legislation. Behind this reproach lies a failure to understand the essence of the European construction process: moving into new fields, changing tools, working around obstacles. Three major changes are also underway that will make open co-ordination indispensable in the very near future:

• the European Union's entering into globalisation and the entry of ten new countries in 2004
• the growing resemblance between the Union and a political confederation (currency, ESDP, 3rd pillar, etc.)
• the proliferation of comparative social policies on social protection, pensions, etc.

The social partners do not seek to encompass all of social life, in particular those practices that might up to now have escaped the attention of a distracted or overwhelmed legislative branch. Restricting the reference framework for social standards to Europe alone would leave it in solitary confinement in a global world.

First of all, social dialogue will widen the palette of tools made available. This is an underlying movement linked to the interdependence of issues,

---

[12] EC (2001b).

the diversity of needs and players, the complexity of markets. Although the text is awkward to use, the European firm statute, the first optional directive, is one of these interesting initiatives.

Secondly, the achievements of the European social dialogue are increasingly relevant. It is capable of assigning itself the issues that employees and businesses alike feel deserve treatment or oversight at the European level. It shows an original approach not only in the choice of issues, but also does so upstream of EU institutions and, as the case may be, in a different way from them. Finally, the functional link between the social partners and the Commission must eventually be loosened up, so that autonomy of outcome is matched by autonomy of *process*. Following adoption of the 2003–5 work programme, this is largely the case *de facto*.

The value of the Laeken declaration on the 'specific role of the social partners in European governance' lies at least as much in the conditions under which it was adopted. The joint declaration of 31 October 1991 had been adopted at the instigation of the Commission, and implemented via three communications from the Commission in 1993, 1996 and 1998.[13] The text drawn up by the social partners for the European Council in Laeken was echoed shortly thereafter by a communication from the Commission.[14]

But many ambiguities remain in the Commission's behaviour. For the EU institution, social dialogue 'constitutes a driving force for economic and social reform' (see EC 2001c), but when there is a contradiction between trade unions and employers, as over temporary work, the Commission defends a 'protector's' *point of view* and not a 'reformer's' point of view. We have already seen (see Supiot 2001) that the social dialogue itself finds it hard to take on this role in agreements. What is really new with the social dialogue in Europe is its methods and outcomes, on the one hand, and a model for a regulatory framework on the other hand.

This movement must not be interpreted as shifting problems up to the European level: general competency must remain 'down below' and attributed competencies stem from more concentrated levels (country, sub-region, Europe). Furthermore, this opening should in no way prefigure a mutualising of norms. I would regret it if Europe were to regress morally by being too quick to sweep away all 'western' thought on the responsibility of the individual, from Epictetus and St Augustine, since the seventeenth-century debate on grace or Immanuel Kant's 'practical reason'. Just as politics is sometimes reduced to the quest for power, so it would be unfortunate if the action of social actors in Europe in favour of solidarity were assimilated solely to the forced collectivisation

---

[13] EC (1993b), EC (1996), (EC 1998).   [14] EC (2002a).

(by law) of resources and expenditures, whether this law be contractual or legislative.

5   Conclusion: promoting a useful law, a law as a tool

True governance requires clear strategies, responsible and empowered players. The lack of progress towards a political Europe brings the Commission and the social partners together. The architecture of the European system does not belong to a specific actor, as shown by the Charter of Fundamental Rights adopted by the European Council of Nice, a major text which will very quickly reveal its importance, in spite of its grey areas, illusions and shortcomings. But if the Commission and the social partners reach a *modus vivendi* on social Europe, then genuine governance can be reached.

This chapter has focused on cross-sectoral European social dialogue because UNICE has a direct role at this level, but it goes without saying that by extension the same applies to all social dialogue, as defined in section 1. These instances could hardly be left out of true governance. It seems to me that dialogue at the sectoral level, to mention this instance only, raises more problems, given certain specific obstacles (differing perimeters between sectors in different countries, absence of sectoral dialogue in certain countries, varying degrees of corporate concentration in each sector, conflicts between negotiating points in different countries, etc.). Consequently governance must be aware not to create conditions leading to uncontrolled standardisation, and regression of democracy.

In its communication on quality[15] the Commission refers to 'modernisation of social policies.' The focus was on benchmarking national employment policies by means of indicators, a recommendation also found in the conclusion of the high-level expert group (see below). The business community, which has experimented with many performance measurement tools, can approve this approach only if it is grounded in a common desire, shared by States and EU institutions, to reform national rules. But this is doubtful, as the exercise might substitute for actual reform. But a new and instructive method of EU action may emerge, if the process does not degenerate into hidden and harmful bureaucracy.

In the same way the high-level group set up by the Commission to investigate *Industrial Relations and Change in the European Union* attempts to explore new pathways. According to this report, 're-regulating [*sic*] labour markets' has come about as a result of the single currency. It is therefore appropriate that 'a new agenda for industrial relations should

---

[15] EC (2001c).

be developed at all levels'. A year and a half after adopting the Social Agenda, the Commission is thus in the throes of a new bout of constructivism. Fortunately, the scope of this text is limited to identifying stakes and reporting on the most interesting experiences. It contains ambiguous phrases, however, that cannot fail to arouse suspicion that the Commission would like to take back control of the issues of the social dialogue, under the pretext of new methods.[16]

Is it reasonable to continue elaborating social initiatives that will impact the future of companies and employees, in the secrecy of expert groups or Commission departments? Do these procedures not lead to a conformist, that is to say a traditional, vision of law? Are the advocates of the public social order inherited from the 1970s and 1980s the best placed to design law-as-a-tool which businesses and individuals will be able to find as levers they can use, and not a prescription for behaviour?

Firms need European action frameworks, but they also need legal tools to get around in them. If frameworks (fiscal, social, financial, technical, etc.) have undeniable binding force, the European Union has done very little to explore optional tools. These give guarantees and possibilities for action, but their use remains optional. I am naive enough to think that they will serve better if the time and way to use them are freely chosen. We are approaching the societal responsibility of business, around which the Commission is still seeking its role as a regulator, after its Green Paper.[17]

The Commission would like to share the role of regulator with the social partners, not only with respect to labour law, but also, and increasingly, with respect to open co-ordination groups, in particular for employment (for a 'strong commitment by social partners', see n. 19). In the co-ordination of economic and social policies in Europe, where the Commission is an invaluable driving force, the latter is still tempted to use the social partners as its instruments to gain support when confronting the Council. Recent texts from the Commission clearly reveal this desire, which employers' organisation and trade unions are not and will not be able to fulfil in any substantial way.[18] Indeed, they focus on their core businesses, and that is hard enough, without attending to areas in which public authorities must assume their own responsibilities. Herein resides all the ambiguity, in addition to the positive aspects, of the expert group on employment instituted by the Council in 2003.[19]

---

[16] 'an efficient procedure to identify recommendations which promote interesting trade-offs.' (p. 8).

[17] EC (2001e).   [18] EC (2002c) and EC (2003a, n. 18).

[19] European Task Force on Employment, chaired by Wim Kok, European Council in Brussels, 21 March 2003.

Social dialogue is moving forward on the following topics: lifelong training,[20] telework[21] and restructuring, along lines that have not been formally adopted at the time of writing.[22]

Initiatives from social partners, European, national and local, are accelerating at all levels. They aim to address European issues in which competitiveness and business needs are at stake. These documents provide topics for action, sources of inspiration and networks. Actors at all levels are stimulated and urged to act, and mechanisms are available to measure their contribution so as to expand on the best practices without creating a bureaucratic process or a legal or contractual obligation. Social partners, for their part, ask only to take the place which is theirs, and in so doing contribute to the general interest. Since the mid-1990s social partners have travelled in the dark, cleared an opening and marked out trails in the maze of European institutions, between economic competition and social policy.

REFERENCE

Supiot, A. (ed.), 2001. *Beyond Employment. Transformation of Work and the Future of Labour Law in Europe*, Oxford, Oxford University Press

---

[20] Following through on the *Framework of Actions for the Lifelong Development of Competencies and Qualifications* (14 March 2002).

[21] Following through on the *Framework Agreement on Telework* (16 July 2002).

[22] *Reference Orientations for Managing Change and its Social Consequences*, finalised in a social dialogue meeting on 13 June 2003.

(EU)

11 The fourth dimension in collective bargaining and social co-operation

Jean Lapeyre

JS2

J08

1 Introduction

The history of social dialogue and of management – labour relations in Europe is an odd story. Some would even say that the very idea of a social model and social dialogue in Europe is a miracle, or a mirage, when we have so many different systems and situations in the fifteen member countries. And yet this model exists and the dialogue is there, although all is not perfect, Community social policy is far from sufficient to address the issues at hand, and Europe-wide collective bargaining is quite modest, whether at the inter-branch or sectoral levels.

Collective bargaining practices are different in the Member States of the European Union, but far from being a handicap this diversity is a resource derived from over 100 years of varied but converging history and social cultures.

In certain countries such as Spain, France, Belgium and Italy bargaining takes place at different levels – national and confederal, federal and sectoral and locally in companies. In other countries, such as Germany, regional sectoral negotiations are predominant, but the first agreement reached in a region (the *Land*) serves as a reference for other regions, whence the importance of a national federal strategy. In other countries, such as Great Britain, company-level bargaining is the general rule.

Whatever the culture of negotiation in a country, three dimensions are present: national, sectoral and company level within its territory. With the construction of Europe a new dimension has emerged – the Community dimension, which brings an added value to bargaining without copying any one country's culture.

With the agreement reached on 31 October 1991 the two partners in industry – management and labour – went from being lobbyists to taking on the role of actors in the implementation and standardisation of the social dimension of the European Union. The inclusion of this agreement, with just two words changed, in the Maastricht Social Protocol and then in Articles 138 and 139 of the Treaty of Amsterdam thoroughly secured the status of actors in the construction of Europe for the social partners. This status was once again fully recognised by the Member States at the Laeken Summit, where management and labour were allotted three seats as permanent observers at the Convention that prepared the upcoming revision of the Treaty and outline aspects of the future European Constitution.

Thirteen years after this agreement, and eighteen years after Jacques Delors launched the social dialogue, in light of the experience acquired, the problems encountered and changes registered, it is now important to review the role of the social partners in the new context. Social dialogue and co-ordination can even better meet the challenges of attaining economic and social cohesiveness, anchoring the enlargement of Europe and its future in a world of globalisation based on greater fairness and solidarity.

2   A short history of social dialogue

It was in 1985 that Jacques Delors, President of the Commission, launched the European social dialogue by bringing together two management organisations (UIECE for private sector employers and ECPE for public and publicly funded entities) and a labour organisation, ETUC.[1]

Three stages marked the development of this social dialogue.

- The first stage, from 1985 to 1989, was a period of initiation and apprenticeship between actors who had to learn to understand each other: a Swedish employer does not necessarily or automatically understand a Greek trade unionist. In order to move towards negotiations of a European scope, all the participants must first comprehend each other's systems. From this stage emerges a common language, and an understanding of subsidiarity that allows principles to be established at the European level, while leaving broad national autonomy for implementation.
- The second stage began in December 1989 with the adoption of the Community Charter of the Fundamental Social Rights of Workers and a Social Action Programme which, thanks to the qualified majority vote (QMV) introduced by Article 118A of the Single European Act (SEA), rekindled the Commission's social legislation initiative which had long been blocked by the principle of unanimity. ETUC, which had always wanted to see a contractual dimension to social dialogue, introduced

---

[1] UIECE is the Union of Industrial and Employers' Confederation of Europe; ECPE is the European Centre of Enterprises with Public Participation and of Enterprises of General Economic Interest: ETUC is the European Trade Union Confederation.

the idea of a social partners' contribution to Treaty reform as a way to open a negotiated regulatory space. The employers then realised that the 'neither/nor' policy (neither legislation nor negotiation) was a Maginot line, and that if they did not want all regulations to be imposed by law they would have to accept negotiations on a European scale.

This second stage came to an end in December 1991, when the Social Protocol of the Maastricht Treaty was adopted. This protocol restated the social partners' agreement reached on 31 October, identifying them as actors in the regulatory process, requiring the Commission to consult them and enabling suspension of legislative initiatives during negotiations on a given point. Furthermore, an agreement reached by the social partners can receive an *'erga omnes'* (of general application) legal validation from the Council, upon proposal by the Commission. This was a 'revolutionary' step in the social dialogue.

- The third stage spans the period from 1991 to the present, with the 'enactment' of European negotiations. Three confederation-level agreements have been reached and have become European law, pertaining to parental leave, part-time work and fixed-term employment contracts. Negotiation at the sectoral level has also become a reality, with agreements on working time in rail, maritime and air transport. This third stage has seen some failures, owing to the employers' inability to open talks (on information and consultation, for instance) or to the breakdown of negotiations, as occurred after over a year of talks on temporary employment.
- The third stage should now pave the way to a fourth stage that will establish a competency for negotiation independent of the Commission, as well as a competency for national and sectoral implementation. Talks on teleworking have been undertaken in this new framework, and will represent a formidable test of credibility for the social partners. While the outcome, if successful, will not be made legally binding by virtue of validation by the Council, it will be contractually binding for the signatories and their components at the national level.

3   Background and framework of European collective bargaining

The European Social Dialogue, more than just a space of peace and democracy, is framed within a model based on three main values:
- *Economic and social cohesiveness* which, via the structural funds, aims to achieve development in all regions of Europe, specifically by compensating for existing structural inadequacies and through the role played by public services and more broadly services in the general public interest which facilitate access for all citizens to quality services, in

particular education and health care. Highly interesting and productive work on drawing up a European charter for general-interest entities and on a project pertaining to 'territorial excellence' has been done by ETUC with ECPE, which represents public, publicly funded and general economic interest firms.

- *Solidarity*, which will promote convergence of social contexts and avert the risks of 'social dumping' by establishing a groundwork of social rights. Solidarity will also be manifested in the preservation, modernisation and extension of basic social protection in qualitative and unitary terms, rather than individual measures, even if complementary systems are allowed to develop.

- *Good management/labour relations* as the most economically and socially effective way to anticipate and handle industrial and technological change and social progress, through collective bargaining. It should be pointed out right away that European collective bargaining cannot exist if it is not rooted in the rich soil of national and sectoral negotiations. Europe represents added value, stemming from the trans- and supra-national nature of the problems arising from the construction of Europe. The objective is to avoid the risks of social dumping on the one hand, so that monetary convergence does not give rise to social divergence, and to take full advantage of the potential of the European Union on the other, to benefit employment and improve working and living conditions for European workers. These are the only ways to inspire confidence among workers in this new and decisive phase of the construction of Europe.

4 A time for clarification

Since 1990 the numbers of forums, forms, instances and actors involved in consultation and dialogue have considerably grown, most often under the heading of 'social dialogue' which has become a miscellaneous grab-bag.

The contribution sought by ETUC and negotiated with UIECE/ UEAMPE and ECPE for the Laeken summit (2001) comprised the following objectives:

- Highlighting the specific and necessary role of *social partners* in structuring the social dimension of Europe in its economic development for the creation of high-quality jobs that respect the environment
- Clarifying the forums for *bilateral social dialogue, and tripartite and institutional consultation*, to better organise dialogue and consultation forums to make them more effective and improve their synergy
- Establishing a more pro-active and autonomous method of *contribution*, better co-ordinated with EU strategy

- Organising the move to truly autonomous management of social dialogue by setting up a *pluriannual work programme* for the social partners and creating a permanent secretariat in liaison with the Commission
- Clarifying the *forums for social and civil dialogue* to ensure that they are complementary.

(UEAMPE is the Union Europeénne de l'Artisanat et des Petites et Moyennes Entreprises.) Apart from the idea of setting up an independent secretariat for social dialogue, which UIECE still finds premature but which we are sure will progress, ETUC was successful in setting out this contribution which was taken into consideration by the Heads of State and Government at the Laeken Council presided over by Belgium.

It can also be emphasised that in their area of responsibility, the social partners' role and contribution is fully in line with the principles guiding new European governance framed by the Commission in July 2001.

The White Paper proposed increased participation of stakeholders, and in particular of civil society. It is thus all the more important to distinguish in this civil-society ensemble the areas which come under the responsibility and role of social partners and those of NGOs.

The growing debate over the importance of civil society must not lead us to confuse and weaken different forums for dialogue, but on the contrary to give them synergy based on areas of responsibilities specific to each one. There cannot be confusion between social dialogue and civil dialogue. The legitimacy and representativeness, the nature of responsibilities and the capacity for contractual commitment are not the same. The social partners have a specific role and capacity for intervention recognised under Articles 138 and 139 of the European Union Treaty.

In various and sundry ways ETUC already has quite a bit of experience in co-operating with NGOs in a context of joint thinking and action or in the new framework of developing corporate social responsibility. The first full-scale action was a joint ETUC/social NGOs' campaign on the theme 'Europe and large-scale solidarity' in 1994. This was followed by focused campaigns with the European Forum for the Handicapped, the Federation of Homeless Shelters and in particular with the European Platform of Social NGOs for the elaboration of the Charter of Fundamental Rights of Citizens. A joint campaign was conducted, leading to a first albeit limited, success, the Nice Charter decision.

ETUC is working on setting up connections and co-operation between different forums for dialogue and action, in order to reinforce the social dimension of the Union. The enlargement makes it even more urgent to involve social partners and NGOs to a greater degree, and anchor the fundamental rights of citizens in the Treaty.

5   Challenges and objectives for the European Union

The Union continues to face a need for better growth that creates more jobs. The economic slow-down and the risk of recession highlight a timid policy on the part of the ECB, obsessed with inflation and budgetary and monetary discipline, while neglecting the action needed to stimulate growth. Whatever criticisms one may have of American policy, at least the Federal Reserve Bank is not a one-eyed Cyclops like the ECB, but has two attentive eyes, one on currency and the other on growth and employment. True economic co-operation between Member States is having a hard time getting off the ground, undermining exploitation of the growth opportunities created by the implementation of the single currency.

Restructuring and redeployment of economic and industrial activities raises the issues of capacity for anticipation and social management to prevent social exclusion and avoid making the territories involved poorer. Technological and organisational changes imply constant upgrading of qualifications and skills, and therefore require that lifelong training be integrated into investment for and organisation of work.

Demography and advances in health care are driving changes in our social protection systems to enable them to continue to guarantee a fundamental solidarity, in an approach that Delors defined with the expression 'change without disowning'. Equality of treatment and equal opportunity for women are still very much current concerns, and the fight against discrimination must be renewed. Reconciliation of family and career, and a more equitable sharing of tasks between women and men, are aims that must lead to cultural and social changes.

In this framework, a new approach to the question of time in general, encompassing both working time and free time, means organising our social lives differently, but also reorganising work and the community. ETUC is thinking about how to move from a situation in which we work roughly 70,000 hours during our working lives, to a total of 50,000 hours, incorporating time accommodating all sorts of life events: working time, training, gradual retirement, parental leave, sabbatical leave, periods of voluntary part-time employment, etc.

The Lisbon Strategy under which the Heads of State and Government decided to follow an economic and labour marketplace policy designed to develop a knowledge society, and qualitative as well as quantitative full employment, is a major reference and starting point for Community policies. Indeed, new Community economic and employment policies have been developed since the mid-1990s. The Employment Title included in the Treaty and the process which ensued after the

Luxembourg Summit had established employment guidelines, were completed by the Cardiff process on structural reforms and the Cologne process for macroeconomic dialogue with ECOFIN and the ECB. These processes have been pursued in various and unequal ways in diverse places and periods of consultation.

The Heads of State and Government decided in Lisbon to integrate the entire economic and employment approach via an annual Spring meeting. The reform of the Standing Committee on Employment, however, did not lead to similar integration of social consultation until now, and thus the social framework no longer meets the demand for coherence and synergy between the different processes in which the social partners are involved.

6   Restructuring the forums for social consultation and dialogue

6.1   Social consultation

ETUC has proposed replacing the Standing Committee on Employment with a Consultation Committee on Growth and Employment that is to be the ongoing management instrument for the full range of macroeconomic and employment consultation processes. The macro and employment dialogues would pursue their own activities under this framework of reference and would issue opinions according to the timetable of the important regular encounters – adoption of economic orientation guidelines and meetings with ECOFIN, the ECB and the Economic and Financial Committee (Article 114), and of employment guidelines and meetings with the Employment and Social Affairs Council, the Employment Committee and the Social Protection Committee under the Council. This work would be integrated by the Co-ordinating Committee which could subsequently prepare an overall contribution for the Council of Heads of State and Government, at a major annual Spring pre-Summit meeting.

6.2   The forum for interbranch and sectoral social dialogue

The term 'social dialogue' originally known as the 'Val Duchesse social dialogue' is used in a great many ways, referring to multiple combinations of participants and situations. The qualitative evolution of social dialogue, both interbranch and sectoral, has fostered among the social partners a greater aspiration to take on a more autonomous leadership of this dialogue.

Thirteen years after the agreement of 31 October 1991, it is time to adapt this social dialogue to the new context and to the new challenges it faces, by achieving greater implication of national employers and labour leaders and by giving a new impetus to the dialogue. The Commission will naturally remain an active partner in this reorganisation process.

An annual Social Dialogue Summit, bringing together all the directors and general secretaries of national and European employers and trade union organisations, in an encounter driven by ETUC, UIECE/UEAMPE and ECPE, could focus on two aims:

- *Formalising joint contributions* and investing them with a greater commitment to implementation at the national level
- Setting up a *pluriannual work programme* for social dialogue, co-ordinated with the European Social Agenda and the employment guidelines.

This summit would create a Steering Committee to implement this work programme.

It is necessary to establish an autonomous 'social agenda' for the social partners. Autonomous does not mean disconnected from the general European strategy. On the contrary it must contain the elements of the social partners' specific contribution to this strategy, complementary to the objectives and guidelines fixed by the EU Member States. Furthermore the Union's Social Agenda assigns to the social partners certain objectives to be attained in the framework of a horizontal subsidiarity. Using a broad range of instruments, from talks to negotiate agreements to the open co-ordination method focusing on common objectives, the Social Dialogue should achieve wider results faster.

A autonomous Permanent Secretariat would be set up, established by the Council and supported by the Commission. It would be made up of permanent delegates seconded from European bodies representing the social partners, to administer the activities of social dialogue. The task of leading the social dialogue could be supplemented later with a task pertaining to joint training for employers and trade unionists in collective bargaining at the European level. The unfortunate demise of CERI, for which ETUC failed to find stable funding, should not lead us to let this very fruitful experience fall by the wayside.

Setting up an autonomous Permanent Secretariat along these lines would also provide a push for 'internal' evolution encouraging European organisations to 'Europeanise' their cultures and actions.

6.3   The sectoral dimension

Mastering industrial and technological change and organisation of work and working time are crucial components of the transnational European sectoral dimension, and can engender a vast domain of social dialogue and negotiation. Anticipating and managing the restructuring and redeployment of economic activity within Europe implies possessing a mastery of information, consultation, participation and negotiation. The cases of Renault Vilvoorde, Levi Strauss, Michelin, Pirelli, among others, have demonstrated the importance of developing these capacities and thus of strengthening existing legislation, in particular law governing European Works Councils and mass redundancies.[2] The capacity for transnational trade union action has already grown considerably, looking at the ground gained between the inability to react at the time of the Hoover case, and the mobilisation of 50,000 protesters at Renault–Vilvoorde. The ETUC Transport Federation has also been able to lead European action in the road transport and rail sectors; ETUC has thus become a force for mobilisation. In November 1997 30,000 militants in Luxembourg were mobilised in a call for a strong employment policy, in March 2000 50,000 European militants gathered in Porto, in December 2000 70,000 in Nice and in March 2001 in Brussels there were close to 100,000 militants from twenty-three European countries. There, however, is still a long road ahead.

Coming back to the mastery of restructuring and economic change, it is equally important that the European Monitoring Centre on Change that has been launched in Dublin develops its activities rapidly, in order to identify trends, verify possible anticipatory measures and implement both quantitative and qualitative provisional employment management policies. This monitoring centre, launched under a tripartite management structure and in which sectoral social partners are meant to be particularly involved, would constitute an excellent way to nourish sectoral social dialogue. It is likewise absolutely necessary for legislation or a European framework agreement to be drawn up requiring firms to submit an annual report to worker representative bodies on foreseeable trends and changes within the company.

The sectoral domain is also that of European Works Councils (EWCs). Nearly 700 such councils have already been set up, out of the 1,822 companies involved. This amounts to some 20,000 militants at the company level involved in transnational trade union work. This is a challenge, principally in terms of training and logistical support, for the European trade union federations and for ETUC. It is not enough to have a mass of information from the European directorate of a corporation, one must also have the capacity to jointly understand that information across a spectrum of trade unionists from different countries in different situations. EWCs must therefore be provided with new tools for analysis and support.

---

[2] See chapter 2 by Claude Didry in this volume.

As mentioned above, the sectoral domain can also establish specific social standards. The negotiation of working time in maritime, rail and air transport illustrates this capacity, its outcome has been legally validated by the Council. The voluntary agreement reached in the agricultural sector and pertaining to working time, health, safety and vocational training should also be noted. There are already twenty-five sector-based social dialogue committees supported by the European Commission. These have achieved common results such as the code of fundamental rights in shoe manufacture, agreements in industrial cleaning, trade, building and construction work, etc. But we have to note that there is an unacceptable void in social dialogue in metallurgy, chemicals and public service.

A co-ordinated approach to wage policy and to collective bargaining agreements has also become an area of work for the European federations. The metallurgy workers in FEM, graphic artists in UNI-Europa, clothing and footwear workers in FETHC – not forgetting the regional space spanning Belgium/Germany/the Netherlands and Luxembourg – have elaborated positions and co-ordination procedures that follow on those drawn up by ETUC at its 1999 congress in Helsinki. Quantitative and qualitative guidelines for wage policies are set each year.

7   In favour of globalisation

Corporate internationalisation, clearly illustrated today by the mergers and acquisitions of multinational and transnational companies, gives them powers that States alone are no longer able to control – the fluidity of capital markets, choice of locations for activities, conditions of social management applied to workers indirectly or directly – all these escape traditional State regulation. The merchandisation of production of goods, and then services, notably cultural and social services, also gives companies the ability to influence and structure the cultural and ideological reflexes of societies.

A consequence of the power invested in multinational and transnational corporations is the need for regulatory innovation, and for more vigorous intervention on the part of the actors of civil society, at a time when States are losing their capacity for intervention and when democracy may be called into question.

The framework of globalisation underlines the need to impose rules of responsibility that will broaden respect for rights within companies in developing countries, so as to not export our bad practices and dangerous and polluting industries to regions where protection is weak or non-existent, where trade unions are attacked and democracy questioned, but instead favour social progress that parallels economic progress.

The failure at Doha to institute social and environmental standards in international trade agreements will weigh heavily in the future. Efforts will now focus on the capacity of the International Labour Organisation (ILO) to take on a leading role in this debate, and on the institution of instruments for the application and regulation of these fundamental rights. The Commission and Member States will now have to put all their weight into the balance to strengthen the ILO. They will also have to involve European social partners.

Europe can and should play a key role in global re-regulation, under a multi-dimensional strategy relying on the ILO and reinforced ILO policies. This capacity for re-regulation should also rely on a stronger role for social partners and their co-operation within geo-economic zones in order to globalise social justice. ETUC has already nourished this co-operation with Mediterranean and Mercosur trade unions. ETUC were also co-organisers of a trade union forum held at the Porto Alegre Forum in January 2002.

The challenge is not how to stop the expansion of world markets, but how to find the rules and institutions that can strengthen governance locally, nationally, regionally and world-wide, so as to ensure that globalisation has a positive impact for people, and not only for profits.

As has been so well put by Amartya Sen: 'Constructing globalisation will be the necessary answer to doubts about globalisation.'

12 The nature of the open method of co-ordination

Philippe Pochet

1 Introduction

Issues such as the struggle against poverty and social exclusion or pensions are now the focus of discussion and practices aimed at stepping up co-operation between the Member States, or even at applying the open method of co-ordination (OMC) to them.[1] In the name of the principle of subsidiarity adopted by the Treaty of Maastricht, they were previously essentially, if not exclusively, treated at the national or infra-national level, and not, other than marginally, at the EU level. Could OMC be the answer for the ideal implementation of subsidiarity?

We will begin by retracing various sources of influence that gave rise to the debates on the vertical and horizontal dimensions of subsidiarity. To this end, section 2 will reflect on subsidiarity's application to the social domain from the early 1990s.

In section 3, we will look at OMC, its development and whether it could be a suitable method for the implementation of subsidiarity. Conversely, we will examine to what degree OMC (as a principle of governance) may undermine the principle of subsidiarity (as a principle guiding the distribution of competencies).

To conclude, we will indicate in section 4 the possible impact of these developments on social dialogue and its actors.

I would like to thank Robert Salais (ENS-Cachan), Pascale Vielle (UCL) and Jonathan Zeitlin (University of Wisconsin–Madison) for their stimulating comments.
[1] To put it in a nutshell (a longer definition is presented in section 3), OMC is a flexible means of working via national plans, which are assessed in accordance with common criteria (indicators), to implement measures decided jointly at European level. Without legal compulsion in the strict sense, the means to ensure that governments adhere at national level to their European commitments is peer pressure (and the force of public opinion). To summarise in one sentence: OMC is an attempt to make official declarations made by Ministers at European level morally 'binding' at national level by the implementation of a set of complex procedures.

2   Maastricht and subsidiarity: a brief reminder of the debates of the early 1990s

The set of issues surrounding subsidiarity emerged at the beginning of the 1990s. In retrospect, its influence can be traced back to 1957 and the Treaty of Rome, which stipulates that directives should leave the choice of the means to be deployed to achieve the defined objectives to Member States. This is also the case for the principle of proportionality, which became one of the main guiding principles for the jurisprudence of the European Court of Justice (ECJ) in Luxembourg. It can also be seen as an integral part of the Spinelli project in 1984 for the adoption of a European Constitution by the European Parliament (EP).[2]

Nevertheless, the debate prior to and following the Treaty of Maastricht was conducted in a new environment, characterised by an incredible acceleration in European legislative regulation. In the wake of the adoption of the White Paper on the internal market and the Single European Act (SEA, 1985), no less than 300 directives were tabled (and adopted over the next few years). The President of the Commission, Jacques Delors, even declared that henceforth 80 per cent of national legislation would be of EU origin.

In the social domain, the adoption in 1989 of the Community Charter of the Fundamental Social Rights of Workers (a solemn declaration made without the UK) was accompanied by an action programme comprising fifty measures, 40 per cent of which were proposed directives (Pochet 1993, 2000). The social dialogue, which had been developing slowly following its inception in 1985, suddenly began to develop at a faster pace. The European social partners adopted a draft to replace Article 118a (old numbering – social dialogue), much of which was to be picked up in the Maastricht Treaty's Social Protocol. We should also recall that the EP regularly threatened to block single market legislation, if the social dimension was not to be developed. Various reports sought to define the main contours of the social dimension of the internal market or of a European social space. Subsidiarity appeared on the Community scene in the context of a debate on strong social regulation, based either on directives or on collective agreements between social partners.

We can distinguish at least three different definitions of subsidiarity, depending on their origin:
- The UK *Conservatives*, worried about the loss of sovereignty, came to see subsidiarity as an insurance policy against the encroachment of the Union and loss of national control. Since the word 'sovereignty'

[2] For more details on the European parentage of this principle, see Wilke and Wallace (1990).

was too strong, or had too many connotations at that time, the term 'subsidiarity' was agreed upon. As Commissioner Brittan said: 'an ugly word but a useful concept'. In this spirit, the principle applies only between the national state and the European Union and not between the national State and its infra-national components.

- The *German Länder* were keen to avoid encroachment by the European Union on their specific powers (poverty, education and the 'television without frontiers' directive were the detonators in this case) and wished to see the German system applied to the Union (notably through the drawing up of a list of competencies) (Schelter 1991). In addition to the German case, a number of regions also supported this approach since it would enable them to (re)negotiate with their central authority and would give them direct access to the EU level.

- Lastly, the concept of subsidiarity originated from the social thought of the *Christian world*. The specific influence of the social doctrine of the Catholic Church can be detected, the most notable manifestation of which is contained in the papal encyclical 'Quadragesimo Anno 1931'. Its definition of subsidiarity is worth recalling here:

We cannot take away from individuals to transfer to the community functions that those individuals are capable of carrying out on their own initiative and using their own resources. It would be an injustice and highly prejudicial to social order to remove from lower-level groupings functions that they can carry out themselves in order to transfer them to some larger, higher-level community.

These origins are obviously not all of equal importance. There is a gulf between the in-depth analysis to be found in the writings of various Christian philosophers (but not exclusive to them, see Millon-Delsol 1992) and the UK Conservatives' tactical use of the term. Nevertheless, the multiple origins and multiplicity of interpretations of the term 'subsidiarity' permitted it to crystallise such a consensus at this particular point in time. As seen on numerous occasions at the EU level, the ambiguity of words and expressions often favours consensus and subsequent progress. Remember the vagueness of the definition adopted in Article 5 of the Treaty, which reads:

The Community shall act within the limits of the powers conferred upon it by this Treaty and of the objectives assigned to it therein.

In areas which do not fall within its exclusive competence, the Community shall take action, in accordance with the principle of subsidiarity, only if and in so far as the objectives of the proposed action cannot be sufficiently achieved by the Member States and can therefore, by reason of the scale or effects of the proposed action, be better achieved by the Community.

Any action by the Community shall not go beyond what is necessary to achieve the objectives of this Treaty. (Principle of proportionality)

The notion of subsidiarity has been clearly adopted and developed as a political principle within the Union for the purpose of addressing issues relating to competences and their exercise, at both the level of the Member States and that of the European institutions.[3] In its interpretation of the principle of subsidiarity, the Commission has stated that:

It is for Community institutions to prove the necessity of Community legislation and action at the level of intensity proposed. This principle naturally works both ways ... For reasons specific to subsidiarity, examination of this principle cannot be disassociated from the content of the proposal or action. (EC 1992: 1)

In that particular context, the issue of legitimacy is an essential one; the assumption is that the actors at a given level are capable of shouldering their responsibilities collectively. Subsidiarity is conceived as a principle of proximity with the citizens seeking to enhance their participation on the basis of an ideal of democracy that is, if not locally-based, at least decentralised. The reason is that the European Union is perceived as a remote place where decisions do not (completely) adhere to the criteria entailed by broadly based participation. Various references are made to the necessity of bringing Europe closer to its citizens.

This principle is general in nature and can be considered as a procedure for governance. Nevertheless, it is in the social domain (along with the environmental domain) that it has most often been invoked (Spicker 1991; Begg *et al.* 1993). In its interpretation of the Maastricht Treaty, the Commission argued that the principle of subsidiarity should not be applied to the whole social domain, but should be used to examine each topic to determine which function – harmonisation, co-ordination, convergence or co-operation – would be the most appropriate, taking into account the needs and added value of the Community level.

From the social point of view, the principle of subsidiarity has had contradictory implications. Firstly, it has supported what is called 'horizontal subsidiarity' – that is, the division at the same level (in this case, the European Union) of responsibilities between social partners (or other organised groups) and the State (for State, read the Commission, Parliament or the Council). One interesting aim was to strengthen the capabilities of the European social partners (UNICE and CEEP for private and public sector employers, respectively, and ETUC, the European Trade Union Confederation) to act. In particular, a procedure for European collective bargaining has been created, which can result in European collective

---

[3] Subsidiarity has also given rise to more economics-focused approaches (such as, for example, that of the McDougall report in 1977) but these have hardly influenced the European debate at all.

agreements. Such agreements can take the form of directives, if request is made by the social partners (see Falkner 1998; Degimbe 1999, especially chapter X; Salais 2001). The use of this new possibility was not obvious for trade unions (Dølvik 1997). However, given that the social partners report back to their respective mandating organisations on the progress and outcome of the discussions, European social issues have become more integrated in national agendas. As a consequence, national implementation has become more dynamic in various Member States.[4] Secondly, the specific design of this pre-emptive right given to the social partners in the social domain, if they reach a mutually agreed-upon decision, has not been of unalloyed benefit. In other words, their primary entitlement to choose to enter (or not) into negotiations on all social topics has downgraded the EP to *second best*. The EP can act only when the social partners decide not to negotiate or if they fail to reach agreement.

The alliance between the ETUC and the EP that the employers' side (UNICE) feared was thus broken. Indeed, even today, the EP has not accepted this division of responsibilities. Secondly, the Commission has shifted from the role of an entrepreneur in the social sphere to that of a more self-effacing, less engaged and less supportive actor. It intervenes less directly in the unequal balance of power between the social partners (which does not mean that its more modest role is insignificant). Commissioner Flynn's White (1993) and Green Papers (1994) on Social Policy indicate a concern for open debate around the social question, but no ambition to regulate it. In this context, the number of legislative proposals shrank dramatically during the 1990s (Pochet 2000). The social partners, by contrast, have succeeded in adopting a collective agreement every two years (parental leave, part-time working, temporary work). This may appear to be very little at first sight, but these figures should be compared with the slump in the number of directives. The failure to reach an agreement on the issue of temporary agency nevertheless indicated that this joint regulation approach is in danger. It opened the way for autonomous agreements between the social partners on teleworking. It also contributed to the adoption of an autonomous work programme (2003–6) including twenty initiatives under three headings – employment, enlargement and mobility – most of them not binding.[5] It is in fact a real innovation, since for the first time the social partners have decided, autonomously, to take matters into their

---

[4] The social accord had provided for the possibility of implementing, via a national collective bargaining agreement on condition that it covered all workers.
[5] See chapter 10 by Emmanuel Julien and chapter 11 by Jean Lapeyre in this volume.

own hands. Until now, the agenda for the European social dialogue had always been drawn up under the shadow of the Commission. Having such a programme should mean that European social negotiations no longer move forward case by case, on the basis of political agendas – or, indeed, of short-term economic events. Three subjects emerged: employment, enlargement and mobility. These will be dealt with using various instruments, from European agreements to exchanges of experience, taking into account opinions, recommendations, etc. (Degryse 2003).

Horizontal subsidiarity has not rectified their asymmetrical relationship; this is because, except when genuinely threatened with legislation, UNICE has taken little interest in negotiating with the trade unions. Conversely, the latter calls for agreements but has no powers to force employers to negotiate. Employers retain a sort of a right of veto over progress on European collective agreements. Branch and Greenwood (2001: 43) underline that

although institutional forces, socialisation and learning have been important, the attitudes of UNICE towards social partnership and social dialogue are nevertheless instrumental. The shift in UNICE's position did not, then, reflect a conversion to a new philosophy. Instead, its attitude was one of 'realpolitik', namely a change in strategy in response to a change in political realities.

In addition, vertical subsidiarity has had the effect of reducing the number of proposals tabled by the Commission. Previously, the Commission had used the Treaty creatively by introducing certain proposals (on working time, pregnant women) on the basis of Article 118A (old numbering), which provided for qualified majority voting. Here, it is worth noting that the UK (unsuccessfully) attempted to have the directive on working time nullified by the ECJ in the name of subsidiarity.

Hence, a paradoxical situation has arisen in which the more powers the European Union has in the social sphere, the fewer directives are brought forward. This means that one cannot explain the weakness of the social dimension solely by the absence of a legal basis in the Treaty.

The ECJ has not become the supreme body for determination of the correct application of the subsidiarity principle. Moreover, the Court has not applied the principle of subsidiarity to itself (De Búrca 1997). This has led to a number of decisions, such as the *Barber* case (male–female equality for pensions) or the *Kholl and Decker* case (healthcare) extending the scope of the social domain (notably through the fundamental principles of free movement and competition rules). While the Court has played a crucial historical role in the development of European social policy (Leibfried and Pierson 1995), it also seems to have deliberately limited its power, never questioning the fundamental principles underlying the organisation of social security (on this point, see Bosco 2000). All of this reinforces our conclusion that the assessment of the European subsidiarity principle is of a political nature. As De Búrca (1999: 3) points out.

But it can also be more broadly understood as part of a language which attempts to articulate and to mediate, albeit within this particular geographical and political context, some fundamental questions of political authority, government and governance which arise in an increasingly interlocking and interdependent world.

It is interesting to observe that ten years later, in 2001, the debate has once again turned to identifying the areas that should be covered by non-traditional regulatory methods, such as OMC and those that should be covered by legislation. However, the order has changed. It is stated in the Social Agenda for 2001–6 adopted at the Nice European Council meeting that:

In the implementation of the Social Agenda all existing Community instruments bar none must be used: the open method of co-ordination, legislation, the social dialogue, the Structural Funds, the support programmes, the integrated policy approach, analysis and research.

At the very end of the negotiations, a phrase was added citing 'the need to take full account of the principle of subsidiarity' (European Council, 2000a: 14).

3 From subsidiarity to the open method of co-ordination

We will first describe the process towards OMC before considering to what extent OMC resembles or differs from subsidiarity.

3.1 Toward the open method of co-ordination

Whereas subsidiarity was a central issue in the early 1990s, a gradual dying down of the debate was then witnessed. There was an increasing focus on Monetary Union, parallel to a decline in the number of directives. The Treaty of Amsterdam (1997) was the pivotal point. In the Treaty, subsidiarity is addressed in the form of a protocol, which reproduces most of the Edinburgh Declaration of 1992, the latter clarifying the Maastricht Treaty's article on subsidiarity. A chapter on employment was added, that was considered later as the procedural template for OMC.[6]

[6] See chapter 8 by Gilles Raveaud in this volume.

As in the case of subsidiarity, it is possible to detect a number of influences and origins leading to the development of this method at Community level.

Firstly, part of the debate around subsidiarity dealt with the question of the appropriate forms of legislation, including the simplification of Community legislation.[7] This applied particularly in the economic domain (after discussion, the social aspect was excluded). The Best task force is a good example of this.[8] Initially, the idea of benchmarking was limited to corporate policy and factors for economic competitiveness. The idea of benchmarking performance then spread to other spheres, notably research and public authorities. In the social area, it can be considered that the 1992 recommendations on the convergence of systems on the one hand and on minimum resources on the other included most of the ingredients (regular reporting, evaluation, comparison, etc.) which were to ultimately make up OMC, but these elements were not backed up by any theoretical approach.[9]

The second influence, more general in nature, was a concern shared by many Member States, first on the types of regulation which should be adopted in a rapidly changing world, and, secondly, on the kind of democracy apt to favour the active participation of citizens beyond the traditional forms of democracy. At the EU level, this led to the drafting of a White Paper on governance and the beginning of in-depth examination by the Forward Studies Unit (see, for example, Lebessis and Paterson 2000).

The third influence came from the attempt to apply the approach that led to Monetary Union, (the convergence strategy), first to employment and then to social exclusion. From an *ex post* point of view, the Portuguese Presidency theorised such practices under the label 'open method of co-ordination', and this was picked up and enshrined by the conclusions of the Lisbon Summit.

OMC (European Council, 2000a: 10) is defined as follows:
- fixing guidelines for the Union combined with specific timetables for achieving the goals which they set in the short, medium and long terms;
- establishing, where appropriate, quantitative and qualitative indicators and benchmarks against the best in the world and tailored to the needs of different Member States and sectors as a means of comparing best practice;

---

[7] The developments in this debate can be followed in the Commission's Annual Report 'Better Lawmaking'.
[8] For more information on this go to http://www.europa.eu.int/comm/enterprise/enterprise_policy/index.htm.
[9] I thank Pascale Vielle for suggesting that I consult the 1992 recommendations.

- translating these European guidelines into national and regional policies by setting specific targets and adopting measures, taking into account national and regional differences;
- periodic monitoring, evaluation and peer review organised as mutual learning processes.

This method would never have been developed and applied so rapidly in various spheres (research, education, information society, etc.) if the various influences described above had not existed (see de la Porte and Pochet 2003). As for subsidiarity, the different versions of OMC have varying levels of depth: OMC can be seen simply as a technique (in the basic sense of the word 'method') or instead can be conceived as an effective procedure for achieving more democratic choice. The interpretation of the precise meaning of OMC will presumably follow an evolutionary path, as did subsidiarity.

3.2   Similarities and differences

It could be argued that OMC is an approach that takes subsidiarity further. In domains where competencies are shared between the Union and the Member States and in domains where the Union has little legitimacy to act, it can nevertheless allow action to be undertaken while respecting the principle of subsidiarity and applying the principle of proportionality. According to this thesis, and due to its flexibility, OMC is said not to compromise the capacity of Member States to regulate such issues as they wish, especially since the Commission's role is conceived more as a supporting agency than as an institution with a monopoly on initiative, as is the case with conventional legislation.

To address this issue in further detail, we need to look more closely at the possible impact of OMC. Does it include the idea of convergence or is it aimed at strengthening existing (intra-)national dynamics, while leaving Member States with the freedom to drive such dynamics? In the absence of unchallengeable empirical data, the future of OMC could be envisaged through three scenarios.

- In the first, OMC masks a *failure to act in the social sphere*, allowing all concerned to continue down their own paths, without paying any real attention to the Community. The 'open method' is then no more than a source of justificatory discourse, without the real social issues actually being addressed.
- The second scenario is that the open method will serve to *limit divergence*, or even bring about a degree of convergence in some cases. To some extent, this idea is defended by Ferrera, Hemerijck and Rhodes (2000), and Scharpf (2000). As there are several social models

(or groupings of Member States) within the Union, the function of the EU level is to provide a common umbrella that allows each country to move forward (or to 'modernise' to use EU jargon) while avoiding individualistic approaches conducive to social dumping (and non-co-operative game).

- According to the third scenario, the open method can lead to paradigmatic and ideational convergence. From this angle, OMC might be considered to have a much more important and real impact on national systems than regulation by directive.

These scenarios point to two issues where OMC (viewed as a principle of governance) could be expected to differ from subsidiarity (when defined as a political principle guiding the allocation of competencies). The first issue is precisely the distribution of competences, the second that of democratic participation.

If, as we have indicated, the principle of subsidiarity is intended to bring decision centres closer to the citizen and 'to delegate to a higher level only those tasks that it would not be possible to undertake at a lower level,' does this also hold for the open method? The principle of subsidiarity is based on the placing of the different domains to be addressed at each level into separate, more or less watertight compartments.[10] The higher level acts in last resort in order to offset, correct or support policies applied at lower levels. The open method is based upon the need to ensure flexible co-ordination between the various levels in order to solve complex problems of governance. Similarly, this approach to regulation tends to address each issue transversally (rather than to take each question separately in the way that they are often dealt with in specialised meetings of the Council of Ministers). OMC intends to establish links between, for example, research, education or training policies and budgetary policy. The re-enforcement of the European Council as a decision-making entity in final resort indicates a will to address issues and choices in a more open manner than before, at a time when ECOFIN has a monopoly on expertise and decisions. OMC has a 'horizontal' and a 'vertical' face, like subsidiarity. But, unlike subsidiarity, it tends not to separate out policies and levels, but rather to address their complex interaction.

Compared with the subsidiarity process, which involves the verification of competencies, then implementing them and undertaking proportionate action, OMC puts another type of sequence in place:

[10]   Some have argued for a less strict division 'Further, the subsidiarity principle has been misconceived as implying an allocation of power to either a higher or lower level . . . The solution might be to use the subsidiarity principle to delineate the respective advantages of each level and to promote collaboration between them, rather than assign exclusive jurisdiction to one or the other' (Bercusson *et al.* 1996: 65–66).

(1) Any policy can be dealt with using OMC
(2) Depending on the precise policy involved, the cursor will focus on a point between simple co-operation and full-fledged co-ordination (an appropriate form of proportionality)
(3) Once the process has been initiated, it is endless (or at least no end is explicitly considered). It is conceived as a repetitive exercise.

This repetition creates the conditions for its effectiveness (Goetschy 1999). The second issue relates to democratic participation.

In the Lisbon European Council conclusions, it was stated that 'the Union, the Member States, the regional and local levels, as well as the social partners and civil society, will be actively involved, using varied forms of partnership' (European Council, 2000a: 10). As pointed out by Telò (2002: 265), one of the architects of the OMC, 'if the actors of civil society are not concerned, consulted, involved at the level of partnership and negotiation, one of the aspects of the "openness" of the new method will be belied'. Maria João Rodrigues, who was the special advisor to the Portuguese Prime Minister Gutteres at the time of the Portuguese Presidency and played a key role in elaborating the OMC, explains that the word 'open' means different things and concludes by indicating that: 'Last, but not least, because the development of this method in its different stages should be open to the participation of the various actors of civil society. Partnership is a tool of modern governance' (Rodrigues 2001).

Where OMC is concerned, one might wonder whether (part of) the government or the technocracy is not endeavouring to use Europe as an external resource (see Ferrera and Gualmini 1999) to bring about the (social) changes it desires. For national elites, the implementation of Monetary Union at national level was undeniably a learning process for the use of Europe as an alibi for forcing through change at national level (see Dyson and Featherstone 1996; Dyson 2000; Martin and Ross 2004). Studies on the effects of monetary integration indicate that certain groups have enjoyed an extra advantage in exploiting European developments for their own benefit, in the absence of any democratic debate.

If so, OMC may be a cause of imbalance between institutional and social actors. By using (or being able to use), either explicitly or tacitly, the resources of an extremely complex European multi-level game, some are better placed to exert influence on the European agenda and to derive domestic advantage from it (see Kenner 1999 on New Labour).[11] Under

---

[11] As Helen Wallace (2000: 233) notes: 'National organisations that manage to get as far as Brussels generally find that they get a fair hearing. The problem is the gap between those that get to Brussels and those who do not. Part of the debate surrounding legitimacy and transparency stems from inequality of access to the Community's decision-making process.'

such circumstances, OMC is different from subsidiarity if subsidiarity is defined as empowering the actors at a given level to find the right solutions at that same level and if they are unable to do so, the level above taking over. Under OMC it is a matter of combining levels and facilitating broad-based participation: participation is allowed but is not compulsory, which explains the meaning of the word 'open' (in a sense, the adage 'the absent ones are always wrong' is accepted). There are no exclusive criteria for participating, as in the social dialogue. The capacity to understand and gain a foothold in the Community game carries more weight than representativeness.

The most striking development has been the role allocated to social partners in the European Employment Strategy (EES). Two levels can be distinguished. The first, and most general, is that their opinions at national level and their contributions (although to very variable degrees from one Member State to another) to the national formulation of the National Action Plans (NAPs) are better taken into account. The second aspect is more novel and consists of virtually delegating to them the implementation of their own Employment Strategy:[12] 'The Member States shall develop a comprehensive partnership with the Social Partners for the implementation, the monitoring and the follow-up of the Employment Strategy . . . The Social Partners at European level are invited to define their own contribution and to monitor, encourage and support efforts undertaken at national level' (EC, 2000c: 9). Until now, the results have been very modest indeed. The European employers' organisation UNICE has stated on several occasions that it has no wish for this type of involvement. Although UNICE has long supported self-regulation and can rejoice at European developments, it is also afraid of an uncontrolled process which could have unexpected results (see the emergence of the subject of quality in work). Moreover, employers consider modernising work organisation to be one of their managerial prerogatives. Some trade unions have thus feared that the process is nothing but talk and will have no practical impact, so why should they get involved? The main problem is to introduce into government documents a contribution managed by the social partners, who do not themselves have full control of the process.

To sum up, in the words of Zeitlin (2002: 3): 'Most Member States have sought with varying degrees of success to involve the social partner organisations more fully in the formulation of their National Action Plans (NAPs), though the very tight timetable and the bureaucratic rigidity of the procedure have remained continuing obstacles, along with disagreements among the parties over the objectives themselves.' Despite initial

---

[12] See an empirical study of this involvement for France (Raveaud 2001).

resistance, however, it appears that the trade unions have stepped up their participation, albeit to varying degrees from one country to another. The European Foundation for the Improvement of Living and Working Conditions has carried out a cross-national survey on the participation of social partners. In seven out of fifteen countries, the social partners have made a direct contribution to the NAP. Most often this is for the adaptability pillar, where the responsibility of the social partners is strongest. A high level of satisfaction of the participatory conditions is correlated with a direct contribution to the NAP in five out of the six cases, the exception being Denmark. It therefore seems that the level of satisfaction of the social partners increases with the quality – more active – of their participation (de la Porte and Pochet 2004).

A more developed conception of OMC would involve combining a European approach with national dynamics. In other words, there would be no sharp division between the European and national levels, but a true continuum extending from the local to the European level. This approach would preserve the principle of subsidiarity and the national forms of debate and collective preference, but in practice its application appears to be far from straightforward (de la Porte, Pochet and Room 2001). We can nevertheless observe that in order to remedy such imbalance between actors, the European Commission now funds the maintenance of European networks directly (under the programmes on non-discrimination or social exclusion, for example).

Finally, another difference is the absence of the ECJ and of any control of the process. As applied ideally, subsidiarity means that a high authority (judicial or political) is responsible for verifying that the principle is applied. In the case of OMC, it is extremely difficult to assess its actual influence on decisions taken at various levels. The mechanisms for reaching decisions remain relatively obscure, as do the guarantees of proper implementation.

4   Conclusion: what about social dialogue?

The shift in the debate from subsidiarity to the OMC, as an overarching principle, has caused all the institutional actors to re-position themselves. Basically, the question of subsidiarity ties in with reflections on a federal Europe with centralised actors, while OMC completes the perspective of multi-level governance with co-ordinated actors. In the wake of the Convention on Europe's future, the 2004 Intergovernmental Conference (IGC) will determine the model of European integration. Monetary Union tips the balance towards a more federal-style model, but enlargement fosters the perspective of an increased diversity, which should be managed more by co-ordination than by centralisation (Pochet 2003).

The shift from a debate on subsidiarity to one on OMC has entailed a redefinition of the positions of the social and institutional actors. This shift has taken place parallel to a serious crisis in the social dialogue and a lack of headway concerning qualified majority voting (QMV) in the Treaty of Nice (the long negotiations during the 2003 Convention for Europe's future have shown how difficult this topic is to resolve). The French Presidency's desire to have more European-level legislation has been supported by only a few Member States, and the 2001–6 social agenda makes provision for only a few draft directives. The asymmetry between the social partners in cross-industry social dialogue and European collective bargaining will not in future be offset by the Commission's capacity to brandish a credible threat of legislation. As for the sectoral social dialogue, the prospect of any real progress in the medium term remains limited (Benedictus *et al.* 2002).

The social dialogue has to find a new way forward. One, suggested by Bercusson (2000), is to regenerate the social dialogue from within the EES. This might be a means of reviving negotiated legislation.

Another, suggested by the high-level group on the future of industrial relations (2002), is to incorporate OMC into the social dialogue. This might be a way of achieving flexible legislation as in the case of the agreement on teleworking in the service sector. The autonomous social agenda between the social partners could be an illustration of this tendency.

We have demonstrated in this chapter that subsidiarity, which enabled the idea of negotiated framework legislation to develop, and OMC, which provides a framework for participation in redefining employment policy, are not merely synonymous. Each has its own logic and assigns different roles and objectives to the social actors. In one case it is a matter of forming European actors and signing framework collective agreements in fields with a recognisable European dimension. As for OMC, it is a matter of Europeanising national and regional policies, opening up the field for participation by a broad range of actors who must interact on several levels. The challenge is to 'redefine' the national social contract. These are clearly two different models, and thus far it is hard to see how they can be combined.

REFERENCES

Begg, D., J. Crémer, J.-P. Danthine, J. Edwards, V. Grilli, D. J. Neven, P. Seabright, H.-W. Sinn, A. J. Venables and C. Wyplosz, 1993. 'Making Sense of Subsidiarity: How Much Centralization for Europe?', *Monitoring European Integration*, 4, London, Centre for Economic Policy Research

Benedictus, H., R. de Boer, M. van der Meer, W. Salverda, J. Visser and M. Zijl, 2002. 'The European Social Dialogue: Development, Sectoral Variation and Prospects', Report to the Ministry of Social Affairs and Employment, Amsterdam Institute for Advanced Labour Studies, The Hague, December

Bercusson, B., 2000. 'The European Employment Strategy and the EC, Institutional Structure of Social and Labour Law', draft contribution at the workshop 'Legal dimensions of the European Employment Strategy', Brussels, SALTSA (a programme of partnership in European working life research run in Sweden), 9–10 October

Bercusson, B., S. Deakin, P. Koistinen, Y. Kravaritou, U. Mückenberger, A. Supiot and B. Veneziani, 1996. *A Manifesto for Social Europe*, Brussels, ETUI

Bosco, A., 2000. 'Are National Social Protection Systems under Threat? Observations on the Recent Case Law of the Court of Justice', *European Issues*, 7, Notre Europe, July, http://www.notre-europe.asso.fr/fichiers/Probl7-en.pdf

Branch, A. and J. Greenwood, 2001. 'European Employers: Social Partners?', in J. Compston and J. Greenwood (eds.), *Social Partnership in the European Union*, New York, Palgrave, 41–70

De Búrca, G. 1997. 'The Principle of Subsidiarity and the Court of Justice as an Institutional Actor', *Journal of Common Market Studies*, 36(2), 217–235

1999. 'Reappraising Subsidiarity's Significance after Amsterdam', *Harvard Jean Monnet Working Paper*, 7/99, Cambridge, MA, Harvard Law School

de la Porte, C. and P. Pochet, 2003. 'The OMC Intertwined with the Debates on Governance, Democracy and Social Europe', Research on OMC and European integration prepared for Minister Frank Vandenbroucke, Minister for Social Affairs and Pensions, April

2004. 'European Briefing: Existing Research and Remaining Questions', *Journal of European Social Policy*, 14(1), 71–79

de la Porte, C., P. Pochet and G. Room, 2001. 'Social Benchmarking, Policy-Making and the Instruments of New Governance in the EU', *Journal of European Social Policy*, 11(4), 291–307

Degimbe, J., 1999. *La politique sociale européenne, du traité de Rome au traité d'Amsterdam* (European Social Policy from the Treaty of Rome to the Treaty of Amsterdam), Brussels, ETUI

Degryse, C., 2003. 'Cross-Industry Social Dialogue in 2002: A Testing Year', in C. Degryse and P. Pochet (eds.), *Social Developments in the European Union 2002*, Brussels, ETUI, Observatoire social européen and SALTSA, 177–207

Dølvik, J. E., 1997. *Redrawing Boundaries of Solidarity's ETUC, Social Dialogue and the Europeanisation of the Trade Unions in the 1990s*, Oslo, FAFO

Dyson, K., 2000. 'EMU as Europeanization: Convergence, Diversity and Contingency', *Journal of Common Market Studies*, 38(4), 645–666

Dyson, K. and K. Featherstone, 1996. 'Italy and EMU as a "Vincolo Esterno": Empowering the Technocrats, Transforming the State', *South European Society and Politics*, 1(2), 272–299

Falkner, G., 1998. *EU Social Policy in the 1990s: Towards a Corporatist Policy Community*, London, Routledge

Ferrera, M. and Gualmini, E., 1999. *Salvati dall'Europa?*, Bologna, Il Mulino

Ferrera, M., A. Hemerijck and M. Rhodes, 2000. *The Future of Social Europe: Recasting Work and Welfare in the New Economy*, Oeiras, Celta editora

Goetschy, J., 1999. 'The European Employment Strategy: Genesis and Development', *European Journal of Industrial Relations*, 5(2), 117–137

Kenner, J., 1999. 'The EC Employment Title and the "Third Way": Making Soft Law Work', *The International Journal of Comparative Labour Law and Industrial Relations*, 15(1), 33–60

Lebessis, N. and J. Paterson, 2000. 'Developing New Modes of Governance', Working Paper, 2000, Forward Studies Unit, Brussels, European Commission, http://europa.eu.int/comm/cdp/working-paper/nouveaux_modes_gouvernance_en.pdf

Leibfried, S. and P. Pierson, 1995. *European Social Policy: Between Fragmentation and Integration*, Washington DC, Brookings Institution

Martin, A. and G. Ross, 2004. *Euros and Europeans: EMU and the European Social Model*, Cambridge, Cambridge University Press

Millon-Delsol, C., 1992. *L'Etat Subsidiaire. Ingérence et Non-Ingérence de l'Etat. Le Principe de la Subsidiarité aux Fondements de l'Histoire Européenne*, Paris, Presses Universitaires de France

Pochet, P., 1993. 'The Social Programme: Review and Assessment', Working Paper, 5, Observatoire social européen, May

2000. 'Le nouvel agenda social européen' (The New European Social Agenda), *Revue belge de sécurité sociale*, 4, 1059–1074

2003. 'Subsidiarity, Social Dialogue and the Open Method of Co-ordination: The Role of the Trade Unions', in D. Foster and P. Scott (eds.), *Trade Unions in Europe: Meeting the Challenges*, Brussels, PIE–Peter Lang, 87–113

Raveaud, G., 2001. 'La dimension européenne des politiques d'emploi françaises. Une analyse de la participation des partenaires sociaux à l'élaboration du PNAE 2001', Etude pour le ministère de l'Emploi et de la Solidarité, November

Rodrigues, M. J., 2001. 'The Open Method of Co-ordination as a New Governance Tool', *Europa Europe*, Special Issue, 2–3, Rome, Fondazione Istituto Gramsci, 96–107

Salais, R., 2001. 'Filling the Gap between Macro-Economic Policy and Situated Approaches to Employment: A Hidden Agenda for Europe?', in B. Stråth, and L. Magnusson (eds.), *From the Werner Plan to the EMU: A European Political Economy in Historical Light*, Brussels, PIE/Peter Lang, 413–446

Scharpf, F., 2000. 'Notes Towards a Theory of Multilevel Governing in Europe', *MPIfg Discussion Paper*, 00/5, Cologne, Max-Planck-Institute for the Study of Societies

Schelter, K., 1991. 'La subsidiarité: principe directeur de la future Europe' (Subsidiarity: A Guiding Principle for Future Europe), *Revue du Marché commun*, 344, 138–140

Spicker, P., 1991. 'The Principle of Subsidiarity and the Social Policy of the European Community', *Journal of European Social Policy*, 1(1), 3–14

Telò, M., 2002. 'Governance and Government in the European Union: The Open Method of Co-ordination', in M. J. Rodrigues (ed.), *The New Knowledge Economy in Europe: A Strategy for International Competitiveness and Social Cohesion*, Cheltenham, Edward Elgar, 242–272

Wallace, H., 2000. 'Some Observations on the Illusions of Institutional Balance and the Representation of States', in E. Best, M. Gray and A. Stubb (eds.), *Rethinking the European Union: IGC 2000 and Beyond*, Maastricht, European Institute of Public Administration, 209–217

Wilke, M. and H. Wallace, 1990. 'Subsidiarity: Approaches to Power-Sharing in the EC', *Discussion Paper*, 27, London, Royal Institute of International Affairs

Zeitlin, J., 2002. 'The Open Method of Co-ordination and the Future of the European Employment Strategy', Presentation prepared for the mini-hearing of the Employment and Social Affairs Committee of the European Parliament on the first five-year evaluation of the Employment Guidelines, 8 July

Part III

What politics of capabilities?

The purpose of part III is to draw out the main features of the capability approach. The overall issue is to study how public policies (whatever their level) provide actors (individual and collective) with the conditions, rights (substantial and procedural) and resources that enable them to effectively participate in the market and to secure their conditions of life. The capability concept has the potential to clarify the relationship between social rights and the market order, as expressed in the discourse of European integration (Jude Brown, Simon Deakin and Frank Wilkinson, chapter 13). Collective bargaining in new working conditions requires collective rights including access to information, and the capabilities to deliberate (Jean De Munck and Isabelle Ferreras, chapter 14). The welfare to work approach cannot properly address equality of treatment between men and women; true equality requires progress toward a capability approach (Jane Lewis, chapter 15). Building a framework of active security means modifying prevailing conceptions of welfare, away from compensating for losses towards providing individuals with capabilities (Noel Whiteside, chapter 16). Pierre Bachman (a social actor from the union side) makes the connection between the capability approach and the new type of "full employment" to be aimed at by the EU (chapter 17). Going further requires institutional innovations favouring democratic participation and deliberation of various intermediary bodies (civil, social and political). The political legitimacy of social Europe remains to be achieved. Incorporating the capability approach into employment and social policies through a renovated open method of coordination can help Europe to escape from political instrumentalism and to positively address social justice and economic development issues (Robert Salais, chapter 18).

13 Capabilities, social rights and European market integration

Jude Browne, Simon Deakin and Frank Wilkinson

1 Introduction

This chapter explores the potential for linking the economic notion of 'capability' to the juridical concept of social rights. The notion of capability which was developed first by Lancaster (1966) and then Sen (1985, 1999) in the context of welfare economics, has more recently come to prominence in the debate over European social and economic policy, as a result of its use in the Supiot report on the transformation of work and employment relations (Salais 1999; Supiot 1999). We will argue here that the particular importance of the capability concept lies in its potential to clarify the relationship between social rights and the market order, as expressed in the discourse of European integration.

We begin by revisiting T. H. Marshall's classic analysis of social rights and their ambiguous relationship to the market (Marshall [1949] 1992). We then introduce Sen's capability approach and discuss how far it provides a framework for locating social rights within a market setting. We argue that Sen's non-dogmatic, context-oriented approach to defining the meaning of capabilities offers a viable way forward for thinking about the current tension between market rights and social rights in the European Union. This argument is illustrated by reference to the role played by mechanisms of corporate social responsibility in promoting gender equality.

2 Social rights

'Social rights' are usually understood as claims on resources in the form of income, services or employment. In T. H. Marshall's classic and still influential formulation, social rights were distinguished from 'civil' and 'political' rights. Civil rights were 'rights necessary for the individual freedom – liberty of the person, freedom of speech, thought and faith, the right to own property and to conclude valid contracts, and the right to justice'. Political rights were characterized in terms of 'the right to participate in the exercise of political power, as a member of a body invested with political authority or as an elector of the members of such a body'. Social rights were loosely defined, but according to Marshall covered a wide range of entitlements 'from the right to a modicum of economic welfare and security to the right to share to the full in the social heritage and to live the life of a civilised being according to the standards prevailing in society' (Marshall [1949] 1992: 8; hereafter, 1992).

Marshall saw social rights as operating in tension with the market order. Civil rights were 'intensely individual, and that is why they harmonized with the individualistic phase of capitalism' (1992: 26). The social rights of the twentieth century, by contrast, displaced the market, at least to a certain degree: the process of 'incorporating social rights in the status of citizenship' involved 'creating a universal right to real income which is not proportionate to the market value of the claimant' (1992: 28). This gave rise to what Marshall called 'a basic conflict between social rights and market value' (1992: 42). Yet he also wrote:

Social rights in their modern form imply an invasion of contract by status, the subordination of market price to social justice, the replacement of the free bargain by the declaration of rights. But are these principles quite foreign to the practice of the market today, or are they there already, entrenched within the contract system itself? I think it is clear that they are. (1992: 40)

In *Citizenship and Social Class*, this claim was followed by a discussion of the evolution of collective bargaining, which stressed its dual nature as 'a normal peaceful market operation' which gives expression to 'the right of the citizen to a minimum standard of civilized living'. However, Marshall later concluded that whatever else the post-war welfare state settlement had achieved, 'the basic conflict between social rights and market value has not been resolved' (1992: 42).

It is clear that Marshall did not expect the courts to play a prominent role in achieving this resolution. The institutions Marshall associated most closely with social rights were 'the educational system and the social services' (1992: 8). He also suggested that in relation to the receipt of welfare services, 'the rights of the citizen cannot be precisely defined . . . A modicum of legally enforceable rights may be granted, but what matters to the citizen is the superstructure of legitimate expectations' (1992: 34). This was in contrast to civil rights which he saw as 'an eighteenth century achievement . . . in large measure the work of the courts'. In this respect, Marshall reflected the emphases of his own time: when *Citizenship and Social Class* was written (1949), social rights were almost invariably seen as the product of legislative action and, increasingly, of bureaucratic provision. The question of the potential juridical basis of social rights was not seen as a significant issue.

3   The origin of the concept of capability: Lancaster and Sen

The concept of 'capability', in the sense attributed to it by Sen, originates in debates within welfare economics. Lancaster (1966) was the first to draw a distinction between *commodities* and the *characteristics* of commodities. He envisaged consumption as an activity in which commodities, singly or in combination, are inputs and in which the output is a collection of characteristics:

A meal (treated as a single good) possesses nutritional characteristics but it also possesses aesthetic characteristics, and different meals will possess these characteristics in different relative proportions. Furthermore, a dinner party, a combination of two goods, a meal and a social setting, may posses nutritional, aesthetic and perhaps intellectual characteristics different from a meal and a social gathering consumed separately. (Lancaster 1966: 133)

Lancaster's paper essentially recast traditional consumer theory, in which utility (happiness or the fulfilment of desires) is the driving force of consumption, in terms of the utility derived from the characteristics of commodities rather than from commodities themselves. In *Commodities and Capabilities*, Sen (1985) adopted the idea that characteristics are the desirable properties of commodities, and that command over commodities may confer command over their characteristics. However, he took Lancaster's insight further by arguing that knowledge of the characteristics of goods does not tell us what a person will do with them. In judging the well being of a individual, it is therefore not enough to analyse simply the commodities to which he or she has access and the characteristics which they are capable of expressing. The *capability* of that individual to achieve a range of *functionings* with the commodity also has to be considered. Sen distinguishes between capabilities, functionings and characteristics by giving the example of riding a bicycle:

It is, of course, a commodity. It has several characteristics, and let us concentrate on one particular characteristic, viz. transportation. Having a bike gives a person the ability to move in a certain way that he may not be able to do so without the bike. So the transportation characteristic of the bike gives the person the capability of moving in a certain way. (Sen 1992: 160)

The sequence is therefore as follows: (1) the inherent *characteristic* (transportation) of the commodity (bicycle) is (2) converted into a certain *functioning* (riding the bike) thereby (3) enhancing the individual's over-all capability set. In this sense, the concept of capability reflects the various combinations of functionings that a particular person can achieve. In *Development as Freedom*, Sen (1999) offers this set of definitions:

the concept of 'functionings' . . . reflects the various things a person may value doing or being. The valued functionings may vary from elementary ones, such as being adequately nourished and being free from avoidable disease, to very complex activities or personal states, such as being able to take part in the life of the community and having self-respect . . . A 'capability' [is] a kind of freedom: the substantive freedom to achieve alternative functioning combinations. (Sen 1999: 75)

As a further illustration, Sen followed Lancaster in using the example of eating as both a nutritional and social activity. Thus:

The conversion of commodity-characteristics into personal achievements of functioning depends on a variety of factors – personal and social. In the case of nutrional achievement it depends on such factors as (1) metabolic rates, (2) body size, (3) age, (4) sex (and, if a woman, whether pregnant or lactating), (5) activity levels, (6) medical conditions (including the presence or absence of parasites), (7) access to medical services and the ability to use them, (8) nutritional knowledge and education, and (9) climatic conditions. In the case of achievements involving social behaviour and entertaining friends and relatives, the functioning will depend on such influences as (1) the nature of the social conventions in force in the society in which the person lives, (2) the position of the person in the family and in the society, (3) the presence or absence of of festivities such as marriage, seasonal festivals and other occasions such as funerals, (4) the physical distance from the homes of friends and relatives and so on. (1985: 17–18)

As these examples show, an individual's capability is to some degree a consequence of their *entitlements* – that is, their ability to possess, control and extract benefits from a particular commodity. An individual's feasible set of utilisation functions is therefore constrained by the limits upon their own resources. However, there are also non-choice factors affecting functioning – for example, an individual's metabolic rate which is a consequence of their physical state. The state of an individual's knowledge may also be a non-choice factor, although this can be improved by education. Here the element of choice may lie elsewhere, at the collective or societal level – that is to say, with policy-makers, government officials and judges. The same questions arise in the choice of commodities. Quite apart from the resources available to an individual, their capability to make use of a commodity may depend at a fundamental level upon access to a legal system which recognises and guarantees protection of contract and property rights.

Crucial, therefore, to Sen's capability approach is the idea of *conversion factors*. These are the characteristics of an individual's *person*, their *society* and their *environment* which together determine their capability to achieve a given range of functionings. *Personal characteristics*, in this sense, could include an individual's metabolism or their biological sex; *societal characteristics* could include social norms, legal rules and public policies (such as norms which result in social discrimination or gender stereotyping, or legal interventions to offset these phenomena); and *environmental characteristics* could refer to climate, physical surroundings, technological infrastructure and legal–political institutions.

4   Reframing social rights: institutionalising the capabilities approach

Sen's capability approach claims to offer a new way of assessing and evaluating legal, social, political and economic interactions. Individuals' well being and substantive freedoms are analysed through an examination of their capability sets, understood as their ability to maximise their potential functionings. An individual's capability becomes 'a set of vectors of functionings, reflecting the person's freedom to lead one type of a life or another' (Sen 1992: 40). Individual well being in the form of equality of capability is regarded as an 'end' rather than as an instrumental device for achieving another goal such as economic efficiency. Nevertheless, the capability approach is not a full theory of justice; Sen states that '[i]t is not clear that there is any royal road to evaluation of economic or social policies' (Sen 1999: 84). Rather, it can be used as an *evaluative tool or space* in which to assess individual's freedoms or potential. Sen's insistence that there is no universally applicable, prescriptive list of functionings and capabilities means that attention is focused instead on social choice procedures by which the content of capability sets can be collectively determined in particular contexts. The implication of this approach is that a procedure which aims at equality of capability should focus on the conversion factors which, in a given society, determine the conversion of impersonal and transferable resources, such as human and physical capital, into functionings and capabilities. The capability approach therefore offers a dual methodology: it aims, on the one hand, at a *set of metrics* for 'quality of life' within a diverse range of settings (such as the 'budget set' in the commodity space which represents an individual's freedom to buy commodity bundles, or the 'capability set' in the functioning space which reflects their freedom to choose from possible ways of living), and, on the other, a *normative framework* for judging particular institutional forms and policy proposals.

The idea we wish to pursue here is that social rights be understood as part of the process of 'institutionalising capabilities', that is to say, as providing mechanisms for extending the range of choice of alternative functionings on the part of individuals. In using capabilities in this way to re-orient the rationale of social rights, we may also come closer to achieving the resolution between social rights and the market order which was left unresolved by T. H. Marshall.

Sen sees capabilities as a consequence not simply of the endowments and motivations of individuals but also of the access they have to the processes of socialisation, education and training. These processes enable them to exploit their resource endowments. By providing the conditions under which access to these processes is made generally available, social rights may extend the scope of the market even if they do so, paradoxically, by interfering with freedom of contract. Thus laws protecting pregnant workers against unfair dismissal, which in neoclassical economic accounts are seen as distorting the operation of supply and demand in the labour market, may instead be serving a social good in terms of enhancing the incentives for women of child-bearing age to enter the labour market and invest in the acquisition of human capital. The passage of legislation may not, in itself, do anything to alter the employment opportunities of women. However, over time, as a consequence of litigation and publicity, laws of this kind may 'seed' social norms which overturn the conventions which lead to discrimination against women workers (for elaboration of this argument see Deakin and Wilkinson 2000). In this case, a social right operates as a *conversion factor* which seeks to enhance real choices for individuals.

An objection to the idea of social rights as underpinning the market is that social rights depend for their implementation upon the existence of a complex public machinery of taxation, redistribution and regulation. By contrast, civil and political rights appear to require nothing more than that the state refrain from interfering with private relations. However, there are good reasons for believing that this is a false distinction. The tradition in human rights law of the 'indivisibility' of civil, political and social rights is a reminder that all rights, whatever their legal form, depend for their mobilisation upon the existence of state machinery. The 'rights' protected by private law, which Hayek, following Hume, referred to as the 'stability of possession, of its transference by consent, and of the performance of promises', are not 'fundamental laws of nature' as Hume claimed (see Hayek 1976: 140), but the product of a certain process of institutional formation in which both evolution and design play a role. As Hayek himself understood (only for many of his latter day followers to ignore this essential point), the so-called 'spontaneous order' of the market rests upon rules of the legal system which cannot be said to have a spontaneous origin. These rules, just like those of social law, require the existence of courts, legislatures and enforcement agencies if they are to be effective. An activist state is one of the conditions for security of property and exchange.

It is also a mistake to see the mechanisms of social law as necessarily having a directory or mandatory character which robs the private parties of the opportunity for autonomous action. On the contrary, a large body of theoretical and empirical work has demonstrated the 'reflexive' character of modern labour and employment law – that is, its capacity to engender self-regulation and collective learning at the level of the social actors (see, in particular, Rogowski and Wilthagen 1994). More generally, the essence of social law in its distinctive western European form is not to be found in guarantees of particular levels of income or resources, but rather in the constitutional recognition of freedom of association and collective representation within a market economy which characterised the post-1945 settlement in a number of countries (Supiot 2003: 135).

This 'procedural' orientation of social law forms a bridge to the idea of a social choice procedure of the kind which Sen sees as providing the most appropriate basis for the achievement of equality of capability. In the particular context of the contemporary process of European integration, any such procedure is required to address the need to locate social rights within the logic of market integration. There are several ways in which Sen's approach might be helpful in this regard.

In thinking about social rights in a manner influenced by Sen, we may discern two categories of such rights: (1) social rights as immediate claims to *resources* (financial benefits such as welfare payments) and (2) social rights as particular forms of *procedural* or institutionalized interaction (such as rules governing workplace relations, collective bargaining and corporate governance). In relating to the first of these categories, we can think of social rights simply as claims to commodities which can then be converted by individuals into functionings or potential functionings (capabilities). The provision of sick pay, maternity pay, or social welfare benefits are social rights in a traditional, well-recognised sense. The second category of social rights is more subtle and links particularly closely to the idea of 'social conversion factors'.

The capability approach suggests that social or institutional settings shape individuals' possibilities of achieving their goals. Resources must be filtered through such frameworks as part of the process of enhancing functionings and potential functionings. Social rights, seen in this way as procedural rights, are the means by which to shape those institutional environments to ensure that all individuals are able to convert their assets – skills, capital – into positive outcomes. This works in both a direct and an indirect way. Directly, such rights can range from the provisions of anti-discrimination laws (which may aim at enabling ethnic minority workers to engage effectively in the labour market) to more indirect forms of intervention (such as the provision of assistance to women with children to enable them more successfully to strike a satisfactory work–life balance). More indirectly, the very existence of social rights can contribute to the development of a different social ethos or set of norms which may enhance individuals' functionings or potential functionings. A society which recognises a wide range of social rights is unlikely to be a society which possesses norms and expectations which create obstacles for particular groups of individuals to engage in lives that they have reason to value. At this level, the objective of public intervention through the legal–political system is to 'seed' social conventions to the extent that they are 'taken for granted' in the way that conventions of property and contract currently are.

Given that social rights can work in this variety of ways, they should be viewed as providing us with a central normative goal – equality of capability – which can then be seen to structure our conversation about social and economic policy, *without presupposing* any particular economic model or policy programme. This leaves open to further argument the particular form of social rights recommended by the capability approach. The capability approach is not in itself prescriptive about the mechanisms that should be employed to realise its goal and thus can be sympathetically disposed to a variety of *means* of ensuring capability equality, including direct state provision of resources, compulsory reshaping of institutions, or voluntary action to refashion widely held norms. The relative efficiency of the mechanisms is assessed through a context-dependent process of social learning, rather than being theoretically or dogmatically asserted. The capability approach is inherently non-dogmatic in asserting what rights individuals should possess at particular times and places. It encourages and enables a debate over the precise meaning of 'capabilities' in different circumstances, thus enabling a reflexive approach to the content of social rights in different circumstances, including in different economic and social situations.

This flexibility, of course, ensures that the capability approach may be more easily rendered compatible with a market model than other forms of social rights theory. In this way the capability approach and its form of social rights should not be seen as replacing or stifling market mechanisms but rather offering a framework for market-steering which results in better and fairer market transactions. Taking this point a step further, in so far as the capability does prescribe a particular overall goal, it is one that might be understood as inherently sympathetic to a market mechanism. This is because the capability approach concentrates not on guaranteeing that individuals possess a given set of resources but rather upon aiming to enable individuals to develop their capacity to be substantively free to make their own effective choices, thus enabling genuine and dynamic interaction in the market.

5   An illustration: the role of corporate social responsibility in European integration

To illustrate our argument, we take the case of corporate social responsibility (CSR) and its recent use in debates about the future development of European social policy. CSR was identified as an appropriate area for intervention at EU level at the Lisbon summit in March 2000, which stressed its links to the goal of building a 'dynamic, competitive and cohesive knowledge-based economy'. The Union is not alone in highlighting this issue: other prominent recent initiatives include the United Nation's *Global Compact* (adopted in 2000), the ILO's *Tripartite Declaration of Principles concerning Multinational Enterprises and Social Policy* (dating back to 1977, but updated in 2000) and the OECD's *Guidelines for Multinational Enterprises* (2000). In July 2001 the Employment and Social Affairs Directorate produced a Green Paper on *Promoting a European Framework for Corporate Social Responsibility* (EC 2001e) which pointed European corporate practice firmly in the direction of a stakeholder orientation.

The Green Paper defined CSR as 'a concept whereby companies decide voluntarily to contribute to a better society and a cleaner environment' (EC 2001e: 5). More precisely, 'companies integrate social and environmental concerns in their business operations and in their interaction with their stakeholders on a voluntary basis' (EC 2001e: 8). The Green Paper insisted, however, that CSR was not a pretext for deregulation: 'corporate social responsibility should not be seen as a substitute to regulation or legislation concerning social rights or environmental standards'. Instead, companies are encouraged to 'go beyond' compliance with existing regulatory controls, and it is argued that legislation is needed to supply a 'level playing field' on the basis of which improved practices can be developed (EC 2001e: 8).

At the same time, the Green Paper stressed the economic advantages of CSR for companies. Thus 'where corporate social responsibility is a process by which companies manage their relationships with a variety of stakeholders who can have a real influence on their licence to operate, the business case becomes apparent . . . [CSR] should be treated as an investment, not a cost' (EC 2001e: 5). Positive direct effects of CSR were thought of as including 'a better working environment, which leads to a more committed and productive workforce' (EC 2001e: 8), while indirect effects included attracting the interest of consumers and investors. The Green Paper noted the importance of strategies for attracting and retaining skilled workers, which included achieving greater workforce diversity and addressing issues of the work–life balance. Stress was also placed on health and safety and on corporate restructuring. Here, the Green Paper raised the theme of employee voice, stressing that restructuring can 'cause the motivation, loyalty, creativity and productivity of the employees to suffer' in the absence of 'procedures for information, dialogue, co-operation and partnership' (EC 2001e: 11). It went on to argue that '[s]ocial dialogue with workers' representatives, which is the main mechanism of definition of the relationship between a company and its workers . . . plays a crucial part in the wider adoption of socially responsible practices' (EC 2001e: 19), and made a reference to the important role to be played in this regard by the (then draft) Directive on Information and Consultation (EC 2001e: 20).

The Green Paper devoted much of its attention to issues of reporting and auditing of companies' social performance and to the implications for investment practice. A number of initiatives for social and environmental reporting advanced by legislation at member state level were discussed, along with standards drawn from industry practice and the involvement of non-governmental organizations (NGOs). It was suggested that 'the involvement of stakeholders, including trade unions and NGOs, could improve the quality of verification' of company reporting on the so-called 'triple bottom line' (social, economic and ethical performance) (EC 2001e: 19). On the investment side, the existence of social investment forums in the UK, France, Germany and Italy was noted. In this context, the Green Paper highlighted the need for standardization in the metrics used by socially responsible investment (SRI) practices. Against the background of the call made at the Stockholm European Council in 2001 to 'create a dynamic and efficient European securities market by the end of 2003', the Green Paper argued that 'European market indices identifying companies with the strongest social and environmental performance will become increasingly necessary as a basis for launching SRI funds and as a performance benchmark for SRI'. However, '[t]o ensure the quality and objectivity of these indices, the assessment of the social and environmental performance of companies listed in them should be done on the basis of the information submitted by the management *but also by the stakeholders'* (emphasis added).

The Green Paper began a process of consultation which eventually resulted, in April 2002, in the adoption of a Council Resolution on the follow-up to the Green Paper on corporate social responsibility.[1] In the manner characteristic of numerous initiatives in the social policy field dating back to the late 1980s, this instrument affirmed the linkage between 'a high level of social cohesion, environmental protection and respect for fundamental rights' with the aim of 'improving competitiveness in all types of business, from SMEs to multinationals, and in all sectors of activity'.[2] The role of the stakeholders in 'encouraging business to adopt socially responsible practices' was stressed, as was a particular role for 'the participation of workers and their representatives in a dialogue that promotes exchanges and constant adaptation'.[3] At the same time, there was a reminder that CSR 'must be understood as complementing regulations or legislation or norms on social and environmental rights, for which it cannot be a substitute'.[4]

For the time being, however, the concrete manifestations of the Union's CSR policy will be few. The Resolution envisaged the promotion of CSR in three areas: initiatives aimed at exchanging good practice; increased awareness of the impact of CSR on economic performance; and training of executives and workers in CSR issues.[5] The Commission was called on to issue a further communication incorporating the conclusions of the parties who responded to the Green Paper and to the debate which it stimulated, as well as to 'query carefully the added value of any new action proposed at European level.'[6]

It would nevertheless be a mistake to regard the Union's CSR initiative as mere window dressing. The agenda advanced in the Commission's Green Paper coincides with calls for greater shareholder activism within corporate governance. Active engagement with management on the part of institutional investors and others is seen as a principal mechanism for advancing an SRI agenda. This agenda is furthest advanced in the one country whose corporate governance system most clearly prioritises shareholder interests, namely the UK. During 2001 the Department of Trade and Industry (DTI) Company Law Review recommended a regime of greater disclosure by companies of information relating to issues of social and environmental responsibility, the 'operating and financial review', on the grounds that this would assist shareholders and other stakeholders in making better informed judgements on non-financial aspects of corporate performance (DTI 2001: 49–54). In addition, legislation requiring pension funds to disclose their voting policy and to state their position in relation to social, ethical and environmental investment

---

[1] 2002/C 86/03, *Official Journal*, 10 April 2002. [2] *Ibid.*, Article 11.
[3] *Ibid.*, Article 10. [4] *Ibid.*, Article 14.
[5] *Ibid.*, Article 17–19. [6] *Ibid.*, Article 21.

matters came into force in 2001.[7] A number of recommendations of the Myners report on institutional investment which was also carried out under government sponsorship in 2001 sought to advance the same end (Myners 2001).

CSR has the potential to bridge the gap between social policy and corporate governance, with some unexpected consequences. In the continental context, multiple stakeholder groups have been to the fore in holding corporate management to account. Continental systems may be moving closer to the shareholder value orientation of UK corporate governance. At the same time, the growing CSR movement in the UK holds out the prospect of humanising the shareholder value concept, and moving it in the direction of ensuring greater corporate accountability on social and environmental issues. There are substantial obstacles to such an outcome in the form of collective action costs and asymmetries of information in the chain of accountability between financial analysts, fund managers and the ultimate beneficiaries of pension funds and insurance policies, not to mention entrenched ideological opposition to CSR in parts of the financial and business community. However, it is precisely this intriguing possibility which the CSR initiative has now placed on the agenda at both UK and EU level.

The issue of gender equality provides a concrete context in which to examine the potential impact of CSR. Although it has had equal pay legislation since the 1970s, Britain's record on pay equality lags behind that of many other European countries. A study of fifteen European countries, the European Structure of Earnings Survey (SES), reported that Britain's record on equal pay was so poor that it was ranked only twelfth when looking at full-time employers – and last, in fifteenth place – when both part-time and full-time workers were included. In response to rising criticism, the Cabinet Office set up the Kingsmill Review to investigate Women's Employment and Pay in Britain (Kingsmill, 2001). The remit for the Kingsmill Review stipulated that it should seek non-legislative solutions to the gendered pay gap. The Review thus relied on the model of corporate governance emerging from the Cadbury Committee report (1994) and its successors, the Hampel Committee report (1997), the Turnbull report on internal company audit (ICAEW, 1999), and the Company Law Review (1999, 2000, 2001). In effect, this meant that the Review was required to focus on developing the 'business case' for retaining and maximising women's skills and experience in the labour market as a way of bringing about a positive impact on the gender pay gap in Britain.

---

[7] The Occupational Pension Schemes (Investment and Assignment, Forfeiture, Bankruptcy, etc.) Amendment Regulations, SI 1999/1849, reg. 2(4), amending SI 1996/3127.

The Review identified the requirements of 'enhancing returns' and 'minimising risk' as the two most fundamental drivers of corporate governance. It is in this context that it suggested that *good human capital management* is crucial to realizing corporate governance objectives. In illustrating the importance of these issues, the Review pointed to some potentially major governance challenges relating to skilled labour shortages. It noted that although UK employment then stood at 74.8 per cent (the highest employment rate for eleven years and approaching the full employment rate of 75 per cent (as defined by the Government in the March 2001 Budget)), the National Skills Task Force estimated that there were approximately 110,000 'hard-to-fill vacancies', largely in industries such as financial and business services, wholesale and retail, manufacturing and public administration and health (Kingsmill 2001: 32). This blockage in the labour supply was reported to be caused by skills shortages – these sectors had grown by 227,000 jobs over the previous year, outstripping the average increase in the whole economy (Kingsmill 2001: 33). At the same time, the UK birth rate was continuously decreasing and had fallen by 41 per cent since the 1960s. The pressure on the supply of labour was set to increase, as it was estimated by the Union that by 2020 the size of the working age population would be largely unchanged but would have to support a further 18 million individuals over the age of sixty-five (*Social Trends* 1996).

In light of such trends, the Kingsmill Review argued that businesses were operating in a climate in which competition for employees was becoming more fierce, especially with technological innovation rapidly increasing the knowledge-intensive sectors of the labour market. As a result, it claimed, the potential impact on businesses of the mismanagement of human capital would become increasingly acute. This was the core of the Review's argument that any business which does not maximise this resource to its full potential cannot expect to maintain its productivity and competitiveness in the face of rising demand for, and falling supply of, skilled labour.

The Review's principal recommendation was to call for greater transparency in terms of gendered pay trends within organisations, in the form of internal pay reviews, with a particular focus on gendered employment patterns. These internal audits should in principle be designed to be comparable across all employing organisations. The recommendation was pitched in terms of the human capital management practices necessary to aid the efficient and well-considered allocation of resources. In language which directly mirrored the CSR debate at both EU and UK level, three types of risks and costs to organisations were identified: (1) the risk and cost of reputational damage (including loss of investor confidence, loss of shareholder confidence and loss of consumer base) from gender bias; (2) the risk and cost of potential litigation against unequal pay practices; and (3) the risk and cost of a rising inability to recruit high-calibre employees, owing to an organisation acquiring a poor reputation as an employer.

In addition, the Review alluded to the high cost of turnover of staff and the associated recruitment and training costs which arise from inability to manage the issue of the work–life balance. DTI figures quoted by Kingsmill estimated that the typical recruitment costs of replacing an individual were approximately £3,500 – ranging from £1,000 for an unskilled manual worker to over £5,000 for a professional employee. These costs increase considerably for employees with specialist training – for example the NHS estimated that £200,000 was lost if a doctor left, £34,000 for a nurse and £22,000 for a physiotherapist.

In keeping with its non-interventionist brief, the Review recommended that the public sector should take a lead in this new initiative, in the hope that the private sector would follow suit out of fear of being 'named and shamed'; only if this failed to work would regulation be considered. Internal pay reviews of government departments and agencies were completed and a campaign undertaken to encourage organizations to conduct similar reviews. If this exercise is effectively carried through,[8] it can be expected to have a far-reaching impact and effect on the understanding of gender inequality in the labour market. The aim of the audits is to track the impact of equality policy in practice. In this sense, it embodies a learning process, revealing information about the structural barriers to equality at the same time as disseminating knowledge about how they may be addressed. By directly highlighting reputational losses from discriminatory treatment and the financial consequences of employee turnover, the review aims to induce employers to internalize the social costs of gender inequality. Corporate governance mechanisms, in particular the processes of internal audit and engagement by institutional shareholders, are called in aid to promote the same end.

This does not meant that a public discourse about equality is excluded: far from it. The Kingsmill exercise was launched against the background of a substantial body of legislation at both UK and EU level on the issue of sex discrimination, which in turn is underpinned by the

---

[8] At the time of writing (September 2003), a further review, *Accounting for People*, has been established with Denise Kingsmill at its head, to look into wider issues of human capital management, including the role of accounting conventions in measuring human capital. See http://www.accountingforpeople.gov.uk/news.htm (website visited 1 September 2003).

quasi-constitutional guarantees of equal pay and equal treatment which are contained in the EC Treaty. The possibility of further legislative intervention exists. The issue here is not whether there should be intervention, but what form it should take. According to the argument we have presented here, procedural mechanisms may be able to play an important role in implementing, at a micro level, the objectives of a rights-based agenda. The aim is to make some forms of social rights effective through a combination of investor activism and the creation of a market in information concerning the social performance of companies. In itself, this implies a public regulatory response to the existing inadequacies of accounting conventions (which do not yet adequately address the issue of non-financial reporting) and the availability to companies of strategies based on low levels of investment in human capital. However, there is reason to believe that it is through just such a combination of economic incentives and public encouragement that learning about capabilities will proceed.

6   Conclusion

Amartya Sen's capability approach has recently become the focus of a debate about how to modernize the European social model in a context where the policy agenda is increasingly set by the language of market integration. In common with other contributions to this volume,[9] we do not assume that Sen's ideas can necessarily be applied to the European debate in a straightforward way; on the contrary, there is a need to adapt Sen's framework to the particular policy parameters of the process of European construction. A further problem is that Sen's theorisation of the notion of capability, while having implications for the content of social law, is silent on the issue of juridical form. This makes it somewhat problematic to apply the capability approach when elucidating the nature of social rights. These difficulties notwithstanding, we have argued that social rights can be seen as a particular institutional form of the 'conversion factors' through which individual endowments are transformed into capabilities. We have also seen that a capability approach links with the development of techniques of *reflexive law*, through which legal intervention seeks both to engender and, in turn, to respond to forms of self-regulation based on collective learning by the social actors. The case study of recent debates concerning corporate social responsibility at both EU level and within member states demonstrates this process: the

---

[9] See in particular the Introduction to this volume (chapter 1) and chapter 18 by Salais.

mechanisms of corporate governance, involving shareholder activism and the evolution of new types of accounting convention, are being called to advance a process of achieving gender equality within organizations.

Above all, this chapter has argued that a capability approach could be highly useful in rebutting some of the criticisms offered of social rights from a neoliberal perspective, namely that they interfere with the workings of supply and demand and compromise the contractual autonomy of economic agents. A capability approach makes it possible to see that social rights, *in common with civil and political rights,* underpin market access and facilitate an extension of the division of labour and knowledge upon which, in the final analysis, a market order depends. This makes the concept of capability particularly useful for understanding the process of European construction, in which social rights and market integration have long been intertwined.

REFERENCES

Cadbury Committee, 1994. *Report of the Committee on the Financial Aspects of Corporate Governance*, London, Gee
Company Law Review Steering Group, 1999. *Modern Company Law for a Competitive Economy: The Strategic Framework*, London, DTI
    2000. *Modern Company Law for a Competitive Economy: Developing the Framework*, London, DTI
    2001. *Modern Company Law for a Competitive Economy: Final Report Volume 1*, London, DTI
Deakin, S. and Wilkinson, F., 2000. '"Capabilities", ordineo spontaneo del mercato e diritti sociali', *Il diritto del mercato del lavoro*, 2, 317–344
Department of Trade and Industry (DTI), 2001. *Business and Society. Developing Corporate Social Responsibility in the UK*, London
Hampel Committee, 1997. *Final Report of the Committee on Corporate Governance*, London, Gee
Hayek, F., 1976. *The Mirage of Social Justice*, London, Routledge
ICAEW, 1999. *Internal Control. Guidance for Directors on the Combined Code* (Turnbull Report), London, Institute for Chartered Accountants in England and Wales
Kingsmill, D., 2001. *Review of Women's Employment and Pay*, London, DTI
Lancaster, K., 1966. 'A New Approach to Consumer Theory', *Journal of Political Economy*, 74, 132–157
Marshall, T. H., [1949] 1992. *Citizenship and Social Class*, London, Pluto
Myners, P., 2001. *Institutional Investment in the United Kingdom: A Review*, London, HM Treasury
Rogowski, R. and T. Wilthagen (eds.), 1994. *Reflexive Labour Law*, Deventer, Kluwer
Salais, R., 1999. 'Libertés du travail et capacités: une perspective pour une construction européenne?', *Droit Social*, 467–470

Sen, A., 1985. *Commodities and Capabilities*, Deventer, North-Holland
1992. *Inequality Reexamined*, Oxford, Oxford University Press
1999. *Development as Freedom*, Oxford, Oxford University Press
Social Trends, 1996. Cited in ONS *Social Focus on Women and Men*, London, Office of National Statistics, 1998
Supiot, A. (ed.), 1999. *Au delà de l'emploi. Transformations du travail et devenir du droit du travail en Europe*, Paris, Flammarion
2003. 'The Labyrinth of Human Rights: Credo or Common Resource?', *New Left Review*, 21, 118–136

14 Collective rights, deliberation and capabilities: an approach to collective bargaining in the Belgian retail industry

Jean de Munck and Isabelle Ferreras

JS2 L81

1 Introduction

Although the industrial society has been overtaken by the so-called 'post-industrial' society, collective bargaining still remains the institutional reference for the construction of Social Europe in the twenty-first century. Policy labels such as 'social dialogue' integrated into EU official language and the Treaty, refer mainly to this paradigm. Nevertheless it is obvious that we now have to tackle the challenge of rethinking the scope and the meaning of collective bargaining. The socialist inspiration which served as a theoretical backdrop for collective bargaining throughout the industrial era has lost its persuasive strength. Economic liberalism, however, is equally unlikely to offer an alternative intellectual framework to capture the essence of an institution which it regards merely – at best – as aggregating individual interests. A new conceptual framework is required to grasp the future relevance this institution in our post-industrial economies.

In order to meet this objective, we propose to cast an 'institutionalist' glance at collective bargaining and the attendant collective rights. This very general formulation is intended to indicate that we take account, in our socio-economic analysis, of (institutional) norms which cannot be reduced to strategic interests or systemic functions. Social action is infused, made possible and limited by such norms. The question we wish to address is: how can an 'institutionalist' theory of collective bargaining be renewed by means of an approach which focuses on the question of capabilities? The central intuition which we shall develop is that a capability-based approach to socio-economic development,[1] akin to that of Amartya Sen, forces us to reconsider seriously the role of deliberation in a just society. We more than ever need a theory of *socio-economic*

Chapter written in the framework of the programme 'Theory of Norms and Democratic Regulation,' co-ordinated by the Centre for Philosophy of Law of the University of Louvain (PAI P4/34, phase IV, 1997–2001).

[1] For a presentation of the outlines of such a framework, see the Introduction, chapter 1 in this volume.

deliberation, both empirical and normative in scope, which is currently sadly lacking in mainstream approaches to socio-economic development. We shall set out this intuition in three stages. First we shall attempt in section 2 to demonstrate the conceptual linkages between collective rights, capabilities and deliberation. Secondly we shall construct in section 3 the concept of 'bargaining conventions', the initial element in a theory of social deliberation. Taking a specific industry (retail food in Belgium) as an example, we shall show how useful this concept is in identifying changes and tensions in specific collective bargaining mechanisms. Finally, in section 4 we shall systematically link these bargaining conventions with *collective, cognitive or political capabilities*. The concept of 'capability' thus becomes an analytical tool for describing and assessing[2] socio-political reality. We shall try to outline the importance of these capabilities and their recent historical transformations in order to envision the future of collective bargaining. Section 5 briefly concludes.

2   Collective rights and capabilities

In what way does a capability-based approach lead us to reconsider the question of collective rights in our democratic societies? In this first section we should like to follow the path opened by Amartya Sen in order to show how the notions of collective rights and of capabilities sustain and complement one another, and exceed a purely deontological theory of freedom and a purely utilitarian theory of capacities ('human capital' theory).

2.1   *Capability development requires collective deliberation and collective rights*

A capability-based approach has far-reaching consequences for the theory of justice and for the compilation of an informational basis of judgements. Let us start with one of these consequences here: the crucial importance of *contextualised deliberation*. The development of individual capabilities requires an extension of the capability for effective decision-making; in the absence of this link between capability and free deliberation, one would be mistaking capability theory (Becker 1993) for human capital theory. Fashionable 'human capital' theories are interested in capacities as productivity factors subject to adjustment constraints. In contrast, a capability theory such as the one we are defending aims to highlight the importance of deliberation in implementing effective freedom.

---

[2] We consider, as Sen suggests, the 'description' as a 'choice'. Our vocabulary is evaluative. On this point, see chapter 18 by Robert Salais in this volume.

In his writings, Amartya Sen often gives a purely individual version of this capability for deliberation. But such a limitation is by no means necessary. Freedom of choice is in fact not just a matter of personal virtues (caution, desire, reflexivity . . .) and is not limited to an absence of censure. Beyond these conditions, it assumes that, for individuals, the real world opens into a variety of *effectively possible* worlds. The juxtaposition of these alternatives obviously presupposes a collective deliberation on ends and means, which goes beyond the solitary, internalised playing-off their own preferences by individual consumers (or producers) in view of the state of the world. This is why Sen attaches great importance to political rights. 'Political and civil rights, especially those related to the guaranteeing of open discussion, debate, criticism, and dissent, are central to the processes of generating informed and reflected choices' (1999: 153). The argument in favour of democracy is not merely instrumental here, as when it is said that political rights allow for a faster and safer circulation of relevant information among economic agents. On the one hand, the possibility of real choices in the *objective* social world presupposes co-ordination among individuals involving public deliberation. On the other, from the point of view of capability theory, individual *subjective* preferences never constitute raw, stable, data, as they do for Utilitarians, but are likely to be the object of deliberation and are subject to revision.[3]

While collective deliberation is understood to be protected by the liberal tradition in the political sphere, collective social rights should take on this role in the socio-economic sphere. Many social rights are, of course, strictly individual: the rights to health or rest, against unfair dismissal, etc. In chapter 13 in this volume, Jude Brown, Simon Deakin and Frank Wilkinson show how we can develop a capability-based approach of such 'individual' social rights. But the rights which create a space for collective deliberation about the common world can rightly be described as 'collective rights'. One could say that the rights to strike, trade union representation and collective bargaining (labelled 'collective social rights') are second-generation social and economic rights, as the rights of political expression and association were the reflexive and procedural counterpart of the first generation of political rights. What these second-generation collective social rights provide for are the democratic means of contextualising the implementation of other, first-generation, economic and social

---

[3] Sen's economic theory allows not only for a classification of preferences but also for meta-classifications, thereby opening up the reflexiveness of the economic agent to moral values, be they individual or collective (Sen 1992). For a commentary on this point, see De Munck (1999, chapter I).

rights. What they potentially do is to open up a public space of deliberation and citizenship in the economic sphere, hinting at a realistic response to the age-old challenge of economic democracy.

In a remarkable article written from the perspective of capability theory, James Bohman (1997) explores the conditions for deliberative equality. He suggests that deliberative capability depends on the 'social capacity to initiate public deliberation about their concerns'. This capability of initiative relies on a number of conditions: for instance, one must be able to speak without fear, especially the fear of being censured or of sparking off a conflict leading to the possible loss of an advantageous (even slightly advantageous) position. Another condition is undoubtedly the capability to initiate a debate and represent a particular issue *symbolically*. This presupposes educational resources and cultural socialisation. Even when this symbolisation capability has been acquired, another condition is the capability to formulate arguments in an appropriate language, considering the structure, history and intelligibility of the public debate. And as public deliberation does not take place overnight but implies an ongoing process, there is also a need for the capability to be present throughout an entire discussion, by means of capabilities likely to collect, process and react to new information. And inasmuch as collective *deliberation* is closely connected with collective *decision-making* structures, the effect of the latter on the former must be assessed: an election by universal suffrage does not lead to the same type of deliberation as collective bargaining, even if the same subject is under discussion.

James Bohman proposes the concept of *political poverty* (1997: 33) to refer to the situation of groups that do not cross the threshold of public deliberation – even though they have the right to legally protected means of expression, and access to institutional mechanisms, and even though parties, trade unions and associations claim to speak on their behalf. It is not just a matter of information asymmetry, such as discussed by economists: 'When citizens are so unequal in capacities to acquire and use information, exclusion is a direct result of the resultant inadequacies of functioning. However, information is best understood as a resource for public deliberation. It is the capability to make use of information and to convert it into convincing public reasons, and not merely to have it, that determines deliberative success' (Bohman 1997: 342).

Unless deliberation is dealt with as a specific act of social co-operation, structured by institutions and dependent on capabilities, there is a risk of falling back on an overly formalistic conception of the public space or the contract. This is undoubtedly a potential flaw in the theory of Jürgen Habermas, as well as in the different versions of classical liberalism.

Democratic public space is a co-operative activity with its own organisation and division of labour.

This stance must be addressed, when reflecting upon collective rights. Evaluating a right as a capability does not only mean measuring its legal scope or asking what standard resources should be distributed to everyone in order for it to become accessible to all; it also means examining its *effective* use, in a given context, in the light of its possible uses. The question worth raising from this perspective is: in today's socio-economic context, does the existing institutionalisation of collective rights foster equality in deliberation? Or does it rather promote the development of (at least relative) political poverty? An answer to these questions cannot be either purely normative or purely descriptive; nor can it be general and out of context. A critical diagnosis of collective bargaining as a multi-layered social and historical institution is therefore required.

2.2   *Collective rights necessitate bargaining institutions*

Collective rights to deliberation can be exercised only through institutions. Collective bargaining institutions form a complex edifice which both *allows for* and *limits* the use of collective rights. These institutions shape the possible outcomes of the socio-economic deliberation. Here the normative thinking of philosophers and economists needs the insights of sociological investigation. How can collective bargaining as an institution be regarded in terms of institutionalising collective capabilities?

We shall now attempt to outline such an analytical framework. Our analysis is predicated on a concept put forward by Niklas Luhmann (1987): the 'thematisation' threshold. The concept of thematisation refers to the process whereby political or socio-economic deliberation explicates the norms of a given social interaction. For the players directly involved, this thematisation process is always hazardous. As Luhmann points out, thematisation involves the risk of 'negation potential', a failure to achieve agreement regarding the norms of interaction. Breaking the routine nature of social exchange, thematisation potentially opens a zone of uncertainty by clarifying otherwise hidden assumptions that underlie deliberation. If a proposal is rejected in this process, the proponent may or may not maintain it. Anticipating this risk and one's ability to deal with it determines the 'thematisation threshold' of a given interaction. Democracy can be understood to lower this threshold by equalising capabilities as far as possible in all spheres of social life.

The level of this threshold undeniably depends on the nature of the norms at stake. It may be very high: it is, for example, very difficult to thematise agreements as fundamental as those studied by Garfinkel (1967), since they are constituents of communication itself. But it may equally be very low: such is the case of specific details which do not threaten the fundamental harmony of an interaction (e.g. an arrangement to meet between two people in daily life). But this level depends above all on the propensity for conflict. Propensity for deliberation is linked to propensity for conflict. This in turn is linked to the existence of institutional mechanisms for conflict resolution *accessible* to the parties to a disagreement. The less the interlocutors fear conflict and its consequences, the greater the potential space for deliberation. Institutions of bargaining are also institutions of conflict resolution. It is therefore essential to have the tools to analyse these institutions so as to gauge the degree to which capabilities have developed in a given economic world, such as that of Europe in 2000.

In order to analyse this mechanism for resolving potential conflicts, we propose to distinguish between three notions: those of *bargaining conventions, cognitive learning capability* and *political control capability*. These dimensions should enable us to study the actual mechanisms of deliberation.

We shall support our theoretical considerations with the lessons learned through a very specific case of institutionalisation of collective rights: collective bargaining in the Belgian retail industry. This industry is particularly representative of the crisis and transformations of the typical 'Fordist' bargaining process currently experienced by the Belgian and other European economies. Indeed collective bargaining is in crisis in many respects, while still remaining the standard means of determining wages and working conditions. We conducted this research into the retail industry: we held interviews, observed joint committee negotiations in the run-up to the 1999–2000 collective agreement, and brought together groups of trade union representatives belonging to the two main unions[4] in the industry. The quotations are excerpts from statements made to us during fieldwork carried out between March 1998 and December 1999.

3   Bargaining conventions in crisis

Collective bargaining is first and foremost a negotiation over *rules*, as was strongly emphasised by Flanders in a famous article (Flanders 1968). Although related to these rules (which, once the process is complete, will become the rules of the *collective labour agreement*), the negotiations themselves are not narrowly circumscribed by explicit rules. Rather, they

---

[4] These are the *Centrale nationale des employés* (CNE) on the Christian side, and *Syndicat des Employés, Techniciens et Cadres* (SETCA) on the socialist side.

coalesce around conventions (understood here not in a legal sense but in the meaning given by the sociologists and economists who advocate the so-called Economics of conventions[5] programme).

3.1   Bargaining conventions

To be clear about terminology, then, we shall distinguish in this chapter between *conventions* and *rules*. Where this distinction proves unnecessary, we shall use the more general term 'norms'. A rule is by definition explicit, whether it be formulated orally or written down. The texts of bargaining agreements, signed by the parties to negotiations and generally sanctioned by the State, are therefore sets of rules. As Bénédicte Reynaud (1992: 48) puts it, a rule quite simply takes the form of a prescription: 'if X, then Y.' But, like a sentence or succession of sentences, a rule is never complete. It has to be *interpreted* in order to be understood in context. Propositions are not fully complete semantically, and implicit knowledge – in principle, it can never be entirely explicit – must be brought to bear on them. When this knowledge is shared between the partners in a dialogue, and when they (implicitly) know that it is shared, we are dealing with *conventional* knowledge. This conventional knowledge allows for co-ordination among players in various aspects of social life; it constitutes a set of shared references, enabling what Parsons called the 'double contingency' of interaction to be removed.

The implicit nature of a convention therefore distinguishes it from a rule. This does not mean that it is totally ineffable: it can be partially thematised in the form of rules. What this means is that a convention cannot be *totally* thematised; like every other convention, a bargaining convention has two intimately connected aspects, which we shall analyse separately for the sake of clarity.

First, bargaining conventions determine the *semantic framework* of the negotiation. We shall refer to this semantic framework as the *field of the negotiable*. Psychologically, this framework enables the protagonists to focus on a common horizon. Logically, it offers a series of categories establishing a discussion *topic* upon which basic *problems* can be constructed. Materially, this framework can be embodied by objects or equally well by the signs exchanged, the arrangement of the meeting room, etc.

Secondly, bargaining conventions also determine a system of normative expectations defining a *pragmatic framework* of interaction. Whereas the

---

[5] See particularly Salais and Storper (1997), Salais, Chatel and Rivaud-Danset (1998) and Batifoulier (2001).

semantic aspect of the agreement determines *what* may be negotiated, its pragmatic aspect determines *where* the negotiations take place, *who* is a 'valid interlocutor' and *when* and *how* these negotiations take place. Seen from this angle, bargaining conventions allow the shaping of mutual expectations in the form of normative[6] benchmarks.

3.2   Changes in the 'field of the negotiable': semantic aspects

By focusing on bargaining conventions, we can identify one of the key changes in collective bargaining since the 1980s. Let us refer for this purpose to the retail industry in Belgium. Bargaining conventions suffered severe turmoil during the 1980s and 1990s. In a nutshell, one fundamental aspect of the Fordist industrial relations regime – negotiability of wages – was gradually eroded. The effect of the pay restraint policy introduced in Belgium as early as 1976 by government recommendation was to restrict wage rises to 3 per cent when the multi-industry collective agreement was signed in 1978, falling to 1 per cent in 1981. A 'competitiveness norm' was imposed in 1983 and extended in the following years; it has since been institutionalised in the form of a '*marge salariale disponible*' (scope for wage bargaining), a ceiling placed over multi-industry bargaining which is calculated with reference to trends in wage costs in three neighbouring countries (Arcq 1991; Lamas 1997).

As a result of this fundamental change in policy, employment took centre stage. In this new scenario trade unions reformulated their claims in terms of number of jobs, social compensation to mass lay-offs and reduction in working time. A *new convention* has been established – not without tension – setting out the interests at stake in terms of social security contributions on the employers' side and employment levels on the unions' side. Wage issues, once a key concern, have since become somewhat secondary.

In this new 'field of the negotiable' it still remains hard to raise questions relating to work organization. Regarding this aspect, the new bargaining convention does not depart from the classical Fordist convention; indeed, many union representatives at the store level complain that they are increasingly coming up against managerial stakes not taken into account by the trade union apparatus. Thus the limitation of the field of the negotiable via the new bargaining convention seems to have somewhat frozen the collective learning process.

---

[6] 'Normative' is to be understood here as meaning both 'normal, routine, regular' and 'mandatory, required, demanded'.

For instance, certain representatives raise a major problem: the introduction of purely financial norms relating to work organisation (WO): WO norms seem to respond to only one requirement: short-term economic efficiency. They are in fact budgetary norms [explains a SETCA representative] because the unit of measurement isn't working time but an amount of money. The question is always 'what does it cost?' No-one says 'such-and-such a task takes 10 hours'; they say 'we'll spend 1,000 Franes on it'. That's why when someone is off sick he can't be replaced, because the budgetary norms and not the WO norms – in the true sense of the term – have been fulfilled: the person is in fact being paid. So his colleagues have to do his work as well as their own.

The working environment is faced with an 'aberration', in that this apportionment and quantification of labour misrepresent the problems faced at work. As a union representative says, they lead to

absenteeism, 'the poor person's strike weapon', and aggressiveness, because employees are expected to serve customers, stock shelves and carry out checks all at the same time. They should give us an extra pair of hands!

It would seem, however, that union representatives regard such matters as being not negotiable, and subject to a productivist logic which nothing can counteract.

And yet certain practical initiatives have been taken, which could perhaps sow the seeds of new bargaining practices, thereby reconfiguring bargaining conventions. A cautious experiment – very localised but very significant – has been under way in a Belgian hypermarket, Bigg's Continent (situated in Waterloo, near Brussels). With support from workplace union representatives, the work of check-out staff is being reorganised according to the so-called principle of 'check-out islands'. This is a new means of setting the working hours of the store's groups of 100 check-out assistants. Each assistant is assigned by management to a group (the 'island') responsible for a number of check-outs. Working hours are negotiated within the island. Considerable attention is paid to the requirement that each island should consist of staff with different profiles (mothers with young children, single women, students, women over fifty, etc.), all of whom have different time concerns (some prefer to work early in the morning, others at the end of the day, weekends or no weekends, not Wednesdays, etc.). The check-out assistants themselves are ultimately responsible for negotiating their hours *among themselves,* under two constraints: they must comply with their contractual number of hours and with the opening hours laid down by management.

The check-out island principle was implemented – at store level – by negotiation between the employer and workplace union representatives.

It undeniably constitutes a new topic of collective bargaining, thereby extending the field of the negotiable. It is worth pointing out that such a 'proceduralisation' of bargaining about working hours could have quite a different meaning if it were negotiated and incorporated, not through an institutional collective bargaining mechanism guaranteed by law, but into a flexible management system ultimately subject to unilateral control by the employer.

3.3   Changes in bargaining conventions: pragmatic aspects

If we are to move towards a theory of institutionalised bargaining, it is worth pointing out that the *place* where negotiations are held is as crucial to the bargaining outcome as their *content*. Conventions laying down the place of collective bargaining have been particularly explicit in Belgium. Economic life in this country is dominated by industry-wide 'joint committees' consisting of employers' associations and trade unions (*commissions paritaires*, CP), instituted by the 1968 Act on the structure of collective bargaining in Belgium. Over the years, five such committees have been created to cover the retail food and non-food industry.[7]

Such fragmentation opens the door to a general lowering of pay standards by means of a trade-off between joint committees. Two examples will suffice. When the GB-Inno-BM group embarked on its huge restructuring programme in 1991, its restaurants immediately formed themselves into an independent subsidiary and went over to the *Horeca* (hotel, restaurant and catering) industry. The entire workforce of the GB-Inno-BM group had until then fallen under the 'large stores' joint committee. Given that *Horeca* rates of pay were 30 per cent lower than those for large stores, one can understand the strategy of recategorising the company's restaurant service. Our second example concerns franchisees,

---

[7] These five joint committees are: CP 312 for 'large stores' (at least two ranges of goods, food and/or non-food, more than fifty workers) which concerns companies such as GB (bought by Carrefour in 2000), Cora, Inno, Hema and Bigg's Continent; CP 311 for large retail sales outlets (non-food, one specialisation, more than fifty workers) which concerns Casa, Ikea, Blokker, Brantano, Brico, Disport, Paris XL, etc.; CP 202a and 202b for food retailing employees (multiple branches, more than fifty workers or a business having at least three shops with the same name, belonging to the same proprietor and employing more than twenty-five workers) which concerns Delhaize Le Lion, Colruyt, Aldi, Match, Barras, Mestdagh, Lidl, etc.; CP 202c for food retailing employees (companies employing between twenty and fifty workers, reducing hours per week from 37.5 to 36.5 hours on 1 May 2001) which concerns Unic, Nopri, Intermarché, AD Delhaize, GB Partner and other franchises; CP 201 for the independent retail trade groups together, in the food sector, small independents and the same names as those listed for CP 202c where these shops/businesses employ fewer than twenty workers, as well as non-food retail businesses with fewer than fifty workers.

whose labour costs are significantly lower than those of traditional super-markets since they elude CP 312, the joint committee for large stores (belonging instead to CP 202c or CP 201). This situation gives the employers the upper hand.

The segmentation of contract and work conditions resulting from this institutional arrangement has no legitimacy in the view of trade union representatives. As they see it, all employees in the industry do roughly the same type of work, so that their experience of the working world is basically the same. This fragmentation is therefore construed as improper and serves only to exacerbate what is already an extremely fierce competition among shops, leading in the long run to downward pressure on working conditions and wages. 'Equal pay for equal work', say the workplace representatives interviewed about this matter.

Furthermore, in the franchised part of the industry (CP 201 and CP 202c), the right to workplace trade union representation has a major implication in terms of control and learning capabilities. Franchises now constitute the 'black hole' of collective bargaining in the retail industry (an obvious case of 'political poverty'): they are virtually absent from the bargaining scene, and certainly never concede much as unions have no power to get them bargain seriously. Indeed theses stores are not organised and these employees therefore extremely difficult to mobilise.[8] It is difficult to find out what is happening in this part of the industry, and so far unions have not found an efficient way to take up its cause.

It would nevertheless appear extraordinarily difficult even for the trade unions to challenge such a cornerstone of the collective bargaining edifice as the convention setting out the CP system. A conflict over bargaining *framework* is more risky than a conflict over bargaining *content*. Whereas a few representatives raise the idea of a single joint committee for the whole industry, it has never been the subject of an official claim, let alone of an education campaign by the union. Instead, the union side opted in 1999 for the strategy of putting a single '*cahier de revendications*' (list of claims) to all five joint committees in the industry, as a strategic means of overcoming the segmentation of bargaining contexts. This strategy did not, however, succeed in harmonising conditions. On the contrary, when reading the 1999 final bargaining agreement one is struck by the fact that as far as weekly working hours are concerned the gap has widened between all the CPs on the one hand and a marginal group of small retailers (CP 201 companies with fewer than twenty staff on the other); these, in actual fact, are franchises.

---

[8] Following the first major conflict involving franchises in this sector, a regional dialogue committee for franchises was created in Wallonia in 1996, but this committee has remained a consultative body.

4   Learning and control capabilities

The above analysis of bargaining conventions, illustrated by means of the example of the Belgian retail industry, does not give a complete picture of the institutional use made of collective rights. It needs to be complemented by an examination of the associated *collective capabilities*. Without claiming comprehensiveness, we shall distinguish below between cognitive capabilities and political capabilities.

4.1   Cognitive and political capabilities

Although conventions are relatively arbitrary (in the sense that they could be different), they are not unmotivated either: they are in fact based on *shared knowledge* which is likely to justify them, demarcate their scope and ensure their implementation. This shared knowledge is of course not given once and for all, constantly available to the players, or devoid of historicity. That is why the protagonists in collective bargaining must be endowed with collective *learning capabilities*. Inasmuch as these capabilities cannot be reduced to individual capabilities, we can speak of a collective cognitive mechanism (*dispositif cognitif collectif*).[9]

Whereas a norm refers to background knowledge, it also depends on the existence of *control capabilities*. The process of establishing the norm and the process of applying it are both distinct and interconnected. On the one hand, the establishment of rules within the negotiating body *anticipates*, more or less realistically, the possibility of their application being effectively controlled within companies. On the other, the possibility of controlling production processes (in particular, through strike action) weighs very heavily on the bargaining processes themselves. That is why any theory of collective bargaining must extend to an analysis of control capabilities.

In a collective bargaining process a key question is to know which group will be *mobilised* as a back-up in case of conflict. The existence of such back-up solidarity largely determines the thematisation threshold. It acts as a 'filter' in any discussions, since solitary risk-taking calls for a certain amount of courage. As Luhmann (1987: 243) reminds us, in primitive segmental societies this role is almost automatically played (for certain types of conflict) by family and clan solidarity, lending a degree of predictability to the future. The same no longer applies in modern democratic societies, however, where solidarity is precarious and has to

---

[9] This notion of '*dispositif cognitif collectif*' is borrowed from Favereau (1989). The point is developed further in De Munck (1999, chapter IV).

be constantly rebuilt as a bulwark against individualisation. The indisputable success of industrial trade unionism was that, after the massive breakdown in corporatist allegiances, it managed to rebuild solidarity at a level transcending the firm in such a way that mobilisation could reasonably be relied upon. The *legitimate reference authority* which will intervene to settle a conflict also determines the thematisation threshold. One particular feature of collective bargaining is that it takes the form of a decision-making authority which is *always dual*, unlike other mechanisms which institute a single, remote, independent authority such as that of the judge or the mediator appointed jointly by the parties in the case of arbitration. Generally speaking, the *technical and institutional means* of control are absolutely crucial.[10] That is, of course, why an analysis of collective bargaining calls for a theory on *strikes* and *lock-outs*, factors overlooked by game theory when applied to collective bargaining (Favereau 1996). Other processes can also turn into means of control – such as the daily presence of trade union representatives in the workplace, health inspector alliances within the internal company hierarchy, etc. – and are no less important, however.

4.2   *Redistribution of capabilities*

The Fordist bargaining convention operated on the basis of a specific distribution of cognitive and control capabilities, but is today in a state of turmoil owing to the introduction of new individualised, flexible and non-bureaucratic management techniques. We shall give two examples, one relating to managerial control capabilities and the other to trade union control capabilities.

On the management side at the store level, this transformation is exemplified by the figure of the Area Manager. Even though each store continues to have its own manager, a new function was added to the existing hierarchy of chain stores – that of 'Area Manager'. His duties involve the supervision of a number of stores in a given region and the direct involvement in the life of these stores on behalf of the commercial group owning them.

This way of working is deemed by the workforce to be 'pernicious', explains a CNE union representative. The Area Manager 'works as an individual and speaks to each worker separately', his aim being to find

---

[10] For instance, in the conflict on the collective dismissal of Renault's workers (Vilvorde 1997, Belgium) analysed by Clande Didry in chapter 2 in this volume, the mobilisation of workers and of the judicial system were important elements of the bargaining process.

solutions to 'problems he can't deal with at regional or national level'. This individualization of bargaining activity is deemed by the trade union apparatus to have a disastrous effect on the working environment, because the Area Manager acts outside of the habitual and legal instances of company bargaining; he individualises labour relations and the solutions to problems by negotiating *as and when they arise*, which is felt to be a real threat to cohesion in the workforce. In terms of both learning capabilities and control capabilities, collective bargaining channels are *short-circuited* by such practices, which are far more destabilising than the traditional practices of the authoritarian 'immediate boss'.

The trade union reaction to this destabilisation of control reveals their failure to grasp what is really at stake, rather than providing for a serious response. Protests against the practices of Area Managers in various Belgian chains have until now amounted to no more than demands for the dismissal of the persons concerned. They have never targeted the organisational model behind the use of this managerial technique. Responding to the individualisation of management practices by personalising the problem will certainly not enable employees to win back control and learning capabilities consonant with the transformations under way.

The development of capabilities is threatened from is the trade union side, too. Their knowledge and capacity to act used to be provided from 'above' (so to speak), from the trade union apparatus. Action is therefore dictated by a political mandate; its cognitive resources (training, meetings, research units, etc.) and political resources (support, funding, communication channels, etc.) are provided by the trade union apparatus. The union agenda is prioritised according to the industry and the national issues, mostly influenced by the crisis of unemployment and not by the new challenges arising from the organisational transformations.

Yet the unions must, on the other hand, get to grips with unvoiced difficulties caused by flexible working. Many of the workplace representatives we interviewed spoke of a real change in the workplace since the 1990s: far from seeing themselves as activists, they now regard themselves as social workers, having to solve a wide range of individual problems in the workplace. They have to handle problems concerning insecure contracts, case-by-case negotiations, time management issues, etc. In such a situation, representatives rely very heavily on *local* cognitive resources accumulated through their own experience or that of their predecessors within the company (more than *central* cognitive resources stored by political leaders); and the balance of power that results from this transformation depends largely on the representatives' own personality, abilities or even charisma.

A lot of representatives don't command respect on the field [said a SETCA Union representative]. So the manager doesn't listen to them. [He added:] In branches where there are representatives who won't take any nonsense, there's no problem putting together a list for the Union elections, because everyone wants to do as the rep does – it's highly regarded. Elsewhere, where the reps are weak, there's no-one to fill the lists. It's all to do with the rep's personality.

One strategy of local representatives may consist in a kind of company patriotism. In the absence of favourable trade union relations at industry level, representatives place their trust in co-operation with their managers. However, the obvious limitation of this strategy is that it depoliticises the role of the trade union, turning it into 'in-house unionism', which is rejected by the trade unions' official policy.

Another strategy may be for representatives to put themselves forward not just as a force for conflict, but at the same time as the 'third party' needed to resolve the conflict. Here the workplace representative (or, in the following example, the trade union officer called to the rescue) sets himself up as an arbiter. A CNE full-timer from the Charleroi region recounted the following incident, which occurred in a franchise store:

In a store in Chimay, the boss insulted a shop assistant. She answered back and the boss decided to sack her. The workers made it perfectly plain that if the boss went ahead with his decision there could be trouble. Because there were union reps on site I was told what was going on. I turned up in the morning and met with management in the early afternoon. We tried to reason with the boss and tell him that he surely didn't mean to dismiss someone who'd been working for him for four years and whose work had been totally satisfactory, just over a trivial personal argument. At the end of the day they both apologised. Management wasn't very happy about this at first, but it accepts this practice of its own free will, even though it does occasionally provoke slight increases in expenditure or headaches of this kind. In my view it's the most basic form of grass-roots trade unionism, nothing to do with putting forward claims.

Are any truly innovative practices arising in the face of such contradictions? Perhaps the 'flying' – or 'itinerant' – union representative might form the basis of an approach aimed at reconstituting learning and control capabilities for the unions. Such representation is a new and original form of trade union action: representatives are no longer attached to a single company but are responsible for a site, a region or a group of stores including integrated stores where union representation is recognised and others – franchises – where they carve out a role for themselves even without legal protection. These 'mobile reps' constitute an attempt to combine in one person the capacity for action belonging both to the union apparatus and to the local area to which they are delegated. Although the only legitimacy they recognise is that conferred upon them by their grass-roots, these representatives are highly professional, full-time employees of the union staff. At the same time, the 'flying reps' have a collective memory of their company's industrial relations. They are familiar with all of its workings and are permanent partners in ongoing negotiations with management.

5   Conclusion

We have attempted in this chapter to outline the main thrust of a possible theory of collective deliberation centring on the notion of capabilities. This theoretical approach illustrates more effectively than others that the capabilities of individuals and groups are central to the reconfiguration of regulatory practices in post-industrial democratic societies. It structures the contextualised use of collective rights into both descriptive and normative categories, thereby identifying some of the very tangible problems to be addressed by collective bargaining in the years ahead: redefining bargaining conventions to tackle problems caused by flexible working; developing organisational cognitive capabilities which are unprecedented in the trade union movement; devising new, egalitarian systems of reference in the context of a coherent conception of justice; and developing new control capabilities which are very localised, flexible and individualised, tailored to company downsizing and to new management techniques. Without this attention to the practical and qualitative problems of collective bargaining as an institution, the European social dialogue may well remain nothing more than a rhetorical formality, ineffectively papering over the cracks in what passes for a European Social Model.

REFERENCES

Arcq, E. 1991. 'La concertation sur la compétitivité', *Courrier hebdomadaire du CRISP*, 1326
Batifoulier, P. (ed.), 2001. *Théorie des conventions*, Paris, Economica
Becker, G., 1993. *Human Capital: A Theoretical and Empirical Analysis, with Special Reference to Education*, Chicago, University of Chicago Press
Bohman, J., 1997. 'Deliberative Democracy and Effective Social Freedom: Capabilities, Resources and Opportunities', in J. Bohman and W. Rehg (eds.), *Deliberative Democracy*, Cambridge MA, MIT Press, 321–348
De Munck, J., 1999. *L'institution sociale de l'esprit. Nouvelles approches de la raison*, Paris, Presses Universitaires de France
Favereau, O., 1989. 'Marchés internes, marchés externes', *Revue économique*, 2, 273–328
    1996. 'Contrat, compromis, convention: point de vue sur les recherches récentes en matière de relations industrielles', in G. Murray, M. L. Morin and I. da Costa (eds.), *L'état des relations professionnelles. Traditions et perspectives de recherche*, Toulouse, Editions Octaves, coll. Travail, and Presses de l'Université de Laval

Flanders, A., 1968. 'Eléments pour une théorie de la négociation collective', *Sociologie du travail*, 1

Garfinkel, H., 1967. *Studies in Ethnomethodology*, Cambridge, Polity Press

Lamas, R., 1997. 'La loi de sauvegarde préventive de la compétitivité: un nouvel encadrement des négociations salariales', *Année sociale 1996*

Luhmann, N., 1987. 'Communication about Law in Interaction systems', in K. Knorr-Cetina (ed.), *Advances in Social Theory and Methodology: Toward an Integration of Micro- and Macro-Sociologies*, Boston and London, Routledge, 234–256

Reynaud, B., 1992. *Le salaire, la règle et le marché*, Paris, Christian Bourgois éditeur, coll. Cibles XXI

Salais, R., E. Chatel and D. Rivaud-Danset (eds.), 1998. *Institutions et Conventions. La réflexivité de l'action économique*, Paris, Editions de l'Ecole des Hautes Etudes en Sciences Sociales

Salais, R. and M. Storper, 1997. *Worlds of Production: The Action Frameworks of the Economy*, Cambridge, MA, Harvard University Press

Sen, A., 1992. *Inequality Reexamined*, Oxford, Clarendon Press

   1999. *Development as Freedom*, Oxford, Oxford University Press

15 The gender settlement and social provision: the work – welfare relationship at the level of the household

Jane Lewis

1   Introduction

Modern states have always constructed social provision around the paid work – welfare relationship; it is this that has in large measure distinguished them from needs-based and arguably universal, but punitively deterrent poor law systems. Governments have always been concerned about the conditions for providing welfare – the nature of entitlements in the language of many policy analysts, but more a matter of conditionality in the mind of government. There has been a long-standing firm conviction, too, that wages are the best form of welfare. In the UK in the early twentieth century the Labour Party fought for a legislative proposal called the Right to Work Bill more fiercely than it did for pensions, while it was not at all keen on the new idea of social insurance because trades unions feared state intrusion into the territory of mutuality. What was at stake, of course, was the fight for the old-style labour contract, to which social insurance was successfully joined and which is now under profound review (Supiot 1999). The settlement at the heart of the modern welfare state was that between capital and labour. But it is increasingly recognised that there was a second key settlement between men and women. The old labour contract was designed first and foremost for the regularly employed male breadwinner and provision had to be made for women.

The gender settlement meant that those marginal to the labour market got cash cover via dependants' benefits. Alain Supiot has described the labour – capital settlement in terms of security traded for dependence. A similar set of arrangements can be said to have marked the gender settlement. The male-breadwinner model was based on a set of assumptions about male and female contributions at the household level: men having the primary responsibility to earn and women to care for the young and the old. This model thus made provision for the unpaid work of care, but at the price of inscribing female dependence on men. The male-breadwinner model that was built into the post-war settlement assumed regular and full male employment *and* stable families in which

239

women would be provided for largely via their husbands' earnings and their husbands' social contributions.

A pure male-breadwinner model never existed; women always engaged in the labour market. But there were historical periods in some countries and for some social classes for which the model more accurately described the social reality than others: for people of the middling sort in the UK and the USA in the late nineteenth century and large tracts of the middle and respectable working classes in the years following the Second World War in many western countries. There was an enormous behavioural change in the second half of the twentieth century, with increasing numbers of women entering the labour market: indeed, this has become one point of convergence between EU Member States. Family change, which has resulted in family breakdown, more fluidity in intimate relationships and a large increase in single-person households has also contributed to the erosion of the male-breadwinner model at the behavioural level.

But the male-breadwinner model also worked at the level of prescription. It was the 'ought' in terms of relationships between men and women and was underpinned by social policies that assumed female dependence on a male wage and by family law, which made the same assumptions about the marriage contract in terms of stability and the nature of the contribution of men and women in families, implementing them through fault-based divorce (Weitzman 1985). Just as the male-breadwinner settlement has been eroded at the level of behaviour, so it has been eroded at the level of normative prescription.

This chapter argues that erosion at the level of prescription has been more complete than at the level of behaviour, and that policy-makers are now inclined to assume that all adults, male and female, will be in the labour market. I also suggest that in and of itself, this 'adult worker model' holds out more promise for women than the dependence inherent in the male-breadwinner model. Given the trend towards the 'individualisation of the social' (Guillemard 1986; Ferge 1997) together with massive family change since the mid-1970s resulting in a huge increase in lone-mother families in many northern and western European countries, women need more access to wages. However, the acceptance of an adult worker model depends on the terms. In many countries outside Scandinavia there has been relatively little attention to policies in respect of carework. Without these, an adult worker model poses severe problems, not only for women, but also for the wider society.

In most western European countries, the central work – welfare relationship is in the process of being re-cast, with an increasing emphasis on the individual's responsibility to engage with the labour market and on labour market activation programmes to make this possible. The aim to make all citizens into 'adult workers' raises large issues about what happens to the unpaid work of care. The capabilities approach offers a means of addressing carework because of the way in which it has defined capabilities as combinations of 'functionings' and insists on the importance of the individual's choice of functioning (Sen 1985, 1999; see also Nussbaum and Sen 1993, Nussbaum 1999). In addition, individuals have to be in a position to make a genuine choice. Money may be important to this, but so may be time, and capabilities encompass political and social life as well as life in the family. The concept thus embraces more than material well being, more than wages and more than paid work (while acknowledging that poverty necessarily restricts choice of 'functionings'). Furthermore, explicit rules and collective provision in the form of cash, services and measures to enhance human capital are necessary to give individuals the opportunity to achieve their potential and to guarantee genuine choice. The capabilities approach provides a way of recognising and valuing care, which is important because too often female family members experience little genuine or effective choice to care (Land and Rose 1985; Kremer 2000). For example, the increasing force of the assumption that all adults will be in the labour market means that lone mothers have little choice other than to seek substitute carers for their children, usually in the form of grandparents or childminders. This chapter makes a case for the need for further research on the principles that are necessary to underpin carework.

2   The erosion of the male-breadwinner model: behavioural change

The male-breadwinner model has been substantially eroded in two key respects: the changing pattern of women's and to a lesser extent men's contribution to the family in respect of cash and care, and the changing structure of the family itself. In both respects there has been increasing individualisation, but nowhere is there a fully-fledged adult worker model. In western Europe there is evidence of substantial movement away from the male-breadwinner model towards an adult worker model (Crompton 1999). However, it is most common to find some form of transitional dual-breadwinner model, with short or long part-time work for women, than a full dual-career model. There may therefore also be convergence between western and eastern European countries, as the latter move in the opposite direction, away to some extent from a full dual-career model.

As table 15.1 shows, the comparative data on women's post-war labour market participation for western countries all show an upward trend and men's a downward trend. However, the variation in the timing and degree

Table 15.1. *Labour force participation rates of population at age fifteen–sixty-four, 1980–2000*

	Male		Female	
	1980	2000	1980	2000
Australia	86.6	83.4	52.0	66.8
Canada	86.0	83.5	57.3	72.1
Denmark	88.3	85.2	71.3	77.3
Finland	79.3	76.7	68.3	72.5
France	81.6	75.7	55.2	62.2
Germany	86.5	81.0	56.2	62.2
Ireland	85.0	79.2	34.7	43.6
Italy	81.9	79.0	39.2	49.9
Netherlands	81.0	79.2	38.2	56.2
Portugal	88.5	82.6	53.4	62.9
Spain	84.5	79.5	32.5	47.9
Sweden	85.4	84.6	69.3	81.6
UK	89.2	83.9	57.0	67.0
USA	83.8	81.5	58.2	70.0

Source: ILO (2000).

of women's labour market participation varies widely between countries. While the figure for The Netherlands remains low, the rate of increase since the 1980s has been higher than for most other countries. In Spain, too, female labour market participation rates remain low, but this masks the fact that since the 1990s they have increased dramatically for younger women.

The nature of women's participation in the labour market also varies considerably between countries. Table 15.2 shows the extent of women's part-time work; men are still predominantly full-time workers.

But the meaning of part-time work differs considerably. In the UK, the Netherlands and Germany, short part-time working is very common. In the Scandinavian countries, female part-time work is also common (albeit declining in Denmark and Sweden), but women usually work relatively long hours, often exercising their right to work part-time while they have young children. This part-time work attracts *pro rata* benefits and is not the 'precarious' employment that is so common in the UK.

Thus the precise nature of the erosion of the male-breadwinner model is complicated. There has been no simple move from a male-breadwinner to a dual-career model. Rather, in most western countries some kind of dual-breadwinner model has become the norm. Often, given women's lower earnings, this amounts to a more-or-less one-and-a-half earner model.

Table 15.2. *Female part-time employment as a percentage of female employment and male part-time employment as a percentage of male employment 1983 and 1999*

	Male		Female	
	1983	1999	1983	1999
Australia	9.2	14.3	35.5	41.4
Canada	8.7	10.3	28.1	28.0
Denmark	7.1	8.9	36.7	22.7
Finland	4.5	6.6	12.5	13.5
France	3.2	5.8	18.9	24.7
Germany	2.1	4.8	31.2	33.1
Ireland	3.2	7.9	17.4	31.9
Italy	3.7	5.3	16.5	23.2
Netherlands	5.6	11.9	44.7	55.4
Portugal	2.9[a]	5.0	12.2[a]	14.6
Spain	1.9[b]	2.9	12.1[b]	16.8
Sweden	4.9[b]	7.3	29.8[b]	22.3
UK	3.3	8.5	40.1	40.6
USA	9.1	8.1	22.9	19.0

Notes:
[a] Data for 1986.
[b] Data for 1987.
Source: OECD (2000).

A more gender-equal model in terms of the division of unpaid as well as paid work has not been achieved in any country, but it is the official policy of the Dutch government, with its 'combination scenario' and the Netherlands has somewhat more part-time work for men (17 per cent of Dutch men work part-time, but a majority of these are either young or over fifty-five).

Thus the social reality is that while a high proportion of adult women are in the workforce in most OECD countries, they are not fully individualised in the sense of being self-sufficient, and they still take responsibility for a large proportion of the unpaid carework that is done, supported to very varying degrees by collective provision. When, therefore the British and Dutch governments swung from treating lone mothers as mothers to treating them as workers in the late 1990s, they did so regardless of the fact that a majority of married mothers actually work part-time.

In respect of growing family instability, the pace of change in the recent past has been greater than in regard to the labour market. In the UK the divorce rate increased threefold and the rate of unmarried motherhood

Table 15.3. *Crude divorce rates, 1973–1998 (per 1,000 mid-year population)*

	1973	1985	1994	1996	1997	1998
Australia	1.21	2.52	2.71	2.87	2.80	2.70
Canada	1.66	2.46	2.72	2.41	2.25	2.28
Denmark	2.52	2.81	2.63	2.43	2.42	2.48
Finland	1.89	1.85	2.70	2.69	2.63	2.67[a]
France	0.98	1.95	2.00	2.01	2.10	2.00
Germany	1.46[b]	2.10[b]	2.04	2.14	2.29	2.30
Ireland[c]	—	—	—	—	—	—
Italy	0.33	0.27	0.48	0.60	0.60	0.60
Netherlands	1.33	2.35	2.35	2.25	2.16	2.10
Portugal	0.07	0.88	1.24	1.42	1.42	1.50
Spain[c]	—	—	0.81	0.83	0.87	0.90
Sweden	2.00	2.37	2.53	2.42	2.37	2.30
UK	2.14	3.08	2.97	2.91	2.70	2.70
USA	4.36	4.95	4.57	4.33	4.34	4.20

Notes:
[a] Provisional data – data not available for this year.
[b] Data for West Germany only.
[c] Ireland passed divorce legislation in 1996 and Spain in 1981.
Sources:
Data for 1973: United Nations, *Demographic Yearbook 1977*, New York, United Nations Publications, 1978.
Data for 1985: United Nations, *Demographic Yearbook 1989*, New York, United Nations Publications, 1991.
Data for 1994–8: United Nations, *Demographic Yearbook 1998*, New York, United Nations Publications, 2000; other sources: Council of Europe, *Recent Demographic Developments in Europe, 1999*, Strasbourg: Council of Europe Publishing, 2000; Eurostat, *European Social Statistics: Demography*, Luxembourg, Office of Publications for the European Communities, 2000; US Department of Health and Human Services, *Monthly Vital Statistics Report, Vol. 47, No. 21*, 2000; Australian Bureau of Statistics, *Australian Demographic Trends.* Belconnen: Australian Bureau of Statistics, 2000; Statistics Canada, *Annual Demographic Statistics*, 1998, Catalogue 91-213-XPB. Ottawa: Statistics Canada, 1998; Statistics Canada, 'Divorces', *The Daily*, 28 September 2000.

fourfold in one generation. Divorce is high and stable in northern Europe, with more moderate rates in continental western Europe and low rates in the South, albeit with rising rates of separation (table 15.3).

There have been extraordinary rises in the proportion of live births outside marriage in northern Europe, wide variations in the increase in the continental western European countries (high in France, low in west Germany), and wide variations in southern European countries (Portugal had a higher rate than many northern countries as early as 1960 and a higher rate than Germany in 1995) (table 15.4).

Table 15.4. *Extra-marital birth rates,*
1988–1998 (as a percentage of all births)

	1988	1994	1998
Australia	17	26	29
Canada	22	30	31[b]
Denmark	45	47	45[c]
Finland	21	31	37
France	26	36	40[a]
Germany	16	15	20
Ireland	12	21	28
Italy	6	8	9
Netherlands	10	14	21
Portugal	14	18	20
Spain	9	11	15
Sweden	51	52	55
UK	25	32	38
USA	26	31[d]	33[e]

Notes:
[a] Provisional data.
[b] Data for 1996.
[c] Data for 1997.
[d] Data for 1993.
[e] Data from 1999.
Sources:
Eurostat, *Eurostat Yearbook A Statistical Eye on Europe
1988–1998*, Luxembourg; *Office of Official Publications for
the European Community*, 2000; other sources: Australian
Bureau of Statistics Australian Demographic Trends,
Belconnen, Australian Bureau of Statistics, 2000; US
Department of Health and Human Service, *National
Vital Statistics Report*, vol. 49(5), 24 July 2001; Council of
Europe, *Recent Demographic Developments in Europe, 2000*,
Strasbourg: Council of Europe Publishing, 2000.

Divorce and unmarried motherhood are routes to lone motherhood
and the proportions of lone-mother families have therefore increased.
Cohabitation is the driver of much of the change; it is now sequel and
alternative to marriage and has contributed to the increasing separation
of marriage and parenthood, which constitutes a more profound shift
that the 1960s separation of sex and marriage. The pace of change is
such that it is tempting to write of the 'rise and fall' of marriage in the
twentieth century (Kiernan *et al.* 1998; Knijn and van Wel 2000; Lewis
1998, 2001a).

It seems that on the work and family front we are seeing more individualisation. Elizabeth Beck Gernsheim (1999: 54) has described the

effects of individualisation on the family in terms of 'a community of need' becoming 'an elective relationship'. The family used to be a community of need held together by the obligations of solidarity. But women's increased labour market participation together with family instability have resulted in new divisions between biography and family. However, individualisation is far from complete and lone-mother households are more likely in all western countries to be in poverty because of the difficulties lone mothers face in becoming economically autonomous.

Yet policy-makers are increasingly assuming 'progress' towards full individualisation in the sense of economic independence, even though such assumptions are in danger of running ahead of the social reality (Lewis 2001b, 2002). Women may also have reservations about putting paid work before unpaid work, not least because of the relative absence of policy-makers' attention to provision for carework.

3   The erosion of the male-breadwinner model: changes in normative prescription

Rational choice theorists such as Jon Elster (1991) may acknowledge the existence of norms, but use them only as a residual form of explanation, to be invoked to explain the awkward bits that are left when the rational choice analysis is complete. Sophisticated economic approaches, such as that using the idea of the 'convention', interpreted by Sugden (1998: 454) in terms of tacit agreements or common understanding giving rise to shared expectations, acknowledge the importance of the cultural variable, but stop short at the idea that norms are internalised. Thus Sugden (1998) has argued that conventional practices can generate normative expectations, which may in turn be significant for the stability of conventions. Others, however, insist that norms and values are embedded in society and are part of the framework within which choices are made. After all, norms by definition are not chosen, and a decision to abide by them may be made consciously or seemingly without any conscious interrogation of alternatives.[1] Thus Sunstein (1997) has insisted that individual choices are a function of norms, meanings and roles, and that individuals may therefore have little control over them. Puzzles of rationality, he argues, are the product of social norms and moral judgements.

In practice, such factors usually remain absent from, or peripheral to, explanation. For example, while Fukuyama (1999) acknowledged the importance of culture, arguing that it allowed Japan and Korea to stave off 'the great disruption' in norms and values that, according to him, began in

---

[1] The process by which this occurs is complicated, see, for example, Suchman (1997).

the 1960s and manifested itself in rising crime rates, a decline in trust and family breakdown, he could see no means of explaining why 'attitudes'[2] in western countries should have begun to change rapidly in the 1960s unless they were driven by something else. He preferred therefore to explain family change in terms of social and economic variables: namely the increased use of artificial birth control and women's greater labour market participation. These in turn changed the norms that constrained men's behaviour and allowed them to behave more irresponsibly. Thus, Fukuyama's explanation prioritised social and economic behaviour; attitudes and norms played a secondary part in the story. He may well be correct, but his relegation of cultural factors to second place meant that, as is commonly the case, little attention was paid to the precise way in which they worked.

In the case of the male-breadwinner model, its use has been descriptive first of a pattern of economic activity in the family. Inevitably it tended to underplay the amount of female labour market activity, but it was not inaccurate in its portrayal of a society in which it was *expected* that men would take primary responsibility for earning and women for caring. Second, the model was internalised by a majority of people, certainly in the years following the Second World War, and this served to condition expectations within marriage. In the immediate post-war decades the gendered division of work, paid and unpaid, was sufficiently in line with the male breadwinner model to give rise to a set of normative expectations about the roles of men and women within the family, that underpinned social policies (for example, in respect of the lesser contributions and benefits paid by married women under the social insurance system), and in turn reinforced the model.

The erosion of the model in respect of the changing labour market behaviour of women might be expected at some point to have been accompanied by a shift in normative expectations on the part of people and legislators, although the shift need not necessarily be entirely congruent with changes in behaviour. As Lessig (1996: 285) has observed, when norm violation increases (as in the case of the shift away from a single male breadwinner towards a dual-earner family) then the meaning of obeying the norm also changes and at some point 'obeying the norm makes one a "chump"'. Indeed, Stacey (1990) has commented that young working class men in late-twentieth century America were not sure whether to regard one of their number who became a breadwinner as a hero or a chump. This is in large measure because normative

---

[2] The relationship between attitudes, values and norms is also complicated and a matter of considerable debate, see Van Deth and Scarborough (1995).

meanings and expectations are far from clear. The norm is now that women will engage in paid work, and attitudinal surveys in the post-war period have shown consistent increases in the acceptance by men and women of female employment at all stages of the lifecourse (Dex 1988). But to what *extent* – full-time or some form of part-time – varies considerably according to social class, ethnicity and sometimes region. Nor are the accompanying assumptions in respect of unpaid work predictable. Indeed, expectations may actually run ahead of behavioural change, especially on the part of policy-makers. The gap between the normative prescription of paid work for adult women as well as men and the reality of a more or less one-and-a-half-breadwinner family with women still carrying out much of the unpaid work has then to be resolved by the couple.

There is, of course, also considerable evidence that women want to do unpaid work, especially carework for elderly dependants and for young children. Hakim (1996, 2000) has argued strongly that the British female labour force divides into a group of committed career women and another group that is content to choose part-time work (and undertake care). Hakim's model is controversial because it highlights choice and underplays constraints. However, as Gustaffson and Stafford (1994) have noted, patterns of provision in respect to care in different countries owe much to historical and cultural factors. Certainly in Britain and the Netherlands there is evidence that lone mothers want to care (van Drenth, Knijn and Lewis 2000; see also Ford 1996; Duncan and Edwards 1999), something long acknowledged also in respect of informal elder care (Finch and Groves 1984; Lewis and Meredith 1987). It may be that alternative moral rationalities underpin women's greater commitment to family work (Tronto 1993; Ahlander and Bahr 1995; Duncan and Edwards 1999) and that given the choice between even a well-paying job and unpaid carework for a child or elderly relatives, some women would prefer the latter. If good-quality, affordable daycare were to be provided overnight, it is not clear that all women in all countries would want to work full-time. British Labour Force Survey data report that 90 per cent of women with children who work part-time did not want full-time work (Thair and Risdon 1999). This is, of course, in a country that until very recently has had little experience of available and affordable formal childcare.

At the policy level, there is evidence that the swing towards assuming that policies can (and should) be based on the shift in normative expectations towards an adult worker model has been rapid. But given the much more complex nature of the social reality, such assumptions as to men and women's equal capability to choose employment threaten to pose as many difficulties as did assumptions regarding the existence of a male-breadwinner model, which assumed (and perpetuated) female economic dependence.

4   The social policy implications of the new assumptions

Evidence that governments at both the national and EU levels are moving towards assuming the existence of an adult rather than a male-breadwinner model is not hard to find. The UK Labour government has made the drive from welfare-to-work central to its social policy. Tony Blair's introduction to the document on welfare reform has been widely quoted – 'work for those who can; security for those who cannot' (Cm 3805 1998: iii) – and contrasted with the Beveridgean promise of security for all. The introduction also made clear that this approach was to apply to women as well as men: 'the welfare state based around the male breadwinner is increasingly out of date' (p. 13). As Goodin (2001: 39) has observed, there is in many western European countries a 'new constellation of work-and-welfare variables'.

There are several strands of thought that have fed the profound shift that government has made in respect of assumptions about appropriate models of work for women (see also Lister 2000). First, a major influence on governments of the early and mid-1990s was the view that all those in receipt of state benefits had a concomitant obligation to engage in paid labour. Lawrence Mead (1986) presented this solution in terms of a model of equal citizenship and something that would bring about greater social integration. Welfare-to-work, implemented first in the USA, embodied these ideas and was applied to all able-bodied adults, lone mothers included (Novak and Cogan 1987; Bradshaw 1996).

Second, social democrats have, like Mead but unlike more radical critics of 'welfare dependency' (such as Charles Murray), also stressed the overriding importance of employment as a means to social integration or inclusion. The effort to get more lone mothers into the labour market has been justified as much by reference to improving the welfare of the mothers themselves as by condemnation of welfare dependency. This position is shared by many feminists who, while they have long stressed the need to recognise the unpaid work of care (Finch and Groves 1983), have also long campaigned for women's economic and financial independence (McIntosh 1981). Welfare-to-work is an idea that is central to 'third way' politics and as Deacon (1998) has suggested, represents a combination of welfare conceptualised as self-interest, as authority and as moral regeneration. But social inclusion on the basis of paid work restricts the choice of participative 'functioning' in societies.

Third, the idea of globalisation and its implications for social programmes has been influential for both Conservatives and Labour. Conservatives subscribed largely to the neoliberal prescriptions of the 'Washington Consensus', which dictated private rather than public provision, allocation by markets rather than on the basis of need, targeting rather than universal provision, charging rather than tax-based finance and decentralisation rather than central planning (Piachaud 2000). However, the effects of what might be termed 'globalisation talk' have been more dramatic in terms of the pattern of restructuring of social programmes than on cuts in those programmes. The increased demands for competitiveness have leant support to major welfare state services that can be perceived as increasing human capital (chiefly education and health), while at the same time serving to justify a tougher approach to cash benefits. The call to ensure reciprocity by matching entitlements to benefit with concomitant responsibilities to train or to work is one such approach, although Labour's strategy in the UK of a minimum wage and in-work benefits has also been a response to the trade-off between equity and employment that became much more unfavourable for the low-skilled during the 1980s as a result of the low-wage, flexible labour market strategy (Vandenbroucke 1998).

The globalisation thesis directs the attention of government to labour markets and competitiveness (Gough 1996). European Commission documents show this clearly; the Commission has stressed the importance of adult labour market participation in the context of a strategy to increase European competitiveness (EC 1993a, 1995b; CEU 2002). In the economic strategy documents of the Commission, there is little reference to the family and family responsibilities, yet there is also obvious concern at the EU level with the work – family nexus – as expressed, for example, in the Directive on parental leave (EC96/34). These two agendas remain parallel and separate, however, and the former predominates. Greater labour market participation is thus seen as the best way of securing competitive advantage, of keeping public expenditure down (especially in respect of the growing numbers of lone mother families) and of promoting social inclusion and reducing poverty.

An adult worker model is not necessarily wholly 'bad for women'. Everything depends on the conditions under which such a model is implemented. The problems of assuming the existence of a full adult worker model are fourfold:

- Unpaid care work is *unequally shared between men and women*, which has substantial implications for women's position in the labour market.
- Given the *lack of good-quality affordable care* in the formal sector (public or private) in many countries, many women have little option but to continue to provide care.

- A significant number of female carers feel that it is *'right' to prioritise care* over paid work.
- Women's *low pay*, especially in care-related jobs, means that full individualisation is hard to achieve on the basis of long part-time or even full-time work.

Just as policy assumptions based on a male-breadwinner model disadvantage women in particular, so assumptions based on a full adult worker model are also likely to do so. Any assumption that wages will enable more self-provision in the social arena, especially in respect of pensions, is fraught with danger for women when both paid and unpaid work are so unequally divided between the sexes. The new welfare contract is moving from social contributions to individually defined contributions, premised on the idea that adults are in the workforce, but this is both an unrealistic assumption in respect of women and one that fails either to value or to reward care. Assumptions regarding an adult worker model pose threats to women unless issues to do with the unequal gendered division of work and hence of life-time earnings are addressed.

The shifts in assumptions regarding individualisation are moving faster than changes in behaviour. It is in any case highly unlikely (and probably undesirable) that informal care will cease. Indeed, welfare restructuring, which has involved both marketisation and decentralisation, has resulted in more fragmentation of services and has made informal care more necessary to fill the gaps. It is therefore important to recognise and value carework, which both policy-makers and academic comparative analysts of welfare states have tended to ignore. We therefore need new principles to both justify and guide the search for policies that give equal place to care. The capabilities approach is promising in this regard. Anything to do with care tends to be poorly valued. Wages in the formal sector are low and benefits and allowances for carers in the informal sector are also low. However, if it is accepted that well being and equality involve the effective freedom of choice between 'functionings', then it is possible to make the argument that steps must also be taken to make it possible to choose to care.

5   Conclusion

Thus far, the new approach to welfare by policy-makers and academics (e.g. Esping-Andersen 2000) has focused on the need for reforms to secure changes to the social security system that will facilitate labour market entry, but given the unequal division of paid and unpaid work between men and women and the fact that the responsibility to care shows no sign of diminution, it is also important that reform and restructuring take account of people's lifetime relationships to the labour market, for example in respect of pension guarantees. Carers are particularly prone to low-paid work and periods with no pay. The capabilities approach holds out the vital possibility of making it possible to choose to care and to acknowledge that for there to be effective freedom to make such a choice, steps must be taken to value it. In order to be able to choose work, it is necessary to provide cash to purchase care, or care services. But if it is also to be possible to choose to care, it is necessary to have the time to care, which involves the regulation of working hours and compensation for carework. These are complicated policy issues and they are made additionally difficult by the issue of gender equality, which a capabilities approach has difficulty in addressing, because of its focus on individual agency. Men's persistent choice not to care effectively threatens women's choice to work. Thus far, the attention of governments has focused firmly on getting women into paid work, and to some extent on the need to reconcile work and care for *women*. The next step must be to focus more on care, and in relation to men as well as women. The point is that much more consideration needs to be given to a new set of principles that will underpin the shift towards an adult worker model family, and that care must enter the policy agenda.

REFERENCES

Ahlander, N. R. and K. S. Bahr, 1995. 'Beyond Drudgery, Power and Equity: Towards an Expanded Discourse on the Moral Dimensions of Housework in Families', *Journal of Marriage and Family*, 57, 54–68

Beck Gernsheim, E., 1999. 'On the Way to a Post-Familial Family. From a Community of Need to Elective Affinities', *Theory, Culture and Society*, 15(3–4), 53–70

Bradshaw, J., 1996. *The Employment of Lone Parents*, London, Family Policy Studies Centre

Cm. 3805, 1998. *New Ambitions for Our Country: A New Contract for Welfare*, London, The Stationary Office

Crompton, R. (ed.), 1999. *Restructuring Gender Relationships and Employment: The Decline of the Male Breadwinner*, Oxford, Oxford University Press

Deacon, A., 1998. 'The Green Paper on Welfare Reform: A Case for Enlightened Self-Interest?', *Political Quarterly*, 69(3), 306–311

Dex, S., 1988. *Women's Attitudes towards Work*, London, Macmillan

Duncan, S. and R. Edwards, 1999. *Lone Mothers, Paid Work and Gendered Moral Rationalities*, London, Macmillan

Elster, J., 1991. 'Rationality and Social Norms', *Archives Europeénnes de Sociologie*, 32, 109–129

Esping-Andersen, G., 2000. 'Challenge to the Welfare State in the 21st Century: Ageing Societies, Knowledge Based Economies and the Sustainability of European Welfare States', Paper presented to the conference, *Comparer les Systèmes de Protection Sociale en Europe*, Ministère de L'Emploi et de la Solidarité, Paris, 8–9 June

Ferge, Z., 1997. 'The Changed Welfare Paradigm: The Individualisation of the Social', *Social Policy and Administration*, 31(1), 20–44

Finch, J. and D. Groves (eds.), 1983. *Labour and Love: Women, Work and Caring*, London: Routledge & Kegan Paul

Folbre, N., 1994. *Who Pays for the Kids? Gender and the Structures of Constraint*, London, Routledge

Ford, R., 1996. *Childcare in the Balance: How Lone Parents made Decisions about Work*, London, Policy Studies Institute

Fukuyama, F., 1999. *The Great Disruption: Human Nature and the Reconstitution of Social Order*, London, Profile Books

Goodin, R. E., 2001. 'Work and Welfare: Towards a Post-Productivist Welfare Regime', *British Journal of Political Science*, 31, 13–39

Gough, I., 1996. 'Social Welfare and Competitiveness', *New Political Economy*, 1(2), 209–232

Guillemard, A.-M., 1986. *Le déclin du social: formation et crise des politiques de la vieillesse*, Paris, Presses Universitaires de France

Gustaffson, S. and F. P. Stafford, 1994. 'Three Regimes of Childcare', in R. Blank (ed.), *Social Production versus Economic Flexibility: Is There a Trade Off?*, Chicago, Chicago University Press and NBER

Hakim, C., 1996. *Key Issues in Women's Work: Female Heterogeneity and the Polarization of Women's Employment*, London, Athlone

2000. *Work–Lifestyles Choices in the Twenty-first Century: Preference Theory*, Oxford, Oxford University Press

ILO, 2000. *World Labour Report 2000*, Geneva, International Labour Office

Kiernan, K., H. Land, and J. Lewis, 1998. *Lone Motherhood in Twentieth Century Britain*, Oxford, Oxford University Press

Knijn, T. and F. van Wel, 2000. 'Does it Work? Employment Policies for Lone Parents in the Netherlands', Paper presented at the *DSS Policy Seminar*, University of Bath, 26–27 October

Kremer, M., 2000. 'The Illusion of Free Choice: Ideals of Care and Child Care Policy in the Flemish and Dutch Welfare States', Paper given to the GEP Conference, *New Challenges to Gender, Democracy and Welfare States*, Conference paper, Copenhagen

Land, H. and H. Rose, 1985. 'Compulsory Altruism for Some or an Altruistic Society for All?' in P. Bean, J. Ferris and D. Whyhes (eds.), *In Defence of Welfare*, London, Tavistock

Lessig, L., 1996. 'Social Meaning and Social Norms', *University of Pennsylvania Law Review*, 144, 2181–2189

Lewis, J. (ed.), 1998. *Lone Motherhood in European Welfare Regimes*, London, Jessica Kingsley

2001a. *The End of Marriage? Individualism and Intimate Relationships*, Cheltenham, Edward Elgar

2001b. 'The Decline of the Male Breadwinner Model: the Implications for Work and Care', *Social Politics* 8(2), 152–170

2002. 'Gender and Welfare State Restructuring', *European Societies*, 4(4), 331–357

Lewis, J. and B. Meredith, 1987. *Daughters who Care*, London, Routledge

Lister, R., 2000. 'Dilemmas of Pendulum Politics: Balancing Paid Work, Care and Citizenship', Conference on *Re-inventing Feminism: Theory, Politics and Practice for the New Century*, Goldsmiths College, May

McIntosh, M., 1981. 'Feminism and Social Policy', *Critical Social Policy*, 1(1), 32–42

Mead, L., 1986. *Beyond Entitlement: The Social Obligations of Citizenship*, New York: Free Press

Novak, M. and J. Cogan, 1987. *The New Consensus on Family and Welfare: A Community of Self-Reliance*, Milwaukee, American Enterprise Institute

Nussbaum, M., 1999. *Sex and Social Justice*, Oxford, Oxford University Press

Nussbaum, M. and A. Sen (eds.), 1993. *The Quality of Life*, Oxford, Oxford University Press

OECD, 2000. *Labour Force Statistics 1979–1999*, Paris, OECD

Piachaud, D., 2000. 'International Social Welfare and the Impact of Globalisation', unpublished address

Sen, A., 1985. *Commodities and Capabilities*, Oxford, North-Holland

1999. *Development as Freedom*, New York, Knopf

Stacey, J., 1990. *Brave New Families: Stories of Domestic Upheaval in Late Twentieth Century America*, New York, Basic Books

Suchman, M. C., 1997. 'On Beyond Interest: Rational Normative and Cognitive Perspectives in the Social Scientific Study of Law', *Wisconsin Law Review*, 1997, 475–501

Sugden, R., 1998. 'Conventions', in P. Newman (ed.), *The New Palgrave Dictionary of Economics and the Law*, 1, London, Macmillan

Sunstein, C. R., 1997. *Free Markets and Social Justice*, Oxford, Oxford University Press

Supiot, A. (ed.), 1999. *Au-delà de l'emploi*, Paris, Flammarion

Thair, T. and A. Risdon, 1999. 'Women in the Labour Market: Results from the Spring 1998 LFS', *Labour Market Trends*, March, 103–127

Tronto, J. C., 1993. *Moral Boundaries: A Political Argument for an Ethic of Care*, London, Routledge

Van Deth, J. and E. Scarborough (eds.), 1995. *Beliefs in Government, 4: The Impact of Values*, Oxford, Oxford University Press

Van Drenth, A., T. Knijn and J. Lewis, 2000. 'Sources of Income for Lone Mother Families: Policy Changes in Britain and The Netherlands and the Experiences of Divorced Women', *Journal of Social Policy*, 28(4), 619–641

Vandenbroucke, F., 1998. *Social Democracy, Globalization and Inequality*, London, IPPR

Weitzman, L., 1985. *The Divorce Revolution*, New York, Free Press

White, S., 2000. 'Social Rights and the Social Contract: Political Theory and the New Welfare Politics', *British Journal of Political Science*, 30, 507–532

Women's Unit, 1999. *Women's Individual Income 1996/7*, London, Cabinet Office

16 Security and the working life: new perspectives

Noel Whiteside

> In dealing with the poor some economists expect from them a virtue that we certainly do not find in ourselves. The poor, of course, have less opportunities of thrift than the well-to-do classes, and it is a little too much to expect of them . . . the extremely penurious lives which would be necessary if they were to make by their own efforts, a sufficient provision for old age . . . I do not think there is any more inclination on the part of the upper and middle classes to make sacrifices for the future than there is on the part of the poor . . . If you told a rich man that he was to give up every chief enjoyment of his life, every recreation, in order to make provision of this kind, I do not think he would make it.
>
> (Joseph Chamberlain, 1894, cited in Thane 2000:186)

This chapter bypasses the well-trodden fields of pension finance and recent pension reform to address the debate on old age protection in the context of changing working lives. By demonstrating how the meaning and objectives of pension provision have changed over time, it argues that there is an urgent need for further reform, if constructive labour market behaviours are to be encouraged by raising personal competencies and offering choice to people as they age. By exploring the weaknesses of understanding labour market experience in terms of the standard working life, it makes a case for new typologies of social support that abandon outdated concepts of social risk, themselves grounded in normative expectations of an earlier age. To foster capability, security must be guaranteed – and that security should promote autonomy, to enable people to plan each stage of their working lives.

1 Introduction

The modernisation of social protection has long been a key theme in communications from the European Commission; pensions have proved

Research for this chapter was funded by grant no. L 216252020 (ESRC Future of Governance programme) and by Zurich Financial Services. To both the author owes her thanks.

central to discussions within the Union when debating reform.[1] Driven by the rising financial burdens imposed by state pensions and the exigencies of budgetary constraints, the key solution is to encourage claimants to return to employment. The EC Employment Guidelines stress 'four pillars' for labour market reform – to promote employability, entrepreneurship, adaptability and equal opportunities – to be secured with the involvement of the social partners through the promotion of lifelong learning.[2] Labour market participation is predicated as a positive utility, advanced to reduce welfare dependency. Under the EC Guidelines, however, the concept of lifelong learning implies rupture in the single career path for a single employer under a permanent contract, hitherto the assumed foundation of a normal working life.

The EU's focus on older workers is driven more by a rationale of public finance governed by short-term objectives, less by the desire to help this target group to secure their own goals.[3] Trends towards early retirement are to be reversed, primarily to secure the financial sustainability of both public and second-tier (occupational) pensions. Less attention is paid to how active ageing might be realised to the benefit of all: the implicit assumption is simply that retirement can and should be delayed. Councils at Stockholm and Laecken (March and December 2001) set targets for the employment rate of older workers (50 per cent by 2010) and stipulated an increase in the effective retirement age by five years. The ground was laid for an application of the open method of co-ordination (OMC) to pensions. In September 2002, the first National Strategy Reports were submitted for assessment. In the context of rising life expectancy and the continuing crisis in pension finance, incentives for older workers to continue in work are increasingly seen as vital.[4]

Current relationships between active welfare and employment promotion rest, however, on uneasy foundations. Historical associations between work and social protection are well known: however, while the nature of working life is to change, there is little sign that welfare systems are adapting accordingly. National schemes of social protection are rooted in conventional labour market behaviour of a bygone age: their adaptability to innovation and new types of employment has proved variable (Whiteside 2000). Classifications of social dependency are grounded in conventions of waged work established in mid-twentieth-century Europe. This 'organised modernity' (Wagner 1998) reflected assumptions based

---

[1] See 'Presidency Conclusions: Nice European Council Meeting, 7–9 December 2000: 5; also 'Communication from the Commission to the Council, the EU Parliament . . . : Social Policy Agenda', esp. 19–20.

[2] EC (2000c: 3).

[3] See Robert Salais' chapter 18 in this volume.   [4] EC & CEU: 50–60.

on a stable, permanent employment relationship and the uniform nature of working life. Social security systems were designed to shape labour markets in accordance with this paradigm and embodied a specific conception of both waged work and the working life. Social dependency reflected (and reflects) individual inability to participate, due to sickness or invalidity, unemployment or old age. State social security still places claimants within these categories, reinforcing standardised norms of employment that are laid down in terms of hours worked per week and the number of years making up a working lifespan. These expectations reflect the world of work in the 1950s.

In the field of pensions, above all, income security at the end of a working life is proving increasingly problematic. The notion of 'retirement' was itself a reaction to the mass unemployment of the Great Depression and the post-war drive for economic modernisation. Both marginalised older workers. Mass unemployment in the 1930s stimulated demands that state pensions, originally designed to supplement falling income in old age, be converted into support for full retirement – to allow the old to make way for the young. Post-war industrial modernisation made higher productivity a central measure of economic success; less adaptable older workers became a burden. Equally, as we have argued elsewhere, a retirement income – whether offered by the state, or by the firm, or both – was designed to attract younger workers into modern industrial employment; this was essential for post-war recovery (Whiteside and Salais 1998). We should also note how the post-war 'modern' labour market invoked implicit assumptions about the gender of waged work and associated social relations. Conventions of marriage assumed the dependence of the wife on the earnings (and social insurance contributions) of her husband; this underwrote a division between waged and unwaged (principally caring) work.[5] Since the 1950s, rising life expectancy, higher living standards, more full-time education, rising rates of female labour market participation, earlier retirement (the consequence of industrial restructuring) as well as changing labour market practices – all have corroded the post-war settlement and its accompanying social and economic relationships. As a result, established pension systems are increasingly unviable.

Yet current welfare systems still reward conformity with old norms. Even though some states, under financial pressure, are modifying their pension schemes, the best pension and the definitive guarantee of financial help in the face of redundancy are given to those who work on a standard contract for a single employer. Whether we look at company pensions or any form of commercial provision, the same conclusion is

---

[5] See Jane Lewis' chapter 15.

reached. Such reward structures countermand official efforts at European level to promote labour mobility, entrepreneurship, flexibility, new working relationships (networks not hierarchies) – or to encourage workers to take time off to acquire new skills, to promote personal capability or to adjust to new work–life balances. The successful entrepreneur may reap rich rewards – but for the unsuccessful, the safety net offered to standard employees is not available. The man who shares caring work with his partner will miss promotion – and sacrifice a higher pension in his later years. These are risks for which there is no cover.

2   Security and the creation of the working life

Conventions concerning the provision of old age income have reflected changing assumptions about the relation between welfare and work. These have varied over time in accordance with the nature of the occupation, the state of the labour market and obligations inscribed within work contracts as well as by national context. The impact of ageing is not solely the province of pensions: the association between age, reduced working capacity and poor health allows the consequent social dependency to become categorised in various ways. The point at which advanced age is associated with invalidity or unemployment or total retirement from waged work will vary in accordance with the law of the land, the nature of the previous occupation, levels of skill and adaptability and personal states of health. Such factors also impinge on the shape of the working life, which in turn is influenced by family obligations, changing technologies and the security available when embarking on new projects.

Equally, apparently uniform systems of social support fulfil various purposes. As far as pensions are concerned, these purposes are highly diverse. Pensions may represent deferred salary (on a socialised or individual basis), the means to secure long and better service from essential employees, a necessary investment in industrial restructuring, a source of venture capital, as well as protection against destitution in old age. These variations in meaning impact on policy. In recent years, political vacillation over priorities has provoked confusion in the employed population. Both cuts in public budgets and falling returns from global financial markets have done substantial damage to personal independence in later life (Clark and Whiteside 2003). Accumulating a pension takes time: a wide swathe of workers is now discovering that their earlier expectations are not going to be fulfilled. This reduced prospect of an independent old age countermands the habits of thrift and hard work: the very behaviour that a liberal political economy aims to develop in the working population. It renders the elderly more dependent, not less.

Current systems are inherited from arrangements that stretch back into the nineteenth century. Through the prism of pension provision, we can read the normative assumptions structuring working life. A complex mix of schemes, each designed to serve multiple purposes, has accrued over a prolonged period. The earliest pensions covering the public sector (the civil service, local government, the armed forces and state-owned industries) were inscribed in contracts of employment that terminated at pre-defined ages (lower for the military and emergency services), with an annuity or generous lump sum. These pensions reflected their objectives: to persuade the skilled, the strong and the literate to enter state service for a pre-specified period. A generous pension counterbalanced a more disciplined (and sometimes more dangerous) life and lower earnings than might be acquired elsewhere. Its receipt implied withdrawal from state service.

The provision of pensions in the nineteenth century was not confined to the public sector. Major firms all over northern Europe developed pension schemes of varied formality that rewarded long-standing company servants with a lump sum or an annuity in their declining years. Commonly confined to skilled and white-collar staffs, the company pension facilitated manpower management. It allowed firms to discipline the insubordinate, reward the diligent and lay off the old, incapacitated and incompetent as required. Such schemes are still highly regarded by national governments and tax concessions for both corporate and professional contributions are commonplace. The company pension was a lure to the independent artisan or journeyman, who might otherwise rely on savings to acquire his own business or property, using quasi- or actual rents as a safeguard against poverty in old age. In such cases, once again advancing years lead to an adjusted working life: personal savings or pensions facilitate transitions from one type of income to another. Finally, mutuality played an important role for nineteenth-century workers, but such funds offered a different type of safeguard against old age destitution. They offered protection to contributors faced with the ill health and infirmity commonly associated with advancing years and requiring the reduction or cessation of waged work.

The first public debates about state-sponsored pensions occurred in the final decades of the nineteenth century. Then, as today, rising longevity and new production technologies had marginalised growing numbers of older workers in industrialising economies, forcing many back on communally funded systems of poor relief. In Britain, then as today, advocates of state pensions confronted a neoliberal ideology insisting that, as earnings were rising, workers could and should save for their old age (Thane, 2000 chapters 10–11). However, detailed investigation by Charles Booth in the late 1880s demonstrated definitively that poor marginal workers, particularly women and casual labourers, could not accumulate sufficient savings by themselves. Then as now, women lived longer than men; then as now, their domestic obligations translated into intermittent work in low-paid jobs that made regular saving impossible. Further, in the large casual labour markets found in London's East End, Booth discovered an army of workers with irregular incomes and poor job security, who lacked the resources for personal saving of any kind. For Booth and subsequent British reformers like William Beveridge, the solution lay in labour market reform, in projects of decasualisation, to transform intermittent employment into regular working weeks (Mansfield 1994). Such a transformation would, reformers argued, eliminate poverty, raise industrial efficiency and promote British economic competitiveness. Regular earnings offered security; this fostered social responsibility and the capacity to create personal savings: quite impossible when workers remained unsure of where the next meal was coming from or how the rent would be paid. In the UK, the introduction of labour exchanges and national insurance (1909–11) was deliberately designed to introduce a normative working week (Phillips and Whiteside 1986, chapters 2–4; Mansfield 1994). Further, by specifying the age at which a state pension might first be claimed, policy began to establish the length of the working life. The gaze of the nineteenth-century social investigator was not turned, however, to the many artisanal and skilled workers who avoided destitution and whose work patterns were not necessarily regular, but whose capabilities gave them choice and control over their own working lives. Employment rationalisation in mid-twentieth-century Britain provoked industrial conflict, notably in the coalmines and on the docks, among the higher echelons of the labour force whose work was too heavy to be undertaken five or six days per week – and whose incomes did not require it either.

Universal social security was predicated on universal common risks, capable of uniform application. This implied the creation of organised work contracts for all, stipulating the responsibilities of employers, employed and the state. As is widely acknowledged, these flowered after the Second World War.

3   Occupation and security

The post-war standardised working week and its associated state schemes of social protection was less an economic than a political product: a mediation between industrial, labour and national economic interests manifested in collective agreements and social legislation. This settlement was historically contingent: there was an urgent need to rebuild war-shattered economies, to modernise industrial production, to secure democracy and to establish universal security following the destructive impact of the Depression years of the 1930s. American paradigms, stressing the production advantages of economies of scale and of the large, integrated corporation, influenced how modernity was conceived. The introduction of new systems marginalised older workers: the association between the receipt of a state pension and retirement from the labour market was established. Post-war labour shortages encouraged firms of all sizes to develop corporate pensions to foster worker loyalty. The drive to rationalise labour distribution and to secure worker co-operation in programmes of modernisation represents an apogee in the promotion of state-sponsored security (Salais and Whiteside 1998, part III).

The first panic about future pension problems occurred not in the 1980s, but in the late 1950s. The elderly were not sharing in rising standards of living, life expectancy was growing and demographic trends threatened the equilibrium of social security budgets. Sections of the population (self-employed professionals and artisans, agricultural workers), whose work did not necessarily conform to recently established norms and who were originally excluded from state pension schemes in countries such as West Germany and France, were demanding to be included. The post-war decades witnessed further extensions in the association between old age security and a rationalised working life. To protect public expenditure from growing burdens, governments in Britain, France and the Netherlands turned to company and occupational pensions to meet rising expectations. In so doing, they reinforced the ties linking each worker to a single profession – even a single employer.

In the Netherlands, this approach was developed relatively early. Although a tax-funded, emergency pension had been established immediately after the Second World War, Dutch governments, in collaboration with the social partners, negotiated a consolidation of occupational pensions in the early 1950s. When social insurance was established in 1958, it was deliberately designed to complement, not compete with, these new schemes. Sectoral funds emerged that encompassed all small and medium-sized firms operating in pre-defined spheres of economic activity. The pooling of assets and liabilities raised levels of worker security while fostering labour mobility within given spheres of economic activity. The funds so accumulated were used for industrial reconstruction. While employers were required to offer an occupational pension, employees were not compelled to contribute: yet the attractions of a secure income in old age encouraged them to do so. Participation reached 60 per cent in 1960 and was well over 90 per cent by 1990 (Clark and Bennett 2001).

In France, complementary pensions for some specified industrial sectors and professions had emerged in the 1930s (Rapport Laroque 1962: 79–82; Friot 1996; Reynaud 1997). These were extended after the Second World War. As many firms committed to offering complementary cover were small, umbrella associations of interprofessional regimes were established to guarantee their viability. For example, ANEP (Association Nationale d'Entraide et de la Prévoyance), founded by collective agreement in 1951, covered 99,800 firms with 780,000 employees in sugar, textiles, wood and furniture by 1971. The largest was the Union des Institutions des Retraites des Salariés (UNIRS), founded in 1957 to co-ordinate provision between regional and sector-based associations of varying size. By 1971, UNIRS covered 298,000 firms with 1.9 million complementary pensioners and 4.2 million subscribing members (ARRCO 1972). In 1961, with direct encouragement from the French government, the employers' organisation (CNPF) and the main trade union federations negotiated the creation of ARRCO,[6] a national umbrella association of complementary pension associations. By the mid-1970s, membership was compulsory for all private sector workers in France and its overseas territories.

British politicians of this era were equally eager to raise pensions without invoking higher public expenditure and also turned to the private sector to solve the problem. 'The growth of private pension schemes is to be encouraged; it produces social stability' a senior Treasury official minuted a colleague in 1960; 'it should reduce the individual's dependence on the government scheme and perhaps even enable the government to get away from the expensive doctrine of universality'.[7] Liberal political perspectives fostered private, company provision devoid of state regulation or state control. In 1959, following West Germany's introduction of earnings-related state pensions, the British government created its own graduated scheme. The object was to minimise state liability while raising pension levels: employers offering occupational pensions could contract out of these new state obligations. Under strong fiscal incentives, the cover of British private occupational pensions peaked in 1967 at 49 per cent of the employed population (Whiteside 2003). Although this figure fell back to 46 per cent in 2002, in the 1980s and 1990s UK governments promoted commercial personal pensions to augment numbers covered by the private sector, albeit with restricted success.

Although similar in strategy, these systems varied in their funding, management and coverage. They also offered different degrees of

---

[6] Association des régimes de retraite complémentaire.
[7] A. J. Collier (Treasury) to Robertson 13 October 1960: T 227/1426, Public Record Office [PRO], Kew, London.

security. In the French case, compulsory membership of an ARRCO-endorsed scheme was based financially on Pay As You Go (PAYG). Growing demands for increased pension finance have necessitated higher contributions (or reduced benefits), which is assumed to add directly to labour on-costs, thereby exacerbating unemployment. Dutch sectoral schemes, by contrast, are funded. During the 1990s, their investment shifted towards global financial markets: highly profitable returns more than met growing demand. The Dutch system emerged as a paradigm for EU financial strategists eager to cut state pension budgets, although market downturns in 2000–3 affected reserves and may cause this judgement to be revised (van Riel, Hemerijck and Visser 2003). In both these cases, the professional basis of pensions allows a mutualisation of risk; labour mobility between firms within sectors is unconstrained and, in France, national organisation underwrites security between all groups. Equally, thanks to management by the social partners, when pension revisions are required, they are collectively negotiated. There is no question of one group suddenly losing pension rights while others retain theirs; this has been the case in the UK.

The voluntary nature of company pensions means that the British system was never as complete or secure as its Dutch or French counterparts. Until very recently, no pension protection existed for the worker in a firm that was taken over, or went bankrupt. Those who change jobs put their pension rights at risk, as the regulations governing transfers were neither widely understood nor respected. Moreover, as the ECJ declared that both ARRCO and the Dutch scheme form part of those countries' respective welfare states, neither is required to comply with EU competition policy. The UK financial services sector is based on market competition, not co-operation. Commercial management did not embrace representation of the insured, nor mechanisms to underwrite failure, although governments have tried to counteract these effects since the late 1990s. All the same, occupational pensions outside the public sector have been a lottery: recent downturns in global financial markets and consequent extensions of new international accountancy rules have revealed extensive debts. Schemes have closed, or been transferred from defined benefit (based on a proportion of salary) to defined contribution, based only on financial returns to a personal savings pot. This transfer of risk from the collective to the individual is justified in terms of promoting flexible employment, but lessens the financial requirement from employers. To the more jaundiced eye, it seems to endorse the late nineteenth-century solution of promoting retirement income through personal thrift.

This variation between Dutch, French and British occupational pensions frequently obscures their common roots. Yet they still share certain features. All have adopted the retirement ages specified by their respective state schemes; they have also imported conventions of manpower management into the provision of old age security. The best rewards go to the loyal employee promoted through the firm's hierarchy and retiring at peak salary. On the continent, the grounding of these schemes in industrial agreement has rendered them relatively immune to direct state intervention.[8] To have more than one profession, to move between different firms or sectors, or to set up an independent business, is to invite risk. '[A]typical workers continue to be less well covered by occupational schemes' as the European Commission reported recently; 'in many Member States, workers who change jobs tend to end their careers with reduced occupational pension rights compared to workers who stay with the same employer'.[9] As state pension rights are reduced, so the significance of these schemes for old age security grows. They reward a standardised working life in a single profession – and assume complete withdrawal from the labour market at its end. Although French and Dutch schemes have long sustained collective guarantees and the UK government is proposing to do the same, none offers transferability and security to cover labour mobility across EU Member States. This is an agenda that needs urgently to be addressed. The historical achievements of state-sponsored agreements between the social partners offer a possible path forward.

Over time, the meaning and significance of pensions has changed. Early pensions had reflected job-specific working lives, recognising how physical attributes and professional experience change with age. Their receipt permitted a transfer to new work, or self-employment, or partial (or total) withdrawal from the labour market. The establishment of universal state pensions invoked a standard time span of employment: a lifetime's subordination to the standard working week, with the prospect of total idleness in declining years. Pensions now had to serve as total income replacement for the elderly. Uniform working lives sustained distinctions between different 'risks': unemployment, sickness, invalidity and retirement. The regulations surrounding state social security still embody incentives to co-operate. Claims from the non-compliant are fraudulent. The pension reflects less the onset of infirmity (and thus work incapacity) than an individual attainment of a specified age.

How far the categorisation of social dependency ever accurately reflected workers' experience is open to question. Social protection

---

[8] Evidence of Camerlynck (Professor of Law, University of Paris), to Donovan Commission: minutes of evidence 7 February 1967: 2876–2877, LAB 28/543, PRO.
[9] EC & CEU: 8.

was designed to shape labour market behaviour: simultaneously, it was adapted to established working practices. How far this has been – or is – conducive to the promotion of personal capabilities is open to question. To this aspect we now turn.

4   The mirage of social classification

In recent decades, the standard working life of the 1940s has gone into decline. For young people, entrance into permanent employment with associated social protection and pension rights is postponed. For the first time in the twentieth century, the current generation has not achieved a higher standard of living than their parents' generation at the equivalent age (Chauvel 2002). There is a rising incidence of part-time and temporary employment among new labour market entrants in most EU Member States (Guillemard 2003: 240–243).

At the other end of the age spectrum, economic activity rates for males in the Union over the age of fifty-five declined sharply in the years 1971–2000: in Germany, by 41 per cent, in France by 43 per cent, in the Netherlands by 36 per cent. The drop over the same period for men aged between sixty and sixty-four has been more marked: 59 per cent in Germany, 77.5 per cent in France and nearly 63 per cent in the Netherlands (Guillemard 2003: 26–29). All EU States have experienced corrosion of their standard retirement age. Even as longevity is increasing, the duration of the working life is falling, a trend also reflected in statistics of higher unemployment and incapacity rates. Once out of work, older workers have greater difficulty finding another job: long-term unemployment is higher among older age groups (Casey and Wood 1994; Guillemard 2003: 35–39) and the quantity of on-the-job training available to older workers is less (Guillemard 2003: 44–47). Invalidity and disability benefits have also helped disguise distinctions between unemployment and early retirement (most notoriously in the Netherlands in the 1970s and early 1980s) (Dreyfus et al. 2003). Advancing years combined with heavy or repetitive manual work damage health and thus productivity, explaining why employers are reluctant to take on older workers. For the old as well as the young, recent labour market change has created uncertainty and insecurity, and the porosity of social classification has been exposed.

Many analysts interpret these developments as the labour market effects of an emerging, new post-industrial economy: a consequence that has engendered a collapse in the standard working life (lifetime employment in a single occupation for one employer). This is a mistake: rather, the situation reflects the consequences of changing economic and political perspectives. Employers are now increasingly reluctant to pay weekly wages to workers surplus to immediate requirements and governments are much less inclined to force them to do so. The financial obligations of permanent work contracts can be evaded by adopting more 'flexible' employment practices: this has secured official approval since the late 1990s. The promotion of a standardised working life has been jettisoned in the process.

However, the tools of labour market analysis inherited from a previous age have not been adapted accordingly. As matters stand, there is no way of knowing whether the young person in temporary employment is there through personal choice (earning money while training, or caring for a child or establishing a new business, for example) or because it is the only option. Equally, some of the ostensibly retired, particularly the early retired, supplement a pension with part-time or casual earnings. This generates another anomaly: the younger 'retired' will sustain a higher income than the old old who, after the age of eighty, can no longer earn. Whichever way it is viewed, current labour market classifications blur the type of distinction needed to understand developments and to promote personal capability.

The classification of social dependency, even in periods of full employment, has long involved distortions of working experience. For example, in the 1950s, sickness rates in factories sited in French rural and wine growing regions rose at harvest time, when extra labour was required on family-based smallholdings.[10] Equally, invalidity and disablement benefits, even in the years of full employment, bridged a gap for manual workers between declining physical capacity and the statutory retirement age. Working capacity and health status are not constant between occupations and over time: given a choice, employers will prefer the young and physically fit over the older job seeker. Studies of the interwar years in Britain show that official sickness and disability rates directly reflected the changing incidence of unemployment. In an economic downturn, employers try to shed less productive workers. As a result, rising unemployment reveals degrees of physical incapacity that, in better times, would probably not be considered as such. In an economic depression, employers exercise their selection preferences higher and higher up the health spectrum of the labour market and, in so doing, discard older workers (Whiteside 1988). The divisions between health and illness, between ages of working incapacity are relative, not absolute.

During the post-war decades, most governments assumed that the interests of national economies, workers and firms were best served by an

---

[10] Labour Attaché, 14 January 1964, Annexes I and II; LAB 10/1933, PRO.

accumulation of experience and skill founded on a lifetime's service by the former to the latter. Such new expectations have fostered inconsistencies. Throughout Europe, higher levels of invalidity among older manual and unskilled workers reflected how a career in heavy physical work forces 'retirement' under another label at an earlier age. The categorisation of social dependency does not operate as originally anticipated – largely because the presumption that the working life can be uniform has proved fallacious.

When viewed from the dimension of gender, this fallacy becomes even more apparent. Throughout the post-war years, in European countries where pension provision remains largely determined by social insurance contributions, pension income for women has remained persistently lower than for men, while their life expectancy has been higher. Pension income has been constructed as the reward for conformity with a working life based on a male-breadwinner model. The child-rearing years in women coincide with the period when employers expect workers to be at their most productive. In France in the 1960s, even though childcare facilities were relatively well developed, the work profiles of mothers with young children were far from the male-based ideal. Frequent prolonged sick leave and other absences indicated how family responsibilities took its toll of a woman's wage earning capabilities, thereby restricting both her chances of promotion and her future old age income. The bulk of applications for supplementary pension assistance were from women, both widowed and single, whose working lives, waged and unwaged, failed to conform to the prescribed norm. Much research has addressed this issue; the results require no reinforcement here (e.g. Ginn, Street and Arber 2001).[11] Even in an era of full employment and apparently uniform working lives, old age security evaded large numbers of people.

The categorisation of social dependency requires re-appraisal. There is a severe mismatch between the analytical tools used to interpret labour market change and the type of employment behaviours to be encouraged. How can the status of the temporary employee or part-timer be understood? How can she be encouraged to develop her skills and take charge of her working life when her job status is uncertain, the bills must be paid and she cannot plan for the future? How can she be protected from a life lived hand-to-mouth, with concomitant risks of poverty and potential social exclusion? How can we prevent her forming part of a new casual labour market similar to the one Booth condemned over a century ago?

[11] French examples drawn from social security records retained at the CPAM, Nantes.

5   Conclusion: promoting capabilities and the future working life

The prospect of financial insecurity in old age provokes risk-averse labour market behaviour that can be counterproductive to the development of individual potential and the promotion of capabilities. In this respect, retirement – now a certainty more than a risk – exerts a huge influence on the shape of the working life. Current EU incentives to promote adaptability and independence fit ill with public and private pension regimes that reward consolidated career structures based on lifelong service in a single occupation and penalising trans-national mobility. They sustain a European labour market completely at odds with the aims of current EU policy. The single currency and the imminence of a single market in financial products promote commercial Europe. The singular immobility of labour, reinforced by old age pension systems, impedes its social equivalent. The freedom of movement for workers is an essential counterpart to the freedom of movement for goods and capital in the generation of economic growth. From a capability perspective, mobility cannot be achieved without concomitant security. The promotion of personal and collective opportunities requires cast-iron guarantees for workers and their dependants. Old age security should encourage, not penalise, changes of career path in accordance with changing physical and intellectual capacities, work experience and personal choice. Accumulated pension rights offer the necessary resources to foster independence and personal capabilities. The creation of European legal rights, negotiated by the social partners and typified by the Parental Leave Directive, offers one possible way forward.

Events in the 1990s exposed the reluctance of politicians to construct a Europe-wide agenda on pensions, or to abandon national social policy frameworks. Demographic crisis is tackled by realigning the existing mixture of obligations on the state, industry and the individual. Far less attention is paid to re-appraising the basic principles of social security and classifications of social dependency. Pensions are discussed uniquely in terms of the burdens they impose on national budgets. The common solution since the 1990s has been to reduce state obligations and to foster personal saving, raising individual risk and thereby imposing further insecurities on workers already discouraged from taking the initiative in planning their working lives. Downturns in global financial markets since 1999 have exposed some of the problems involved with this strategy. The rest remain similar to those identified by Joseph Chamberlain in the 1890s, as cited at the start of this chapter. Personal pension saving offers no security, but penalises those on lower incomes – particularly women with interrupted working careers, who are the great majority of present and future pensioners. Most importantly, by reducing employers' obligations, this represents another step towards a 'drive to the bottom' in social protection.

The challenge that Europe faces is less about the transformation of public accounts to meet the expectations of global financial markets (the driving force behind current policy) than about how to adjust social support to the restructured working life in a more deregulated and uncertain job market. Security is essential to lifelong learning, to encouraging adaptation to new situations and to promoting capabilities. Capabilities change in the course of life: physical strength (still a prerequisite in construction and transport) declines with age, but expertise and acumen grow. There are health and other advantages in encouraging workers to move with their changing capacities: a lifetime of repetitious manual work will lead to early retirement and inactive, totally dependent ageing later on. Transference between different careers should be fostered, not punished by forcing workers to take greater responsibility for their old age income security. Taking time out in earlier life, or switching to part-time work – to accommodate child-rearing, or caring for elderly relatives, or retraining – should not impede the right to support in extreme old age. Similarly, allowing partial retirement in later years (as currently promoted in the Netherlands and Finland) would enable pension income to rise when it is most needed, when total incapacity strikes. This is not rocket science: simply a recognition that work can be adapted to changing personal capabilities rather than the other way around. Old systems of universal classification of social dependency should no longer impose uniform treatments for pre-defined groups of social dependants.

The idea of flexible security recalls Alain Supiot's report (Supiot *et al.* 1999, chapter 5); work participation should endow individuals with 'social drawing rights', to finance career breaks and to facilitate change in the pattern of a working life. Although the report does not detail how such a system might be funded or run, it is attractive and pertinent because it offers individuals the chance to take charge of their lives: the concepts of choice, responsibility and empowerment, all central to the promotion of capability, underpin its realisation. It does not seem insuperably difficult to imagine how people might negotiate partial (or total) suspension from waged work on a temporary basis in exchange for partial (or total) extensions in a working life in later years. The convention of labour market withdrawal on retirement is currently not respected: prolonged life expectancy has translated – by and large – into incapacity for people in their late seventies and eighties, when a retirement income is no longer an option, but a vital necessity. There is space here for negotiated arrangements and, thanks to its close association with work, the involvement of the social partners. Of course, such arrangements must be voluntary. However, if Supiot's idea of flexible security is to be taken up, then current debates over pensions might be used to promote this agenda.

So what may the future hold? The demise of the single-career, forty-year working life appears imminent, allowing a revival of older, more diverse working patterns. There is, however, the real risk that this diversity will generate the tiered labour market observed in late nineteenth century Britain, with a renewed casual residuum living hand-to-mouth on the borders of legitimacy, quite unable to provide for their own future needs. It is possible for people to develop more varied strategies towards work and employment, to allow specific periods of life to reflect different types of working capability. This would imply that retirement renews its meanings; a withdrawal from waged employment need not necessarily imply a transfer to passive dependency, but could offer a pathway into another life that utilises accumulated skills and knowledge that would otherwise become redundant. Allowing the concept of lifelong learning to further such a strategy, to offer citizens a second or third active life, to help the transition towards inevitable infirmity, presents one future option. The challenge must be to further such ambitions, to offer the security required for persons to seize opportunities to retrain, to gain new experience, to participate in socially desirable activities – all essential for them to realise capabilities that offer them liberty to control their working lives. Here is an agenda for the modernisation of social protection, to allow it to focus on how time is spent, rather than on spurious categories of social dependency. This could be taken up by the social partners, to allow negotiated solutions to develop in accordance with new working lives.

REFERENCES

ARRCO, Tenth Anniversary Report, 1972
Casey, B. and S. Wood, 1994. 'Great Britain: Firm Policy, State Policy and the Employment and Unemployment of Older Workers', in F. Naschold and B. de Vroom (eds.), *Regulating Employment and Welfare*, Berlin, De Gruyter, 363–394
Chauvel, L., 2002. 'Social Generations and Life Chances', Unpublished paper presented to seminar, Paris, Sciences Po, July
Clark, G. L. and P. Bennett, 2000. 'The Dutch Model of Sector-Wide Supplementary Pensions: Fund Governance, Finance and European Competition Policy', at http://papers.ssrn.com/so13/papers.cfm? abstract_id = 228949
Clark, G. L. and N. Whiteside (eds.), 2003. *Pension Security in the 21st Century: Redrawing the Public – Private Divide*, Oxford, Oxford University Press
Dreyfus, M., E. Nijhof, P. Pasture and N. Whiteside, 2003. 'Syndicats et Etats sociaux', Unpublished paper for colloque, *L'Apogée des syndicalismes*, Paris, November

Friot, B., 1996. *Puissance du salariat*, Paris, La Dispute

Ginn, J., D. Street and S. Arber, 2001. *Women, Work and Pensions: International Issues and Prospects*, Buckingham, Open University Press

Guillemard, A.-M., 2003. *L'age de l'emploi: les sociétés à l'épreuve du vieillissement*, Paris, Armand Colin

Mansfield, M., 1994. 'Naissance d'une définition institutionnelle du chômage', in M. Mansfield, R. Salais and N. Whiteside (eds.), *Aux sources du chômage*, Paris, Belin, 295–325

Phillips, G. and N. Whiteside, 1986. *Casual Labour*, Oxford, Oxford University Press

Rapport Laroque, 1962. *Rapport de la Commission d'études des problèmes de la vieillesse*, Paris

Reynaud, E. 1997. 'France: A National and Contractual Second Tier', in M. Rein and E. Wadensjo, *Enterprise and the Welfare State*, Cheltenham, Edward Elgar, 68–72

Salais, R. and N. Whiteside (eds), 1998. *Governance, Industry and Labour Markets in Britain and France*, London, Routledge

Supiot, A. *et al.*, 1999. *Au-delà de l'emploi*, Paris, Flammarion; published as *Beyond Employment: Changes in Work and the Future of Labour Law in Europe*, Oxford, Oxford University Press

Thane, P., 2000. *Old Age in English History: Past Experiences, Present Issues*, Cambridge, Cambridge University Press

Van Riel, B., A. Hemerijck and J. Visser, 2003. 'Is there a Dutch Way to pension reform?', in G. L. Clark and N. Whiteside (eds), *Pension Security in the 21st Century*, Oxford, Oxford University Press, 64–93

Wagner, P., 1998. *A Sociology of Modernity*, London, Routledge

Whiteside, N., 1988. 'Unemployment and Health', *Journal of Social Policy*, 17, 177–194

  2000. 'From Full Employment to Flexibility: Britain and France, 1960–2000', in B. Strath (ed.), *After Full Employment*, Brussels, PIE/Peter Laing, 107–135

  2003. 'Historical Perspectives and the Politics of Pension Reform', in G. L. Clark and N. Whiteside (eds.), *Pension Security in the 21st Century*, Oxford, Oxford University Press, 21–44

Whiteside, N. and R. Salais, 1998. 'Comparing Welfare States: France and Britain, 1930–1960', *European Journal of Social Policy*, 8(2), 139–155

17 Social needs, development, territories and full employment based on solidarity

Pierre Bachman

1 Introduction

The present chapter is driven by the personal conviction that a European identity must be built around a new form of full employment to be inscribed in the reality and history of its nations. At its heart is *solidarity*. This chapter seeks to define some of the conditions essential for full employment. Section 2 looks at a straightforward definition that might be provided for full employment based on solidarity. I then go on to examine the consequences of such a definition with respect to how political action is conceived (section 3), different forms of democracy and collective projects yet to be invented (notably where territorial administrations are concerned) (section 4). I conclude in section 5 with a discussion on the role a European Social Dialogue could play in the design of a system of 'professional social security' based on a defined status of 'person potentially in work'.

2 How might full employment based on solidarity be defined?

A concept of full employment based on solidarity starts out from human aspirations to achieve happiness, to take pleasure in life, to realise one's potential, to succeed in life and in work. Such aspirations are expressed in social movements and are part of the underlying psychological bedrock of each and every one of us. However, there is nothing spontaneous about the solutions to be provided in response to those needs, which we can classify into three broad groups.

First, there is the need for various types of *security*, guaranteeing the human right to existence in a number of different domains: training, work, employment, freely chosen and satisfying mobility, resources, income and salaries, access to healthcare and to health itself, and security in old age. When translated into guarantees and collective institutions, such forms of security provide the foundation for solidarity between individuals, between different activities, between generations and between geographical regions.

Next comes the need for *time*. Human time is not financial market time. The temporal rhythms of the production of wealth, the acquisition of qualifications, of expertise, of active citizenship are the rhythms of life, not those of money. In order to learn, create, co-operate, reflect, choose – in short, to live – clock time synonymous with profit, obligations, work rates, efficiency, stifled individuality, uniformity and exclusion must be rendered less important, and the time marked by the rhythm of human lives,[1] including life at work, given greater weight.

And, lastly, there is the need for *choice*. To have one's life under one's own control, to develop and change, to take on responsibilities, to create, to work, to act, all require a capability for individual choice far beyond the rights, and above all the practices prevalent today in the world of labour. The demand for genuine choice to be available to all implies that relationships based on domination and exploitation of all kinds must become a thing of the past. Democracy and real equality in civil society and at work must become, in new forms, norms for measuring economic, social and political efficiency.

Full employment cannot therefore be defined simply as putting the unemployed back to work. It is quite possible to reduce unemployment to a level considered acceptable using means that are in fact counterproductive for work, income, and the forms of security described above. Is this not to some extent precisely what we have witnessed in France since 1997?

The notion of full employment is therefore not based on any consensus, and is a major goal for the trade union movement. In recent French literature, we can find several definitions of it, ranging from market equilibrium to the right to an activity irrespective of its precise nature, or the demand for the socialisation of all. But the concept may also be fleshed out by input from experience gained in past trade union action. Thus considered, full employment is employment that satisfies at one and the same time the social needs and aspirations of those who wish to live from the proceeds of their work. In this case, it involves the simultaneous development of the capabilities of individuals and their genuine freedom of choice. The form of solidarity created by this type of full employment is not simply a passive solidarity, such as that involved in assisting others to help repair damage, or the provision of charity or aid. It is a genuine, active solidarity founded on the mastery of one's own fate in the context of a collective approach carrying with it consequences for the structure

---

[1] See most notably Le Duigou and Le Bris (1998: 55), Lallement (1998).

of society. In France, social security and public services are the structural tools for this form of solidarity.

Full employment based on solidarity can thus become a vector fostering radical structural changes in economic, political and social relationships. The coherence that arises in living and working environments between aspirations, actual possibilities and potential opportunities calls for a new conception (or rather, an older conception to be rediscovered) of political action, and democratic choice (in economic and employment terms). One central proposal flows from this: European social dialogue should be creating the components of a defined status as a 'person potentially in work'. We will look at these points in the sections which follow.

3   Political action and local – regional projects

A balanced and fertile construction of Europe should take on the goals and issues inherent in satisfying the needs discussed above as its own. However, not only has this requirement not been met, but the economy has in fact been characterised since the mid-1970s by underutilisation or waste of human, financial and physical capacity.

European countries in general, and France in particular, are in fact comparatively rich. There is room for a national strategy, dependent neither on the size nor the level of development, but on the existence of a *national project* springing from confrontation of points of view borne collectively within society and integrating the European dimension. Political agreement, and *coherence*, should be sought on the basis of full employment based on solidarity and of an interfacing of national development strategy and common European policies. Such a strategy would act in relation to national and European institutions, to invoke the 'law' of peoples, of the satisfaction of their needs, as against an essentially monetarist or financial stance. The free movement – or, to be more precise the free accumulation – of capital, must be constrained by individual rights at a higher level, notably in the domain of work, in order to meet the criteria of *social efficacy*. This means that the State[2] must take back the lead in political and social matters. Compelling the State to play its role as organiser of society, as the wellspring of medium- and long-run vision, as the vehicle and the partner of development projects designed to respond to social needs, is increasingly an imperative goal.

Nevertheless, projects which combine the economic, social and political dimensions are rare. How then might it be possible to build projects whereby companies and local – regional administrations can work together proactively to create genuine wealth? Local – regional diversity

[2] Roger (2000).

is, from this point of view, an asset, a potential, and can be seen as a factor for reduction of uncertainty and a more independent vector[3] for the creation of resources.

Consider the case of France. The task would be:

(1) To drive *local – regional development dynamics* by co-ordinating central government policies, the role played by regional administrations, agreements on long-term objectives between central authorities and local governments and corporate strategies.

(2) To bolster the capacities for *expert analysis and forward planning* of regional government councils by creating genuine capabilities at the regional level for strategic guidance and evaluation to serve development, innovation and enrichment of activities.

(3) To broaden the conception of *infrastructure and land use planning*, based on the spatial allocation of created or planned wealth, in order to move in the direction of a concept of territorial development as a source of new wealth and employment, with the aim of combining the satisfaction of needs with a holistic conception of economic efficiency.

(4) The role played by the *business community*, which is essential, must be re-examined in order to create a denser fabric of genuine small and medium enterprises (SMEs), with a view also to developing the relationship between companies and their regions. All too often this relationship goes no further than competitive tenders or dependency.

In this way a political, social and economic legitimacy could be created, capable of avoiding the excesses relating to corporate relocation and windfalls. We also need to move away from public financial aid and towards action and incentive. Hence the need to evaluate the effectiveness of the funding provided and to limit productive configurations that are abnormally work-intensive or which incorporate abnormally low labour costs.

To achieve this, instead of direct aid, it would be necessary:[4]

- To promote the building of a local fabric of *co-contractors* and certain *corporate seeding practices*.

- To *pool economic and social risks* at the level of the region or any other relevant territorial unit,[5] and to mobilise savings at the local level. For example, the planning agreements signed between central and regional governments in 1999 and 2000 should have announced the creation of a fund for development, employment and innovation, setting out clearly its instruments, arrangements for decentralised regional management, resources and objectives.

---

[3] As compared with the dominant idea of submission to 'external constraints', real or imagined, stemming from the processes of globalisation.
[4] These proposals are based on Colletis and Levet (1997).
[5] For example, the employment catchment area, or an economic unit such as a major port.

- To see innovation *holistically* in all its dimensions, and not focused solely on technology as harnessed to heavyweight or prestigious programmes. In particular, the task must be to bring together the business community, research and training potential at the local level, under arrangements that are effective in promoting innovation and the general interest.

Mastery of complex systems is a capability which allows the most coherent form of development, for it creates new jobs which tend themselves to generate further employment (in specialist or neighbourhood services, for example). It tends to push the level of qualifications upward and broadens job supply in the labour market. For example, the regional commissions described below could play another role: the co-ordination of labour qualifications, capacities, needs and prospects in the geographical areas for which they are responsible.

National legislation and European law must be used to stress that layoffs must be a final resort, to be used only if economic difficulties are genuine and grave, with all parties having their say in the assessment that this is in fact so. Redundancy programmes cannot be based solely on the desire to make a company more profitable in financial terms. Employers must bear joint and several liability, notably within the same branch of industry or the same local or regional area, for arriving at concrete proposals to be put to their workforces (e.g. new jobs, retraining leave, redeployment, vocational training courses).

The validity of such proposals must be monitored by *tripartite regional commissions* (composed of local elected representatives, trade union organisations, employers' organisations). This should also apply to national and international corporate groups whose strategic decisions impact not only the workforce they employ directly, but also the jobs generated indirectly by their business activity, in sub-contracting companies and elsewhere.

4   Deepening the democratic process

If the modes of political action are to be transformed, and if we are to see them lead to projects achieving solidarity-based full employment, there must be a deepening of the democratic process. Democracy based on the delegation of power to political and trade union representatives[6] must be combined with a new and direct process for the definition of strategies, projects and decisions. This is so because the geographical

---

[6] The CGT's proposal for a new type of trade union representation is a move in this direction.

space relevant to any given decision rarely coincides with institutionalized divisions, such as local municipalities, cantons, *départements*, regions or even nations. The relevant territorial unit today is increasingly the geographical space for which a project[7] or an activity is designed, developed, implemented and monitored. The nature and magnitude of such projects vary, as do the geographical areas in which they arise and are implemented. This shift stems from changes in the scale of companies' projects, activities and goals. We look below first at powers (section 4.1), an issue which will lead us on to the major distinction between negotiation and deliberation (section 4.2).

4.1 The various levels of powers and democracy

In order to resolve the issue raised by powers and democracy at all the levels where decisions can be taken, it is not enough to simply point to the labour movement. It is necessary to build a movement capable of acting towards the goal of acquiring powers, and all the more so that political parties, the State and European institutions can no longer be the only bodies in which choices are decided. At the same time, the latter must regain credibility, effectiveness and legitimacy to ensure that their policies are perceived and assessed by the public, without ambiguity, as changing people's lives in line with their own aspirations.

In any society, confrontation and conflict are healthy, as long as they are channelled by democratic, civilised rules. Any society that sets out to deny its own internal conflicts is a society that is constructing itself on a bed of frustration. That frustration will undermine it to such a point that society itself will be at risk. The concept of 'social cohesion' belongs to this category of frozen, conservative notions, the purpose of which is to stifle conflict. The concept of 'coherence' is much to be preferred, when it is applied to the dynamics of social development. There is an urgent need to take a leap forward in terms of our conception of democracy and democratic rights, in order to legitimise individual aspirations and link them into the relevant general interest shared by all.

Even today, leaders make choices and seek to rally citizens around their decisions. We are living in a democracy based on validation and sanction. We might well wonder what 'democracy' really means when it is confused with management or governance techniques.

Powers must thus be reviewed and their relevant areas of application redefined. Within these spaces, we must *negotiate* and *deliberate*.

---

[7] Where the trade union movement is concerned, we could define a project as the rational and analytical formulation of needs and aspirations with a view to ensuring their satisfaction within a coherent and sustainable vision of development.

4.2   Negotiation and deliberation

Social negotiation must be put back at the heart of social relationships, corporate strategy and work processes, along with its objectives and its rights. Its scope must be broadened to cover every topic of concern to employees and all the physical spaces relating to them, ranging from the places in which they live and work, to Europe. But negotiation is a *trade-off*. Its outcomes can be challenged when the balance of power changes. It cannot substitute for the capability to deliberate with which all actors in society must be empowered in order to reach decisions.[8]

Neither the State nor public authorities should delude themselves by believing that social negotiation alone can regulate society. They have a crucial role to play in providing a shared framework for negotiation by taking political power back from economics.

The process of *deliberation* brings together on a voluntary basis – if needed, the political authorities should provide encouragement – all stakeholders, in order to design, decide and implement a project. Deliberation has an extra component compared with negotiation, and this is the effective commitment of the resources possessed by all, with the aim of collectively reaching by the end of the process of deliberation, a fair outcome. To achieve such an outcome there must be a common good, a higher interest that none of the actors will dare contradict. For example, regional economic development, genuine freedom of choice, or new jobs in the corporate sector may all achieve such a status of 'common good'. This means that private sector interests are obliged to demonstrate during their action that they are in phase with the general interest. In this way, the role of *civil or organised society* is expanded: the legitimacy of an organisation will come from its clearly identified contribution to the shared goal as defined above.[9] Such an approach is not easy. It will necessarily imply numerous debates, confrontations of points of view, partial outcomes and conflicts before a sustainable agreement can be reached that will give structure to public opinion, to political and social behaviour.

In addition to political institutions and their associated elected representatives, the definition and collective management of decisions, actions and policies are the concern of parties, trade unions, voluntary associations and all citizens wishing to become involved. Structures and practices embodying direct democracy are needed at these levels in order to redistribute and reinvigorate responsibilities and capabilities for decision and

[8] See chapter 14 by Jean De Munck and Isabelle Ferreras in this volume.
[9] See Salais (2000).

management. We *might, for example,* imagine the setting up of 'committees or councils for civil or civic deliberation' which would be entrusted with responsibilities. They would thus become a crucible enabling direct and immediate intervention by the general population, a force for driving and calling to order the actors at all economic, social and political levels, alongside elected assemblies, which would have the final power of decision, as well as more transparent and more easily overseen public responsibility.

Today, the fragmentary beginnings of this type of practice or structure already exist in European countries. In France for example, there are the development councils instituted under small regional entities (*pays*) and conurbations, the economic and social councils, the railway line committees encouraged by certain regional administrations, the purpose of which is to collaborate with the SNCF (French Railways) in order to find the best ways of improving public transport services. Nevertheless, all too often this is simply consultation without any real decision-making capability granted to the bodies concerned. If such capabilities were to be granted to them, their make-up would need to be changed, along with their profile and role, in order to achieve the genuine diversity required for the exercise of these new powers, and to give them unassailable legitimacy. At the very least, it would be possible to experiment with structures appropriate to such new practices for the involvement of citizens. The task for such bodies might be to prepare the way for decisions to be adopted by elected assemblies and to place implementation on a contractual basis for example – or, in relation to employment and lay-offs, to assess the relevant dynamics, reasons and validity in each case, working through the tripartite regional commissions suggested earlier.

Such proposals are not aimed at the sharing of power,[10] but at an extension of the democratic domain to encompass a number of domains in which at the present time decisions are either not deliberated or not taken at all, or are deliberated and taken under a system in which elected representatives are responsible for relations with the general population – sometimes to the point of adopting a demagogic or populist stance – and in which technical executive staff appropriate for themselves, within a technocracy, the actual definition of strategy, working through institutions that elude public oversight. They are aimed, by the same token, at opening up the scope of democratic action.

---

[10] The argument relates very much therefore to capability, i.e. the collective power to act, or to choose, and not to the attribution of power, i.e. delegation of power to a public figure who takes decisions in lieu of the community or its administration. In this context, the role and responsibilities of elected representatives acquire greater value and the trade union movement a new role, the legitimacy of which it must proceed to demonstrate.

5   **Conclusion: European social dialogue and the right to professional social security**

There will be no major progress on rights and freedoms in the corporate sector unless there is an effective right to *employment*. The right to employment is enshrined, for example, in the French Constitution. Could it become, through national and/or European legislation, an individual right that workers would actually be able to invoke to challenge their employers when dismissals are planned? This 'defensive' dimension would be accompanied by an 'offensive' one, the latter both a logical extension of the former and its most effective safeguard. This presupposes both an improvement in labour law and a revision of business law to take employee demands into account, and this has not as yet been attempted at the European level.

Despite this, the time has come to change the excessive privileges and disproportionate importance given to property rights in corporate governance. The real wealth of corporate networks is, and will increasingly be, the expertise they accumulate and which circulates within them, the actual creators and holders of which are the salaried employees. 'Professional social security' is a right that must be gradually instituted in order to give priority to investment in human beings, by creating conditions conducive to secure social and professional mobility. If this is not done, economic domination, instability and uncertainty will stifle any freeing up of the human initiative and capacity that it will be necessary to deploy if the fundamental needs described at the beginning of this analysis are to be satisfied.

In this context, the European Social Dialogue is not all that it should be – but, even worse, such a dialogue is not seen at the present time as a driving force for the construction of the European community. Specifically, the development of employment is made subject to the *employability* of individuals through a selection of their *competences*.[11]

Faced with these barriers, in the interests of European Social Dialogue itself, it is legitimate to devote thought to concepts that would provide more effective vehicles for social development. The concept of *capability* leads to such reflection if it is given all three of its meanings: the property of being able to contain, the contents, and the ability to do, to understand and to act. The argument relates in fact here to the potential in each individual and to the application of that potential through action for the self, for others and through others.[12] The prospects defined by

---

[11] See chapter 3 by Bénédicte Zimmermann in this volume.
[12] Schwartz (1988).

this volume, as I understand them, would make it possible to go beyond approaches that are too strictly economic, towards other methods that are more anthropological, ethical and political. This means that it is essential that

Each person should be able, practically and locally, to verify in his or her work and life that commitments are being met and are leading, for themselves and those close to them, to genuine improvements and to genuine consideration of their needs (which are themselves modified by ongoing changes in the economy and work). The issue here is one of social ties. Individuals should be able to see and feel that they actively participate in a collective project whose progress they are accountable for, in a system of mutual expectations.[13]

This defines the condition to be met for effective freedom of choice along with the condition governing responsibility to the community.

We might, given this, imagine an essential dimension of added value for a European identity, of which the European Social Dialogue could be the source, as a structure for substantive deliberation (in the meaning defined above) rather than conventional social negotiation. This would be a innovation designed to ensure recognition of the capabilities of individuals in a community made up of the diversity of European cultures, by the diversity of its nations. It would involve granting to every man and woman a defined status as she enters working life. Such a status of *'person potentially in work'* would affect the whole range of economic, social and political rights for each individual in a European democracy. Enjoyment of such a status and its symbolic force could be a strong means conferring a more robust, reinvigorated meaning to the notion of European citizenship. It would give practical reality to the guarantees benefiting individuals and could be adapted in different versions to match the range of real-life situations: work, public services, students, elected representatives, trade union activists and voluntary association workers, those deprived of employment, household work, etc. By integrating the structures already in place or to be created (e.g. corporate rules, collective bargaining agreements, the right to work, social protection), the implementation of such a right (fundamental to the meaning of Europe) would provide the foundation for a genuine *'professional social security'*.[14]

This status would thus become a factor for regulation of economic life by placing the fundamental components of security – personal development and capability for choice – outside the market, and in the sphere

---

[13] Salais (2000).

[14] Bernard Thibault, General Secretary of the CGT, to the Assembly of the National Confederation Committee convened on 24 and 25 April 2001, and in the newspaper *L'Humanité* (11 May 2001).

of individual rights. It would be a factor of utmost importance for freely chosen mobility between activities, jobs and training courses and living spaces. Such a status of '*person potentially in work*' would be more than an umbrella concept for purely formal rights – it would be an effective factor for integration and for social and civic development, reflecting a change in the focus of policies in the European Union and its Member States in the direction of human development.

REFERENCES

Colletis, G. and J.-L. Levet (eds.), 1997. *Quelles politiques pour l'industrie française?*, report issued by the *Commissariat général au plan*
Lallement, M., 1998. 'Rationalisation du temps et mutation des rapports sociaux', *Problèmes économiques*, 2, 677
Le Duigou, J.-C. and R. Le Bris, 1998. *Demain l'emploi*, Paris, Editions de l'atelier
Roger, P., 2000. *Vers l'Etat charitable*, Paris, Editions de l'atelier
Salais, R., 2000. 'Vers un nouveau plein emploi', Minutes of the CGT workshop held on 2 December 1999; brochure published by the Centre confédéral d'études économiques et sociales
Schwartz, Y., 1988. *Expérience et connaissance du travail*, Paris, Messidor

18 Incorporating the capability approach into social and employment policies

Robert Salais

I30
J68

1 Introduction

Implementing the European Social Agenda[1] has been skewed by two major handicaps. The first well-known handicap is that the definition of 'European competencies' has been narrowly circumscribed and framed in relation to national prerogatives. The second handicap, which has had more far-reaching effects, is that, until now, its general orientation has been determined by a different agenda, namely ECB and ECOFIN monetary and economic policy, which is less concerned about social issues *per se* (social justice, equality, expenditures suited to needs) than about their impact on the public deficit and employment rates. Yet, for reforms to be sustainable, they must reconcile economic objectives with social aims in a delicate balance. Our thesis is that, in order to attain such a balance in an unfavourable political context, Europe's social agenda must be based on a social theory of its own. There must be a clear connection between theory and policy, and the implications of the theory must likewise be clear-cut. It must give prospective actors a well-defined, mobilising role and provide a specifically European definition of social progress.

The capability approach, as developed by Amartya Sen, could well be this theory, provided it is adapted to the construction of social Europe. This chapter will develop two main arguments in its favour, the first factual, the second, political. To begin with, the capability approach offers solutions suited to work transformation. Work is changing, demanding flexibility and autonomy; its practice raises the issue of effective freedom and contradicts the logic of subordination. The three models of the Welfare State[2] implemented in European countries no longer provide an adequate framework. In order to evolve, they need a reform principle that, instead of calling them into question, allows them to reconfigure in order

---

[1] By 'Social Agenda' we mean not only the 2000–6 Social Agenda designated as such by the Treaty of Nice, but more broadly, the entire field of European social policies and employment.

[2] As popularised by Esping-Andersen (1990).

to cope with new expectations of security. From a political standpoint, it will be argued that by adopting the capability approach, social Europe will come into its own as a legitimate political construction, a position it has yet to attain (perhaps even to seek, though it must do so). In true accordance with the principle of subsidiarity, a renovated open method of co-ordination would use the capability approach as a benchmark for national actions.

Section 2 criticises the instrumental design of European social and employment policies. Section 3 presents the capability approach in the light of Amartya Sen's work. Section 4 looks at how this approach could be turned into a European reform principle. We will conclude with the conditions required for its implementation (section 5).

2   The instrumental design of European social and employment policies

European social and employment policies are designed to achieve maximum impact, given the resources allocated, on anticipated overall quantitative results. For example, in the case of the European Employment Strategy (EES), measures are targeted according to the rate of return to employment. For pensions, the preferred adjustment variables are the rate of replacement (the relationship between revenue from work and the pension received) and the duration of working life. In brief, the design of these policies is, above all, instrumental. Reforms are first assessed according to the criteria of the Stability and Growth Pact (SGP). Though the consensus is rather broad on this orientation (which can be explained by the failure to grasp its implications) it neglects the contribution of the social dimension to European economic development. We will take a brief look at two examples: pension systems and employment. The relevance of the objectives is not in question in any of these examples; everyone agrees that population ageing requires a re-examination of the rules for attributing and financing pensions or would welcome a genuine improvement in employability and social provision. However, the order of priorities, the earmarked resources and the societal implications all raise problems. Objectives are being used to serve utilitarian ends other than their own. What counts is maximising quantitative targets, whatever the means used and the content of achieved outcomes.

The integrated approach, developed in 2001, aims at guaranteeing secure, viable pensions.[3] It presents a set of objectives to guide the reform strategies of Member States. Expected outcomes are firmly emphasised,

[3] EC (2001d: 2–8).

one concerning public spending, the other flexibility. Member States will have to make sure 'that pension spending remains at a level in relation to the GDP that is compatible with the Stability and Growth Pact'. The steps to be taken 'may result in adjustments in the pension amounts paid out to retirees and the contributions and taxes paid mainly by the active population'. Furthermore, Member States must see to it that 'the pensions systems are compatible with the demands of flexibility and security' and that they do not discourage non-standard forms of employment or self-employment. Calling public pension schemes into question has been programmed. People who wish to preserve good pensions will have to rely, more systematically than before,[4] on the second pillar (professional pension plans) and third pillar (personal pension plans), both of which are described as 'private pension schemes'. The inevitable consequence will be an increased inequality towards ageing, socially stratified according to revenue. Those who can afford it will have to increase their savings above and beyond their social contributions and taxes. The rest, in accordance with a well-known pattern in countries with a liberal Welfare State,[5] will have to make do with a basic public pension.

Like the previous strategy, the EES[6] uses the Open Method of Coordination (OMC.)[7] It has the same core objectives as the 'integrated approach': maximising the employment rate and labour market flexibility. The main variable of EES action is individual employability in the labour market. This pillar is virtually the sole subject of benchmarking indicators. The five-year review in 2002 was unable to demonstrate that the EES had had any direct, substantial impact on improving the employment situation or the labour market. Instead, it emphasised the resulting convergence of national policies regarding EES objectives and guidelines. In other words, the gains were purely procedural. The likely explanation for this,[8] which unfortunately was not explored by the review, is that the strategy had deviated towards instrumentalism. Improvement in benchmarking indicators was mistaken for actual improvement in the corresponding situations. In fact, statistical observation of an improved rate of return to employment has not so much to do with progress in real employability; it depends on how one defines 'employment' and the rules and categories for managing job seekers, which are factors that vary over time and from one Member State to another. Conception of the

---

[4] 'It is possible that the contribution from private pension schemes will have to be increased insofar as the Member States attempt control the effects of rising pension spending on public finances', EC (2001d: 8).
[5] See chapter 16 by Noel Whiteside in this volume.
[6] See chapter 8 by Gilles Raveaud in this volume.
[7] See chapter 12 by Philippe Pochet in this volume.   [8] Salais (2004).

labour market is truncated and static; it lacks a variable as important as vulnerability to unemployment.

In these policies, two central issues that form the core of the capability approach have been neglected or brushed aside. The first concerns social justice which, in itself, is a fundamental objective of any public policy. In every society, political debate and the search for solutions are oriented by the principles governing the evaluation of inequalities between persons and decisions about who is entitled to which sort of aid and the criteria to be used in identifying the person's situation. The second issue concerns the quality of employment. In many respects (including working conditions, professional qualification, lifelong security, mobility, promotion, reconciling home life with work), employment quality contributes as much to preventing social contingencies as it does to increasing productivity. This is especially true if the quality of a job is defined by the range of real opportunities it offers to the person who performs it.

In short, European policy in these areas tends to use an order of priorities – strategy first, then technique followed by policy – that reverses the way things should be (policy should inform technical decisions, which in turn should be implemented by a suitable strategy). The justification for this paradox has been repeated and theorised so often it is familiar to everyone.[9] In the name of the principle of subsidiarity, policy decisions are to be left to Member States; it is up to them to work out problems relating to social justice, equality and spending content with their own population and electorate. This demonstrates threefold naïveté. Competency in monitoring public deficits and business competition puts monetary and economic authorities in a position to strongly influence policy decisions by imposing instrumental assessment criteria. Problems with implementation are blamed on Member States, whereas in many instances their 'unwillingness' is due to the fact that the solutions are fundamentally inadequate. Last but not least, European policies have yet to be elevated to the status of public policy. Demonstrating that means (criteria of efficiency) are justified by ends (criteria of justice) and submitted to them is the very essence of public policy.[10] By refusing to discuss such a connection publicly on a Europe-wide level, European social institutions cannot achieve political legitimacy. Lacking any fundamental ethical conception, the danger is that they will limit themselves to rules that can be manipulated.[11]

Nevertheless, a careful reading of the premises of the Social Agenda shows that it has other prospects in mind. On the one hand, the need

---

[9] See EC (2001f).   [10] Especially, but not solely, in social areas.
[11] Here we come back, by a different path, to the conclusion of Streeck (1996), who maintains that a European social policy cannot be created due to lack of autonomy.

to base policy reform on a debate about social justice is recognised. It is even asserted that social protection and inclusion of all in society should first be viewed as 'productive factors'[12] rather than as costs for society. A number of points in the agenda reveal an intuition similar to the capability approach. Its concern for equality of opportunity between women and men is targeted on specific situations: access to employment, revenue, career prospects and the possibility of reconciling family with professional life. The lifelong development of competences may refer to 'human capital', but it finds its real scope in terms of capabilities. Employment quality calls for an analysis of the scope of working and living possibilities offered by inclusion in employment. The lack of capabilities provides a more accurate analysis of social exclusion than the poverty line.[13] Hence, this approach does contain the seeds of a truly European social thought, along with a method. Would it not be better if this hidden agenda were brought to light?

3   The capability approach in the light of the Amartya Sen's work

Another striking aspect is that all policy targets construct the person's choices in their areas as arbitrating between money and work.[14] There can be nothing fundamentally erroneous about that; however, the critical question raised by Amartya Sen's work is that these ratios do not take into account a widespread fact of decisive importance for policy effectiveness. Given equal resources, when faced with the same contingencies, people do not have the same ability to overcome them. They do not have the same power to convert the means at their disposal into valuable outcomes (in other words, into *functionings*). To neglect this reality is to run the risk of being neither fair nor efficient. Inequalities will remain between individual situations. The overall result will fall short of hopes of efficiency, which are distorted by not taking these inequalities into account. The policy cursor should thus be shifted from inequality of resources to inequality of capabilities (figure 18.1).[15]

All too often, especially in the individualist approach developed by microeconomics, variability in outcomes is said to be due to inherently individual properties. This hypothesis is sometimes an inexplicit by-product of the technical constraints of econometric models. Certainly,

---

[12] EC (1997a).   [13] Sen (2000).

[14] The same can be observed in the fight against social exclusion. Monetary poverty is assigned a primary role (see Atkinson *et al.* 2002 in their report on social indicators in matters of social inclusion).

[15] Diagram inspired by Sen (1985a).

Evaluating the state of the person

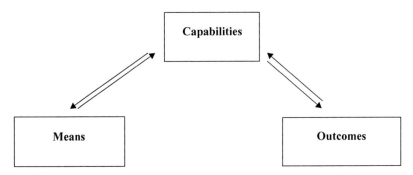

Figure 18.1. Capabilities as operational mediation between means and outcomes

part of the unequal success rate of a social measure is due to individual factors beyond anyone's control. Other inequalities, however, although related to the person, are due to objective social and institutional factors. These factors condition living and working and should be included in public action through prevention and compensation. In many instances, married women with small children have a lower capability of finding high-quality employment when there are no childcare facilities close to their home or workplace (not to mention other conditions). Without laws guaranteeing the possibility of returning to one's previous job, the extension of parental leave can end up a dead letter. To achieve real freedom of transport for the disabled, it is better to ensure that public transport offers special access ramps than to pay disability compensation. In addition to general job-placement services, long-term unemployed workers need personalised services tailored to their specific cases to make up for reduced capability of finding a job on their own.

This shift of focus may seem modest, but it actually has far-reaching consequences when designing and implementing social and employment policies. Insisting on the need for individualised follow-up, for example, is a way of coming to grips with the reality of long-term unemployment. At the same time, it is ambiguous: does it mean encouraging or obliging people to take jobs corresponding to their current employability level (the instrumental approach) or will they be allowed to take advantage of available resources to achieve a genuine improvement in their employability (the capability approach)? Dissipating this much too systematic ambiguity is a priority for the capability approach. Three points stand out: capabilities as the scope of effective freedoms; giving priority to factual objectivity; management based on capability evaluation.[16]

3.1   Capabilities as the scope of effective freedoms

Sen's work refers to the relationship between social justice and economic development.[17] Sen has an original theoretical position. His experience as an expert for international organisations (the UN, World Bank, ILO, etc.) led him to search for the effective conditions for economic and human development that would be both efficient and fair. One of the conditions is the range of possibilities that are really (and not merely formally) available to anyone, anytime and anywhere. The more fully this condition is satisfied, the more individual and collective initiative can be deployed, especially if the participants have the capability of doing so. The concept of capabilities thus contains several overlapping meanings. A 'capability' belongs to the person or group in question. It includes not only a competence but also the power of *achievement*. To exercise this power, an area of opportunities or 'capacitation' must be created.[18] This is largely the responsibility of public authorities and collective bargaining. Creating such areas requires laws, policies, rights, facilities, etc. Nevertheless, human action has the final word; only the responsible exercise of one's own freedom can transform a potentiality into a reality. If a 'virtuous circle' is generated, the scope of achievements and of effective freedoms will expand together. This dynamics involves a *learning process* (on the part of both the actors and the political decision-makers) and *self-examination* (a reflexive development of institutions and policies so they can improve through the process). This approach does not neglect responsibility, but is aimed at equipping individuals with the effective means to assume responsibility and to enjoy effective freedom as a result. This is a complex question of judgement and the response must be constantly re-examined.

The implications are obvious for the European issues mentioned above. Instead of focusing on 'quantifiable' employability (the number of action plans offered to unemployed workers), EES co-ordination would evaluate the effective employability of the workers upon completion of

---

[16] This chapter has benefited from the survey conducted by Farvaque (2003), for a thesis now under way. Sen's thinking remains relatively unfamiliar and misunderstood. All too often it is reduced to basic income or the HDI (Human Development Indicator), whereas Sen has distanced himself from these areas.

[17] The best we can do here is provide a few references: Sen (1982, 1983, 1985a, 1985b, 1990, 1993, 1999).

[18] See chapter 14 by Jean de Munck and Isabelle Ferreras in this volume. Also Robeyns (2003).

the action plans and again later on: did they find a job; did they stay with it; what was the job's quality? Only such effective employability expresses effective freedom of choice in the labour market. This evaluation would provide lessons concerning the content of action plans and measures to improve them. Extending the retirement age would not be decreed in advance for the instrumental purpose of balancing the budget. It would result from prior in-depth examination of the economic and social conditions for effective freedom of choice on the part of ageing workers to continue working or to retire. Such an extension would therefore be founded in justice. This presupposes an analysis of the facts (statistics, monographs, surveys of the interested parties, both companies and workers) and full debates in which all the relevant parties are given a hearing. With regard to social protection, the first question would not be how to spend less, but rather how to spend better to meet social challenges (particularly healthcare). If better spending were to require additional spending, then there should be a policy debate on how to finance it.

3.2   Giving priority to factual objectivity

In line with Rawls' works, the debate on justice is often confined to reaching an overall political compromise on normative models of society. The nature of 'good institutions' is deduced prior to any functioning of society. Amartya Sen has shifted the debate. In his view, the criterion of justice belongs to the realm of facts. In social matters, Sen proposes what might be called an ethics of *objectivity*. What is important is to evaluate whether or not the selected policy or institutional system actually helps enhance effective freedoms and capabilities. What is required, he says, is a judgement about the 'state of persons', to measure what they achieve or would have the freedom to achieve according to a 'metric of capabilities'. Since the comparison is between persons, it must be possible to make this judgement at the level of each individual. The capability approach is therefore non-dogmatic. It may be that, from a general normative standpoint, the market is the best possible framework for building social regulations. In that case, as we know, only means-tested allocation (along with increasing activation) is considered useful, and it is reserved, moreover, for deserving applicants only. Such an approach may be enough in some cases; in many others, impartial observation shows that it is notoriously insufficient and ill-adapted. Other rules are needed in the field. The fact that they are derived from other general normative models does not keep them from being fair, when the facts demonstrate that they are.

It is important to fully understand the scope of this approach. The aim of any liberal policy (in the proper sense of the word) is equal opportunity.

It must therefore contain general rights. What Sen adds is that the policy must ensure that it is effectively translated into *real* possibilities for everyone, taking into account their state, their situation and their environment. When such conditions are created, each person is free to take part or not, and the choice is his or her individual responsibility. In other words, if inequalities are created, they should be the result, not of inadequate policy, but solely of effective free choice. This counterfactual criterion is essential for assessing the relevance of a policy and finding out empirically how to improve it. Even if social progress applies to everyone, the range of real possibilities is *de facto* narrower, if not non-existent, at the bottom of the social scale. The first and absolute constraint is to ensure real improvement in the situation of the least advantaged. The second constraint on any social reform is to avoid increasing inequality of capabilities. Both of these constraints are clearly violated by the instrumental approach.

In Sen's view, social institutions are founded on an informational basis of judgement in justice. This basis delimits the 'territory of justice' as applied by the institution:

The informational basis of a judgement identifies the information on which the judgement is directly dependent and – no less important – asserts that the truth or falsehood of any other type of information cannot *directly* influence the correctness of the judgement. The informational basis of judgement of justice thus determines the factual territory over which considerations of justice would *directly* apply. (Sen 1990: 111, italics in the original)

This basis determines the relevant facts, the information which, given its rules, an institution needs in order to act upon the person's state and situation. To put it simply, it is made up of rules and criteria relating to eligibility and aid characteristics.

'Description is choice.'[19] Observation cannot be separated from evaluation. Determining the relevant facts does not mean compiling data. It would be ridiculous to include the colour of the walls as an aspect of quality of employment. On the other hand, effective access to possibilities of apprenticeship is important in relation to lifelong training, for it can increase real freedom of choice. The functionings to which development capabilities correspond must be valuable, precisely those that public policy thinks it should support, and observation should be limited to them. The weight assigned to the various valuable functionings may vary according to individuals and communities. Drawing up a list of valuable functionings will depend partly on the conventions in force (what everyone

---

[19] Sen (1982).

considers necessary for a decent life and a decent job in that society) and partly on a political choice supported by public deliberation. Sen thinks that partial agreements can work. It is possible, for example, to reach agreement at the European level on the components of job quality, and still disagree about the weight that should be assigned to each one. Owing to this incompleteness, the capability approach allows for flexibility in use that can be exploited through gradual implementation. As Sen notes:

> The capability approach is inescapably pluralist. First, there are different func-tionings, some more important than others. Second, there is the issue of what weights to attach to substantive freedom (the capability set) vis-à-vis the actual achievement (the chosen functioning vector). Finally, since it is not claimed that the capability perspective exhausts all relevant concerns for evaluative purposes (we might, for example, attach importance to rules and procedure and not just to freedoms and outcomes), there is the underlying issue of how much weight should be placed on the capabilities, compared with any other relevant consideration. (Sen 1999: 76–77)

Here, too, the guidelines are relatively simple. If Europe were to follow a capability approach and adopt an ethics of objectivity, it would refuse to assert normative priority among the three classical models of the Wel-fare State (Anglo-Saxon, Continental or Scandinavian), or between them and the market. A precise meaning would be assigned to the fundamen-tal objective of 'improved working and living conditions, so as to make possible their harmonisation while the improvement is being maintained' (Article 136, TEU). Europe would realise that national data, categories of evaluation and observation are so thoroughly permeated with norma-tive choices that it would be difficult to build on them. Hence, there is nothing neutral about the selection of OMC indicators. What does an employment rate mean independently of the quality of the jobs making it up, if not that preference is being given to a model in which labour leg-islation plays a minimal role? On the other hand, learning about unequal capabilities would become the priority. Determining the relevant facts in areas such as healthcare, employment, retirement, social inclusion, etc. would allow European action to impact Member States' policies.

3.3   *From outcome-based management to evaluation of capabilities*

Like a number of other European initiatives, the OMC came into being by default. Lacking 'positive' direct competences in social and employment policy, the idea was to monitor the Member States from a downstream position (on the basis of outcomes) and leave the upstream (the means) to them. Compared to the three aspects in figure 18.1 (capabilities, means, outcomes), this type of management strengthens the instrumental pressure applied in designing national policies. For Member States, what counts is *quantitative performance*, at the lowest financial cost. Member States are therefore encouraged to neglect the question of justice in their reforms, as well as efficiency, beyond merely improving their scores. This is a paradox for a European approach, which ends up being highly 'economically oriented' in nature.

Contrasting with such a view, Sen's approach emphasises the median term of 'capabilities'. Capabilities are what turn means into outcomes and what a well-conceived policy should contribute. The development of capabilities is the crux of public policy efficiency. Neglecting them leads to wasteful public spending. If the training offered to a young unemployed worker is of such poor quality or so short that it does not improve his employability, there will be virtually no conversion of the means spent (however minimal) into successful inclusion. If financially balancing social protection were to result in a deterioration of quality of life and healthcare possibilities for the poor, the cost will have repercussions on the state budget in the long run. The virtues of initiative and autonomy (effective freedom) within the range of public policies will be put aside or restricted to an elite, which is contrary to the essence of the European project. Sacrificing the short term (often evoked to justify unpopular reforms) in favour of the medium term may, in fact, obliterate the medium term. It is a gain from an accounting standpoint. In reality, it increases the losses.

4   The capability approach as a principle of European reform

The relevant ground for European action on social and employment matters is not to manage national policies on the basis of results, but rather to evaluate the capabilities they develop. The OMC should make the evaluation of capabilities its core.

In section 3, we noted a number of contributions and possible applications of this approach in various sectors. The capability approach does not dominate at the present time. Nevertheless, it has some support in the Treaty as well as in European policies. First, we will take a look at research projects aimed at applying this approach. Finally, we will summarise the constraints and possibilities of making it a part of European policy.

4.1   Putting the capability approach into operation

Since the early 1990s, research has tried to make the analytical framework operational and now offers a potential starting point. Research has been concentrated on key points such as drawing up the list of valuable functionings or measuring capabilities, either *ex post* (starting from achievements), or *ex ante* (the scope of effective freedom). They aim at demonstrating how this approach can contribute to issues such as quality of life, employment, unemployment, gender equality and social exclusion in Europe. We will mention only three examples here.

Burchardt (2002) insists that employment be considered a capability, an option among a set of opportunities that are all real possible choices. This consideration takes on its full meaning when seen in the light of the European employment rate objective. Indeed, some people – particularly women – choose not to work, but others, who do not work, lack the capability to do so. Finally, we should add, some people work because they have no alternative. Hence the pertinent question is the opposite of the one suggested by the concept of employability. One should not be seeking the means to ensure insertion in the labour market at any price, but rather ask whether the people under review have the real capability for employment. Contrary to appearances, ensuring that everyone enjoys the conditions required for an effective choice between working and not working is the best way to achieve inclusion in employment. Such inclusion will result from a decision based on an effective choice. Working on British data, Burchardt shows that at the end of the 1990s, about three-quarters of the women who were not working lacked the capability for employment. Only one-third of them were included in the official unemployment statistics.

Basing themselves on questionnaires given out to unemployed people in Belgium, and to RMI[20] recipients in France, Schokkaert and Van Ootegem (1990) and Le Clainche (1994) independently sought to determine the functionings which these populations valued the most. The first group came up with six: escaping from social isolation, gaining self-confidence, being in good health, having social contacts, being able to plan one's future and not having financial problems. As a consequence of the overlapping between observation and evaluation, policy-makers should be given the evaluations made by the people concerned with their own situation. Active participation of potential beneficiaries or their representatives in developing the informational basis comes under the ethics of objectivity mentioned in section 3.2.

4.2   *Work as a value and the capability approach*

Considering work as a valuable functioning for people and society is a promising direction for research (Supiot 2001; Salais 2002). As in the works discussed above, extending Sen's analysis to this field is easy and helps us see the limits of the Welfare State models more clearly. As the

---

[20] The *revenu minimum d'insertion* (minimum insertion income) or 'RMI' is distributed, under certain conditions, to people excluded from any other form of aid.

Introduction of this book points out, the theory developed by Esping-Andersen (1990) to justify the models and its later developments are outdated as far as the conception of work is concerned. 'Negative freedom' neither encompasses the transformations of work nor the fact that social spending is an investment in people's capabilities. On the other hand, if work is looked upon as a valuable functioning, it takes on additional politically relevant characteristics including participation in a group activity, appraisal of working and living conditions and how they are connected, self-esteem and enriched social relationships. In Sen's words, work should be considered as an 'agency goal'. Furthermore, Welfare State models have been wrongly associated with countries. Being technically constrained to use national statistics has nothing to do with the theoretical relevance of the national level.

Figure 18.2 re-formulates the three models in terms of informational bases required for welfare provision. It does it along two lines:[21] the foundation of rights in terms of freedom in relation to work; the definition of the social safety net in terms of equality of *what*. The first contrasts negative freedom (individual work as disutility) and freedom of action (work as participation in a collective activity). The second opposes equality of means (aid as compensation for a loss) to real equality of opportunity (giving effective access to functionings deemed valuable). For lack of room, we will not go into the advantages of formulating Esping-Andersen's three 'worlds' in these terms. Let us merely note that the Scandinavian model is refocused on quality of life.[22] In other words, it aims at ensuring that every person acquires the capabilities corresponding to the achievement of well being.

We shall insist, however, on the fourth case, which remains blank *for current Welfare States*. It is blank, not because there have been no concrete achievements, but because it has not yet been developed as a policy approach. But the underlying policy approach in this fourth 'possible world' is a capability approach. It gives priority in reform to equality of capability and encourages effective access to basic functionings that constitute a 'good' life and a 'good' job. By enhancing the values of inclusion, participation, autonomy and effective freedom, it also fosters the transformation of work. This could offer a positive compromise between flexibility and security.

4.3   Including a capability approach in European policy

The seniority of Europe's current Welfare States makes their self-correcting development extremely difficult. Social Europe, on the other

---

[21] The developments are shown in Salais (2002).   [22] Nussbaum and Sen (1993).

			Equality of *what* (form of aid)	
			Ensure real access to functionings	Compensate for a loss
Freedom for *what* (foundation of rights)	Freedom to act	Work as collective agency	IBJ: possibilities	IBJ: work
			Capability world	**Status world**
			TO BE POLITICALLY ADDRESSED	*CONTINENTAL*
	Freedom from want	Individual work as disutility	IBJ: well being	IBJ: basic income
			Well being world	**Market world**
			SCANDINAVIAN	*ANGLO-SAXON*

Figure 18.2. Redefining welfare state models according to their informational basis of judgement in justice (IBJ)

hand, is a new political construction. While not totally unfettered by the weight of history, should it not build its political legitimacy on foundations of its own? In other words, should it not promote the capability approach as a principle of reform in the social and employment field? The challenge requires a profound change, not simply discourses or superficial consultation. It would be up to a renovated OMC to co-ordinate national policies using the capabilities approach as a benchmarking method.

Significant data support the realism of this proposal. Most social protection systems and employment policies in Europe and within the OECD are still operating on rules belonging to or combining the worlds of status and well being.[23] In the mid-1990s, out of the 163 systems found

---

[23] Or, if one prefers, the continental and Scandinavian worlds. Statistical data in Salais (2002). Data have been built by combining the OECD SOCX database with the ILO ISSADOC database.

in OECD countries, only twenty-two were based on means-testing, in other words on the informational basis of the market world. They are widely found in Anglo-Saxon countries (e.g. the UK and Ireland in Europe), although these countries are not strictly limited to this model. The reforms undertaken in these countries have encouraged *workfare*. Far from enhancing the effective freedom to work, the workfare system adds a criterion of merit to already existing income criteria, merely refining the old approach. On the other hand, 108 systems distributed work-related aid and thirty-three aid according to a universal principle. These systems therefore already possess one of the two components of the capability approach: they either value work or they aim at effective access to functionings. Establishing a capabilities-based benchmarking for Europe would create a strong incentive for Member States to reform their policies and systems by introducing the component they lack.[24]

Objectifying political controversies to keep Member States from equivocating is a right orientation. But the OMC will not succeed in practice unless it adopts an ethics of objectivity.

First, the method must shift from its downstream application (outcome-based management) to the median area (evaluation of capabilities). The aim of public communication (to show that action is being taken) would give way – not easily, of course – to the imperative of political truth (taking real action). It would rule out a pure accounting approach and instead evaluate the intensity and content of mobilised resources in relation to the scope of effective freedom of choice they open up. That, for instance, the amount of *per capita* expenditure on unemployed workers and their inclusion in employment can vary from 1 to 7 in Europe cannot but influence the quality of their inclusion.[25] Does changing pension system parameters increase effective freedom of choice between working and not working? Does it widen the range between these two extremes? Or does it worsen the living conditions and limit the choices of the least advantaged?

Secondly, the European Union should responsibly assume a position of impartial actor evaluating of inequalities of capability in Member States. Such a position requires rigorous scientific methods. The technical project of determining indicators would have to change its aim and organisation. The oft-repeated argument[26] of simplicity and availability to every country is unacceptable, for it is a question of political

---

[24] Or both for workfare-inspired policies. The challenge in figure 18.2 would be to bring about shifts towards the 'blank' box in the upper left-hand corner.

[25] Data established in Salais, (2002). *Per capita* social expenditure is divided by the country's mean worker remuneration.

[26] For example, in Atkinson *et al.* (2002).

responsibility. The renewal in 2005 of the European households' panel on living and working conditions[27] offers an opportunity. Empirical data do exist, such as the studies by the Dublin Foundation. Among the 100 indicators proposed by the Employment Committee[28] to manage the EES in 2002, only a few of them would come under a capability approach. They concern areas in which the reality is too obvious to be dismissed altogether: lifelong training, apprenticeship, health and security at work, gender inequalities, reconciling professional life with family life. Not a single indicator, not even those concerning job quality, passes the test for the main pillar (employability). There is still a lot to be done.

Thirdly, determining which facts are relevant to social and employment policies is indissolubly descriptive and evaluative. The information rests on cognitive categories that have yet to be constructed and debated; it is never an immediate reflection of reality. The exchange of best practices would profit from an explanation of their national cognitive foundations. Data become comprehensible and transparent only when every step in their creation (questions, survey method, coding, ranking, aggregation) is made explicit and public. The devil hides in the details. The relationship between indicators and policy should be much more elaborated than it is now.

5   Conclusion

The search for objectivity and equality of capabilities does not dissolve policy. On the contrary, it requires explicit, organised policy when choosing indicators – and, more broadly, for the OMC. Social Europe could pioneer deliberative democracy, and thereby earn the political legitimacy it lacks. It will not be easy, because success will not be measured by procedural sophistication, but rather by the real content given to the reforms that adopt the approach. Deliberative democracy is certainly not what we are accustomed to: a group of experts, a final conference and one more committee. An economist is not in the best position to present the broad outlines. Nevertheless, establishing a European informational basis of judgement in justice (in Sen's sense, see section 3) on capabilities carries with it certain requirements. At the very least, it assumes that proposals will be drawn up by researchers and submitted to social, political and civil actors for in-depth discussion. The debate should be concerned with the possible cognitive framework for such a basis and the procedures for

---

[27] SILC panel.

[28] See *Indicators for monitoring the Employment Guidelines 2002 (endorsed by the Employment Committee)*, European Commission, 2002, www.europa.eu.int/comm/employment_social/employment_strategy/indic/list_from_compendium_jer2002.pdf.

developing it. This collective effort must be allowed all the time it needs, for the path towards political truth is filled with obstacles, diversionary tactics and strategic manipulation. Discussion must take place regularly and conclusions must be revised if necessary (for instance, as a result of new facts or unexpected outcomes). This is the condition for a true learning process. It is conceivable that Member States, social actors or civil actors may disagree with conclusions and request a counter-expertise, provided it is subject to the same constraints of objectivity. European legislation calls for social dialogue and requires it in making reforms. Judging by their statements, European social and civil actors are ready to participate, and as representatives of the interests of social groups and categories they would have an important role to play in a capability approach. They have everything to gain from seeing Social Europe advocate an approach that would allow them to make their proposals heard. But what about the Member States and the various EU bodies?

REFERENCES

Atkinson, T. B. Cantillon, E. Marlier and B. Nolan, 2002. *Social Indicators: The EU and Social Inclusion*, Oxford, Oxford University Press
Burchardt, T., 2002. 'Constraint and Opportunity: Women's Employment in Britain', Paper prepared for the Von Hügel Institute Conference *Promoting Women's Capabilities: Examining Nussbaum's capabilities approach*, Cambridge, 9–10 September
Esping-Andersen, G., 1990. *The Three Worlds of Welfare Capitalism*, Cambridge, Polity Press
Farvaque, N., 2003, 'Les tentatives pour rendre opérationnelle l'approche par les capacités et la place de l'évaluateur', *Document de travail IDHE*, April
Le Clainche, C., 1994. 'Niveau de vie et revenu minimum: une opérationalisation du concept de Sen sur données françaises', *Cahier de Recherche CREDOC*, April, 57
Nussbaum, M. and A. Sen (eds.), 1993. *The Quality of Life*, Oxford, Clarendon Press
Robeyns, I., 2003. 'Sen's Capability Approach and Gender Inequality: Selecting Relevant Capabilities', *Feminist Economics*, 9(2–3), 61–92
Salais, R., 2002. 'Work and Welfare. A Capability-based Approach', in D. Trubek and J. Zeitlin (eds.), *Governing Work and Welfare in a New Economy: European and American Experiments*, Oxford, Oxford University Press, 317–344
    2004, 'La politique des indicateurs. Du taux de chômage au taux d'emploi dans la Stratégie européenne pour l'emploi', in B. Zimmermann (ed.), 2004. *Les sciences sociales à l'épreuve de l'action: le savant, le politique et l'Europe*, Paris, Editions de la Maison des Sciences de l'Homme, 287–331
Schokkaert, E. and L. Van Ootegem, 1990. 'Sen's Concept of the Living Standard applied to the Belgian Unemployed', *Recherches économiques de Louvain*, 56(3–4), 430–450

Sen, A., 1982, 'Description as Choice', in A. Sen, *Choice, Welfare and Measurement*, Oxford, Blackwell, 432–449

1983. 'Poor, Relatively Speaking', *Oxford Economic Papers*, 35, 153–169

1985a. *Commodities and Capabilities*, Amsterdam, North-Holland

1985b. 'Well-Being, Agency and Freedom: The Dewey Lectures 1984', *The Journal of Philosophy*, 82(4), 169–221

1990. 'Justice: Means vs Freedoms', *Philosophy and Public Affairs*, 192, 111–121

1993. 'Capability and Well-Being', in M. Nussbaum and A. Sen (eds.), *The Quality of Life*, Oxford, Clarendon Press, 30–66

1999. *Development as Freedom*, Oxford, Oxford University Press

2000. 'Social Exclusion: Concept, Application and Scrutiny', Asian Development Bank, *Social Development Papers* 1

Streeck, W., 1996. 'Neo-Voluntarism: A New European Social Policy Regime?', in G. Marks, P. Scharpf, P. Schmitter and W. Streeck, *Governance in the European Union*, London, Sage

Supiot, A. (ed.), 2001. *Beyond Employment: Transformation of Work and the Future of Labour Law in Europe*, Oxford, Oxford University Press

Appendix 1 EU bibliography

Council of the European Communities (CEC), 1994. 'Council Directive 94/45/EC of 22 September 1994 on the establishment of a European Works Council or a procedure in Community-scale undertakings and Community-scale groups of undertakings for the purposes of informing and consulting employees', Official Journal, L 254, 30/09/1994 P.0064–0072

Council of the European Communities (CEC), 1996. Council Directive 96/34/EC of 3 June 1996 on the framework agreement on parental leave concluded by UNICE, CEEP and the ETUC, Official Journal L145, 19/06/1996 P. 0004–0009 CONSLEG – 96L0034 – 16/01/1998

Council of the European Union (CEU), 2002a. 'Annex: The Employment Guidelines for 2002. Horizontal Objectives – building conditions for full employment in a knowledge-based society', Official Journal of the European Communities, OJ L60/63, Annex of a Council Decision of 18 February 2002 on guidelines for Member States' employment policies for the year 2002 (2002/177/BC)

Council of the European Union (CEU), 2002b. Council Resolution on the follow up to the Green Paper on corporate social responsibility, Official Journal of European Communities, OJ 2002/C 86/03, 10 April

Council of the European Union (CEU), 2003. 2003/578/EC: Council Decision of 22 July 2003 on 'Guidelines for the employment policies of the Member States', Official Journal of European Communities, OJ L 197 05.08.2003, p. 13

Court of Justice of the European Communities (CJEC), 1998. Ruling of the Court of First Instance, Social Policy Field, Case T-135/96, Union européenne de l'artisanat et des petites et moyennes entreprises (procedure language: French) *UEAPME* v. *Council*, Court of First Instance, 17 June

Court of Justice of the European Communities (CJEC), 2003. Judgement of the Court of Justice in Case C-280/00, *Altmark Trans GmbH and Regierungspräsidium Magdeburg* v. *Nahverkehrsgesellschaft Altmark GmbH*, the Court rules that financial support which merely represents compensation for public service obligations imposed by the Member States does not have the characteristics of state aid, 24 July

European Commission (EC), 1992. Communication from the Commission to the Council and the European Parliament 'The Principle of Subsidiarity', SEC(92)1990 final, 27 October

European Commission (EC), 1993a. White Paper on Growth, Competitiveness, and Employment – *The Challenges and Ways Forward into the 21st Century*, Commission of the European Communities, COM(93)700 final – Brussels, 5 December

European Commission (EC), 1993b. Communication concerning the application of the agreement on social policy presented by the Commission to the Council and to the European Parliament, COM(93)600 final, 14 December

European Commission (EC), 1995a. White Paper on Education and Training – Teaching and Learning – Towards the Learning Society, COM(95)590

European Commission (EC), 1995b. Equal Opportunities for Women and Men: Follow-up to the White Paper on Growth, Competitiveness, Employment. Report to the European Commission's Task Force (DGV) Brussels: DGV European Commission V/5538/95-EN (report of the 'seven wise women')

European Commission (EC), 1996. Commission Communication concerning the Development of the Social Dialogue at Community level, COM(96)0448 final, 18 September

European Commission (EC), 1997a. Communication from the European Commission, 'Modernising and improving social protection in the European Union', COM(97)120 final, 12 March

European Commission (EC), 1997b. Proposal for a Council Directive concerning the 'Framework agreement on part-time work concluded by UNICE, CEEP and the ETUC', COM(97)392 final, 23 July

European Commission (EC), 1998. Communication from the European Commission, 'Adapting and promoting the social dialogue at Community level', COM(98)322 final, 20 May

European Commission (EC), 1999a. Cohesion report, 'Sixth Periodic Report on the social and economic situation and development of the regions of the European Union', DG Regio, February
This is the last in a series of reports on the socio-economic situation and development of the EU regions. In accordance with Article 159 of the Treaty, the Commission publishes triennial reports on Economic and Social Cohesion.

European Commission (EC), 1999b. Communication from the European Commission, 'A Concerted Strategy for Modernising Social Protection', COM(1999)347 final, 14 July

European Commission (EC), 2000a. Initial Proposal from the European Commission, 'Acting Locally for Employment – A Local Dimension for the European Employment Strategy', COM(2000)196, 7 April

European Commission (EC), 2000b. 'Social policy agenda', Social policy agenda: following the European Councils of Lisboa and Feira, Council of Nice December 2000 procedure, COM(2000) 379 final, 28 June

European Commission (EC), 2000c. Initial Proposal from the European Commission for a Council Decision on 'Employment: Guidelines for Member States' Employment Policies for the year 2001', COM(2000)548 final, 6 September, followed by the final act LEX 2001 D0063, 19/01/2001, L022 24-JAN-01

European Commission (EC), 2001a. Report from the Commission to the Council, the European Parliament, the Economic and Social Committee and the Committee of the Regions, Second Report on Economic and Social Cohesion, COM(2001)24 final, 31 January

European Commission (EC), 2001b. Communication from the European Commission 'New European Labour Markets, Open to All, with Access for All', COM(2001)116 final, 28 February

European Commission (EC), 2001c. Communication from the Commission to the Council, the European Parliament, the Economic and Social Committee and the Committee of the Regions, 'Employment and social policies: a framework for investing in quality', COM(2001)313 final, 20 June

European Commission (EC), 2001d. Communication from the European Commission, 'Supporting national strategies for safe and sustainable pensions through an integrated approach', COM(2001)362 final, 3 July

European Commission (EC), 2001e. Green Paper – Promoting a European Framework for Corporate Social Responsibility, COM(2001)366 final, 18 July

European Commission (EC), 2001f. White Paper on European Governance, COM(2001)428, 25 July, OJ C287 12-OCT-01

European Commission (EC), 2002a. Communication from the European Commission, The European Social Dialogue, a force for innovation and change, submitted to the Council a proposal to create a tripartite social summit for growth and employment, COM(2002)341 final, 26 June

European Commission (EC), 2002b. Communication from the European Commission, 'Taking Stock of Five Years of the European Employment Strategy', Communication, COM(2002)416 final, 17 July, the first five year-evaluation of the employment guidelines Procedure INI/2002/2152

European Commission (EC), 2002c. Communication from the Commission on streamlining the annual economic and employment policy co-ordination cycles, COM(2002)487 final, 3 September

European Commission (EC), 2003a. Document enclosed in the consultation procedure CNS/2003/0068 *Employment: guidelines for Member States' policies, review. Employment package*, European Commission, 'The future of the European Employment Strategy', COM (2003) 6 final, 14 January

European Commission (EC), 2003b. Proposal for a Council decision on Guidelines for the employment policies of the Member States from the European Commission, COM(2003)176 final, 8 April

European Commission and the Council of the European Union (EC & CEU), 2003, ECOFIN. ECOFIN 51 SOC 72, Draft Joint Report by the Commission and the Council on adequate and sustainable pensions, Brussels, 3 March

European Council, 1997. LUXEMBOURG EXTRAORDINARY EUROPEAN COUNCIL MEETING ON EMPLOYMENT, 20/11/1997 – Press: 0 Nr: SN 300/97, 20 November 1997, launching the European Employment Strategy (EES)

European Council, 2000a. LISBON EUROPEAN COUNCIL: PRESIDENCY CONCLUSIONS, 24/3/2000 Nr: 100/1/00, 23 and 24 March

European Council, 2000b. NICE EUROPEAN COUNCIL: PRESI-DENCY CONCLUSIONS, 8/12/2000 Nr: 400/1/00, 7–9 December

European Council, 2000c. EUROPEAN SOCIAL AGENDA adopted at the Nice European Summit, Part V. A new impetus for an economic and social Europe, Social Europe, points 15 and 16, see Annex I. European Social Agenda, pp. 3–23, 7–9 December

European Council, 2001. EUROPEAN COUNCIL MEETING IN LAEKEN: PRESIDENCY CONCLUSIONS, 14/12/2001 Nr: 00300/1/01, SN 300/01 ADD1, 14 and 15 December

European Parliament (EP), 1997. A4-0052/97, Report on the Communication from the Commission to the Council, the European Parliament, the Economic and Social Committee and the Committee of the Regions 'European Automobile Industry 1996' (COM(96)0327 – C4-0493/96), 'European Automobile industry: progress in the structural adjustment of the industry. Report' (rapporteur: Donnelly Alan John) of the European Parliament, Committee on Economic and Monetary Affairs and Industrial Policy of 17 February 1997; Official Journal C115 14-APR-97 003

European Parliament and Council of the European Communities (EP & CEC), 1996. Directive 96/71/EC of the European Parliament and of the Council of 16 December 1996 concerning the posting of workers in the framework of the provision of services, Official Journal L 018, 21/01/1997 P. 0001 – 0006

European Convention, 2003. 'Draft Treaty establishing a Constitution for Europe', Articles 47,104.4,105 and 106, CONV 850/03, 18 July 2003, http://european-convention.eu.int

Eurostat, 2000a. European Social Statistics: Demography, Luxembourg, OOPEC

Eurostat, 2000b. Eurostat Yearbook 2000: A Statistical Eye on Europe 1988–1998, Luxembourg, OOPEC

Appendix 2   Information on EU official documents

Publication reference in the Official Journal in the European Union (OJ)

Series
L = Legislation
I = Information and Notices

followed by
OJ issue number, Volume number, Publication date

European Commission's documents' references
COM = COMmission documents, i.e legislative proposals and other documents of general interest (White Papers, Green Papers, communications)
SEC = SECretariat documents

Luxembourg: Office for Official Publications of the European Community (OOPEC)

Index